The Life and F
of Mickey Plum

CW01506559

Michael Spencer

To Steve & Maureen

With Best Wishes

From Michael

Printed in Australia

Published by Centreforce Pty Ltd

ISBN 0-646-42560-9

All enquiries should be addressed to
      Michael Spencer
      c/o Text Management
      PO Box 1157
      Mornington Victoria
      Australia 3931
      or murray@centreforce.com.au

Prologue

What I can't understand is why on earth anyone should have to write an introduction (I'm calling it a prologue) to their book, it really is beyond me after working tirelessly to get it written I now, for some unknown reason, have to rack my brains and come up with something to put in front of what I think is my best stuff. So to all those people out there who are thinking about writing their own story, here is my recipe (for what it's worth):

> Reams upon reams of paper, other ingredients should be; a fine pen and a good imagination (or vice-versa); then (Micks in) a great sense of humour that won't quit; and then all the fun you'll have trying to put it into some sort of order.

I think the hardest part was writing about ten pages then realising that a piece of your life should have been plonked in there somewhere, so on a few occasions it was, of course, too late to go back but I think I got through it reasonably well (without having a nervous breakdown). Yes, all in all folks it certainly kept me on my toes (I must admit, it made me look taller).

Most of the names I've used are real people that came into my life at some stage or other, except a few that have been changed to protect their innocence. Now, I can assure you there's never been a book like this before (and you'd better believe it) and I guarantee there won't be another one again (unless, of course, I write it). I had an absolutely fabulous time putting all this together, your journey awaits you, enjoy!

With Special Thanks To…

Angela and Daniel and Rodders and Colin, for your computer skills, to Allan, Bill, Gus, Jock and Terry who helped me with names (a word of warning, I could be picking your brains at a later date), and also to Sue at Text Management, David and Malcolm at Bookmark, ta very much.

And how do I put into words to show my appreciation to all my family and numerous friends (for your support, and I always think of you when I wear it) so I suppose a big thank-you will tide me over for now and while I'm dishing them out the same applies to all those people who kindly lent me photos, especially to Keith Fort (you made my day).

Now you can all take a bow but be careful in case you're facing each other.

Chapter
1

Happy New Year, folks. Well, we've made it to the 21st century, some people reckoned the millennium started in the year 2000, then others said it was 2001. I'm sitting on the fence at the minute, I thought I'd make doubly sure just in case these so-called experts change their minds, they have a tendency to do that.

Right, I know you're itching to give me your best rendition of "Auld Lang Syne", but we'll put that on the back burner for a while, and go back in time to what they called "The Good Old Days".

I wasn't even a teenager but I remember it like it was yesterday. I used to think; I wonder what I'll be doing at the turn of the next century, blimey Charlie, that's nearly fifty years away, if I should make it that far. Never in my wildest dreams did I think I'd be writing about my life or trying to put it together in a book format, and of all the places to be living, in Australia. Not that there's anything wrong with that!

All of my tributes in rhyme (that's what I call them) you, the reader, will see they'll be strategically placed throughout the book. Now, they were all written before I decided to do this, so that's the way I have to go. It's not what I want to do, it's a case of I have to do it like this (I know what I mean).

You would not believe the trouble I've had trying to get a foot in the door, I feel like I've done all the spade work, but just don't know how to get something in print. I've lost count of the heartaches I've had and the times I got my hopes up, only to have them come crashing back down again.

Now, how do I keep you, the viewers, entertained as we go "Around The World In 80 Days"? Well, I know what I like, so hopefully if you're on the same wavelength as me, I've cracked it. The only other hurdle at the moment is that I can come up with enough stuff to put in between the tributes, but knowing me as I do, once we've set foot on the old Memory Lane, it should be all downhill as it comes to view in my mind's eye.

Now these tributes, most of them are about famous people. I can assure you though, they are autobiographical, as there is a lot of me in every one of them. It scares me to think where this comes from, but as of now it excites me where it's going. I shall give you a bit of a run down as we get near to one of the tributes, and as you are intelligent people, it shouldn't take you long to catch on. Then again, on the other hand if it does, I'll just twiddle my thumbs and hope you didn't get too far behind. Be careful, as you could get trampled to death, what with me going backwards and forwards. And if I do confuse you somewhere along the way, hopefully it will all come out in the wash.

Oh, I nearly forgot... I'd just like to tell you how I came up with the title. Would you like to know? (No, you say), good, then I'll tell you. Now, I used to love that film title "The Life And Times Of Judge Roy Bean", so with a little bit of switcheroo on my part, that's what it became. Oh, don't tell me you've forgotten it already. Go on then, you can go back to the front and take a peek. I'll wait here for you and have a quick twiddle... ah, you're back! There you go, that's why I decided to call it what I did, because it's about me and my rhymes. Very clever, eh? (Hoy, there's no need for that language!). It's not that long ago I was calling you an intelligent lot.

Now, what was that line Mae West used? Something about keeping a diary and one day it will keep you. I don't regret not keeping one, but it would be good to remember every little detail, I suppose. So while the memory is still intact, a word of warning is to be prepared for anything. Now, I'll try to remember as much as I can, so I'm going to use all my resources, and as long as I don't change them midstream, or something like that, it shouldn't be a problem.

I'm just thinking, I have only one chance to write this, so if I make mistakes I'll just have to slap my wrist and say, "Basil, you're a very naughty boy." (I'll most likely keep throwing lines like that at you just to see if you're paying attention, as I could be asking questions later).

Now, to be perfectly honest with you, goodness knows where this is going, but as long as I get to the last page before you that's all that matters (and no, the butler didn't do it). So I'll tell you what I'll do. If I get there first I'll draw a line and if you get there before me you can rub it out. Right, it's head down, bum up and "Let's Get Physical". We'll rewind to the early fifties.

So here I am in the yard at Rosegrove Junior School on Owen Street, when one of the kids shouts, "Hey, Mickey Plum, yer Granny's here." So I raced up to the railings, as fast as my wittle legs would carry me, and there's dear old Grandma (sorry, I was miles away there for a minute), it was just like that though. Then Grandma would produce a big piece of homemade parkin (cake), or ginger biscuits. All the other kids would flock around like seagulls on a hot chip and, of course, Grandma would always have some to spare for the other kids, all the while making sure her youngest grandson got his share first.

Then it would be my turn to show off in front of Grandma and to try and make her laugh by pulling faces behind the teacher's back, or to pick my nose and pretend to flick it, or better still, push a fat kid over, that was always good for a laugh.

It must have been somewhere about this time that I realised having a sense of humour was a good thing to have in my possession, and as they say, laughter is the best medicine, or a chuckle a day keeps the Doctor away. I think I must have inherited my humour from Mum, as hers got her through some very tough times and I can assure you, there were plenty of those over the years, from what she told us.

I was only very young when Dad left home so Mum had to bring up three lads, of course Grandma and Grandad were close by, plus a few more relatives who would help out. After Dad had gone, the burden Mum had been carrying went as well. We always knew she had the gift of the gab, but now she was armed with an incredible wit. When she was talking to people she'd throw in these classic one-liners, which would have them, and us, in fits. One thing she used to say, and it's just come to mind, was, "I wish I had six kids, I'd drown three." I can laugh at that now, but it wasn't funny at the time as I used to think, fancy drowning three, she'd still have the same number left, so which ones would she do in? I prayed I would be reprieved as, of course, I couldn't swim.

That's why I was always scared to death at bath times, I remember being very little and it was my turn for the dreaded tub. Now, John and Bob (me bruvvers, and big bullies in the bargain) would whip off my clothes and toss them in the air, then they'd grab an arm and a leg each, I quickly screamed, "For goodness sake, don't make a wish!" Then on the count of one, two, three, I was hurtling towards the murky water.

Now, you would be surprised at the number of different things that stick out, as one is plunging towards a frightful destination. They say your life flashes in front of you in situations like this, well in my case, I hadn't lived much up to this stage, so if I'd have blinked I would have missed most of it. Then again, when you are in a position like this you see certain parts of your body that you've never visualised before and this is no time to be looking up your relatives, or stocktaking to see which little piggy went to market.

Now, in my time of trouble, I couldn't sing out, "Mother Mary come to me," as my Mum was called Margaret, but unbeknown to them I had my wits about me, they were dealing with Superboy. Yeah, I was quicker than a speeding pullet, able to leap tall bounds in a single building, faster than a Hornby train. Yes, I'd ricochet off the water like that specially made bomb in "The Dam Busters". I was in and out like a fiddlers elbow, my socks and jocks hadn't had time to hit the floor, I was as naked as a jaybird and a slippery little sucker.

Then Mum was at the foot of the stairs, wanting to know what all the commotion was about and she'd be up, quick smart, to leather the three of us. I'd shout, "You'll only be able to belt two of 'em, as you'll never find me, I'm hiding under the bed, oops!"

Great Grandma, Mum, Me and Grandma

With little stories like that one, they may be slightly fabricated, but as long as no one gets hurt or offended, that's the main thing. And if we have a laugh or a bit of fun along the way, then well and good. By the way, medical authorities say a smile is a frown upside-down, so if I can put a smile on your dial, it's all been worthwhile.

Now, if I remember right, the bath used to be under the back bedroom window on Liverpool Road. I don't think our house was classed as a two-up, two-down, as we had what they called a scullery. Now, we couldn't have been that bad off, to have a bath, as Lowerhouse Lane and Saltburn Street, where we would live after, didn't (more later).

I think the furthest I can go back to in my mind is about age five or six. Sometimes I would go in next door to Mrs Walton's for a bath, she would twirl the corner of the towel and say, "Let's get those potatoes out of your ears." I couldn't for the life in me think who on earth would do that to a little fella like me. It's a frightening thought that some stranger in the night would come into a kids bedroom and plant spuds in their lugholes. I actually did a bit of research at school about this and to my amazement quite a few kids agreed we were in the same boat, and besides that, we even had tidemarks (baffling). Maybe because we were in a boat together… who knows? I had heard of being up the creek without a paddle and never did work that one out either.

Then, of course, there was the Tooth Fairy, who seemed like a nice chap, a bit down in the mouth, but by gum it wasn't his fault. As I'm writing this right handed, my left hand is on the bible and I swear that's the tooth, the whole tooth, and nothing but the tooth, so help me God.

Grandma and Grandad lived on Saltburn Street in The Grove, and Uncle George (Mum's brother) was still at home. At this time there was Uncle Tom and Aunty Edna, plus their daughter, Edna, and son, Gordon, they also lived on Liverpool Road. Uncle Tom was Grandma's brother. Uncle Tom and Aunty Maggie were on Dorset Street, the latter being Grandma's sister. Next door to us at number 30 lived Aunty Alice and Uncle Ted with their son, Bobby. Aunty Alice was one of my Godparents, they weren't related, we just called them Aunt and Uncle out of respect, as we did with Clara and Stan who lived a few doors down.

In those days it was very hard to keep track of them all. In fact, we had more Aunts and Uncles than you could poke a stick at. One Aunty we always looked forward to seeing was Aunty-cipation. Another one, who never knew what time it was and had trouble finding a direction in life, we called Aunty-clockwise. Then there was a posh one who only ate smoked meat or fish, she was Aunty-pasto. And yes, I've saved the best for last, this will knock your socks off, she was always complaining how cold it was and I wasn't surprised at all, in fact, I'd seen more meat on a butchers pencil. Mum reckoned she was so thin, every time she went to Gannow Baths she had to run around under the shower to get wet. Once, she turned sideways and poked her tongue out and the attendant thought she was a zipper. Now, you can most probably see this coming a mile off (drum roll), yep, we called her Aunty-freeze. (That sounded good in the think tank, I hope I didn't build you up to an Aunty-climax). Right, let's get back to some sort of order… also on Saltburn Street were Uncle Harry and Aunty Beattie (Grandma's sister).

They had a daughter called Beatrice, who married Alan, and they had two daughters, Pat and Pamela. They weren't our first cousins, but we called them cousins and yes, like everybody else, we had cousins removed. Of course, they were disposed of very discreetly. Just thinking back now, there were quite a few kids my age around The Grove, but what I'm going to try and do is name most of them (hopefully nobody will take offence with that), and it should be a challenge in itself and that will be the pattern throughout the book. Who knows, one of my readers might be thrilled that I've mentioned an Aunt, Uncle, Dad or Grandad, Mum or Grandma.

John, me and Bob

My two best friends were Colin and Billy Iverson, they lived on our row; then Elaine, Tom and Charles Henshawl, they lived on the next row; John Parkinson lived on Lower Rosegrove Lane; Bob and Ann Markham; Alan and Ann Etherington; John, Billy and Pauline Lupton; the Leeson family; also the Bolans; Brian Baker; John Stubbs; Kenneth and Kevin Berkins (their parents had the butchers in The Grove); Irene Turner; Jeff Eastwood; Jean and Betty Eastwood; Hilda and Alan Wood; Sandra and Michael Varley, Bernard Platt and Malcolm Allen all lived on Dorset Street. Phew, I haven't thought of these people for a lot of years, so the old brain is working overtime. Right, back to the rollcall: Alan Eel, Eric Fox, Alan Bushby, John Edmondson, John Morgan, Jimmy Miller, Derek Leather, Arthur Hines, Michael Starkie, Raymond Washington, Keith Stacey, Len McIvor, Fred Hunt and Colin Spencer (no relation). The last four were my good friends outside The Grove.

I'm sure there's still a few more I can't think of, but if they come to mind later, I'll give them a mention, I promise you.

I spent quite a lot of time at Grandma's and Grandad's. It must have been when I was around seven or eight, about the time Robert had Rheumatic Fever. It would have given Mum a break, as she was going through a bad time with Dad. Oh boy, I thought it was great at Gran's. I'd never received so much love and attention. Believe me, I was like a cat with a saucer of milk. I lapped it up. Looking back now, it must have been Grandma's idea, as I was frightened to death of my Dad and a nervous wreck most of the time. Now my teeth would chatter and the knees would knock. Half the time they didn't know where I was, but they could hear me knocking about. Of course, my nerves being what they were, the end result was Enuresis (bed wetting). I suppose it had to come out some way.

That in itself would be an embarrassment for a lot of years to come. But looking back now I can make fun of it, and I was the first kid on the street with a waterbed. What's that song of Billy Joel's? "River Of Dreams". I had mine many moons before he had his (I didn't wear pyjamas, I wore trunks). The kids at school used to say, "Poo, you pong!" Quick as a flash I'd say, "It's that little moggy we've got, it piddles everywhere," (gee, I got out of that well).

I always remember Mum telling me that Grandma used to say to our Dad, "Jack, if you're going to belt the lads, please don't hit them on their heads." To this day I don't have any marks on the outside, but I'm badly scarred inside. As they say, you learn to live with it and I think I release a lot of it through my writing, which is therapeutic. So while I'm dealing with it, lets go back further, to day one.

They had moved their bed downstairs, to what we called the front room or parlour. That's where I came into the world. The day I was born, Dad came home from work in the afternoon and Mum said, "Do you want to see your son?" But he had his tea first and saw me later. You know I often think, what sort of man would do that to his own flesh and blood? Maybe he didn't realise the heartache and pain I would have to carry on my journey through life.

Today I'd like an hour or two with him just to answer a few questions, but then again, maybe towards the end of his life he would have had to deal with that and put things right in his own mind. I am not bitter towards Dad, but I can't understand his rhyme or reason for doing what he did.

Well folks, I dug a bit deep that time, so I'm going to rest on my laurels (and spade). Let me tell you about when Mum was carrying me. Three months earlier they had a day trip to the zoo, now in England there's a lot of what they call 'old wives tales'.

After the bath

One was that if a lady was expecting a baby and she'd been frightened by, say a savage dog, when her baby was born there would be a small tuft of hair somewhere on its body. This was a result of the shock that the woman had received and the baby would carry that, call it a birthmark, for the rest of his or her life and I'm living proof of this. Just a minute, this spade is not comfy, it's hurting under the old armpit. Yes, that's much better, but they don't make them like they used to.

So Mum and Dad had taken sandwiches for lunch and there were a few scraps left. Mum thought she would give them to the bear, who was sitting there contemplating his navel. Well, when he saw Mum coming, he jumped up and stood against the bars and he was about 6'13" in the old money (and that's tall), well it scared Mum half to death as she wasn't expecting that (she was expecting me).

They managed to calm and sit her down and someone got her a drink of water, then after about twenty minutes she was alright, but what a hair raising experience. You know what? When I was eventually born I had bear feet (I'll show you a photo later). I knew this spade would come in handy again, I'll just get rid of this pile of manure, all in favour say "Aye," the ayes have it.

Now, let's go to Grandma's for a quick visit. Please wipe your feet and come in. I can't offer you a sherry, that's for the insurance chap. It used to be so funny at Christmas time as these blokes would get offered a drink at nearly every house they went to. Mum used to say to Grandma, "For goodness sake, don't strike a light near the Prudential fella, or he'll be off over Bowkers like a skyrocket." Do you remember, most of them used to ride bicycles? They'd ride round the spare ground, just like the Injuns circling those covered wagons. They'd be singing, "Riding around on a push bike, honey," while the inebriated ones were giving it, "Show Me The Way To Go Home."

Grandma did a lot of work for St. Marks (so did many of the other ladies). I used to enjoy the whist drive nights. At half-time I'd take the sandwiches and cups of tea to the people Grandma pointed me towards. By the time I got there the tea was half cold and most of it was in the saucer anyway. Then after the break they got back into it. Grandad loved his cards and he liked to smoke. As the saying goes, he smoked like a factory chimney and some near him would cough and splutter. I never got a cold or a runny nose, I'd just have a fall of soot every now and then.

There was walking day at St. Marks and Habergham Garden Party. Now, I'm not sure if these both fell on the same day, I can't remember, but I have photos of both and I think we're wearing the same clothes? Must try and find them now to include in the book. Behind Liverpool Road was Mr Iverson's Woodyard and that would have to be the greatest place to play for any kid, not only knowing Colin and Billy, we went to school together, that more or less made me a season ticket holder. We'd pretend to be "The Three Musketeers" or play cops and robbers, another good one was hide and seek as there were tons of hiding places, but the best of all was where they dumped the sawdust.

The Garden Party

Believe me, we would play there for hours (and we did "The Full Monty"). So much laughter and fun, we would get filthy then have to clean ourselves up before we could even think about going home. There was one section of the Woodyard where they would saw the wood up, in another building was where they put the firewood into bundles. Now, the wood had been cut into kindling size, then you had to put so many pieces in a round type vice. You then pulled a lever and it tightened the wood, then you placed a wire around it and made that as tight as possible and released the lever and you would end up with a neat bundle of wood. I think there were a few people worked in there, but I can't remember exactly how many. I know Colin and Billy were a dab hand at it, they would say to me, "Have a go," so I thought, I'll be in this. Well, when I'd done a couple, they looked something like blind Freddie had made, one bundle would have fourteen to fifteen pieces in it, the other one eight or nine, that was because I'd tried to show off.

I've never heard so much laughter or, for that matter, finger pointing, and with all that sawdust around I'd sneeze about four times, which made it hard for me to stop myself from going conk first into the woodpile. More laughter and digits directed in my direction, then Mr Iverson became curious, I don't think he wanted to hurt my feelings, as he gave me sixpence. I never did find out why he'd crossed my palm with silver. Was it in appreciation for a job well done or was it severance pay? You know, I think it was the latter.

Throughout my life I've always liked jokes, limericks, rhymes, one-liners or anything else that tickles my fancy, but could never put it to a better use until say, six years ago. I think most of this comes from where it has just been filed away, waiting for a chance to pounce…

A limerick, to be sure
Should have five lines, no more
But if you're slick, you can get away with six
Whilst others require only four

I think that just about sums up the style of a (verse or) limerick but I do seem to struggle with the length of my lines, this is not mine either but it's a classic example…

There was a young man of Japan
Who wrote verse that never would scan
When they said 'But the thing
Doesn't go with a swing'
He said 'Yes but I always like to get as many words into the last line as I possibly can!

So now the floodgates have burst open, man the lifeboats, as it's women and ankle biters first. Let's get back to the future. I can't remember the exact date, but somewhere about August 1995, she who must be obeyed had gone to bed and I was staying up to listen to the radio. I would tune in to the BBC World Service, in the hope that my football team would win (sorry Aussies, soccer). I was most probably sitting there waiting to jot down the results and where we lived we had a potbelly stove which was pretty old, but did a great job. I remember it was getting a bit cold, so I put some wood on the fire, sat back down and I wrote:

Here I sit looking at the potbelly stove
Wishing I had one as a kid in The Grove
Getting fuel for the fire wouldn't be hard
I'd get heaps from Mr Iverson's Woodyard

And I said to myself, heck, or words to that effect, where on earth did that come from? I was still in a state of shock, but by chance a bell rang, which got me thinking about a couple of years before this. I'd had an idea to write something about The Beatles and I had stashed away a few lines into those four dark corners of my mind (that's why sometimes I answer to blockhead). And now it was starting to emerge in a different form so I thought, I'm not going to fight it, by Jove, I'll write it.

So there and then or then and there, depending on which side of the line you're from, I let it rip. My missus shouted from the bedroom, "Are you going to stop breaking wind and come to bed? I thought you wanted a bit."

Under my breath I said, "Why, haven't you got much?" As I was busy writing I sang out, "I'll be there in two shakes of a lambs tail." I thought, I'll wait till she drops off, then I heard 'thud'. "Good, she's gone," I said, now I'll get on with it, as the ideas were coming thick and fast.

So I must have knocked out about eight pages, some verses good, some fair and quite a few that needed working on which I still jotted down. They didn't look much good, but I knew at least I could go back to them at a later date. I said to myself, "Self, it's time to call it a day, yeah, that's a good name for it."

I woke up bright and early the next morning, I thought, I'll just do my exercise and punch the bag for ten minutes. To which she replied, "Alright, I'll get up and make a brew," (she'll punch me when she reads this).

I grabbed the writing and showed her the rough draft and I said, "What do you think of that?"

She said, "Heavens to Betsy, where on earth did this come from?"

I said, "I wrote it last night."

Quick as a flash, she said, "Why?"

I said, "How the hell do I know? It just came from nowhere."

Now don't get me wrong, I knew it wasn't Nobel Prize winning stuff, I read it through a few times, then changing a line here or there till I got it how I liked it. I still couldn't believe that I'd written it, so Audrey typed it up for me and it looked good, and boy, was I chuffed! Then I thought, what do I do with it? So I put it in one of my desk drawers and tried not to think about it. So now I'll whip it out and let you read all about…

That's My Rosegrove

Growing up in The Grove was great as a kid
And I've written this ode of the things that I did
Would you care to take a flashback with me?
Then you and I can re-live what we see

Liverpool Road was the place I was born
I ran around in clogs and pants that were torn
Mr Iverson's Woodyard where we would play
Grandma & Grandad's where we'd spend Christmas Day

Shops in The Grove, there were quite a few
Let's stop and think how many you knew!
Berkins, Vincent's Butchers, Bushby's, Turner's Shoes
Adam's Stores, Hargraves, people standing in queues

Farrers, Rockcliffes, Sweeny Todd's (where you'd stare at the floor)
Because we the kids believed he had a trap door!
Mitchells, Teals and Salkelds, where they sold toys
Sherburns, The Selling Out Shop and also Foys

Pickfords, Hasties, Scholes and Shorrocks, what great toffee!
Duckworths, Redmans and the smell of fresh ground coffee
Stackhouse, Potts, Newbolds, Bob Bird's Fish & Chips
The taste of salt and vinegar still lingers on me lips

Places near The Grove, time to think, let's see
Are you ready for the journey? Then come along with me
The railway where John worked, Collinge's Farm, Hiltons Bleach
Rosegrove Methodist, where my brother Bob did preach

Red House and Junction, Bridge Inn, Unity Men's Club
I was too young then to go in a pub
Mr Briercliffe's Woodyard, sad to see the landmark gone
I suppose that is progress and time marches on

Butts & Dicks, Harling & Todds, the library, Cherrylea
Those buildings as a kid, looked very big to me
The Co-op, Billy Holts, Nuttalls & Crooks, The Engine Shed
Most of the folk who worked there will now be dead

Ginny wagons, the Cemetery and Happy Valley
In those days people seemed so pally
Bowkers & Smallshaw Bridge, both off Gannow Lane
I loved to play there and tried to race the train

Then up to Gypsy Bridge, or down Molly Brook
The Gypsies would say, "Take your bloody hook!"
Can you remember the things that you did?
Let's take the magic box and lift the lid

When we were young we made our fun
I'd write 'kick me' and stick it on someone's bum!
There were no computers, videos or tellies
We played on the Loco pond in our wellies!

I wore a pop bottle top in my lapel
I would show off 'cause I thought I looked swell
The Owen Street 'little swings' were great
But I would get told off for swinging on the gate

There was 'mummying' and 'conkers' and candles in jars
Who'd have thought one day they would land rockets on Mars?
Men would kill chickens, their heads on the floor
They were dead, yet they would still try to find the door

Saturday afternoon, Flash Gordon & Three Stooges at the Coli
Flying down Livie Road on our fruit box trolley
We loved going down to Grandma & Grandad's
They held such sweet memories for us three lads

The long drop toilet, the tippler and the slop stone sink
Stanton's pop, Ginger beer and Sarsaparilla that we did drink
The man with the horse and cart shouting, "Rag'n'Bone"
Grandma would get a 'donkey' or 'yellow stone'

The sideboard and on it the Britannic Insurance Book
The oven near the fire, where Grandma would cook
Her cooking was something to be tasted
With appetites like ours, not a crumb was wasted

There was potato pie, sad cake and oven bottoms, so good
And the silver thrupny bits in the Christmas pud!
A penneth of kali and a ha'penny Spanish
When it was time for bed we kids would vanish

Rosegrove Junior School, the Secondary Modern next door
All that education, who could ask for more?
The school yard where we used to play 'bobbers'
Sometimes football, kiss chase or even cops and robbers

The girls would skip and topple, or play leapfrog
Whilst the boys smoked 'dog-ends' up in top bog
Well it's time to go, so I must move on
So thank you my friends for coming along

I do hope these memories you won't quickly erase
And sincerely hope they brought a smile to your face

R   *is for   Rosegrove, the place I was born*
O   *is for   Owen Street, where I played on a frosty morn*
S   *is for   Spencer, that's the name we had*
E   *is for   especially, especially Mum and Dad*
G   *is for   God, for he is always around*
R   *is for   relations, who in a crisis could be found*
O   *is for   obedient, what we were taught to be*
V   *is for   verse, to make this poetry*
E   *is for   everyone and the Lord above*

That's My Rosegrove, which I dearly love

Just a couple of things to clear up, there might have been a few words that some of you had trouble with. Butts & Dicks was short for Butterworths and Dickinsons (and not what you lot thought), it was a foundry at the bottom of our row. I mentioned dog-ends, that was a term we used for cigarettes, not canine posteriors; and the word bog was another name for a toilet; the Loco was where we played opposite The Engine Sheds.

Chapter
2

Colin, Tom, me, Roy and Billy

I'll just try to put you in the picture. At the back of our house and in between the Woodyard were pens or allotments. I can't remember too much, but I know Dad kept hens and we had to smash old pots or plates, I think it was like a grit for the hens. I'm not sure if it was Mr Walton who chopped the hens heads off, but it was a sight in itself to see them running around like that. Behind the Woodyard was the Loco and the pond in the corner. To the left of the Loco was The Engine Shed and Lower Rosegrove Lane, and that ran down to Collinge's Farm, then down to Molly Brook, as we called it. Now, let's step forward a few years…

Where I was born

Liverpool Road, The Loco and The Engine Sheds

Someone had sent us a copy of the Express, the local paper in Burnley, and Rosegrove is one of its villages. Burnley is situated in Lancashire, the north of England, which was famous for it's football team in the fifties and early sixties (more about that later). Right, where was I? I seem to be up and down like a toilet seat, but that's my prerogative. I'm reading the paper, checking out the comings and goings (births and deaths), as a lot of people used to call it. The readers' letters and of course the sports page. Then I started thinking about one letter that I'd read and that just triggered something off. I quickly flicked to the index; there was the address you could write to and the editor's name. I thought, my new-found friend, you'll be hearing from me ASAP.

I went down to the newsagents in Rye (which I call Wayne's World, where there's everything at ones fingertips) with the written goods firmly tucked under my arm; got it photocopied (not me arm), grabbed an envelope, then went down to the Post Office singing, "I have often walked down this street before." Once inside I went to the bench, wrote the name and address on the envelope, then got it weighed, gave it a big smooch for good luck and merrily sent it on its way.

I then plonked a few bets on the TAB (Totalisator Agency Board), or as they call it over here 'The Lucky Shop', went home and had some lunch.

Now under the house was a carport or garage, depending on which way the wind blew, so there was plenty of room to store firewood for the stove, which I used to do, till I was ready to saw it up into pieces that would fit the fire, saw I thought I'd go down and so some would. Hands up all those who spotted the spelling mistakes? Very good, glad to see you're on the ball. To the rest of you, now you're gonna have to try a little harder.

So there I was, cutting the wood and I just started thinking about The Grove. Our Uncle George used to be the organist at St. Marks and he had a smaller version that he practiced on which was in the parlour on Saltburn Street. As Uncle George was deaf, he used to have headphones, which doubled for the organ and the radio. I loved to play with the headphones. If I remember right they were big cumbersome things, and I would pretend to be a jet fighter pilot.

Now in those days the radio was the only home entertainment (unless your parents were rich, then you had a piano), with music, plays, sport, news and, of course, comedy. I kid you not, we would actually watch the wireless, especially with the comedy shows, I sat there fascinated. Who were these funny people? We couldn't even see them but loved everything they said and we'd hang on every word. The selection of the comedy shows had to be heard to be believed. Now I thought Peter Brough was great, I couldn't see his lips move, well, on radio you couldn't see anything move and come to think of it, Archie Andrews was probably not even in the same studio. He would have been stuck in a dressing room somewhere, giving therapy to another ventriloquist's dummy who'd been circumcised with a pencil sharpener.

But my favourite and first love was The Goons. I remember crying through laughing, numerous times. Of course they'd lose me with their double innuendos, and I'd think, what did they mean by that? It would be years later that I'd realise what they were really on about (you filthy swines). Those crazy people still give me a knee-slapping laugh to this day and every so often I'll have a mad impulse to play one of their tapes. I have every show that's available except series 1-2-3. I don't know if these are in the Beeb (BBC) archives or if anybody out there in Goonland that is reading this has copies. I would love to hear from you.

Besides the collection of cassettes that I have, I've got heaps of books by Spile Milligan; six by Hairy Secombe, plus three on Petor Sellers, two by Mitchill Bentine (those well known typing errors). Those five words in brackets were for Goon fans only. If you don't fit that description, I hope you didn't read them (get it, got it? Good). Now, if there's any Goon fans out there who haven't got a copy of "The Goon Show Companion" by Roger Wilmut and Jimmy Grafton, as the saying goes, do yourself a favour, go out and get it right now as it's a Goon fan delight. We'll wait here for you, so toddle off and take your time.

Right folks, we got rid of those idiots, didn't we? So over the years, all that I've heard, read or seen, it had been filed away somewhere in the noggin. Then like it was meant to be, I got a couple of good ideas. I quickly stopped sawing the wood (if you remember, that's what I was doing while I was day dreaming about The Grove), I ran upstairs, saying these lines over and over again so I wouldn't forget them. I stuck the kettle on, then made a quick brew, grabbed some paper and a pen, and I started jotting down the words that were gushing through. It was like this had been simmering for a while and now it was coming to the boil, but what scared me the most was the number of verses I finished up with (over sixty). I'll let you judge for yourself, as…

It's All In The Mind You Know

Let's sit upon that time machine
Go on a journey back in time
Come with me on a rhyming adventure
Into the basement of me mind

I think the first I heard of them
Yes, that's it, now I remember
It was very early fifties
Somewhere around September

To me they were influential
Those four crazy fellas
I mean the one and only
Spike, Harry, Mike and Peter Sellers

I would turn on the old steam radio
And then I pinned back my ears
Because, yes folks, here they were
My four idiotic musketeers

Yes, my eyes would protrude
Oh, how my cheeks did glow
I tuned to the home service
For the all leather Goon Show

Listen all Goon Show fans
I'll let you make the choice
When you're reading my rhyme
To use the characters voice

I wonder if you know much about them
Will you let me try and fill you in?
Perhaps we should start with Spike
If you're ready, then I will begin

He'd rise early in the morning
Take a stroll to a London park
And talk to his friends the birds
It was so cold and dark

That brain of his was active
Who knows what it could find?
The birds, he confided in them
And that certainly eased his mind

He was a writing genius
Who wrote reams of words
Were those ideas there
When he first spoke to the birds?

He was a frantic 'writerholic'
Just writing against the clock
His mind confused, his heart bruised
And his body in a state of shock

He was a 'manic depressive'
How on earth did he cope?
It was a constant battle
But where there's life, there's hope

He had a series of nervous breakdowns
No wonder with all that stress and strain
Plus, to boot, a broken marriage
But we didn't feel any of his pain

Whilst he was in hospital
And ordered to have complete rest
The swines took all his pencils away
When he felt he could have wrote best

The need for funnier scripts
Was a consuming obsession
Larry Stephens & Eric Sykes were close by
Which certainly lifted his depression

John Antrobus and Maurice Wiltshire
Who could write series' as well
This would have freed Spike
From fierce fires of hell

Even when under the weather
His mind was always bright
Wrote, "My love is like a red red rose,
But my underwear is off-white"

He'd write 'one-liners'
Time and time again
Like, "By gad, that's sun's hot"
"Well, don't touch it then!"

Any subject or novel
He'd really turn it around
It could be a current affair
Or if they'd devalued the £ound

Could you imagine Spike
Being anything but a Goon?
If writing romantic novels
He'd put humour in Mills & Boon

He argued with the hierarchy
By the gow he was a terror
Referred to as Spike Milligna
That well known typing error

Fights he had with them
Spike knew it was greed
You know who I mean
The old Beeb Beeb Ceeb

Had arguments with the Beeb
What on earth could he do?
His hands were tied by Aunty
He was just another Nephew

It's time to meet the actors
Or should I say those funny men
That's taking part in my rhyme
Adapted from a Milligan gem

Peter and Michael were RAF
While Spike and Harry were Army
But when they got together
Absobloominglutely barmy!

A sense of humour in common
And on a mental wavelength
This amalgamated combination
Surged from strength to strength

Spike wrote himself into the show
Became the main cog in the machine
At first it wasn't clockwork
But then it chimed his dream

Now, my patient readers
It's time to bring on a Goon
"Hooray," I can hear you say
And not a moment too soon

As they step onto the stage
To start the rhyming story
They surround the microphone
Their applause is a crowning glory

For Neddie, Major Bloodnok and Willium
Plus Henry, Min and Eccles
Grytpype-Thynne, Moriaty, Little Jim
Boy Scout Bluebottle and his freckles

Now Eccles was the original Goon
Everybody's got to be somewhere
And to anybody who listened
He'd go around saying, "Hello dere"

Neddie always shouting, "Heeelllpp!!"
It definitely made him madder
While poor Bloodnok was always fighting
His mortal enemy, "The Red Bladder"

Grytpype-Thynne & Moriarty
A cunning pair of thieves
Trying to con Neddie, our hero
Did no one hear his pleas?

Moriarty said, "You've got to go owww!
It's all the rage you know
If not, sing the song entontled
Ying-Tong-Iddle-I-Po"

Henry says, "Listen Minnie
You can't get the wood"
Then Willium pipes in with
"Two years in the Army mate, do 'em good"

Bluebottle pauses for audience applause
Not a single sausage he got
This little cardboard cut-out said
"Ye-he-he, I hate you rotten lot!"

Every week one of the characters
Was blown to smithereens or shot
Whilst Neddie's always clucking
"What, what, what, what, what"

Jim Sprigs was responsible for
"Hello Jim" pronounced 'Hello Jeem'
Another raving lunatic
Part of the idiotic team

Led by Eccles talking to Bottle
"My good man, have you any hobbies?"
"Yes, my girlfriend Freda Cringe
And eating me Granny's pobbies"

In the team was Andrew Timothy
Who was known as Tim
The Goons gave him a hard time
Didn't they have it in for him!

Then there was John Snagge
He was used as the announcer
But couldn't outsmart The Goons
They always had the answer

Then Moriarty says, "Oh Sapristi!"
From Neddie, a needle nardle noo
And just for good measure
Throws in a 'raspberry' or two

They thrived on achievements
And never had a rest
Even went and conquered
The inside of Everest

They'd go on expeditions
And take listeners by the hand
To an exotic island of dreams
"Oops," says Eccles, "It's quicksand"

The antics they got up to
What would happen next?
Poor Wallace, you could tell by his voice
That he was getting vexed

What about the Orchestra?
More commonly known as 'The Band'
A quick chord or an ad-lib
Yes, they were always on hand

Henry singing and Min on the sax
Belting out that crazy modern rhythm
And you could bet your bottom dollar
That The Band would join in with 'em

There were ticklish situations
And Bluebottle tried to be manly
The poor lad had Athletes Foot
Because it ran in the family

Other voices on the program
Dick Emery, Kenneth Connor and Graham Stark
Who were just as idiotic
And would do anything for a lark

Eccles and Bluebottle were sent to work
Willium said, "Hoy, you're non compos mentis"
"You can't talk to us like that," they said
"Because Major Bloodnok sent us"

That braggart, Major Dennis Bloodnok
Military idiot, the biggest coward by far
Absconded with the regimental funds
But could be found in the nearest bar

Peter could change his voice
At the drop of the proverbial hat
Loved him impersonating Michael Caine
You know, not many people know that!

Neddie and his speaking Trumpet
It always came in handy
Especially for "Right lads,
Round the back for the old Brandyyy!"

There were two musical interludes
And those gave The Goons a rest
They were provided by Ray & Max
Who were on a Musical Conksquest

The most famous catchphrase
Nearly always got it in
"He's fallen in the water!"
Exclaimed little Jim

With Big Ben chiming in all directions
All over London Town
Oh well, in that case have a tree
No thanks, I'm trying to cut them down!

Now back to young Bluebottle
By himself in the pictures
But a lad was never alone
With some string and Dolly Mixtures

They could take us anywhere
Once they got inside our head
No rules to Goon humour
They were only 'playing dead'

Here's some crazy people
That produced this great show
Just thought I'd mention them
They'd like that, you know

Bridgemont and Dennis Main Wilson
Brown, Ronald, Dixon and Spear
The Goons were like wild animals
And no one could get near

Peter Eton & Charles Chilton
Not forgetting John Browel,
*Who produced **The Last Goon Show Of All***
And then threw in the towel

I must mention Jimmy Grafton
And the pub where it all started
Plus The Little Camden Theatre
That's where they finally parted

Yes folks, it was all over
As Spike moved forward to shout
He looked them squarely in the eyes
And said, "Listen, now get out!"

I tune in whenever I can
You know they're never tireless
It's donkeys years ago
I heard that talking type wireless

I could get honoured for this
Have letters after my name
M W Spencer G.A.M.P.
But only in case of rain

Now I'll go on being a fan
Yes, for the rest of my life
To the annoyance of Angela
Plus Matthew, and Audrey, my wife

I would have given anything
To be part of that zany team
But alas it's all too late
So that's my impossible dream

Though to meet Mr Milligan
It would be just great
If not here on Earth
Maybe at the Pearly Gate

So all you fans in Goonland
Please stand up and be counted
Our Spike deserves a Knighthood
If not, he should be 'mounted'

Bluebottle got dreaded deaded
It was inevitable and so tragic
Should I write him back to life
And then "It Ends With Magic..."

Well, I hope you liked it
I'm near the end of my rhyme
Let me know what you thought
By dropping me a line

Thanks Pat, for pies & mushy peas
And Bob, for patience and assistance
My sleepless nights are over
I've finished my piece de resistance

So it's time to say goodbye
I hope you enjoyed the ride
My sea of rhyme is going out
I'll see you on the next tide

My rhyme machine has ground to a halt
As we say, "Bon Voyage" to the show
Hit the applause button, Wally
"It's All In The Mind You Know!!"

I've read most of the books written on The Goons and I've never come across a concept like mine, so as the saying goes, when you're on to a good thing, stick to it, just give me a minute, I've got to think where I was.

By the way, I'm writing this slowly because I know you can't read fast, but you've surprised me, you're keeping up.

Yeah, that's it, it was the following Tuesday, I was going up to John (me brother) and Rhonda's. You see, John is the Secretary/Treasurer for The International Sinatra Society and they have their meetings at the North Melbourne Social Club.

As the meetings finish about elevenish, I'd stay with J and R overnight. Then the next morning, after brekkie, I started to make tracks as I had to get a tram from Kingsbury to Melbourne, then a train from the city to Frankston and get the connecting bus home to Rye. I love travelling on the public transport, as it gives me plenty of time to read or write, depending on what sort of mood I'm in, plus there's always someone with a tale to tell.

I think I once read that Benny Hill used to do that. He could just get ideas from people talking, honestly, you would be surprised what you hear, that's why this pen and paper come in handy, or a good book to read as a back up.

When I got home, Audrey was all over me like a rash and I thought it must be tonight. She said, "Mickey Plum, I'm very excited."

I do seem to have that effect on women (that's if they're breathing) whenever I walk through the door (especially if it's open). So I said, "It's tonight, isn't it? C'mon, let's have an undressed rehearsal right now."

"No," she said, "and you can get that gleam out of your eyes and keep your hands off them as it's nowhere near your birthday."

Curses, I thought I was in with a chance, but quickly glancing at the calendar I saw she was right, July was a long way off. She then proceeded to go through the old 'guess what' routine. Don't you just hate that, fellas? You've got your mind on a bit of the old afternoon delight and if you do happen to guess what right away, you get nothing for it. Even a dog gets a pat on the head or a biscuit (especially a Schmackos) for being a clever boy.

By now I was going blue in the face from guessing what, to which she kept saying, "You're not even close, Fernackapan."

By this time I'd managed to scramble onto the roof with the rope around my neck and I'm thinking I'll have climbed up that golden staircase and I'll be knocking on those Pearly Gates and St. Peter would say, "Guess what?" (That would be my luck). When she had talked me into coming down I said, "It can't be my bath night, I had one last week," so I started singing, "Jimmy Crack Corn And I Don't Care," as I don't have another guess left in me.

Then she hit me with it. June had called from the States to tell us her sister, Lilian, had called her from Burnley and "That's My Rosegrove" had been printed in the local paper. No wonder I couldn't guess what, as it wasn't a question, it was more like a conundrum.

So by now it was bedtime. She said, "Do you want a bit?"

I said, "Guess what? I have a headache." See, us men are more subtle. We don't drag it out like you lot do, we get straight to the point, as normally there is beer to be drunk and sport to be watched. Most times, chicks have to have the once over, especially those ones wearing low cut blouses or wonder bras, and over the shoulder, boulder holders. Once you start wearing them you lose your right to complain about having those stared at, as us guys are notorious for this and we've been known to sneak a peek at any given opportunity. I think it's in our jeans, but you know where it is girls, we don't have to point it out to you, and when all's said and done, nothing beats mothers' milk. Those containers don't break like bottles would when bashed against the bedpost overnight and, of course, the cats can't get at them. However, I know a few dogs that are always trying to get their hands on 'em.

So yes, girls, you're always making it hard for us (if you'll pardon the pun), and if it itches it shall be scratched, or if adjustments have to be made, we men do that. I'm sorry fellas if I've told a few tales out of school, but someone had to tell them and I happened to draw the shortest straw. Anyway, it's about time they knew the facts. So that's the reason why we haven't got time for idle chit-chat. Oh, by the way, while we're on the subject of the brassiere, one of those well known plastic container makers (I won't mention their name in case of libel) have brought out a bra, but girls, although it doesn't give you better support, by the gow it keeps them fresher.

I went to buy a bra once (for a pair of friends) and the young girl said, "What bust?"

I said, "That little clasp at the back."

"I meant what size?"

I said, "15."

"How do you know it's a size 15?"

So I told her, "I take a 7½ in a hat and it fits over one of them."

What did the bra say to the top hat? "You go on a head and I'll give these two a lift." (What do you want, champagne comedy? If you behave yourself I might open a Magnum later).

Right, if you remember, there I was in print. I hadn't seen it as yet, but I thought, at least those wheels are in motion and it made me feel quite good. But it wasn't a case of saying to myself, what I'm going to do is write about such and such, I'll just play it by ear and all these, that I thought were good ideas and coming from goodness knows where, so I said there and then, from now on in, Mickey Plum, anything you think is good and worth keeping, write it down. You never know when you will be able to use it. And this way it will be stored for future reference.

I quickly made myself a list of Do's and Don't's that I'd numbered from one to ten, which I pinned up over my desk and they are:

1) Do be disciplined. Snatch these moments when you can use them.

2) Don't let anyone tell you that you can't be a writer or that your work is no good.

3) Do bounce ideas off other people. You shouldn't be afraid to talk to them.

4) Don't try to impress people with long words. Clarity is the essence of good communication.

5)   Don't worry if you have writer's block. The ideas will come in the end.

6)   Do check newspapers for ideas, sometimes something small will get you started.

7)   Do keep a notebook and jot down any ideas as soon as they pop into your head.

8)   Do save everything you write, no matter how bad you think it is.

9)   You do need to make mistakes to learn.

10)   Do believe in yourself.

Chapter
3

Now, I have quite a few books on The Beatles, plus videos, records, tapes and CDs. In a lot of the books I've read, they mention the one by George Martin "All You Need Is Ears". This particular day, I thought, I'll go up to town and try to find it. I always carry a list of books that I'm looking for, then I put my plan of attack in motion and do my round of the bookshops (new or second-hand). By accident I picked up a book that I didn't know existed and it was called "A Day In The Life". It was the day-by-day diary of The Beatles from 1960 to 1970, written by Tom Schultheiss. Boy, I'm glad I didn't have to pronounce that.

I couldn't believe my luck that I'd found this book, so I paid for it, then shoved it in my bag, feeling quite pleased with myself. I still had a couple of shops to check out, but couldn't find the one by GM. I went to the TAB, as I noticed one of my gee-gees was running in the first race. I put the bet on while I was there, otherwise I would have been on the train and wouldn't be able to get to Frankston in time. So I thought, I could be lucky (who knows?). I jumped on the tram to get to Spencer Street Station (I was going to put SSS there, but I thought you would have trouble working that one out, he's very kind, I hear you say). By the way, isn't that a great name for a station?

I only had to wait a few minutes for the train, then I was on my way home. But straight away I thought, oh no, don't tell me her indoors has another 'guess what' lined up for me, because I couldn't go through all that again. I've only just gotten over the last one and I'm still taking the tablets. So quick as a flash I thought, when I get home I'll shout, "Hello Sugar, I'm home. Guess what?" Good I thought, there's Plan A, waiting to swing into action.

I got myself comfortable for the journey, then I took the book out of my bag. I thought, I'll give it a bit of a squiz, and if I remember right, it had over 300 pages (it would have to rate as one of the best books on The Beatles that's available). I must have read over 50 pages on the way, I couldn't put the book down. It's a good job the train terminates at Frankston, or I could have finished up in Tassie.

I popped into the TAB, the nag came nowhere, but I thought, I've had my luck for one day by finding this book. What's that saying? What you lose on the tote, you gain in the bookshop.

I got the bus and before long I had to whip out my pen as the words were swirling around inside my head. I did about fifteen verses, some I thought were passable, others maybe needed a better first or third line, which I could fix up later. I sometimes find that if I can get two words that rhyme I'm halfway there. Mind you, there's not a week goes by I don't get a couple of words from people, you know the two words that I mean (I shouldn't have to spell them out for you). Then for good measure they'll throw in a few more about, of all things, my nationality, and to top it off, they seem to question whether my parents were married or not (as Grandma used to say, there's nowt as queer as folk).

Now, getting back to what I was writing about before. That's why I call them tributes in rhyme, because to me, poetry is to rhyme first and third lines and ditto with the second and fourth, which I don't normally do.

Eventually I got home. I stuck my head through the door (should have opened it first) then shouted, "Sweetie Pie, I'm home. What guess!" Of course she thought I'd been drinking. Took me quite a while to explain that. So after tea I watched Seinfeld, which I love and I can't get enough of him (brilliant).

Then I went into the spare room, which on one side had the ironing board, sewing machine and the typewriter. On the other side was a bookcase, the stereo, plus the desk. I remember once we were in there and Audrey was doing some sewing. We both must have been drinking that night, or in the words of Billy Joel "We were sharing a drink called loneliness". After all, it's better than drinking alone.

Right, I'd decided to get stuck in and do as much as possible on the current tribute. I put on a Beatles CD for a bit of inspiration. Before long it was like someone had turned up the gas under my pot of ideas. It didn't take long to knock out the rough first draft and I was amazed how quickly it all just seemed to fall into place.

Now folks, I must tell you, my writing is so bad, I'm a terrible letter writer. In fact, over the years I've written some shocking letters, so I belted out a better copy, because if I'd given that to Audrey like it was, she would have said, "I'll pop into the chemist, he'll make it up for you."

Isn't it funny how you can think about something when you're not thinking about anything? You know what I mean (good thinking). Now there I was, sitting, thinking about nothing, when Audrey said, "What yer thinking about, Mickey Plum?"

I said, "Nothing."

"You can't be thinking about nothing."

I said, "Well, that's what I just told the readers, so why should I lie to them? They've been behind me all the way and believing every word I say." Then out of the blue, Spike Milligan came into my mind, I said, "Get out, you fool, are you out of your mind?" As there's only room for one in here and hopefully my lease isn't up for a while. But then it came to me, I had Spike's address somewhere, I quickly found it and said, "That's enough for one day."

Next morning I went through the same procedure as I did with the one about The Grove. Well, I thought, I've done my best, I'll just keep everything crossed and wait, and then we got some bad news. Audrey's mother was very sick. We had a good talk about it and both agreed there was nothing she could do here. So I said, "Off you go, because if anything happens you'll be kicking yourself."

I had quite a bit of painting to do outside the house, so she said, "Make sure it's done before I get back."

I stood to attention, then quickly saluted and said, "Yes, ma'am! I'll just dust off your broomstick and you can be on your way."

Have you ever been belted with a broomstick folks? (It hurts). You know I was only in hospital a couple of days. Audrey came to see me before she left. Wasn't that sweet of her? Plus she brought me a box of her favourite chocolates and one of those crossword books that she likes doing. She said, "See you later and don't forget that painting."

"What painting?" And then it went dark again. That's twice now that's happened. In my subconscious I said, "As soon as you see a Doctor, tell him, as you're in the right place."

Then when I opened my eyes, a Doctor was stood there with a brandy glass in his hand. He said, "I just brought you to."

I said, "I didn't taste them. Bring me two more."

To be honest with you, I didn't know if I was Arthur or Martha, I thought, I must be Arthur, as I'm in the men's ward. I met the bloke in the next bed. In fact, he was an Aboriginal and a very funny fella. He reckoned he swallowed a boomerang, he'd been discharged twelve times. After the laughter had died down, he said, "I'm really in for what they call diarrhoea, as it scared me to death, I thought I was melting."

I said, "Have you tried Gravox?"

"Will that work?"

I said, "No, but it should thicken it."

Now I ask you, have you ever been kicked in the didgeridoo? It puts you right off your performance, I can tell you. Especially if you just happen to play the ruddy thing.

I managed to get all the painting done and, of course, I'd knocked out loads of writing. I had about three different stories on the go at once. In the meantime, Audrey's Mum had picked up, so Audrey came home and that night we'd had a few drinks. I must have been under the influence as I could see two of her. Quick as a flash, I thought my chances could be good. If one's got a headache, I'll make a play for the other and with a bit of luck, I could get the good looking one. Guess what? I got neither, I'm gonna sue that airline, jet lag has a lot to answer for.

If you remember, I'd written out a better copy of my tribute and as Audrey was in the spare room ironing, I said, "Would you like to type that out for me? When you get a chance, thanks."

She said, "Put it next to the pile of ironing and I'll iron out your mistakes later," (very clever that). I've trained her well, readers, plus I keep lobbing iron tablets into her coffee. So she typed it up and I thought it looked good in print, about me being a...

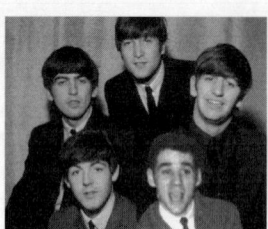

Beatlemaniac

I've written a rhyming story
It reads like a spoken song
If you're a fan like me
I'll ask you to sing along

Volumes have been written
Millions of words said
This you are reading now
Is categorised in my head

Too many songs to mention
Those I do I Will underline
Now I Feel Fine Because
I have started my rhyme

Let's use that crystal ball
A clear picture we will find
And see that memorabilia
'Way Down' in my mind   *E

We'll take The Long And Winding Road
To Penny Lane, that's a good start
And we'll purchase a Ticket To Ride
This Magical Mystery Tour of my heart

In the beginning there was John
"What You're Doing?" he said to Paul
"Me and you should Come Together
To revolutionise rock'n'roll"

Paul's mother, Mary, had died
And Julia was killed so young
"We Can Work It Out," they said
The writing geniuses had begun

Paul mentioned his pal George
John said The Word, "Bring him along"
The foundation was cemented
For the construction of a song

A drummer was recruited
This Boy was called Pete Best
The eggs were ready for hatching
But needed a stronger nest

They'd impressed the Germans
With My Bonnie and Ain't She Sweet?
Those Frauleins did Dig It
That crazy Beatles beat

"So Don't Let Me Down!"
Said Koshminder, mach schau
Eight Days A Week they sang
And for very little dough

Then Bill Harry told Brian Epstein
"Go to 'The Cavern' on Mathew Street"
He saw the lads Act Naturally
And arranged a place to meet

Brian became their Manager
A smooth talker with style
"I'll Get You to the top soon"
He said with a wry smile

They wanted another drummer
"I Wanna Be Your Man," said Ringo
They agreed he was the one
With words like "Eureka" and "Bingo"

The building was completed
They'd built a musical wavelength
"All Together Now," John said
"We'll go from strength to strength"

George Martin put them on £arlaphone
As soon as he heard that sound
And with the lads liking for Money
How appropriate the emblem was a pound

Early sixties I heard them
Seems like Yesterday, remember?
A Taste Of Honey on my palate
Oh, how sweet that September

I Want You to know that
I adored Love Me Do
Please Please Me made Number 1
And so did From Me To You

I liked I Call Your Name
Also If I Fell and Misery
You've Got To Hide Your Love Away
Now the rest, as they say, is history

"You Won't See Me," they said
To a Blackbird Flying over the Kop
The mates had only one goal
To be in unison at the top

John said, "What Goes On fellas?"
"We're going to the top," they'd boast
And where is the top, fellas?
The toppermost of the poppermost!

When they wrote She Loves You
They'd used every possible permutation
Those Words Of Love became the anthem
Sung by a Beatles crazed nation

I Saw Her Standing There they sang
I Want To Hold Your Hand
This was the second top seller
From England's most loved band

Who'd stormed the music scene
As they had previously pledged
Can't Buy Me Love hit the top
Now they're fully fledged

Characters like The Marx Brothers
Four Stooges instead of three
Sang I Love You Too, Dear Prudence
You Really Got A Hold On Me

They were our Lancashire lads
Who sang Only A Northern Song
The One After 909
Was bound to come along

When it did they went to Scotland
I've Got A Feeling they did rave
Here, There And Everywhere
Conquering Scotland The Brave

"Your Mother Should Know," I said
"This group is going to kick on"
Dr Robert examined Ringo's tonsils
While the Taxman was after John

"Fair dinkum," those Poms said
"I'm Down Under, it's great"
Sang For You Blue, Hello Goodbye
As they mimicked "G'day mate!"

Found an Old Brown Shoe
When they visited the Kiwi's
Now such a polished act
Shining over The Tasman Seas

The USA was Beatle plagued
With Limey's on their plight
They gave those exterminators
A Hard Day's Night

In LA, Mexicans shouted
"Hey Hey Hey Hey amigo"
They liked Every Little Thing
Performed by J, P, G & Ringo

John and Paul sang most songs
Odd times Ringo would sing
But Something that George sang
*Tugged at my 'Heartstrings'   *EK*

There was Ringo's Honey Don't
Think For Yourself, what's your choice?
I loved Paul's She's A Woman
With his interchangeable voice

They helped a lot of romances
By singing All You Need Is Love
And caused a musical Revolution
With Lucy In The Sky With Diamonds up above

'Audrey' and I were redecorating   *DB
While listening to those Scouses
<u>Twist And Shout</u> shook the foundations
And deafened those poor mouses*

*The <u>Two Of Us</u> liked <u>It's Only Love</u>
Paul's rendition <u>The Night Before</u>
<u>Got To Get You Into My Life</u>
We loved, plus quite a few more*

*There was <u>Baby It's You</u>
And George's <u>I Me Mine</u>
<u>All I've Got To Do</u>
Is mention <u>Good Day Sunshine</u>*

*Now these Fab Four mop tops
Who harmonised from Scouseland
So with their <u>Rock'n'Roll Music</u>
Were <u>Sgt Peppers Lonely Hearts Club Band</u>*

*Their music was played in pubs
Navvies were <u>Fixing A Hole</u> in the street
<u>Lovely Rita</u> was checking a meter
Tapping her feet to that Mersey beat*

*The Liverpudlian Ambassadors
<u>Getting Better</u> <u>Across The Universe</u>
By Jove I couldn't resist that
Just to <u>Help</u> me with my verse*

*A song came <u>Anytime At All</u>
<u>It Won't Be Long</u> was sang
Till Father McKenzie buried <u>Eleanor Rigby</u>
Then a lonely church bell rang*

*So <u>A Day In The Life</u>
Of those magnificent men
Wrote <u>Ob-La-Di-Ob-La-Da</u>
With their lyrical pen*

*The <u>Things We Said Today</u>
Those words will leave me never
<u>Do You Want To Know A Secret?</u>
They wrote <u>Strawberry Fields Forever</u>*

*Then went on a <u>Yellow Submarine</u>
<u>And Your Bird Can Sing</u> once more
To great songs like <u>Hey Jude</u>
<u>Hold Me Tight</u> <u>When I'm Sixty-Four</u>*

They sang about <u>Her Majesty</u>
The Fireman with his portrait
The Barber shaves another customer
While the Banker has to <u>Wait</u>

Ringo was in an <u>Octopus's Garden</u>
Far from the stormy skies
What about <u>Rocky Raccoon</u>
Was he shot between the eyes?

There was <u>Anna</u> and <u>Michelle</u>
<u>Long Tall Sally</u>, plus <u>Maggie Mae</u>
<u>She's Leaving Home</u>, sang Paul
*And 'Tomorrow' is 'Another Day'   *P*

"<u>I Need You In My Life</u>" he said
"<u>And I Love Her</u>, don't <u>Ask Me Why</u>
<u>PS I Love You</u>," he begged
"Please <u>Don't Pass Me By</u>"

<u>Being For The Benefit Of Mr Kite</u>
Has come to my recollection
<u>With A Little Help From My Friends</u>
My books and record collection

To me they were an island
In the middle of a stream
Like four colours of that rainbow
In my <u>Golden Slumbers</u> dream

Then the rumour Paul was dead
What a weird imagination
He was a <u>Paperback Writer</u>
In <u>Kansas City</u> on vacation

<u>It's All Too Much</u> they sang
Their lives became a song
Unhappiness reared its ugly head
While Beatlemania was going strong

Now I reckon those <u>Chains</u>
They were still there at night
John sang, "Oh <u>I'm So Tired</u>,
Please turn out <u>The Inner Light</u>"

Then came the break up
*They went their 'Separate Ways'   *E*
It was agreed <u>Let It Be</u>
*Yeah, 'Those Were The Days'   *MH*

Then John's murder was a callous act
And my tears fell like <u>Rain</u>
Julian and Sean were <u>Baby's In Black</u>
The group will never <u>Get Back</u> again

The <u>Boys</u> were in a state of shock
No more Lennon, McCartney penned
<u>Norwegian Wood</u> (This Bird Has Flown)
While three lads grieved a friend

<u>Lady Madonna</u> will <u>Carry That Weight</u>
<u>Maxwell's Silver Hammer</u> brings sorrow
For <u>The Fool On The Hill</u> and <u>Nowhere Man</u>
I think the sun will shine tomorrow

George paid tribute to John
Acoustically with Paul and Ringo
<u>There's A Place</u> where they'll meet
And reminisce about 'All Those Years Ago'   *G

Well it's time to <u>Slow Down</u>
In this whirlpool of rhyme
I just went under once
But <u>Not A Second Time</u>

Now <u>I Want To Tell You</u>
That I am not a sinner
<u>I'm A Loser</u> with the lottery
But this could be my winner

Might be in the <u>Birthday</u> honours
And receive the odd MBE
Would I 'Return To Sender'?   *E
Hey, no way José, not me

So <u>Roll Over Beethoven</u>
Tell Tchaikovsky the news
<u>I Should Have Known Better</u>
But there I've rhymed <u>Yer Blues</u>

I started writing under <u>Mr Moonlight</u>
Look out <u>Here Comes The Sun</u>
So I'll send <u>All My Loving</u>
And <u>I'll Follow The Sun</u>

By gum I've enjoyed this
What will become of it all?
I could be a <u>Day Tripper</u>
With Ringo, George and Paul

Beatles 'It Had To Be You'   **FS*
That gave this idea to me
If you read my story
<u>*Tell Me What You See*</u>

I 'Imagine' people will read this   **J*
Maybe some I've never seen
For <u>Tomorrow Never Knows</u>
It could open the door of my dream

<u>Please Mr Postman</u>, hear my plea
Take these words of mine
And don't be <u>Bad To Me</u>
That's the bottom line

<u>I'll Be On My Way</u> now
It's been a <u>Long Long Long</u> time
Come on, <u>You Know My Name</u>
So please drop me a rhyme

There's only one single left
And <u>The End</u> is now in sight
God bless you all, <u>Yes It Is</u>
<u>The Ballad Of John & Yoko</u>
<u>*Goodnight*</u>

I know in one sense, while writing that, I set out to name all The Beatles' singles, twenty-two in fact, and I achieved that, which to me was a challenge in itself. But out of the hundreds of song titles I could have put in, I think I only named about 150-odd of theirs, for the simple reason it would have been a mission impossible to mention them all.

I had read somewhere that John and Paul were notorious nickers. They would pinch words from "Here There And Everywhere". I think somewhere along the way I'd been brainwashed by "Penny Lane" and they'd mentioned everything in and around that area. Now don't get me wrong, I didn't steal their words, it was them that gave me the idea which is where 'That's My Rosegrove' came from in the first place.

So after reading the typed-up tribute to them I was quite pleased with myself. As the saying goes, I was over the moon, then suddenly a cold shudder came over me that brought me back down with a thud. Now what on earth do I do with it, or does it just get shoved in the drawer with the others? Then, as if by chance, a small flicker of light appeared in the lighthouse of my subconscious. So I searched through The Beatles books and Eureka! I found the address for Paul's home and the one of his office in London. So I sent a copy to MPL Communications and one to Waterfalls Estate, which is not far from where Spike lives in Sussex.

The longer it went, the more I thought I'm not going to hear anything. Now, what I should have done was not to affix a stamp, then I would have heard from them one way or another (yeah, their solicitors). Oh, by the way, remember those idiots I told to go and buy that book, they're not back yet, so should we wait for them or move on? (Moving right along).

Now I reckon it's a classic, so just go with me on this. What I should have done was to send a copy of The Goons tribute to Paul, and The Beatles one to Spike. Yeah, you're on the same track as me, now read on MacDuff. So you've got to imagine if and when these two should meet, their patter might go something like this:

Sir Spike first, "Hello, Sir Paul."

"How ya doing there ar kid?"

"I'm good, ta very much. Oh, by the way, Sir Paul, I received a story through the post the other day about The Beatles. It appears some cuckoo has got his wires crossed."

"That's a coincidence," said SP, "and you wouldn't believe it, I got one sent to me, and of all things, it's about The Goons."

"When you come to think of it," said Sir S, "it seems to me a very clever ploy to get us to write back to those bird brains. You know what? They're a cunning lot."

"Oh yeah, you can say that again," said Sir P.

"It seems to me a very clever ploy to get us to write back to those bird brains. You know what? They're a cunning lot."

"No," said SP, "when I said you could say that again, I didn't mean what I said."

"If you didn't mean what you said, Henry, why did you say it?"

"What, what, what, what, what," Sir Paul said.

Then Sir Spike quipped, "That's a nasty stammer you've got there. In fact, Neddie Seagroan (that well known moaner) had one just like it, all through The Goon Show series."

"What on earth are we going to do, Minnie? As this loony has gone to a great deal of trouble to get his foot in the door, and besides that, he's Down Under," SP said.

"So he should be. That's a good place for him," said Sir Spike.

"What's the best thing for us to do? We can't just ignore him," said SP.

"Send him a copy of that song of yours."

"Which one's that?" queried SP.

"No Reply," said Spike.

When I get setbacks like that it hurts, but if I can make it into something funny, it seems to take a bit of the pain away when that rejection rears it's ugly head.

Chapter
4

So about this time my team, Burnley, were on the improve (not too loud). Over the years they'd been up and down like a don't know what. Just take notice you lot, the next time you see a don't know what, if it's going up and down that's what I mean.

Now in the early sixties, they were a danger in the First Division. That was the top league then, as they didn't bring the Premiership in till much later. So there I was thinking about The Clarets, and what a top team they were and, of course, they had the greatest player who ever put on a pair of boots, the one and only Jimmy McIlroy, or to the Claret & Blue Army, Mac.

The book I was reading at this time was called "A Complete Record" by Edward Lee and Ray Simpson from 1882 to 1991 (and boy, do they know their onions). I read about games from yonks ago. It was good to have a book like this with all those facts, as in dates, years, attendances, home and away (sounds like an Aussie soap opera) details, those who played in the matches and, of course, the scores. I could have any game to check up on, right at my fingertips. So thanks to Messrs Lee and Simpson for a job well done.

I was just thinking about nothing, when I thought about the books I've plugged so far. I could be in line for some royalties, or they could be hearing from my solicitors, Marten, Barton & Fargo. Hands up all who thought the last word was going to be in reference to flatulence (disgusting).

Now do you, the readers, know what's coming? Spot on, you've hit the nail on the thumb. It's time for a tribute, and with this one not being as long as The Beatle one, it was a lot easier and a bit quicker to knock out. So what I'm going to do now is grab a cup of coffee while you, the viewers, read…

My Hero, My Friend

This boy from the village of Lambeg
Never thought he would play against Hamburg
Influenced by Uncle Willie and Harry, his Dad
When first capped, so proud of the lad

This talented footballer with a touch of "blarney"
Was a "Major Influence" in this "Claret & Blue Army"
I'd meet John under The Culvert in case of rain
Saw them beat Man United, "What a great game"

We'd stand in't corner on Turf Moor
When Mac got the ball, the crowd would roar
McIlroy and Adamson, brains in the engine room
Swept The Turf, like a new broom

Anyone who witnessed this combination
Saw two shining stars in a constellation
You'd think a coronary had hit the full back
Wrong, it was just a massive "Mac attack"

A deft flick, a precision pass
Like a hovercraft skimming over the grass
Pointer would hit it, you could bet
Any second, "kapow" in the back of the net

The final whistle blew, what a score
Manchester United 2, Burnley 4!!
Another game, Burnley were playing Spurs away
As long as I live, I'll never forget that day

Before half-time they were 4–0 down
There was a hush all over the town
I'd go to watch the reserves play
Many did when the first team was away

Burnley pulled one back, then two, then three
One more, and that would just do me
Over the speaker came the final score
Clarets had equalised with a deafening roar

Division 1 Championship against 'City'. What a win!
I was one of the hundreds that couldn't get in
The whole team deserved a medallion
Harry Potts victorious battalion

When the coach came down our street
The loyal fans got a great treat
Mac's glint in his eye and hands on the cup
Seemed to smile at me as he raised it up

Blacklaw, Elder, Smith, Joyce, Talbot, Angus
Over the seasons they did please us
Adamson, Harris, Cummings, Meredith, Miller
They plugged the gap like 'Polly Filla'

Connelly, Robson, Pointer, Lochead, Pilky & Mac
Interchange these for a great attack
Then dreaded news, he'd been given a transfer
Fans were flabbergasted, "Was this the answer?"

Begosh & begorra, situation was tragic
The magician disappeared with his magic
Boys and women cried, a thousand grown men
Vowed never to go through turnstiles again

The Clarets' loss, was Stokes' gain
To us supporters, heartache and pain
These are my thoughts and how I felt
I'd been given a horrendous 'belt'

I won't cry, I'll be brave and manly
So I switched to "Accrington Stanley"
But I committed a cardinal sin
When I asked what colours Accy played in!

Week after though, I was back at Turf Moor
I forgave them, but my heart was still sore
Not the end of the world and life goes on
As we reminisce, me and our John

It's a few years since I met that great man
Hope to meet him again one day if I can
So my tribute has come to an end
For Jimmy McIlroy, My Hero, My Friend

I enjoyed that cuppa. As I was a few lines in front, I thought I'd give you a chance to catch up. Ready? Let's move.

So I sent a copy of the tribute to the local paper, thinking, well, I've done my best again. Now I'd heard on the grapevine that there had been a couple of responses to That's My Rosegrove. This gave me a terrific feeling. There was no money coming my way, but this was a great reward in itself, that these kind-hearted people had actually written to the paper and thanked me personally for writing about The Grove and bringing back a lot of memories for them. I was as high as a kite for weeks.

Then came a distressing time, Tuppy was on her last legs, so to speak. A beautiful black Labrador, she was about fourteen or fifteen at this time. We weren't sure if her hip had gone, or she had arthritis, we decided to let her go to that great kennel in the sky. Bob and Pat took her to the vets for us, as neither Audrey nor I could find the strength. It took me quite a few days to get over that very traumatic time. Then just when I thought I was alright, this one particular morning I'd gone down to get some wood and the first thing I saw was where Tuppy had sat the last time we were down there together. I can honestly tell you, that cracked me right up. I cried like a baby for what seemed a long time and I made myself laugh by saying, "There's no women lining up to breast-feed you." (Well, you can't win them all).

Now, it had taken Audrey a while to get over it and then, of course, she was looking for another pet (yes, I did say pet, not pest, as she's got the latter). Apparently, she had done some enquiring, very cluey, these women. From what I could gather, rumour had it that a dog was on death row at the Rosebud pound. Time was running out, we only had a couple of days to reprieve him, so Audrey told me, and if not, into the electric chair he would go. He'd be strapped and zapped in that order if we didn't save him (talk about Chinese water torture).

By this time I was on my hands and knees pleading with her to go get him. Picking up her car keys she said, "I'll catch you later."

I sang out, "Hoy, what about a treat for this boy? And give us a quick nibble on one of them there dumplings."

She said, "Certainly not, they're for tea. So stir them once in a while till I get back."

After she'd gone I thought, I really came in, hook, line and sinker. And you know what, chaps? When it comes to these women, we've got them right where they want us. It's marvellous isn't it? The kids are grown up and all of a sudden we have a new addition to the family, what have I done to deserve this?

They say as one door closes, a window will slam on your fingers. I must admit though, the dog was so funny, and I christened him…

Spike

This is my story of a rascal called Spike
He came from the pound did this lovable tyke
I didn't want him at first, though I gave him his name
Really a substitute for Tuppy, but I loved him just the same

When Audrey saw him, she fell in love
With this shining star, from the heavens above
He was just what she wanted, the answer to her prayers
That day she brought him home, he soon lifted those cares

Spike should have been available on Prescription
Personality plus, was his description
Just what the Doctor ordered, it was so ironic
The exact amount of a recommended tonic

We didn't have him long, or so it seems
And now he has gone it's shattered our dreams
He was hit by a car, trying to scamper across the road
We watched, horrified, me and Aud

I placed my hand under his body, his little heart was pumping
Up the golden staircase on those Pearly Gates, he'd be thumping
And then Audrey and I, oh how we cried
We just could not believe little precious had died

I love anyone who makes me laugh
Like Spike did from the start
But when he passed away in my arms
Oh God! He broke my heart

I'd witnessed a grieving experience
And so had my wife
I wanted to place my mouth over his
Then bring him back to life

This cheeky chappie was only a kid
Didn't deserve to die the way he did
Then with Bob and Pat we laid him to rest
At the bottom of the garden where he loved it the best

I dug a hole and placed him in
Then with my hands cupped, I filled the soil in
Bob said a prayer to the Lord above
Take Spike in your care and give him our love

Yes, the little Scallywag was such a funny puppy
He's in that doggie heaven, right next to dear old Tuppy

After I'd read it through, I thought, where on earth did that come from? Just as I'd done with the others. It was very hard for me to accept, it baffled me that I could write something like that, as it's all true, I think it helped my grieving by dealing with it the way I did.

So I'm going to try to explain to you people what these tributes mean to me. That is, I can write what I wanna and the beaut thing is, it gives me a tremendous charge that I can voice my opinions and feelings like this, especially as of now, by writing my life story before and after the tributes.

It's actually funny to me that I can slip words in that weren't around in the early days, and when you see them you'll say, "He's right, we did get by without those words." Yet today we can't.

Here's an easy one for you. When you go to the cinema, you must have seen this heaps of times, a movie will start and the next thing that happens is you are in the middle of a flashback. "What's your point?" I hear you say.

My reply is, "Let's go back."

Chapter
5

With Dad gone, our abode became a home sweet home, so it must have been about this time I turned into a little cheeky bugger. From that moment on, I'd get that name a lot. Sometimes it was a full time job for not only Mum, but John and Bob, just to try and keep me in line. With a clip here, a clip there, here a clip, there a clip, anytime a clip, clip. Even on the streets, people would strike out with a well-timed cuff that was skilfully applied to the back of one's bonce. Yeah, it was open slather and their way of saying, without putting it into so many words, that we are your elders and if you've any manners you'll use them and respect us. Then for good measure, they'd throw in, "Children should be seen and not heard."

It didn't really hurt that much, I suppose it was just the shock of it. In fact, it did more good than harm, but sometimes it was so funny, if you came home and told Mummy, as you were looking for a bit of sympathy, she'd turn around and say, "You most probably deserved it, so tell someone who cares."

Just before I go on, earlier on in the piece I mentioned Grandma's brothers and sisters and their offspring. So I must have gotten sidetracked somewhere, as the other ones have just come to mind. I'll do my best to try and name them, so here goes; another brother was Bill and his wife Ethel, they had four children; Bill, who married Marion, their children were Janet and Bill; then there was Ronnie who married Joyce and they had Robert; the daughters were May, who married Harold and they had a daughter Kathleen; the other girl was Dorothy and her husband Albert, their children were Colin and Dorothy.

Now Grandma had another sister, her name was May and her husband was Ralph, they had Harold who married Jenny and they had two boys, Kevin and Keith. Then Grandma's other brother, Bob, and his wife Lizzie, they had a daughter who died very young, her name was Wyn.

Grandma used to tell us about one of her Great Aunts who had a liking for a wee dram or two the noo. Even her husband reckoned she had a drinking problem. "Balderdash," was her reply, "when I want a drink, it's not a problem." Every time there was a family get together, she was always on her balanced diet, yeah, one in each hand. They thought she was amazing for her age, she was eighty-five and didn't need glasses, she drank straight outta the bottle. Grandad would have this blank expression on his face and that's all he said.

There were no complaints at school, I've got many fond memories of this time, and life was good, but we didn't know what was lurking around the corner. I don't mean it was the end of the world, but it would be a big change. I didn't go to the school canteen much for lunch, as Grandma's was only a few minutes away. I remember she made bread in the oven next to the fire, you'd cut off a couple of slices and, as we used to say, thick as doorsteps, which were then smothered with jam, treacle or lemon curd. But then other times I'd make a beeline for the crust (I still do, folks). Then a big blob of marge or best butter, as we used to call it, whenever it was available, would be spread as thick as possible. When you took a bite you could see your teeth marks in it. You'd swear it was a homemade Venus's Flytrap. So that meant the other thing you never wanted to happen before demolishing it was (are you ahead of me?) the old Murphy's Law, best butter side down.

If you were quick enough (like me) you could flick it up with your left foot, then bounce it off your right knee. Then once you've got it spinning through the air, you're half way there and you've got a good chance it will stick to something (to save it from hitting the deck) and hopefully it's not the ceiling. Just imagine the repercussions, Grandad would hit the roof, saying, "You'll never be a footballer, you don't use your loaf," shaking his head and saying to Grandma, "crumbs woman, that kid should have his crust examined, he's a couple of butties short of a picnic."

Then it would be, "Is that the time? Superboy's got to fly, bye Grandma," a quick pat for the dog, then tweak his nose, which made him sneeze.

If the cat was at the back door waiting to come in I'd pick him up, then sling him just inside the door, as I knew the dog was trying to get out. So this meant the dog and the cat had their noses about a couple of inches from each other, then of course, it was on for young and old. Now, you'll have to excuse me you lot, as I'm going to use it. They fought like cat and dog. There I was, closing the door and poor Grandma didn't know what the commotion was all about, she was always telling them off and, "If they couldn't get on together, one of them would have to go," she'd say. And as the sneck went down I could hear Grandma, I was laughing to myself.

She always had a tea towel over her shoulder and she was the fastest Granny in The Grove who could whip a spoon off the table into the sink at two paces. It was only a small yard at Saltburn Street, and as I closed the back gate behind me, I could hear her whipping the tea towel while saying, "You're on you're last flipping warning you two."

While on the subject of food, my favourite would have to be yellow fish or

Scotch fillet, as we used to call it (Cape Cod, Aussies) with plenty of potatoes. I could eat that till it came out of my ears.

I'll never forget some of dear Grandma's words of wisdom. Crusts are good for the hair and fish for the brains. When people asked me, "What are you going to be when you grow up?"

I'd tell them, "A curly haired scientist."

Grandad, Grandma and Laddie

Christmas times were great. Grandma's table, which was a snooker table, would be chock-a-block with food and the family had a laugh at my expense. There were a few veggies that I didn't like, they were: cabbage, parsnip and swede. So they would only put on my plate what I could eat. For example, Brussels, carrots (as they were good for your eyes, who ever saw a rabbit wearing specs?), cauliflower, peas, spuds and chicken, because at that stage I loved chicken, but hated turkey. Maybe this was because it was a darker meat.

And, of course, who could forget pickled onions? If you remember, we used to get pickled onions and cauliflower in the same jar (I think it was a brand name like Crosse & Blackwell). We used to call the cauliflower 'trees'. And just thinking about it now, Grandma used to make her own pickled onions. I still make them, but unfortunately I haven't got Grandma's recipe. Then if my plate was empty and I was still licking my lips, Mum or Grandma would say, "Do you want a chicken butty to finish off with?"

"Yes please," I'd say. The turkey was shoved between two slices of bread and their dastardly deed was done. So unbeknown to me, I ate it, but really, I should have twigged, what with all that smirking and twittering and not necessarily in that order. I know one thing for sure, I've loved it ever since.

I don't know if there's many of you intelligent people still with me (I hope so). Just at the minute I'm having trouble growing up, as I'm enjoying this, so it could take a while. Well, I've got a lifetime in front of me.

At school there were a lot of budding comedians. Everybody wanted to get in on the act. Mum didn't know this at the time, but she was my scriptwriter, as I'd pinch funny lines that she'd used and I'd just twist them around to suit me.

One joke that she would tell was about the couple during the war. The night raids were on over England, the sirens were blaring and that was their way of telling the masses to get to the air raid shelters as quickly as possible. So this couple were in their bedroom and double checking to see if they had got everything, when the wife noticed her old man was frantically going through the drawers, she said, "Hurry up, or we'll be blown to bits where we stand," then she said, "come to think of it, there's better places than this I'd rather be killed in."

He shouted, "Just give us a minute, woman, as I'm having trouble finding me choppers."

She screamed at him, "They're dropping bombs, not bloody sandwiches!"

Mum went to the fishmongers once, she said, "What have you got today that's cheap?"

He said, "We've just had a large delivery of whale meat."

She said, "I'll take some, but I can't afford a lot. How much is it?"

He said, "It's not that expensive, in fact, it's only a penny a pound."

She put a farthing on the counter saying, "Give us a quarter of a pound."

He said, "Will that be all then, Margaret?"

To which she replied, "Yes, but can you do us a favour and wrap its head up for the cat?"

"Bye now," he said, "will we see you tomorrow?"

She said, "There's no guarantee, but whale meat again. Don't know where, don't know when."

Then she'd pop into Sherburns and say, "Have you got a sheep's head? And can you leave its legs on?"

Now at school, as any kid would know, is where you get your nickname and I was no exception, as I was christened Michael, so of course, I copped Mickey Plum. I'm not sure where this comes from, but I remember the girls would sing, while skipping, "Salt, mustard, vinegar, pepper…" I don't know if that's the right way round, but it went something like that. And the girls would sing one with my nickname in it (I wouldn't mind having a couple of bob each way it wasn't a skipping song) which went like this…

> *Mickey Plum with the gas tar bum*
> *Went sailing down the river*
> *A big fish come and bit his bum*
> *And it made his belly shiver*

I remember once I scribbled on the blackboard 'Mickey Plum is the best kisser in the class'. The teacher saw it, "Okay, which one of you is Mickey Plum?"

Somebody said, "Please Miss, it's him with the dollop of lard on his head," pointing straight at me. Well, it wasn't my turn for the Brylcreem and a kid had to do what a kid had to do to look smart.

So the teacher said, "Mickey Plum, I want you to stay behind after class, is that understood?"

"Yes Miss," I nodded.

After school I walked up to the top gate, and there waiting for me were a few little floozies. Now, I don't know whether they really liked me or they were just trying to lick the jam from the corners of me gob (now you may not know this, but I'm going to tell you. That's why we have lips, so as to stop your mouth from fraying at the edges). So I managed to fight them off and had tucked everything back into my pants that belonged there. For example, shirt and Post Office savings book (I never left home without it), which contained about nine pence (you could buy quite a lot of kali and Spanish for that). Maybe they were after the money. Who knows?

No sooner had I thought that, when this snotty nosed kid said, "Mickey Plum, I'm a Philatelist."

"Well, I'm Church of England but you don't hear me broadcasting it to everybody."

She said, "That means I collect stamps."

So I stamped on her foot and said, "You can add that to your collection."

Now by this time, the rest of them were dying to know what went on with the teacher. And how did I back up the statement that I was the best kisser in the class? While nonchalantly wiping the drip that was just about to hit my top lip (and ruin this young lad's image) I said, "I'm not telling you lot." But it pays to advertise.

Now our school was like every other one. There were good and bad kids. But the teachers knew who the real terrors were and they would blow the whistle on them, so to speak.

While we are still at school, do you remember the four colours? And we also wore some sort of a band. I don't think they went in any sort of order so here they are: Buttermere (yellow), Grasmere (green), Thurlmere (red) and Windermere (blue). While you're still remembering, here's some rhymes that were doing the rounds…

> *Mary had a little lamb*
> *She also had a bear*
> *I've often seen her lamb*
> *Never ever seen her bare*

I don't know if it was the same girl, but here's another one:

> *Mary had a little lamb*
> *It's fleece as white as snow*
> *Everywhere that Mary went*
> *The lamb was sure to go*
> *It followed her to school one day*
> *And a big lorry squashed it*

Now this next girl was different altogether:

> *The Captains' daughter, Mabel*
> *Whenever she was able*
> *She gladly gave the crew*
> *A portion on the galley table*

There were loads of these being passed around, which of course we kept secret from the teachers (who used to say, "Isn't it nice to hear the kids chuckling at playtime."). This one's clever:

> *Now there was a crooked man*
> *Who had walked a crooked mile*
> *And he found a crooked tanner*
> *Then stuffed up the fag machine*

I cleaned those last two up, just a little bit, in case there are any whippersnappers reading this. Mind you, they've probably read worse before today. Here's one more:

Simple Simon met a pie man
Who was going to the fair
Said Simon to the pie man
"What have you got there?"
He replied, "Pies, stupid."

Or what about when the teacher would say, "Is there anyone who'd like to stand up and say a few words about going on a holiday, and to mention Timbuktu?" I was the one that was jeered on by all the kids as a dare. So I stood up, quickly wiping my nose on my sleeve, it came out something like this:

Tim and I went down to Kent
There were three girls in a tent
Now then I bucked one
And of course Timbuktu

Well the class was in an uproar, but the teacher was not amused, she said, "Guess what?" (I thought, don't tell me I've got to go all through my life listening to these women saying, guess what? That really is something to look forward to). "I want you to stay behind after class. Is that understood?"

While blushing like a don't know what, I mumbled, "Yes Miss."

Now, if you've ever seen a don't know what and it was blushing, that's exactly what I'm talking about. Wait a minute, I said to myself. That'll be the second time this week I'll have been kept in after school. This could mean only one thing. She's crazy about me and just wants my body. Well I was half right (bottom half). As she bent me over, then spanked me with a ruler to within an inch of my life.

One day a skeleton was brought in, as we had to learn about certain parts of our bodies. One kid said, "She's thin."

"Yes, that's Anna Rexic," I said. A lot of them didn't get that joke. Maybe it was ahead of its time. And here's another one for good measure… she used to like dancing, but it's a long time since she's been, as she has nobody to dance with.

The teacher would ask some girl to point to somewhere on their own body and then say what part it was. And then the teacher would point to the same place on the bag of bones and say, "That's quite right, Daisy."

Then the teacher said, "Gilbert, where is your index finger?"

And some smart remark would come from the back of the classroom, "Where it normally is, and that's halfway up his hooter, digging out crows," (medical authorities warn that nose picking can lead to one's cranium caving in).

"Half of that is enough, thank you very much," the teacher said, pointing to the index finger on the skeleton, she said, "that's where it is, isn't it children?"

"Yes Miss," they would chorus in unison.

"Now, Mickey Plum, I want you to tell the girls and boys where your bowels are."

"I don't know, Miss, as me Granny makes me move 'em every morning." I think you know what's coming folks.

So she said to me, while looking at the kid who was sitting opposite. Oh, I forgot to tell you, the teacher had a wandering eye, in fact, the other one was so lovely, this one couldn't stop looking at it. Yes, she was very attractive really.

I could have slept in her eyes as there was a sty in one. Her ears were like flowers (cauliflowers). Her teeth were like stars, they came out at night. She had lips like petals, not rose petals, more along the lines of bicycle pedals. Remember that first time I was kept in after school, well it was then I asked her about the wonky eye (she rolled her eyes at me, I picked 'em up, then rolled them back).

"When I cry, the tears run down my back," she said, "then I finish up with bacteria." Then she threw this at me, "Sometimes I really have trouble controlling my pupils."

I could see she was getting teary eyed. I thought, for goodness sake, don't tell me she's going to scrike her eyes out, as I wouldn't have a clue which way the tears would go, so I said, "Fair maiden, what you need is a bit of a squeeze (and I'm just the lad for the job)."

"Oh, yes please," she said.

It was then that I noticed her chest region. It looked like two kids fighting under a blanket and there was a thumping sound. I knew it was her heart that was pounding. In fact, I'd never heard a noise like it, and with me being only a little tyke, mine was a quarter pounder. I looked into her eyes. One of them was looking out the window. I would have won a coconut if I could tell you where the other was gazing. We raced towards each other in slow motion. Well, that's what they do in the films, so why should we be any different?

> *Oh no, I thought but I could see*
> *My napper was in line with her knee*
> *Whew, I knew it wasn't meant to be*
> *When she went gliding past me*

Throwing her arms around the skeleton, "We've got to stop meeting like this," she said, "I have to get somebody more my age, as you're losing too much weight. So remind me first thing in the morning and I'll make an appointment for the quack to see you."

I thought, I hope he has more luck than you, I said, "Er…um…yes, Miss," and

I quickly closed the door behind me.

I didn't "Look Back In Anger", but I glanced over my shoulder. I could see she was staring around the room to try and find out who had just walked in and the poor old skeleton looked like a cross between Shaking Stevens and Mister Bo(ne)jangles. I swore I could hear it singing, "Dem Bones, Dem Bones, Dem Dry Bones."

Now where did I dig that lot up from? I think I surprised myself then. But while it was coming, and from who knows where, I thought, Mickey Plum, you've got to go with this and if you lose a few readers along the way, that's how the mop flops.

Well folks, I'm gonna put the kettle on (and who knows, it might suit me). So we'll have a cuppa and meet back here. Let's synchronise. Now I make it a quarter past something, I'll have to get a little hand for this watch (I couldn't resist throwing that one in. It was a classic that Hylda Baker used), so I'll be back shortly.

Chapter
6

I'm here. Now, anybody not back yet, kindly put your hand up. Well that's not bad, there's only a couple missing. I'll just go slow until they catch up. Remember the ones that went for that book? There's no sign of them. I think they've gone down the dreaded gurgler. So should we have a minute's silence? All in favour say, "Aye." The nays have it. Well, if they don't show up, I'll just have to write them back in. And then "It Ends With Magic", a book written by Spike Milligon (that well known typing error).

Now, if you can cast your minds back, I was telling you about the teacher who was talking to me while looking at this other kid. And she asked, "How do the initials GW grab you?" Straight away I thought, they're the same ones as my dream girl, who just happens to be Gina Wollabridgeider. Go on, laugh, it's alright for you lot, people should understand that Wollabridgeider is not that easy for a young lad to pronounce.

So before you bring your minds forward, I think I was telling you about rhymes. This one almost got under my guard. Mum used to say this one to us a lot, but I wouldn't have a clue where it came from. I'll tell it to you as I know it and hopefully someone out there might know where it originated:

I went round a back street front corner
There I saw a dead donkey alive
I took out my knife and shot it
And that's how the dead donkey died

I went to the pictures tomorrow
I took a front seat at the back
A lady gave me a banana
I ate it and gave it her back

While we are on this one, there are another couple of lines, but I'm not sure where they fit in. It goes something like this:

I fell from the pit to the gallery
And broke a front bone in my back

So as far as I know, there's only two verses and I'm not sure which one is first. I think I've been pretty patient with you up to now, and as we are all in this together, I'm a little bit disappointed. When I was telling you about GW, suddenly I went off the rails again (seems to be a pattern there). Next time you can see it's going to happen, give us a whistle. So those initials, they stand for 'guess what'. Then I replied, "What Miss?"

"I won't keep you in after school," she said, "as I'm looking for somebody that's strong." Under my breath I said, "Try Henry behind me, he's very strong. I can smell him from here (and I wish he'd 'Take It From Here')."

A good job she didn't hear me, or it could have been on again. And who knows where I might have gone with that story? So think yourself lucky.

Let's go back to Liverpool Road for a while. Now, we weren't a very musical family, but we all had to attempt to sing as there was no lock on the toilet door. The toilet was in what we called the air raid shelter. The coal was kept in there, which sometimes would be chucked down the loo. I remember one time a kitten had been pushed down. I suppose you could say it was its turn for the long drop. Mum had a helluva job getting it back up. Talk about soggy moggy. It wasn't in it. I don't know what mood it was in, or its colour for that matter, but it seemed browned off when it came out.

It was a good place to play, but at night a young lad didn't know what lurked out there. We used to have to take turns to bring some coal in. I hated it when it was my turn. Mum only had to say, "Michael The Great," and that was it, I had to get the shugel. I told you I had trouble with words, and that was another (there could be some more like that, so you have been warned).

If you were anything like me, you would leave the curtains open and the door ajar (when is a door not a door? When it's ajar) for a bit of extra light while you were going on your death defying journey. And if it had been a warm day, there would be midges about. Now, it was a hard task in itself, to whistle while your teeth were chattering and to swat things you couldn't see, especially with a thing that weighed about 3lbs in your mitt. You'd push the door open pretty quick while shouting, "Is anybody there?" Goodness knows what would have happened if someone had spoken. I could have gone down in history by breaking the four minute mile before Roger Bannister. Then you'd slide your implement along the floor and if you were lucky you'd get a few cobs and a bit of slack (as long as the cat hadn't crept in, crapped and then crept out again), you were feeling pleased with yourself but still shaking.

Not only were you wearing short pants, your breath was in short pants. You would come out of the shelter and see that the curtains had been drawn, but the furniture was real. Do you realise if it wasn't for Venetian blinds it would be curtains for the lot of us. It was then that I noticed someone had thieved the jar and the door was pushed two. Not only had they closed it on me, they'd done it twice for good measure. I shouted, "Let me in!"

The brains trust sang out, "Who is it?"

"It's The Great Michael," I replied, then Mum opened the door, I said, "I was passing and saw your light on. So I just called to say I love you." (Good title for a song that, in fact, coal me, I have a sack full).

"Just in time lad," she said, "it's your turn to wash up."

While still shaking, I said, "I'm sure there was a bogey man."

"The dead won't hurt you," she said, "it's the living you've got to keep your eye on." (There's many a true word spoken in jest).

While on the subject of toilets and making fun of them, this is not a joke, but it's in loo of. Question: What is 25 yards long and usually hangs in the kitchen?

Answer: It's a toilet roll.

I hear you say, come, come, Mickey Plum, surely a toilet roll doesn't hang in the kitchen? And I say, you're right, any bum knows that. Are you implying this is toilet humour? (Well it's none of your business).

I think I was talking about singing. I know I'd make Mum laugh, being on my knees on the oil cloth (or if you were posh, Linoleum) with a stick in my hands using it as a paddle, while warbling, "'Can I Canoe You Up The River?' Can I canoe you up the stream?" So if I had to sing for my supper I'd most probably starve to death. About singing, I tell a lie. There was a singer in the family. Yeah, the sewing machine, and as the other saying goes, I couldn't play a musical instrument to save my life. The funny thing was, we were always up to date with the current music, which was just great. With no TV there was stacks of music on the radio. Even the comedy shows all had a musical interlude. Then, of course, there was the best station ever for music and it was 208 on your dial, Radio Luxembourg.

I suppose you could call us the original Back Street Boys. Oh yeah, we were rough and ready, guys. And we did our damnedest to harmonise. You know to this day I can still close my eyes and see young Billy flying along Owen Street on our latest mode of transport with me and Colin running behind in hot pursuit and singing out, "Clang, clang, clang goes our trolley." What great fun.

Other good times would be spent going down towards The Engine Shed on John Parkinson's three-wheeler bike (a red one, I think). Talk about The Edinburgh Military Tattoo. You know where there's all those blokes hanging off a jeep of some sort? We'd never actually seen this, only on radio of course (who needs a TV as long as you have a good imagination). I don't know what our record was, but we'd pile on as many kids that managed to hang on. I think one time we had about six on board. There would be fingers and thumbs everywhere and a muffled voice would yell, "Get yer nails cut!"

And if you didn't balance this weight properly, you'd be holding on for dear life. With having two wheels at the back, they were okay, but you had trouble keeping the front one down. So that meant whoever was trying to steer had all those bodies hanging over him. People just watched in amazement.

Two dogs were passing. One said to the other, "Should we throw a bucket of water over 'em?" Even birds were hurting themselves by falling out of trees while laughing at our antics. I don't know what happened to Uncle Ics. Maybe he was having a bit of a siesta. If you've seen Ester, you'd most probably like some yourselves (as for me personally, I'll have half). So the song we belted out was based on the "Twelve Days Of Christmas", which went something like this… now on the count of 1,2,3, c'mon, sing along with me…

Six kids on a bike
Five thrown off
Four broken limbs
Three black eyes
Two teeth missing
One busted nose
And a partridge with a fractured knee

Well done! You're not bad singers you lot. Not good, but not bad! We'd stagger home like the walking wounded. We had been battered from pillar to post. I'd get home feeling sorry for myself and looking like the wreck of the Hesperus, "All I really wanted was a cuggle," I said to me Mum.

"I'm all out of them just now, and I thought you were my brave solider, anyway," she said.

"I am, but believe me it's a bloody battle ground out there."

"I'll have less of that language in this house," she said.

"Shakespeare says it."

"Well," she said, "you don't play with him any more and, by the way, there's two d's in kuddle."

"To d's or not to g's. What's the difference? So is my request going to be granted? Because I'm under the weather just now."

"I wondered why you were wearing your sou'wester and wellies," she said.

Now, I don't know if you've ever noticed this or not, but girls seem to have the ability to scream at Will (and honestly, he wishes they'd stop, as the poor bloke's heading for a nervous breakdown). So my scream came out like a mouse breaking wind. Mum said, "What was that deafening noise?"

"It's me, I'm trying to keep your attention, remember? And 'Mama Mia', if you don't help me now (and 'Please Please Me', stop ad-libbing) I'm going to need therapy in years to come. Do me a favour, just 'Rock Me'."

"Certainly," she said, "if I can find a rock big enough."

She made me giggle. So instead of that cuddle, I settled for a chuckle.

Then right out of the blue we were on the move, but still within spitting distance of The Grove. So we moved to 65 Dorset Street, which I suppose was only about five minutes walk from Liverpool Road. I would keep my friends, plus making one or two more. And as it worked out, the Junior School was almost on our doorstep.

I remember early one morning, we hadn't been living at the new house long, when there was a knock on the door. Mum said, "I wonder who that can be at this time of the day?"

"I'll get it, as it could be an opportunity," I said, "and as everyone knows, it only knocks once." I opened the door and the Milkman was standing there.

"Would you like to do me a favour? Go and tell all the people that I deliver to 'On The Sunny Side Of The Street', the cows have got tuberculosis, so there won't be any deliveries," he said, "you will see where I take the milk to, as the empty bottles will be on the step. I'll give you a shilling for your trouble."

"I'll do that small thing just for you," I said, "so show me the money." He handed me a photograph of a half crown. I gave him a photo of 1/6 change, and the deal was completed.

I shouted over my shoulder
"Back in five minutes, Mum"
Yes, it's a job for Superboy
And by gum, it shall be done

I was "Gone In Sixty Seconds". I made for Aunty Maggie's first, as she would give me a thrupny bit. I thought, when I leave here there's moolah to be made if I play my cards right. "You're early," she said, "what's wrong?"

"No need to hit the panic button," I said. Then I sang out as best I could, "'No Milk Today', the cow had twolikklehorses." After a while I'd picked up some pennies, plus washers, a couple of safety pins and a piece of chewing gum. There's some bent people out there. Now a bit of mileage is left on the choddie so I'll keep that. As for the washers and safety pins, I know a place for them, I'll stick 'em in the collection plate at a later date.

On the way home I could hear the neighbours saying, "That's little Mickey Plum and he's doing such a good job, but the simpleton doesn't know there's three t's in twolittlehorses."

I got back and told Mum what had happened. She laughed so much. Then she said, "You're very funny. You should be on the stage, painting it."

I said, "Oh Mummy
Now you're so funny
And I'm not a dummy"
I showed her the money

Then she said, "I'm keeping you off school today."

"Yippee," I said, "but I'll bet you've got some dirty jobs lined up for me to do."

"It's nothing like that," she said, "but you can still go if you want to. Mind you, you'll be the only one there, as it's Saturday." (I never saw that coming).

"So give us a cuddle," she said.

"Oh, that's your sneaky plan, is it now," I said, "it's alright for you to say that. But when it was my turn all I got was cold shoulder (and you know I only like chicken). So the shoe is on the other hand, also the chairs are turned. How do you like those oranges? That's a different kettle of chips."

I knew all the one-liners. In fact, there was one for every occasion, so it was just a case of getting them the right way around so once I did that they seemed to just roll off the tongue. Mum used to amaze me how she would pull those great quips, from what seemed nowhere, just when she needed them.

It's so funny when a young lad knocks on a door and a pretty girl opens it. So not much chance of that happening in The Grove, as there were some real little horrors according to the lads at school. In fact, they reckoned one lass was so ugly they had to tie a chop round her neck so that the dog would play with her (weren't they cruel?), I would never have said anything like that. Do you believe me? I bet you don't know what to think. Folks, I've been racking my brains for ages on how to get that one in, but as I say, where there's a will there's always a relative.

It's back to the kids on the doorstep, or "Hello Young Lovers" (that's where we were, if you remember) and then you would stare at each other for what seemed a lifetime. You'd both still be blushing and feeling slightly embarrassed, then you would glance at your shoes. If by chance they were dirty, you then hurriedly tried to polish them by putting your foot behind the other leg and then giving them a quick once over on your sock.

While all that was taking place, you were still really fidgety, which generally meant twirling some piece of your clothing. Suddenly an idea came to you, then there would be a frantic search through your pockets to give her a present. She can't have that piece of string as that's a back up for my pin for. I hear you ask, what's a pin for? It's to hold my trousers up just in case me braces snap. There was no way I would give her the bus ticket. It might come in handy one day. All that remained was my lucky rabbits foot (it didn't bring him much luck). Yeah, I thought, that's the only way to go, to give it as a token of my love. I gently placed it into her tiny hand (no it wasn't frozen, it was quite warm actually).

At this stage we still hadn't exchanged words, and then her sparkling eyes gazed straight into my big brown ones, she said, "You can shove that scabby thing as far as it can go. Now sod off!"

Did you know I invented the knock, knock ones, so lets give it a go. Knock, knock. Who's there? Ammonia. Ammonia who? Ammonia little kid who can't reach your doorbell.

They say love hurts. It starts when you're young and goes on forever and ever. My little heart was broken as if it had been belted quite a few times with a sledgehammer. I thought, there's plenty more pebbles on the beach, but not shaped like that one. I gently closed the gate behind me, then pushed their moggy into the privet hedge.

Right behind us on Dorset Street was Hilton's Bleach. Sometimes I'd help around the yard. Does anyone remember how they used to have those great big bottles which had some sort of straw on the outside and then wire around that? I didn't really know what that was for. Looking back now, maybe it was a safety precaution, in case of spillage or breakage. Whoever came up with it, they hit on a clever idea. Once you got used to handling them, you could actually move them with ease.

I think the bleach itself was industrial. I was a bit young to get into that side of things and I think if you were really interested you would ask questions. Other times people would say for no reason, "Hey young fella, can you see that thing there? Well it's used for such and such." I thought, I must remember those words of wisdom for later in life if ever my such and such is broken. I'll use one of those instead.

Chapter
7

By this time John had started work and Robert had gone on to Towneley. Now at the back of Gannow Lane and Saltburn Street was Mr Briercliffe's Woodyard. It wasn't as big as Mr Iverson's and maybe not as productive, but still a reasonable sized place. There were Mr Briercliffe's sons, John and Wesley, plus a few more worked there. I'd do a few small jobs, like cleaning up and making teas. This was mostly Saturday mornings.

Then one day, the lad who used to go to Hargraves Pie Shop for the morning teas hadn't shown up. So, of course, I was shoved into the spotlight. Now you had to get them all to write down what they wanted, for the simple fact that if there were any mistakes they couldn't blame you and it was best if you got correct weight so you wouldn't have to carry much money. You also had to get back quick or the pies and pasties were cold, and believe me, that didn't go down too well with some of the blokes. Yes folks, there were some "Grumpy Old Men" in those days (good film that).

I would dawdle on my way to the shop, poking my tongue out at some kid on the bus or a quick swing round the lamp-post. I'd been known to stand outside Shorrock's Toffee Shop and slaver for a couple of minutes, then come back to earth with a crash as now the job had to be done.

The list was handed over, then the goodies were placed in separate bags with the right person's initials on. The job lot was then put into a cardboard box. Now, the money I kept in an old tin that Grandad had given me. I think it was some sort of a toffee tin which he used to keep his cigarettes in so they wouldn't get squashed. Then, of course, when he got a new one I was always next in line for the other. There weren't many kids around The Grove that could say they had their own tin (I've still got one to this day).

The teenage girls that worked in the shop would wink at me or offer me biscuits. Yes folks, it's true, I was cheap in those days (every young kid has his price). Then I was outta there in a flash, running as fast as I possibly could. I was likened to a blur. Women who were mopping steps or sweeping the flags (footpath, Aussies), (sidewalk, Americans), their turbans would fall from their heads and curlers would drop out. While those wearing pinnys, they were ripped off, and as I went past the moggy who was doing his contortionist act, his legs every which way, his head tucked somewhere near the lower Hebrides. Actually, he looked like a set of broken bagpipes and then when he got the back draft from the whoosh, he was off, as the saying goes, like a scalded cat. People were saying, "Was it a bird? Was it a plane?"

I disappeared around the corner shouting back over my shoulder, "No, it's Superboy with the grub."

I think they used to knock off at lunchtime on Saturday. So when they were ready for going home, some of them would give you a penny or tuppence. I'd sometimes joke with the blokes, saying, "Give us a tanner. I want to go to the flicks this arvo." (Well, it was worth a try).

And they'd say, "That's all the change I've got besides a two bob piece."

Quick as a flash I'd say, "I've got change, in fact, the change will do you good."

So then it would be, "Get out of here, you little cheeky bugger!"

I'd go and say, "So long," to Mr Briercliffe and, "See you next time." He'd reach into his pocket and give me some loose change.

> *So on a good day*
> *You could walk away*
> *With a shilling or three*
> *Thanks, that'll do me*

I mentioned earlier about what we called a Post Office savings book. I think it was Grandma that had put me on the right track with that (or so she thought). I'd give her a shilling and ask her if she would get some stamps for me on Monday. Then I was off to get the toffee and it would be Saturday afternoon at the Coli, upstairs (there's posh for you). A bag of crisps and a Tizer (lovely jubbly) which came in very handy in case you just happened to bite that small blue packet which contained the salt.

So all in all, it turned out to be a great day. Remember other times when you had a bit of money in your pocket? Then some kid would hear it rattling about, creep up behind you then stick a finger in your back (I think it was a finger, or they might just have been pleased to see me) and they would say, "This is a stick up. Give us your money or your life."

And I would say, "Take my life. I'm saving up."

Now, I'm going to test your memories, about the American kid who came from Texas. In fact, we called him Tex for short. But it was Grandma who said there's something fishy about that young fella. I don't think you should be playing with him (it was funny how she spotted this). He was a real menace, not really for thieving things, just borrowing them for good. Grandma would say, "Where's that tennis ball got to? I haven't seen you playing with it. Don't tell me you lost it?"

"No," I said, "Tex has got it."

Then it was, "Where is the pencil you had? You haven't given that away, have you?"

"No Gran, Tex has got it."

Then she said, "Grandad was looking high and low the other day for his penknife and he couldn't find it anywhere. Have you seen it?"

I took a big breath and sang out, "It's 'Deep In The Heart Of Texas'."

So I was popular with the kids, having gone from Mickey Plum to Mick The Knife. Is there no stopping this bloke's determination, as he keeps trying to pull the wool over our eyes, by slotting in these anecdotes? If you think I'm scraping the bottom of the barrel, you're very much mistaken. In fact, I've only just skimmed the surface, or to use the words of Al Jolson, 'You ain't heard nuttin' yet!

As you've already read, I've named a few people. The hardest part I find now is trying to remember the exact year that the others came into my life. As this pans out, you will see that there will be a cast of thousands. I can assure you, you're on my file. So it might take a while, you'll just have to wait till your name is called.

Mums friend, Alice, was going out with Eddie. He worked "On The Buses". They got married and had three children: Andrew, David and Julie. Not so quickly, but in that order, I think?

Chapter
8

You know folks, it's been a while since a 'Guess What?' (Well, we're due for one, like it or not). So Mum said, "Guess what?"

"Good Golly Miss Molly," I said, while doing a double take at the furniture van that just happened to be idling outside our door. I thought, why are we on the move again so soon? I was just getting used to this place. Now all I had to find out was if I was included in their plans as everybody was avoiding me like the plague. So I sang out, "'If You Leave Me Now', you'll take away the biggest part of me." And somebody, one day folks, will most probably write a song about that. What's that you say? Why don't I write it? Well, I'll tell you, at the moment I'm struggling to keep in front of you and if I stop to write a song, you'll be off and I won't see your heels for dust. As for the ending, it's no good asking me, I'm not within striking distance of it yet. So trust me, you'll be the first to know. That's after me, of course.

"Listen, number three son," Mum said (she always called me 'Listen'), "if we don't take you, we'll have no one to belt or shout at for no reason at all."

When she put it like that it was an offer I couldn't refuse, I breathed a sigh of relief, it's nice to be wanted. Not knowing where we were going, I wondered if passports and visas would have to be in order. We'd had jabs the last time we moved, so maybe we need boosters, they say it's better to be safe than sorry. It's funny what gets into a young lad's noggin. What if we are emigrating? Now that's what I'd call an adventure. The mind boggled, then I quickly realised we couldn't be going overseas, not with the motor running outside the door. Then someone said, "Will you get from under the feet?" (They often called me 'Will You').

Now I feel a tangent coming on… so excuse me while I go off at one. Better still, if I go off on a tandem, you can come with me. Then you'll be behind me all the way and won't you look sweet? (On a bicycle made for two). Now, it's funny how according to the adults, that kids, no matter where they are, they're always under someone's hoofs. We have a disadvantage, as we're down at heel to begin with. I wish I had a quid for every time I'd been walking along, minding my own business, when this big clodhopper would come from out of the blue, then catch me right on the back of my shoe. The first words uttered from those in higher places. It wasn't a 'sorry, young un', quick as a flash you'd get, "Why don't you look where you're going?"

And I'd flash back just as quick (under my breath), "Because I was going where I was looking." And if you had have done that, I wouldn't be telling the readers all about it, as I have a deadline to meet.

So I have to find out where we are going to. I took Mum to one side. We both agreed it wasn't the right place. The lighting was all wrong, for one thing, so we sidled over to the other side. I sang to her:

"Now we ain't got a barrel of money
Yes, maybe we're ragged and funny
But where are we moving to, Mummy?
Is it somewhere exotic and sunny?"

"Yes, it's Lowerhouse," she said…

"And really we haven't got time
To be singing 'Side By Side'
One day you may put it in a rhyme
Then look back on it with pride"

It's all very well saying that now, "But Lowerhouse?" I said, "that's only a hop, skip and a jump as the crow flies. There's no chance then that we're going Down Under?"

Mum said, "I'll give you a shovel. You can start now, and whatever you do, don't forget to turn left at Singapore."

I didn't know a great deal about Lowerhouse, but I thought, lock up your daughters, I'm on my way. When Mum told me where the house was, it wasn't all that far from Dorset Street. At a rough guess, I'd say it would be about twenty to twenty-five minutes walk from where we were. So it was still within walking distance of the school. Once I'd settled, I thought, this is not bad, lots of great new places to play and, of course, friends to be made, but I knew quite a few of the kids through school.

I haven't mentioned this before, so I'll bring it up now. I always have a bit of a snag with the names Alan and Ann. So if yours is spelt wrong, it's not done on purpose. Just as long as I get your surname right, that's all that matters. And as I said earlier, if I miss you this time, I'll try and get you later.

I'll start with Frank, Clifford and Harry Berry. They had a sister, Pauline, and an elder brother, Peter. Their parents were Rita and Aaron, who had a brother Frank.

Let's put you in the picture, just where we are. We're living in the top house, near the Ash Pad, as they called it (it's now called Greenbrook Road). Don't you go a worrying AP, you'll always be Ash Pad to me. I suppose I should tell you the number, like I did with the other places, it was 274. Mr and Mrs Spencer were at 276 (no relation). She was always borrowing cigarettes, so we nicknamed her Faggy.

> *She was on the wrong track*
> *Trying to borrow off me*
> *As mine were hard to come by*
> *I wouldn't give 'em for free*

There was Mr and Mrs McEvit, their daughter, Wyn, who married Arthur and they had Janet; Norman and Olive Leoroyd, and they had Joyce and Malcolm; Mr Thexton, Richard and Eileen; then Silcox's, they ran the shop.

Higher and Lower Water Streets were at the bottom of our row. There were the Bleasdale and the Campion families; Mrs Cole and her son Bernard; Lillian and Billy Wiggin; June and John McGough; Jean Scott; Alan Smith (Acko); Mr and Mrs Rhodes, their daughter, Brenda (they had the Post Office); the Lyons; Ann and Jeff Barnes; Derek and June McCartney; Mary and Ben Smith and their son, Ken, they had the pie shop (scrumptious). Then down on Bear Street there was Donald and Duncan Howarth and Charlie Sanderson. We'll go back up to our place and then I'll name a few that were on the opposite side to us.

There was Mr and Mrs Coulthurst (I'm not sure if I've spelt that right) and their son, Stan, who married Barbara Bland; there were the Pembertons; June and Malcolm Graham; Frank and Jean Holmes and they had Ian and Janet; Doris and John (Frank's brother) and their children, Julie, Steven, Trevor, Stuart and Kath (I think); Bert Howard; Mr and Mrs Judge; and the Shackletons…

If I have missed some out (and I could have) I'll have to set the old noggin to deep thinking for about ten minutes, that should do it.

> *Right, let's take a stroll*
> *We'll go up to The Fold*
> *Mum says, "Take a jacket"*
> *"Mater," I say, "It's not cold"*

Do you remember Gerties (Padget) fish and chip shop, with the flagstone floor? Ron and Elsie's shop (it's still there). There was Chippendales, the Fentons, Tommy Thistlewaite (I think that's how you spell it). A lot of kids knew him as Tommy Ticklemouse, he was the night watchman at Drew's. Do you remember a young fella by the name of Robert Wiggin, who lived with Tommy? I don't know what their relationship was (so I will have to do a bit of research on that), I'll keep you posted, but for goodness sake, don't hold your breath!

There was Mr and Mrs Ware and their children, Ted and Teresa; May Smith;

Marion Howarth; Margaret Ingham; Mr Latham…now I'm not sure if he used to live on Rosegrove Lane, because when we were a bit younger and lived on Liverpool Road, I remember we would go to this house with Dad, as Mr Latham used to cut hair there, and I think he worked at B & D's with our Dad. I can't put a year on it, or how old I was (isn't it funny what comes to mind, so I don't think I'm doing too bad without a diary). But I do know he used a taper on the back of your neck and when you're a young lad and you see someone coming towards you with a naked flame, you suddenly realise what Joan of Ark went through when she was tied to the steak, as the poor girl was a vegetarian. Did you see the misteak in stake? Did you see the mistake in mistake? Very good, get yourself a Mickey Mouse badge.

While on the subject of barbers, I knew one who had no legs, he used to cut hair on crutches. And when I mentioned about the vegetarian before, that reminded me of the explorer who was captured by the cannibals (no, it was his brother who was dragged off by the bullocks). The wives had been told to grab all the vegetables they could possibly get their hands on, then they would chop them up and toss 'em into the big pot. They would make sure there was enough water in it to come up to the explorers neck, then it was a case of in you go, you big Jessie. Then vigorously rubbing two Swan Vestas together (English matches, as lighters hadn't been invented yet), they got a light and lit the fire.

I bet you're thinking what on earth has all this got to do with The Fold? And we won't half cop it when we get home. Don't worry folks, I'll find a clearing and then get us out of this jungle, as soon as I've told you the punch line…

So it's back to the plot
As our explorer's in the pot
Who said, "By the gow it's hot
I wish I'd have been shot"

Now he'd been simmering for a while
Plus getting hot under the collar
The chief's eldest son, Two Dogs
Jumped up and started to holler

Bunga Unga Wunga
And sliced off our hero's head
Dad asked, "Why U do that?"
"Him eat the veggies," TD said

We're outta here and lucky to escape with our lives, eh?

But what if they caught me?
Drats, it'll be the end of me book
Folks, I'd poo in their stew
Yeah, that'll make 'em crook

I bet you're saying to yourselves, he certainly goes on. Well after all's said and done, it is the go on show (Goon gag). That sounds like a good title for a book. I'll keep that in mind. Let's get back to The Fold (and the story).

Now, we'll start to walk up Lowerhouse Lane. On our right is the Cricket Ground, they used to have some great Derby games against Burnley and always had a good crowd. Going past the Cricket Ground on the other side there was Mr and Mrs Duckworth, and they had Alan, Joan, Peter and Roy. There was Peter Wade and also Ernie Marsden and his Mum, Joan. Over the road was the little park, you could go through there to get to Liverpool Road, or go past the phone box and you would be at the bottom of Liverpool Road, near enough opposite the Rec (recreational ground).

I think that's all for now, so I'll call it a day, unless you've got a better name for it. We'll meet on the Ash Pad tomorrow after school. Ciao for now!

Chapter
9

Right, is everybody here? Good. Sorry I'm a bit late, I had to get rid of some Gypsies, as a lot of times they won't take no for an answer. Plus they were flogging allsorts (not liquorice). I was in no mood to buy any pegs, they said, "Have you any knives that want sharpening?"

I said, "Tex has got mine," they didn't get that one.

Just switching off for a tick. There was a bloke who used to come down the back of Livie Road (he used to sharpen knives). He wasn't a Gypsy (just an average chap, trying to earn a few bob). Does anybody out there remember him? What do you mean you never kept a diary? That's my excuse. Did you notice with the Gypsies how most of the men wore earrings? I'm off again for a minute. These days they have rings everywhere, it was only about a month ago I saw a young bloke on the train, I kid you not, he must have had four or five in each eyebrow. As I was getting off the train, I said, "What are you getting for Christmas? A pair of curtains?" I don't think he heard me, as he was wearing headphones and deafening anybody in earshot. In all honesty, he didn't bat an eyelid. Maybe he couldn't with all that weight.

If you can remember, I was trying to get rid of this clan, when Gypsy Rose Lee said, "Well, what about some knick knacks?"

I told them, "I don't want anything that has been nicked and I'm right for knacks, thanks."

> *As a last resort, a bloke said*
> *"Do you want your tea leaves read?"*
> *I said, "If you don't mind, Jack*
> *Honestly, we prefer ours black"*

They were looking daggers at me by this stage (it looked as if they'd just sharpened them too). But then they got the joke and said, "You're a funny little chap. You should go far with that sense of humour (Australia), we hope." Then hitching their covered wagon to a star, they were off in search of a new galaxy. Don't ask me where those last seventeen words came from, they just seemed to fit, so in they went.

Let's go up the Ash Pad
And see how far we get
You'll be home for tea
There's no need to fret

We'll put one foot in front of the other as that always seems the most sensible thing to do when one is going for a ta ta. Mr Berry's allotment (pen) is on our left. On the right is Lowerhouse Methodist (Meths or Chapel we called it). Then further up on the left were some fields owned by Mr Robinson, who lived at the top of Holyoake Street, and if you went through his land without being caught, you came out (after squeezing through the railings) near Liverpool Road Bridge.

So back to the Ash Pad again… on the right, past the Chapel was Mr Judge's allotment (more later). We keep going up till we come to what they called the Green Hill. Mum would tell us they used to sing it at Sunday School, "'There Is A Green Hill Far Away', without a city wall", and she always believed it was one and the same.

By the way, to show you I'm not trying to pull the wool over your eyes (unless, of course, your balaclava is working loose), as the one they sang just happens to be number 180 in the Methodist hymn book, or if you are female, the number is the same in the Methodist her book.

So while we're stood standing on the Green Hill, you could actually jump onto the cut (canal) bank. Then looking straight across, you'd see the bottom end of Butterworths and Dickinsons. If you walked to your left, that would take you to Livie Road, or if you took the other direction, you could either come out up the old lane, then carry on up to Gypsy Bridge, or stay on the bank and walk along to Hapton.

Here's one for you that was doing the rounds at that time… why is a river rich? Because it has a bank on each side.

Now I feel like "The Grand Old Duke of York" (would someone get him for me?). As I took you up to the top of the Green Hill, now I'll take you back down again. Continuing on, we pass the buildings of Collinge's Farm. On the left is a big house, the house that faces the canal was built by Richard Ormerod and the back of the building was Old Oak Cottage which, of course, was more or less opposite Collinge's farmhouse. When we get to the end of the road, then it becomes what we called the old lane. But really, to give it a proper name, it is the continuation of Lower Rosegrove Lane, as this was once used as the road from Burnley to Accrington. And if we go left we pass The Engine Sheds. Opposite is the Loco and then you come out on Liverpool Road. But if we'd turned right, we would have gone down the old lane to Molly Brook, and guess what? (Seeing as you haven't had one for a while). You would finish up at Gypsy Bridge again (it seems all roads lead to Gypsy Bridge).

Now I bet you're thinking, what did we do to deserve that load of old twaddle? But as a matter of fact, I have plenty younger than that and if by chance I get stuck for a few words, it could be getting a run. What I'm going to do is write 'Abracadabra' and hopefully we will be taken back to where we started from. Now, if we all hold hands, we'll try to contact the living, as there are a few of you that look like death warmed up (as the saying goes). And I think I've walked some of you too far, let's have a bit of a breather here, and while you're resting, I'll tell you a story (so you're not going to get any rest at all, R U?).

It goes… once upon a time there was a family of skunks. It was made up of Daddy and Mummy, with their two boys who were named In and Out. Well this day, In and Out were in and, of course, under Mums feet (as usual), who just happened to be in a bad mood. The simple reason being because their Dad had been drinking and he was flaked out on the couch. He was drunk as a skunk, so they say (now for goodness sake, don't ask me who they are, but apparently these people are always coming out with these clichés). That's why Mum was losing her patience, so she yelled out to In and Out, "Will you two go out and come in when it's time for tea?"

Then after a couple of hours, seeing as the lads hadn't come in, Mum shouted out, "Come in, In and Out!"

Out came in, grabbed the milk out of the fridge and poured himself a drink, then he sat down at the table where he saw two funny looking tablets.

He said to his mum, "What are these?"

She said, "They're wedge shaped aspirins for your Dad, as he's got a splitting headache and it serves him right," she giggled.

> *With the lad being a skunk*
> *He thought that joke stunk*
> *Said to pop, "give us the facts*
> *Now who hit you with the axe?"*
>
> *Dad was like a skunk with a sore head*
> *And vowing never ever to drink again*
> *If somebody had handed him a pledge*
> *He would have signed it there and then*
>
> *But Mum knew what he was like*
> *And she'd heard it all before*
> *As soon as her back was turned*
> *He'd be into it once more*
>
> *Mum bellowed out, "Where's In?*
> *Don't tell me he's still out"*
> *Dad said, "Shush, me head's sore*
> *So you don't have to shout"*

Then Mum went out to tell In to come in for his tea. She was out for about half an hour and couldn't find him anywhere. She went back in and she was furious. She screamed out to Out, "Go outside and try to bring In in."

He said, "Why should I? I'm not my brothers keeper," mumbling, "so it's always me that gets the blame."

So Out went out and came straight back in with In. Mum said, "How on earth did you find him so quick?"

Out said, "Instinct."

Well after that, I think we could do with a walk. So if you're ready, we'll cut through and go behind the church and that leads us down to the bywash. This was, in fact, the overflow from the top lodge and it ran past the bottom of Higher and Lower Water Streets. More commonly known as the Brook Row. It then continued past the bottom lodge and ran through Alexander Drew & Sons, which some people knew as Lowerhouse Printworks, but it always got called Drew's. What we might do now is go up Higher Water Street. Then we'll follow the main road down and I'll point out a few places as we go. Now, on our left is Wellesley Street, we pass Rhode's Post Office, then come to Mary's shop, which is near enough to the top end of Fox Street.

Over the road is the Lowerhouse Mills Club or Canteen, as it's called. Back on our side we come to the Joiner's Shop, then Spring & Textile Engineering and, of course, Bob Lord's Butchers. He was Burnley Football Club's Chairman. Just around the corner was Knotts Lane, with the bottom lodge on one side and on the other side, Drew's (so now you're in the picture).

I think we'll double back to the Canteen. It would be nice if we could whet our whistle (but we're a bit young for that yet). Then if we cut through this field it'll lead us towards Ivy Bank. If you could get across the overflow there without falling in, an apple orchard is on the other side, so there's a reward waiting for you. We'd get caught a few times (just to let the Groundsman think he was doing his job properly). Otherwise it was no fun if we won all the time. The worst one was being three quarters of the way up the tree and your mates would shout, "He's here!" before scarpering to save their own necks. The funny part of that was you had apples in every pocket, plus a couple in each mitt and one in your gob. There was no chance of escaping so, of course, you were gone for all money and when you did look down, there he was. You knew he had you by the short and curlies (I was short and curly anyway, so it didn't matter). But if you were cheeky enough, you could try and bluff him with...

> *We are doing a project at school to see*
> *How many apples on the average tree*
> *He said, "That's clever, I'll guarantee*
> *274 is the answer, but you don't fool me"*

Most of the times they'd let you off with a stern warning. Okay, how many of you were on to the fact that the number of apples on the said tree and our door number were one and the same? (Very good, to those who got that). Actually, I was going to put 548, which is the number in question doubled. I thought that would have been a little bit of a challenge for some of you.

Let's get back to the orchard. I think what they used to do was to rotate the Groundsmen (yeah, they would put them on a rotisserie, but you had to get there early, or you could get a tough one). So in a sense, you had to be stiff to get caught by the same bloke. The only other punishment you got was if you had scoffed a couple of bad ones (apples that is). You'd be sat on the throne for what seemed like ages till your bellyache had gone, but you could read the News Of The World (that was on a nail behind the toilet door).

So the Ivy Bank overflow ran down and went under Scott Street. Just near where it went under SS, there was a big old derelict house which we would play in...

> *Till we were told to, "Bugger off"*
> *By some old grumble bum*
> *"Yeah, same to you," we'd reply*
> *"We're only having a bit of fun"*
>
> *"I'll call the Rozzers," he said*
> *We quickly said, "Ah, but what"*
> *He came back with a classic*
> *"You kids are all cheek and snot"*
>
> *Wiping our noses on us sleeves*
> *It was time to go on our merry way*
> *And still laughing at his remark*
> *We'd shout, "Mister, have a nice day!"*

It's funny, Mum would give us strict instructions about going too far, plus staying out of trouble. We covered more miles than Burnley's forward line.

While we're on the subject of travelling, I didn't tell you about our Great Uncle Eno, he migrated to Australia, in fact, he was one of the first early settlers.

> *Folks, I just had to get that one in*
> *I don't care if you think it stinks*
> *That's been on my list for a while*
> *And there's more like that, methinks*

I mentioned we were told to keep out of trouble. Well, it just seemed to follow us wherever we went. One of the lads would say, "Who's that snotty nosed kid at the back?"

Somebody piped in with, "He's trouble."

"Well then, for goodness sake, don't let him get in front of us, or boy, will we be right in it!"

And, of course, if you didn't come in on time, when you were told to, oh boy it was "Double Trouble".

That was the thing that amazed me about adults, they made the rules up as they went along. I don't know about you, but they would give me different names, I got called 'Hurry' a lot. In fact, for the first few years I thought that was my name, as it was; Hurry across the road; Hurry into the shop, and most popular of all; Hurry up (when they were trying to get me out of bed in the morning).

And when a young fella is a certain height, two things come into contention; elbows and corners of a table. Yes, these are the things that we always seem to be running into on a regular basis. Somebody would plonk some marge on your head (not best butter) while saying, "Well you kids are all the same, always hurrying."

Then it would be funny at school to see your mates with bumps. You'd ask, "Where did you get yours?"

They'd say, "Elbow," or, "Table," or vice versa.

There would be one kid with a real shiner, his story was he tripped over the moggy and went head first into the hearth. We'd all agree that we should see the Gypsies and have our lumps red, as any other colour would look better than black or blue.

Well would you look at the time? It certainly is getting away from us.

> *With a little bit of mystique*
> *And, of course, my trusty pen*
> *Now we'll be transported*
> *Back to the Chapel again*

Here endeth the first lesson (and let that be a lesson to you).

> *We're all here, safe and sound*
> *You'll agree we had some fun*
> *Sorry, but I must go home now*
> *Tea's ready, I can hear me Mum*

As there was still quite a bit of discharge from the nasal area, I said to Mum, "My nose keeps running."

She said, "What do you want me to do, run after it? Why don't you use your sleeve, as that's what your gang seem to do while going around singing 'Green Sleeves'."

"That's only because our snot rags are full," I said.

"You know something? The trouble with you kids," she said, "is that you are built upside-down."

"Why is that so, Mum?" I said.

"Because your nose runs and your feet smell," she replied.

Now, imagine me trying to have a battle of wits with Mum (I was way out of my league). It was a great learning experience and looking back I wouldn't have missed it for the world.

Chapter
10

Now, just between me and you, and that's the way it's going to be because I'm the writer and you're the reader. I don't know if you've noticed those little rhymes that just seem to bob up sometimes during the course of a story, and yet in other stories there is no sign of them. There is a simple explanation for that, I couldn't think of anything. But I will say this, that when I start to tell a tale, if a verse comes to mind, I'll put it down on a piece of paper and only if I think it's good enough then it shall be used (so I bet you're wondering where they came from). I think you should give me eleven out of ten for being honest. If you didn't understand a word of that it really doesn't matter, as neither did I. But I will tell you this, and that is right now I need as many words as possible. I'm convinced they'll help immensely from now on until the finish line (meaning the last one). No clues just yet as I'm still working on it.

Then came the day we had to sit for our Eleven Plus. As most of you will know (boys, that is), if you were successful, you could either go to Towneley or the Grammar School. Of course, the norm for passing was the kid would get a very expensive gift, which was of his own choice as a reward for using his noggin. Then just before we got our results, I remember it well, saying to Mum, "If I get to go to Towneley or the Grammar School, please (and there was plenty of emphasis on that word) can I have a brand new bike?" (With drop handle bars).

She looked me squarely in the eyes (I think I got square eyes from watching too much radio), her exact words were, "If you pass, you can have a bloody jet!"

Now, let's have a show of hands for those who think I'm a jet pilot. Wrong. So to all the kids who passed and got bikes, I would shout at them, "Clever clogs!" Then other times, if they'd left their bikes outside home or a shop they had just popped into, I'd look around to see if the coast was clear (I don't know why, as we didn't live anywhere near the beach), I would then sneakingly let some air out of the back tyre. When they saw the wheel in question (if I hadn't had a chance to get away) I'd try to look innocent while rattling the loose change in my pocket. They stared at me as if to say, how did that happen? I'd glance at them as if to say, you're the one with the brains, and the school uniform, you work it out. So if you lived in Lowerhouse or The Grove about this time, now after all these years, there's your answer.

> *Or is Mickey Plum*
> *Having a bit of fun?*
> *Isn't he a son of a gun?*
> *If you'll pardon the pun*

We have finished at the Junior School and said our goodbyes to the teachers. Now I'm challenging the old memory at the moment and you might remember some that I've forgotten. The names of the women that come to mind are: Ruddock, Tateham, Hanna, Lambeth and Hatton. I'll just cover myself here by saying I hope they're spelt right. I might have to do a bit more research on that, I'm not talking about the spelling, I mean the actual names. The men were Fletcher, Magnall and Speakman, and, last but not least, was Miss Coulburn, the Headmistress. I don't think anyone could forget her, she was a tireless worker and always gave support to families who were going through a rough time (there seemed to be a few around). And she certainly was there for us with Robert losing schooling through Rheumatic Fever. I do remember taking schoolwork home for him during this period so that he could keep up with his studies.

I seem to be stuck in some sort of time zone…

> *I've still got years to write about*
> *I'd better start growing up quick*
> *I'll put some horse muck in me shoes*
> *I think that should do the trick*

So the summer holidays came and, of course, they were great fun as always. Then before we knew it, it was time for the new term to start at the Secondary School, which was right next door to the Junior. So really there was no extra travelling to do like the other kids who went to Towneley or the Grammar School.

Some of our older friends had told us about the 'big school', but it was totally different to what we expected and what we were used to. I didn't realise how much I loved the Junior School until I left. I'm not saying we got away with murder, but at the big school the teachers would soon bring you into line. On the other side of the coin, it brought us in contact with a lot of other kids from all parts of Burnley, so you made new friends.

But there were a few who thought they were better than us. There would be a couple of scraps, once or twice a week. They say fortune favours the brave. There would be about five or six in groups and sometimes for something to do, you'd yell at some kid under the shelter shed, "Come out you coward, and fight the six of us!" My problem was that I wasn't that tall, but I could give 'em a quick gobful before they clobbered me. So if I happened to hit the deck (which I did a few times), I'd be taller laid down than I was standing up.

Right, where am I? Oh yes, crawling along the schoolyard, but quite fast I might add, while licking my wounds as I went. Looking back now, it wasn't really all doom and gloom, it just seemed that way. Here's some of what I call the main things that I enjoyed: metalwork, woodwork and science.

The best thing in the science class
You had permission to bisect a frog
Others would put a straw up his bum
He was then blown to bits in the bog

And, of course, I loved sports, which included football (at Lockyer) and indoor cricket in the main hall (great fun). Do you remember that (German lad) good bowler, nearly always took three wickets in a game (wait for it), Jerry Hattrick (well, I think it's good material for a young bloke).

So in the other subjects I think I always tried to look interested (like most of the other kids) just so the teacher wouldn't bounce a piece of chalk off your bonce, as some of them got great pleasure out of this and, I must admit, they weren't bad shots either.

Do you remember those tests they used to give us? For example, say that A can do the project in three hours, B can do it in two hours and C can crack it in one hour… how long would it take if… ? This is the bit that intrigues me, just get C to do it in the first place.

We used to go over to the grounds of St. Marks and do some gardening. I enjoyed that, plus the fact you could have a bit of a skive, especially if the teacher was having a smoke or gasbagging to some old geezer through the railings. That was a good chance for us to swap fag (cigarette) cards or bobbers (marbles) because sometimes, if you attempted this back at school (you were alright in the yard), it was a real buy and sell place, but in the classroom you'd have your goodies confiscated.

Then, of course, there was the cross-country run which, just thinking about it now, it was a fair hike. I used to call it "The Great Escape", if only for a couple of hours. So any chance I would get, I'd do my best, believe me, then if and when you did manage to get out of a class, there would be kids floating about everywhere. Some of the excuses were pretty tame. The most obvious one was the toilet. I liked to try and come up with clever ones, I'd say, "Please Sir, I've forgotten to lock up my bike, can I just nip out for five minutes?" But then you'd be in trouble when you got back, as some kid had put you right in it by telling the teacher you didn't have a bike. This could mean a visit to the Headmaster where you could get a warning or the cane. If it was the cane, he'd say, "You know something? This is going to hurt me more than it hurts you."

To which you would say, under your breath of course, "Well give us a couple more then."

I bet you're thinking, he's forgotten to tell us about the cross-country run (good). Well, if I had, do you think I would be silly enough to admit it? (Pull the other one, it's got bells on). So, if you're ready for a run (if you've got a note from Mum, that's alright, you're excused), we start opposite Rosegrove Station. Then on the count of 1, 2, 3… we're off!

Turn left into Lower Rosegrove Lane, down to Molly Brook and up the other side to, guess what, you got it in one, Gypsy Bridge. Once you were on the bridge you'd stop there to get your breath back and have a quick fag. It seemed a bit pointless stopping for a breather and then sucking on a cancer stick, but we were kids and didn't know any different, or any better. Mind you, if you had a full cigarette you were well off. If you happened to have a couple in a packet you were called Rockefeller. My dog-ends were that small, if I shouted to somebody to give us a light I had to be very careful, I could go up in flames or even lose half an eyebrow in the process. Then I'd get the third degree, trying to explain that to Mum (and seeing as we're having a rest) then it would go something like this:

"What the heck have you been up to this time? You'd better have a good excuse."

"Well, 'Mommie Dearest'…" (that's the Christina Crawford story about her Mum, if you can't get it in the bookshops it should be available at the library).

"There was this kidiot (that's a kid who's an idiot) in the science class and he was clowning around with the Bunsen Burner, saying he was going to blow up the school and take everybody to kingdom come. Personally, I think he'd seen one too many James Cagney films, especially 'White Heat', 1949 (I'm on top of the world, Ma)."

Now, as luck would have it, there were some older boys in the next class and they just happened to be making 'paper' mache, which was then made into various things that would be used in the Rosegrove Theatre Group (and they put some good plays on). I think you lot must have noticed this by now, that I do seem to have the ability to drag out a story (call it a gift). Now, the boys couldn't help overhearing all the commotion, so quick as a flash, four of them barged in and pulverised him to a pulp. So would I lie to you, Mum? She'd most probably give me one of those looks where there's a lot of frowning thrown in and then say, "You couldn't lie straight in bed."

We'd better get a move on, or they'll be sending out a search party for us. So throw your butts away, we'll get rid of the evidence (you don't want Mum to find 'em in your pockets) and back to the marathon. We turn left over the bridge, then go along Accrington Road. On our right is the way to Hapton Valley Colliery (the pit) and then, of course, there's the Valley Gardens. On our left is the canal, once past that we have the long hard slog up towards Billy Holts (Burnley Billiard Works). We'll turn left and that will bring us back to the station. By now it would be lighting up time. We'd be so late it's a wonder the teacher never had his pyjamas on. Normally his first words were, "Where the bloody hell have you lot been?"

We were very tempted to say
"Sir, it was such a lovely day
We thought we'd have a walk
Do nature studies, plus talk"

But someone would come up with, "Please, Teach, it was so and so, he hurt his ankle and we all had to take turns to piggyback him." It amazes me to this day, when there's fear involved or a rumbling around the bowel region, how the mind will come up with a gem.

Did you notice how the teacher would seem to disappear for no reason at all? One chap we used to call Houdini. He was always at it, every chance he got. Maybe round the back for the old brandyyy (Goon gag) and while they were absent someone would be put in charge. But just before the teacher left the room, he would turn to the class and say, "I'll be back before you shower can say 'Jack Robinson'."

It's funny how a lot of people mentioned that bloke (never did find out then who he was) and to this day I still don't know who he is. The teacher would whisk his brandy flask out of his pocket, then he was gone, and all hell broke loose. Now, the kid who was in charge, he would have more chance of putting butter on a red-hot needle and sticking it up a porcupine's bum than to keep us lot in order. And for his trouble he got called 'Scott'. So whoever was put in charge by the teachers, most of the lads just assumed they were on the opposition's side anyway. I hear you say, why was he called Scott? (And I say, I'm writing as quick as I can). Because if he was the teacher's pet, he's Scott no friends. All this time hell was still loose and we had no intentions of tightening it just yet. The poor lad would get bombarded by all sorts of missiles…

Elastic bands were fired at him
Paper planes went that way too
Blotting paper dipped in ink
Made Scott a little boy blue

There were kids who'd do their party piece. Nearly everyone wanted to get in on the act, so I thought, I'll have a go at this. After bucking up courage, I nervously said, "What goes tick woof, tick woof, tick woof?"

They said, "Pray tell us, what goes tick woof, three times?"

"A watch dog."

After the pelting had stopped, a budding poet took my place, saying, "He should be on the stage."

The reply would be, "Yeah, sweeping it."

Or an even better remark was, "There's one leaving town in ten minutes, be under it." (I like that).

He'd waited for a couple of minutes till the din had died down, then he was straight into it, saying, "Friends, Romans, Grove-ites, lend me your lugholes."

> *Now little Miss Muffet*
> *Was sat on the buffet*
> *Eating her curds and whey*
> *Then down came a spider*
> *Moved alongside her*
> *She said, "Nick off, hairy legs"*

He quickly raised his hand, saying, "Don't fire yet, I've saved the best for last."

> *Now little did he know*
> *But we'd run out of ammo*
> *Then he was on with the show*
> *Till we found more to throw*

And tapping on the teacher's desk, he said, "C'mon lads, give me a break, I promise you it's the last one."

> *Jack and Jill went up the hill*
> *To fetch a pail of water*
> *Jill came down with half a crown*
> *It wasn't for carrying water*

Most of the time we knew how long we had to cause mayhem, as…

> *We'd have someone on the door*
> *He was known as the lookout*
> *So when Sir was getting near*
> *Hey lads, "Look out!" He'd shout*

The race was on for young and old, we just made it with seconds to spare…

> *So we were sat at our desks*
> *As he waltzed into the room*
> *"Jack Robinson," we all chanted*
> *You could tell he felt a Goon*

"I called you a shower before I went out," he said. Then, after that wise-crack, and while trying to give us his best Terry Thomas impersonation, "I should say, you are a complete shower, what about that then lads?" he said, "do you think I should be on the stage?"

"Yes Sir, repairing it."

Things seemed to go along steadily, but there was one teacher that stuck out. Just briefly, when I started this book, I had no intentions of rubbishing people. And having said that, let me say this, I can assure you I'm not going to start now, so I won't even mention the art teachers name (I got outta that well, didn't I?). So anybody who went to The Grove will know who I mean. He just had the ability to spot little cheeky buggers at ten paces. Of course, when we met, it was love at first fight. I always tried to keep on the right side of him and any of the kids who knew him will verify this, as once he got you in his sights, you were a goner. There will be more later on this subject (it will come into the story better further down the track), so you'll have to be patient.

Chapter
11

Now, with living down Lowerhouse, it was too far to go home for lunch and with the grub being what it was at Grandma's, well, wild horses (or delirious donkeys) wouldn't keep me away, plus a great program on the (steam-driven) radio called 'Workers Playtime', and that consisted of musicians, comedians and singers. My favourite singer was Vince Hill and they would visit a different factory each day. Now, I'm not sure if they came to Burnley (but I'll have a quid each way they did). I think what the idea was, it must have been recorded and maybe edited as it seemed to run for say thirty or sixty minutes (that's just a rough guess) and be broadcast at the same time (Monday through Friday).

Now, in all honesty, I don't think me Gran can feed you lot at such short notice, unless you're keen on tripe and onions, but I can't see her parting with that, as it's Grandad's tea. So I've got an idea, if someone will race up to the chippy and get a couple of pieces of fish (must be Bob Bird's), then somebody else grab a few loaves, who knows, maybe we can perform a miracle and feed the rank and file? So hurry up!

Right, the rest of you can come in as it's drizzling and this is the ideal opportunity to do the project for school, which is to see how many kids we can possibly squeeze round the table, while listening to Workers Playtime. Well gang, it sounds good on paper, so do you think I should give the paper to Grandma? I'll say it's from the teacher. Nah, she'll never believe that, as the wireless is in the parlour.

Did you know, the quickest way to make a radio is to take a medium-sized box (not cardboard), then after that get about three wires, but whatever you do don't get them crossed (it could be painful). Grab a few valves and a plug, not forgetting antenna, or if she won't come to the party, ask Uncle Tenna (but don't bring Lulu). After doing all that, the last thing you do is remove one of the original wires, then before your very eyes, you have a wireless. I think more people bought Marconi's model than mine.

Right, let me do all the talking, as I have the gift of the gob, er gab. I'll tell her you're my Fan Club, so if I get hot under the collar, start fanning (not clubbing). Grandma says it's alright to come in, first make sure your shoes are clean, then take your caps off and wipe your noses (no, not on your caps!).

She's put the folding card table in the parlour, we should all fit around that and we'll listen to Workers Playtime. Would somebody get the door, as the lads are here with the tucker. Now, I'll just get some Stanton's pop, Dandelion & Burdock, eh? (Remember the big pot jars that used to double as hot water bottles?). I might have to water it down a bit, then hopefully it should go further. A word of warning, no mess, as one of Grandma's golden rules is, don't drop food on the floor unless (Laddie) the dog's in. So will one of you say grace and then we'll get cracking.

Then little Arnold bowed his head
Placed his hands over the spread
Lord, bless this food upon these dishes
As thou dost bless the loaves and the fishes
And now, just like the sugar in our tea
Yes, may all of us be stirred by thee

After the laughter had stopped, I said, "I'll bet my bottom dollar Grandma will try and embarrass me. She'll tell you a couple of stories about when I was younger, so I'll tell you this one and steal her thunder, so to speak."

You know how us kids are always told not to run with scissors or a knife and even, of all things, toast. This is because you could have someone's eye out, especially with the piece of toast. So here I was, a little chap galloping with a carving knife, shouting for Cheekie (the moggy). It was then that Grandma had hold of my collar (just before I had someone off by their stocking tops), saying, "Why are you looking for the cat?"

And apparently, I said, "Because when Grandad was playing cards, I heard him say there's fifteen bob in the kitty."

Then as if on cue, Grandma came in and said, "Do you know when Michael was younger, his Grandad asked 'would you take this vinegar back to the shop? And tell them there's too much sediment in it'."

So he went into the shop and the fella said, "Yes, young man, what can I do for you?"

Michael says, "Me Grandad said there's too much element in your vinegar."

And the shopkeeper came back with, "You mean sediment."

And then Michael said, "I honestly don't know what the hell he meant, but that's what he said he meant."

Hey, c'mon lads, we've got to go. So Arnie, will you wrap this up for us.

Again, the lad lowered his head
Clasped his hands, then he said
Thank him above for what we've getton
If there'd been more, it wud a been etton

It didn't pay you to be late back to school, as you'd cop the double whammy. You would get a rollicking from Mr Churchill (the Caretaker, who we called Winston) and then one from the teacher.

Chapter
12

Now, do you people remember when I wrote in the introduction about having a great imagination? I think you'll agree there's nothing lacking in that department, as I keep taking it to the limit one more time.

So let me just put the record straight (as it keeps falling off) and I could finish up with a slipped disc. Then while you're still remembering, I said earlier that the tributes would be strategically placed. I'll be perfectly honest with you (as I have been all along), my strategy seems to have gone haywire, but I can assure you normal service will be resumed as soon as possible. Now that I've softened you up a bit, we'll stay in the fifties for a while yet.

You know, I hadn't thought about Mr Churchill for a lot of years, then his name just came to me out of the blue. I'm glad in one sense that it did, or I would have forgotten all about this next little tale.

Let me be your Michaelangelo
And paint a picture for you
I'll put snow on the ground
In the bottom yard the noo

Now, this was great fun for us, but for anybody a bit unsteady on their feet, it could be quite treacherous. So what did we do? (Besides write our name in the snow). We made great slides, as it was a good slope, but you know, sometimes it would take forever to get a decent slide going and to make it, as they'd say, like shot ice.

But then some tell-tale-tit had blabbed and who should come sailing around the corner but Mr Churchill and he'd be armed to the teeth (some days, if he forgot his choppers, he was legged to the gums) with all sorts of stuff like ashes or salt to put the damper on our little game. But he made a near fatal mistake, instead of starting at the bottom and working his way up, guess what? Good guess, he started at the top, so it was only a matter of seconds before he lost his footing, then he was at that point of no return and whoosh, off he went.

There were cheers from the kids
Who had been booing and hissing
Some were crying with laughter
While others started peeing

What's the difference between roast beef and pea soup? You can roast beef but it's impossible to pee soup!

Now, I'll let you into a little secret, oh, that's brilliant Michael, isn't it? There could be thousands of people reading this (millions I hope) and here I am sharing secrets. So, if I'd have rhymed the word beginning with P (you know the one I mean) with hissing, I wouldn't have been able to work the pea soup gag in.

> *Now, there's no flies on me*
> *(You can see where they've been)*
> *So this is a way of keeping*
> *My writing attempt clean*

Anyway, after Mr C had come to a screaming halt…

> *The kids would shout, "It's good fun*
> *But you shouldn't go down on yer bum"*
> *He said, "Who's responsible for this?"*
> *Guess what? We all played dumb*

Now, about this kid who told over us (as they say). We took him to one side and gave him a good seeing to, then we moved him to the other side so our seeing to could be seen in a better light. We were pleased with what we saw. We said to him, "Why on earth did you tell? Was it because we used your jacket to make the slide better?"

"Yes," he said, "but I wouldn't have minded if you had asked me to take it off first, as it was my best blazer."

A young lad, quick as a flash, whipped out his matches, struck one, and set fire to the garment, the boy yelled, "What did you do that for?"

To which the culprit replied, "Well, now you've got yourself a smoking jacket."

That's enough of that frivolity for one day, and school.

I mentioned about the Cricket Ground, it was great playing there. If you were on good terms with the Groundsman, which we were, sometimes we would help him, as there were always odd jobs to do. So he let us have the run of the place, but the bottom lodge was where a lot of lads would hang out, plus, there were always a few blokes fishing. We got to know some of the blokes and they would talk to us. There was one chap, we called him The Preacher, as he was always trotting out quotations from the good book (not this one, ha ha). He said, "Always read the Bible, and remember, cast your loaves upon the waters, then it shall come back tenfold." I thought, that sounds reasonable (we might have to do a project for school about that, I wonder if we can talk the teacher into it). But you could finish up with a lot of soggy butties.

This is a good opportunity to slip the one in about the famous Eccles. This one day he'd decided to try his luck, so he was sat there with a big bucketful of worms, and some character came up to him (I forget which one) and said, "How are you today?"

He replied, "Fine, fine, fine."

Then the bloke asked him, "Why so many worms?"

Deadpan Eccles said, "I get just as hungry as the fish do."

You'd get the odd bloke fishing who always seemed a bit nasty. One of us would try to get on the right side of him, while the others would get on the left side, as that's where he kept his bait. So if the lads were lucky, they'd pinch a bit (then we'd go and feed the ducks on what we called Drews Pond, at the back of Bear Street). I bet that poor bloke would go home scratching his head and saying, "I'm losing me marbles, I thought I took plenty of bait."

Another good place to play… the only trouble was it was a bit far. You had to go down Bear Street, over the little bridge, then up the other side, as if going towards Padiham. On your right was a park, which had swings, a bowling green, tennis court and miniature golf, where we had lots of fun.

On our way back, somewhere along the line, we'd bump into Tommy Tittlemouse. He always had a sack over his shoulder and his little dog with him. If there was a new kid in the gang, we'd say, "Ask Tommy what his dog is called."

Me, grandma and grandpa

TT said, "Some days I call him Carpenter, because he's always doing little jobs around the house. Then after he's done them, I call him Blacksmith."

The young lad couldn't help himself and fell for the old three-card trick by asking, "Why do you call him Blacksmith?"

Tommy said, "If I kick him up the bum, he'll make a bolt for the door."

"So what have you got in the sack, Tom?"

"Wabbits," he said.

Straight away, I said, "Can I have one?"

"I'll tell you what I'll do," he said, "if you can guess how many I have in the sack you can have them both."

One idiot said, "Three."

Well, I don't like rabbit anyway, so putting that behind us. Do you know the best way to catch a bunny is to stand outside his burrow (or hers) and make a noise like a lettuce? Let's get back to the tale.

The place where we played most was, of course, the Ash Pad which was, as I said, literally on our doorstep. One of the many games we played was what we called 'Tin in't Ring'. The idea being we'd put stones in a circle, then an empty tin was placed upside-down in the ring. Whoever lost the toss would stand inside the circle, close his eyes, and count to one hundred while the rest of us would scarper and hide. When he found someone, he'd shout their name and that they were caught and they would have to stand in the circle. Then it was up to one of us to get back to base and relieve them by slinging the tin as far as it would go.

A couple of good ones were lobbing the can onto Collinge's cart as it went past and to watch some kid trying to clamber up on the big cart was a task in itself. But the best one was to put a couple of pebbles in the tin and throw it up, as there were big trees in the Chapel grounds that hung right over the Ash Pad (there should be a photo in the book, if I remember to put it in). With a well-aimed shot, you could manage to wedge it on one of the many branches. The kid would have to throw sticks and stones (but names would never hurt) to try and knock it loose and that was a job and a half.

Or the last resort was he'd have to climb the tree. Sometimes the game had to be stopped, as it was impossible to get near the can, no matter how hard we tried. Then someone came up with a brainwave, we'd borrow a clothes prop, which was five foot or more in length (maybe six?), then one kid would have to get on another one's shoulders and swing or poke at the tin, while the kid underneath was running around like a chook with its head off, as he didn't dare look up.

Now, the lad on the shoulders was swinging madly (and badly, I might add) while hitting every branch in sight, except the right one. With only being a little fella he was getting more nervous by the minute and then, without giving any warning, wind was expelled from the rear passage. The kid that was underneath quickly dumped the offender into the long grass, while hurriedly wiping the back of his neck. Then, after calling him a smelly little sod, he said, "Why didn't you tell me you were going to do that?"

Quick as a flash, the kid said, "I didn't have time, and you're lucky I didn't follow through, as I had diarrhoea ache yesterday."

What a sight it was, kids doubled up with laughter, tears streaming down their cheeks, while wisecracks came thick and fast from all directions, like, "You should get a cork to fit that," or, "we know where to shove the clothes prop till next time."

Can you just imagine this day and age, what with all this modern technology, for example, the mobile phone, it certainly would take all the fun out of 'Hide & Seek'. You know, we thought we were well off with a couple of old cans and a long piece of string. We painted our cans yellowish-brown, so it was a mobile fawn. With one on this side and the other across the road, then we would shout at each other. I wish we had a quid for every time we almost decapitated a cyclist!

Cricket was popular, we always started out okay, but it could flare up at any time. Like if someone hit the ball into one of those big green things with branches (they came into play quite often). Sometimes they'd run about thirty before we'd get the ball down. It was always six and out over Mr Berry's pen, unless of course, you could manage to belt it into the ground first and it would bounce over. Then you could run for ages, or it would be a good chance to go for a leak in the bushes, but you had to be careful on a windy day, you could get your own back.

One time there was a couple in the bush. I said, "What's your game then?" It seemed better than the one I was playing, theirs looked more like all-in wrestling. His excuse was he was in slips, having a rest, as he'd just bowled a maiden over and from where I was standing, I must admit, she had a fine leg.

So back to the game, if they couldn't find the ball, even the ones batting had to join in the search. Then a ball would be found, but it was from last week's game. If it was in good nick, it would be used. Any kids who owned a pill would be allowed to play. If, by chance, you had a brand spanking new one, you could bowl first, but you didn't seem to be able to hit the old ones as far as the new ones.

There would be times when a four was needed to win. The batsmen (or lads) had run three and one of the fielders would have his foot on the ball (in the grass) while pretending to be looking for it (pretty sneaky, eh?). Then there would be shouts, "Yes!"

"No!"

"Stop!"

"Go!"

"Wait!"

"C'mon!"

"Get back!"

By this time, the ball came flying in to have one of 'em stranded by a mile. After being run out, and if he wasn't happy, he'd take his bat and go home. So that would be the end of the game anyway.

Then there were occasions when somebody refused to walk, saying, "I'm not being out to pea-rollers or donkey-droppers." So it was a case of three bat handles, the bowler had three chances to get him out. If he got through that without being dismissed, he would then be allowed to bat on. It's maybe a good job I didn't go on to be a world-famous cricketer, because if I had my way it could be three bat handles, rather than the third umpire (very interesting).

Now, I'll tell you this story, so park your carcass. On a Saturday, we'd go up to the Coli (matinee), hail or shine, while Mum would go shopping downtown (Burnley Market). This one day, we'd been home for a while, she came in with this chap and she said, "Look what I picked up on the market…"

Sit down, and if you're sitting comfortably I'll begin. She started off that when they were kids, both of them lived in The Fold. That was their playground and he would win all Mum's marbles. I think it's still called The Fold, even though the houses they lived in have gone. They went to the same school, then after leaving they'd go their separate ways and take life's course. Now, Mum was divorced, while his marriage wasn't going too good, and by this time we were champing at the bit, so to speak. But Mum was dragging it out, as usual, as she had centre stage (I wonder if that's where I get it from?). But now we were jumping up and down like the 'Where The Hell Are We Tribe' (I've cleaned that one up a lot) saying, "Tell us where you two met!"

She said, "There I was at Barmy Mick's, minding my own business, when I noticed this bloke across the stall smiling at me, so I thought to myself, looks like they've let him out for the weekend. Now, if I just ignore him he might go away or, hopefully, they'll round them up and take 'em back soon. But they didn't, and all this time he's grinning like a Cheshire cat..." (I've never figured out why our Lancashire counterparts don't flash their pearly whites). She continued, "…and then of all things, he started winking at me. You know, you can never find a copper when you want one."

Then she told us she thought… "that's it, he must be one of the assistants that takes the teapots to the customers, more like a crackpot if you ask me, especially when he keeps winking. Then again he might have something in his eye, but if he comes over here he'll get the pointy end of me brolly in the other one… the next news was he was standing right beside me."

"Hello, Margaret," he said.

"You've got the train driver's name right, but you're on the wrong track, hard lines." she replied.

He said, "But Margaret, it's me."

"There must be thousands of me's in Burnley, you'll have to be a bit more specific."

"It's Bert," he said.

Of course, a lot of water had gone under the bridge (and over it when flooded), so they hadn't seen each other in something like twenty-odd years, plus the fact he had a moustache now. And Mum made us laugh by saying, "If he had one when he was eleven, I would have recognised him a lot quicker, instead of thinking he was from the funny farm."

So they went to a café opposite the market, had a bottomless cuppa (not a Café Latte) as well as a good old-fashioned chinwag. In a sense, it was like a fairytale, that their paths would cross again, then Mum dropped the 'F' word and said, "Do you want to meet the family?"

He said, "How many have you got?"

Then like lightening, she said, "How many do you want? I used to have six, but I managed to drown three," knowing Mum, she most probably threw that in to test him out.

Now it was our turn to put him under the spotlight (so to speak). There were quips flying about, left, right and centre. One was, "What happens if you take him back? Can you swap him? I wouldn't mind a donkey." (I could even go to school on that). But unbeknown to us, he was armed, yes folks, he had money (with a capital M), I think he gave me a shilling. I thought, I can always have a ride on a donkey next time we go to Blackpool, and seeing as he had come into our lives, that could be sooner rather than later. So yes, he'd won me over, no more questions asked. He could have my vote any day of the week, I thought, this bloke can move in tomorrow, he could even have my bed (providing he's a good swimmer).

I was still a bit young to really understand all that jazz about separation and divorce (besides, I still had to find out how much a return ticket to Blackpool cost). I didn't have time to listen to people rabbiting on about decree nisi (in fact, I thought it was the latest foreign film showing at the Continental, it would have a chance at winning the Academy Award). So I left all that to the adults to sort out, which they did, in due course.

Now I'll move forward by saying they got married. I suppose you could say, in one sense, we had a dad, but none of us could call him 'Dad'. We weren't being disrespectful and I think he understood that and he said we could call him whatever we liked (without being rude). I wouldn't have the foggiest where the name came from, but 'Pop' was top of the list and it just stuck.

So he came into my life right when I needed him most. I knew he would never be my real dad, but he gave it a damn good try (and I was as happy as a mouse in a cheese factory).

Me, Pop and Mum. The Ash Pad with the big trees.

I'll tell you this, in all honesty, not many men would do that in those days, take on three (ruffian) lads, what with our senses of humour, then me being cheeky in the bargain. He told us straight that he would do his best (then leaned over and said it again). Alright, we'll do the comedy, if you don't mind, if you want to be a clown in our circus you'll have to put your name down. So he copped a bit of ribbing but, just quietly, he gave as good as he got.

Now, all jokes aside (well, for a tick), he was actually a very handsome man. Mum would say to me, "Don't you think he looks like someone out of the films?"

"Yeah," I'd say, snapping my fingers (and putting up with the pain), "oh, what's that bloke called? No, don't tell me, I'll get it in a minute," and there was Pop, giving it his best angle, "it's on the tip of my tongue," I said.

"Roll it out and give us a dekko," he said.

I came back with, "It's not a carpet," while sticking my tongue out at him, "so there!"

Mum must have been saving this one for a rainy day, as a quick glance out of the window I could see it was lashing it down, she said, "Get that back in your gob before someone jabs a fork in it, last time I saw a tongue like that it was in Berkins window. And that reminds me, I don't know what we're having for tea, I haven't christened it yet, maybe some lettuce and a couple of those big tomatoes would go nice with that tongue and we'll do a few boiled eggs." (Mum, I don't think the readers wish to know that!).

So back to the film star, "I've got it, yeah, that's him, Fatty Arbuckle!"

Then Pop would chase me around the table a few times, never did catch me though. He'd push his false teeth out, which always made me chuckle, and Mum's back in with, "Don't you think he has a look of Clarke Gable and Errol Flynn?"

"More like Gable End, if you ask me." Then the chase was on again, but this time I'd be taking short cuts under the Cain and Abel (table). I ducked first, or I'd be seeing stars (even in the daytime) without a telescope. Most of that story is true. So with my elastic pen it just got s t r e t c h e d a little.

To those people who know rhyming slang that I've used, there's no need for me to explain, but for the ones who don't, the meaning will be in brackets so you won't be in the Thompson Park (dark). I just love me rhyming slang, and I've got a book that has quite a lot in it so, from here on in, it shall be slipped in at different places.

Chapter
13

Let's get back to Pop.

He had two half brothers, there was Norman who married Joan, they had Melanie and they lived on Gannow Lane. And there was Kenneth, he was in the Forces, he'd give us a visit when he was on leave and he would take me for a ride on his motorbike. Pop used to take me down to his mother's, she lived somewhere near Westgate, I forget the actual street, I don't think it was all that far from Massey's Brewery. Sometimes we would go down and wallpaper a room for her, he also did rooms for his workmates, I don't know how much he charged them. He'd give me a couple of bob for helping, I don't know if I was more of a hindrance because he never said a dicky bird (word).

It was great going places and doing things. I remember we once went on a holiday to Rhyl, in Wales. The place we stayed at was some sort of chalet or shack, depending on which way you looked at it. You would swear any minute it was going to collapse.

It was one of those holidays that was advertised as being only two minutes from the beach. I remember Pop walked out onto the veranda, then breathing in a big lung full of fresh air. He had his hand up to his forehead and over the top of his eyes, like you would when scanning the far horizon. He cracked everyone up within earshot by saying, "Two minutes to the sea. What, by bloody jet?" And just think, if I'd passed my Eleven Plus I could have taken them in my private plane!

I think it's time to head home after the holiday, so look out Lowerhouse, here we come!

No, you can't get rid of us that easy. Now, don't have heart failure, folks, but I reckon I should put another rhyme in about here. After the first attempt (on The Grove), a few more ideas have been popping up. So, in my own round about way of storing these rhymes (I hadn't really been all that strict with myself), some of them had been put on the smallest pieces of paper. My filing system has to be seen to be believed, but the ironic thing is, I know where it is (yeah, all over the place).

So, at this stage, I had a few different ones on the go, but didn't know what to write about next. I had a quick glance at the Rosegrove ideas and I thought, Mickey boy, you've got enough for another rhyme. Then once I'd put my thinking cap on again it just seemed to come from nowhere. There aren't as many verses as the first one, but places and things I didn't even think about using in the other are used. So in a way, something was telling me to go ahead and do it, but all the time I was thinking, what if nothing comes of it? And this was where I put my foot down with a firm hand. So I said to myself, "Listen, write it all out, then it's done, because we don't know what's around the corner (most probably another corner), but I'll cross that bridge when I come to it."

I've always liked that Willie Nelson song title "On The Road Again" so let's go up Lowerhouse Lane, then we will be…

In The Grove Again

Well, hello my friends from me to you
If you liked the first one, here's part two
Right, let's think back and remember when
And see those days yet once again

I was born in the summer of '42
On Liverpool Road at number 32
John was born on Dorset Street, number 65
Number 7 Saltburn Street was where Bob did arrive

We had lots of hope and not many fears
Barrels of laughter and buckets of tears
Thousands of dreams plus a million ideas
To last us for the rest of our years

When we were kids there were no confusions
We weren't scared of death or blood transfusions
Where have those years gone? They have flown so fast
But my treasured memories of The Grove will always last

I was very little when my Dad went away
In fact, too young to remember the actual day
We never received his love or affection
The only thing we ever got was rejection

Our Dad to us seemed so cold and callous
Yet to this day we bear no malice
We didn't know what Mum was going through
Tried to help, but what could children do?

Mum has a heart of gold and a sense of humour
We weren't rich, it was just a vicious rumour
Very knowledgeable was our Mum and oh so funny
Gave us liquorice and castor oil and a good run for our money

I ate crusts for my hair and for strength plenty of Brussels
I was a curly haired kid with a shirt full of muscles
There were always lots of things to do
And plenty of places which we did travel to

Those outside The Grove seemed so far away
Sabden Roughlee or Worsthorne where we'd spend a day
We'd take jam butties, ginger biscuits and Corporation pop
A special treat was an ice-cream from the village shop

Remember the dungeons at Towneley and the Big Bear
If my memory serves me right, I think he's still there
There was the Habergham Garden Party and The Lucky Dip
I'd see a kid with a Tizer and say, "Give us a sip"

There would be Pendle to climb, just for a change
Or go up to Hameldon past the rifle range
What about Lucas Sports Day and Peg Leg Pete?
He would amaze us with his death-defying feat

The old open market, where the rain ran down your collar
"Lean or fatty one," the black pudding chap did holler
We'd go to the Pot Fair but you had to be quick
To get near to the front to see Barmy Mick

The pantomime at the Vic, we sat up in the gods
That's when there were no Rockers, not even Mods
And behind the Odeon was where they held the fair
When up on the big wheel we never had a care

St. Marks was on Owen Street, it's now up Rossie Road
It was to be years later, that's where I'd marry Aud
You remember Griffin, Hapton and Valley Streets, that was Little Cornwall
The two Doctors in The Grove they were Spira and Gornall

We played with gas masks and drank Mrs Shorrock's goats milk
In those days no Beatles or even Acker Bilk
Tommy Higgins and Jack Lee, they both had a horse and cart
And boy, with my new pumps, I'd give them a good start

On a hot day we played with gas tar that had melted
Came in like Black & White Minstrels, didn't half get belted
We had a washboard and dolly tub and an old fashioned mangle
I'd put the cat's tail in and then turned the handle

Do you remember 1953 at the school canteen
Gave us a new shilling when they crowned the Queen?
On the school cross-country run, I never was a winner
My intentions were good, but didn't get back before dinner

After school we followed the rainbow for that elusive pot of gold
We started off on the Old Lane and finished up in The Fold
As we leave The Grove, we'll close the door
And it will be preserved in our memory forever more

Then I'll say TTFN as I'm running out of time
I hope "We'll Meet Again", same place, another rhyme

It's been a while since I've seen that and just reading it again, I think it worked in well. And we finished in The Fold, so we're not all that far from there. If some of you got stuck on TTFN it means, ta ta for now, and pumps were runners, trainers or joggers or whatever other names they use these days. I said to Pop, "I really go zoom zoom with them on."

He said, "Race down to the shop and get me five Woodbines then."

I was gone and back before he knew it, I said, "What about a tip?"

"Certainly," he said, "never tie your shoelace in a revolving door."

A couple of days later I said to Mum, "You know, with these new pumps on I ran home from school behind the bus and saved a tanner."

She said, "Run home behind a taxi next time, you'll save about five bob."

Now, Uncle George had met a young lady named Mona. I'm not sure if they got to know each other through the church. The wedding had been arranged, the service was at Habergham and they had their reception at The Junction. There was plenty of liquid refreshment, I could feel myself getting sozzled. Then it was my turn to get them in, I'd stagger to the bar (I think someone had to lift me up) and I said, "Garcon, give us a bucket of your best lemonade and five straws, by the way, get one for yourself."

Next morning I had a mouth like the bottom of a parrot's cage. While on the subject of getting hitched, sometimes when we saw a wedding, on the count of three, we'd give it…

Here comes the bride
Fair, fat and wide
See how she wobbles
From side to side

And then for good measure, we'd throw in…

So, oh how we danced
On the night we were wed
We danced and danced
As the room had no bed

So let's continue. Robert leaves school and goes to work at Drew's. Pop was at the gas works at the time and, as it was a bit of a way to travel, I think Bob pulled a few strings (so to speak) and got him a start at Drew's. I was taking papers for Mr Rhodes, which was very heavy work for a little chap like me (a lot of lads did it), but the dough wasn't bad.

For anyone who knows the area, you had to go up Scott Street, Poets Road, Byron Street, Johns Street, Hambledon View, Moore Street, Campbell Street, Lytton Street and you would finish on Burnley Road, right down past Whitegate. I would always carry a few spare papers in case someone wanted one. If you didn't, and you had to sell one, it was the last drop that missed out. You had to be careful they weren't missed too often, as they used to get quite annoyed, and that didn't go down too well with Mr Rhodes. Fridays were tough, with the big edition of the Burnley Express.

I started to go up to Collinge's Farm and soon got involved in doing part-time work after school and weekends. There was Mr and Mrs Collinge, and they had Winnie, Jim, Hazel, Gerald and Donald. Of course, in the school holidays, I more or less lived there. Mrs Collinge was just like Grandma, always did her own cooking, you know to this day, every time I get a whiff of cooked bacon it takes me right back to their kitchen.

Some mornings I'd go in to see if Donald was ready (as I used to help him take the milk) and there would be bacon crackling away in the fry pan. Mrs Collinge would cut two thick slices of homemade bread, then slapped on some marge. She piles heaps of bacon on it, then with a big glass of fresh milk, gave me a wink and said, "You're a growing lad, here, get your laughing gear around this."

Then as I bit into it, it was even hard to hold onto without the marge (I can't believe it's not butter) running down your sleeve. So I've got this thing which almost needed a block and tackle to lift it, there and then I said to myself, "This is without doubt a small sandwich for mankind, but one humongous butty for Mickey Plum."

The cheeks were bulging, the peggies (teeth) were going twenty to the dozen. Donald would come in, take one look, then he'd do a double-take and say, "They'll have to operate to get that out of your hands! You'll certainly be able to work on that full belly." I thought, I don't know about work, it'll take me a while to walk. I'll most probably be waddling around like a duck for about half an hour.

I was jumping up and down on a snail once, Donald said, "What are you doing that for?"

I said, "It followed me around all morning and it passed me twice."

(I don't care if they are old ones, if I think they are appropriate, I'll give them a mention).

There was always plenty to do. One big job was cleaning out the shippen. I didn't know where the word came from, there were no ships to be seen. We had to sweep most of the cows' droppings to the bottom end, we'd shovel it into the wheelbarrow, then wheeled it across the yard. It was dumped on the manure pile, I never did find out what they did with it. Maybe they sold it to the gardeners.

I learned a very valuable lesson while working there on the farm, that nothing was wasted. Even Mrs Collinge kept a waste food container and all their scraps went into that, then it would be dished out to the pigs. They were so funny (those big fat things), I used to love feeding them.

Now here's a play upon words, just for a bit of fun. A piece of wood inside the pigsty was called the pigstick, to show them who the boss was. One piglet was so small he got named The Pigmy. The others looked after him by taking turns to give him a piggyback. The pigheaded one used to butt the gate, he was Pigiron, and Pigface was Daisy. Now I've put you in the pigture, if you will pardon the pun. I think you know what I pigment. There are still quite a few more I could have used, but I didn't want to boar you.

So I'd start to feed them by throwing in some tomatoes and lettuce, then thinks I wouldn't mind a BLT, nah, it won't catch on. And yes folks, they knew when the grub was coming (they'd carry on like pork chops) and squealed as if their bellies thought their throats had been cut (I don't know where that saying comes from, but I just thought I'd use it).

Well, I piled on the dung that time, I'll bung it in the barrow, then it's back to the cows (had you forgotten? I hadn't). After the cows had been milked and the floor had been hosed down it was shippen shape and Bristol fashion. We'd let them all out, you could tell the cows liked the place as they left a deposit on leaving, and if you happened to be standing right behind them, without warning they just stopped, propped and plopped. It always seemed to be me who got the lot. They say, muck for luck, or words to that effect, but it's not nice to cop something like that from a great height and then to slip on it and go bass over oboe.

The cows were beautiful creatures; so big and yet gentle; also very trustworthy. I loved them. The way they would look at me, they'd watch my every moo-vement and what amazed me was they never seemed to stop chewing their cud, and of course they had those gorgeous, big, brown eyes.

Now, Mr Collinge would watch his p's and q's when he was around the kids, I never heard a foul word, even when the chickens got under his feet. In fact, he wouldn't swear but he used to shout, "Get those heifers into the bottom field!" We knew he meant the cows.

This one day, a cow was having a drink out of the trough, which to me looked a bit dirty, so I said to her, "If you don't tell the udders (sorry, others), how would you like a nice drink of milk? Nod once for yes and shake your head for no."

Then she nodded (well, of course she did, if she shook her head there would have been no story). I quickly put some milk in a bucket, then double-checking to see that no one was watching, I gave her a drink and she lapped it up. Then my luck ran out, I got sprung by Mr Collinge, he said, "What on earth are you doing, giving her milk?"

The brain quickly sent down some words which came out, "I thought it looked a bit weak, so I'm putting it through again."

Now, most of the time he called me Mickey Dolittle, not for the amount of work I did but, by the way, I would talk to the animals. Other times I'd whistle or sing to them, "What Do You Want To Make Those Eyes At Me For."

They looked at me as if to say, "Change the record." I don't think they liked that, it seemed to put them right off their fodder.

One day I told them the story of the zebra, who I'll call Zsa Zsa. She escaped from the zoo and walked into a farm. She said to the chicken, "What do you do here?"

The chook said, "Apart from getting under everyone's feet, I provide the farmer with eggs."

She saw the pig wallowing in the mud and said, "What do you do around here?"

The pig said, "I supply the bacon for people's butties."

She then went up to Daisy and said, "How, now, brown cow, what do you do on the farm?"

And the cow said, "I give gallons of body building milk (not lite, organic, Physical, Rev or Skinny)."

And then she saw the bull and asked him what he did, the bull just sorta snorted and then gave his best Humpty Gocart impersonation, "Listen shweedheart, you get those pyjamas off, then you'll see." (That's no bull).

So three cows booed
Some of them clapped
Then six just mooed
The rest crapped

I can truly say I milked that one. Then once, we were cleaning up the yard and this motorcyclist came staggering in. He was limping and blood was pouring from a deep gash on his forehead. I said to him, "Have an accident?"

He said, "No thanks, I've just had one," he then said to Mr Collinge, "if you're the farmer, I've just run into your bull and he's dead. I'd like to replace him if I could."

Mr C never batted an eyelid, then said, "Sure, young man, the cows are in the barn, help yourself."

Another day, while doing some repairs to the fencing, we just happened to be singing, "Don't Fence Me In," when this bloke came up to us and said, "It's 11.15 now, so if I go through here to Rosegrove Station, will I get the 12.20?"

Donald said, "If you do take a short-cut and our new bull sees you, you'll catch the 11.55."

I said, "You won't miss him, he'll be riding a motorbike."

They were great days. Mind you, they were long ones too, if you'll pardon the pun, sometimes I was there till the cows came home. Haymaking was hard work, but I was getting plenty of fresh air, being out in the sunshine, depending on what day summer fell on, so with the grub and money thrown in, it was a good learning experience. I thought, how long has this been going on?

I remember about this time I got an old bike given. Pop said, "It looks like a million dollars, all green and crimpled, so what if it needs a lot of work?" (I'm just the lad for the job).

Now, every time I got some money, it went towards doing it up. After a short time and plenty of elbow grease, it didn't look that bad, plus it got me from A to B (and back again). Some of the lads asked, "What sort is that?"

I'd say, "It's a BSA."

"Who are you trying to kid," they said.

"You, because it's got Bits Stuck Anywhere."

Now, I thought with all this moolah coming in, all I need to do is get some muggins to work for me, then pay him half of what I was getting (if that was possible). I could turn it into a nice little nest egg and if I played my cards right, I could leave school at fifteen and retire. Guess what? I was a lousy card player.

Then something happened, and looking back now it was great, but at the time I just took it in my stride. I wish I'd have written down the exact details, as in prices, but I'll do my best. We had a chance to buy the allotment off Mr Judge (which we did) and it was only four to five hundred yards up the Ash Pad, it ran alongside the Chapel. I do remember taking the payment book over to pay on a weekly basis. It was something like ten bob a week and the pen must've cost nearly fifty quid? It was a great big block, it had on it a hen hut, a greenhouse and quite a big veggie patch. When Pop first took it over, Mr

Judge said, "We can come to some agreement about the poultry."

So besides the hens, there were a couple of gooses, I mean two geeses, hang on, I'll get it right in a minute. There was a goose, and there was another one! I don't know if you've ever been chased by a goose, but they can really move. It's so funny, plus the racket they make.

We were in the hen hut when Mr Judge said to Pop, "It's like this Bert, the ones in the brooding boxes are ten bob each and the ones above them are five shillings down and a bob a week for the next six weeks."

I thought, hold your horses, it doesn't take a Rocket Scientist to work out that they are a shilling dearer, so I said, "I couldn't help overhearing your little confab, but how come those up there are more expensive?"

At that precise moment they both nudged each other and winked, then Pop said, "Because they're on higher perches."

There's nothing worse than two grown men nudging and winking at each other (nudge, nudge, wink, wink, if you know what I mean). I'm onto you (and about my other leg, you can pullet). So have you ever tried to push a couple of hysterical blokes into a brooding box? (It makes it easier if they're eggheads).

We had a little pig, I can't remember what his name was so we'll call him Percy. But I do know we had a pith helmet, which I would wear at every given opportunity, especially if it was pithing down (I couldn't resist that one).

We were always playing tricks on each other and this one day, Pop, he got me a good one. We used to have a barrel that caught the rainwater off the greenhouse. He must have put some water in the helmet (not much, but enough) and of course, when I put it on, I said, "How the heck did that get in there?"

"Percy must have pithed in it," Pop said.

Well, you've never seen a hat (or helmet) come off so quick and get booted that far. Then a glance at Pop and he would be smirking, then saying, "That's one to me." I don't know what happened to Percy, he most probably filled a lot of butties (burp, excuse me).

We also had a tortoise that we kept in the house more than anything. I can't remember his name (that's if he ever had one), we'll call him Tommy. So I'd take him up the pen and let him frolic in the grass, then we'd have to get the search party out when it was time to go home. Sometimes it would take ages to find him. Now, this one time, I had a brainwave. I thought, I'll stick a dart in him with a piece of string tied to it, the idea being to reel him in. Have you ever tried to throw a dart at a tortoise (when they're in full flight)? They bounce off and go every which way. Once I got two chooks and a leg of pork, you don't get prizes like that at the Burnley Fair!

Now, if you cast your mind back to when I was talking about the bath on Livie Road, I said Lowerhouse Lane didn't have one, meaning there wasn't a fixed one, it was a tin bath. We used to place it in front of the fire and we would fill it from the sink with a bucket. After having the bath you had to drag it to the back door. You'd tip it up, then empty it into the yard. By the way, you had to make sure that the window cleaner wasn't on his way in, or he'd cop a bath, buckshee (free) and I don't know if you've ever seen a window cleaner trying to tread water with a ladder on his shoulder (it's a funny sight).

You also had to double-check on the tortoise to see if he happened to be out there, or pretty soon he'd be headed towards the whirlpool at the drain (where he would get beheaded) and if you weren't quick enough, he'd go round a few times before you could grab him.

One time I thought about putting a thimble on his noggin, then he would have some sort of protection when battling against the current. And when he went up the pen, the hens wouldn't peck him, but Mum soon put a stop to that saying, "The thimble stays in the sewing box."

You know folks, I was a little genius just waiting to hit on the right invention. So this brings me to the canary. Whenever I had a new playmate, he'd come to our place and say to the bird, "What's your name then?"

And the canary would say, "Cracker wants a polly, Cracker wants a polly."

The bemused kid said, "He's got that the wrong way around."

"No," I said, "that's his name, Cracker."

This one day, when I was changing his water, I said to Pop, "Did you know this bird has haemorrhoids?"

"How can you tell?" He said.

"Because there's piles in his cage, OTM."

"What on earth is OTM?" He said.

"I've just equalised, as that's One To Me, Pop off," I said.

Then he chased me out the back door so I was off around to the front, but he had the same idea and he locked the door on the inside just as I got there. "Let me in," I shouted, "you'll keep, as every dog has his day."

I heard him laughing, he said, "You've got to get up early to catch me, and that's another one, Fido."

It's back to the birdie. I don't know what they put in that millet, but sometimes he was as high as a kite and there were times we'd let him out in the kitchen, but we had to keep him away from the fire, the whistling kettle and the chip pan, and not necessarily in that order. So you had to have eyes in the back of your head and a tea towel at the ready in case you had to give him a quick waft. For a bit of fun he would dive-bomb Tommy the tortoise and land on top of him, squawking, "Mush, mush!" Then before you knew it, he'd be on the kettle handle. After a couple of seconds he would be into his dance routine and giving it, "Who's a pretty boy then?" And with the steam still coming from the kettle he'd whistle "Misty" or "Smoke Gets In Your Eyes".

The entertainment was going along very nicely when suddenly he lost his footing, maybe because of the condensation on the handle. He'd gone beak over claw and plummeted into the chip pan in his best Johnny Cash voice singing, "I fell into that burning 'Ring Of Fire'."

There was a real commotion, Mum screamed, "For goodness sake, will someone fish Cracker outta there, the chips have to be done first!"

> *But alas it was all too late*
> *Yes folks, he'd met his fate*
> *Tom said wrap him in lettuce, mate*
> *Then stick him on me plate*

I said to Pop, "Let's go into the food business."

He raised his eyebrows and said, "Why?"

I lowered them back down for him and said, "Y is a crooked letter that can't be straightened. So just think, we could call it Lowerhouse Fried Canary, or LFC for short."

Pop said, "It'll never catch on."

Oh folks, you don't know how close I came, as some fella brought out KFC and didn't he hit the jackpot with that? Ah well, them's the breaks, and while on the subject about birds, here's one for you. What succeeds? It's a canary without teeth.

I assure you, we did have a pig, a tortoise and a bird, but I just fibbed a little (well, it was fun). Before I go much further, this has baffled me for a while. If tin whistles are made out of tin, what are foghorns made from?

Now viewers, I think I've earned a coffee break, and it will give me a chance to get my notes together, as there could be a couple of things I've overlooked. So don't get me wrong, it's not that I'm struggling (far from it), in fact I've got plenty to write about, but seeing as I'm doing a life story it would be good to get most of the events near enough in the right places. I think that's a good excuse and you people should accept it. I was going to say, if you don't I'll throw the book at you, but I won't say that as it's not finished yet.

Chapter
14

This was one thing that slipped my mind and after a bit of double-checking I've managed to come up with some facts.

Now, I do remember everybody was talking about this and it got a lot of coverage on the newsreels. It was the SS Flying Enterprise (1944-1952), while going from Europe to the U S of A she was hit by a severe storm in the North Atlantic. A few ships came to help her and managed to get the passengers and crew off on the 29th December 1951, but the ships master, Captain Carlsen, wouldn't leave her and stayed on board for a couple of weeks as they tried in vain to tow her, eventually he had to abandon ship. Then on the 10th of January 1952 she went down about forty-odd miles from Falmouth (England) and to this day it remains one of the many stories of courage at sea.

Now, here's something else I want to share with you. It's about, of all things, boxing, so a lot of lads my age should be interested in this. There were a couple of boxers (if you'll pardon the pun) doing the rounds, the first one was Don Cockle and the second, Bruce Woodcock. I don't know if they fought each other or even at the same weight (as I was only a little tot at the time).

I'm still checking on Don, but here's what I found out about Bruce; he was born in Doncaster (England) in 1921; he was European and British Empire Champion (1945-50); he fought Jack London (I'm not sure if he was Brian's father, Brian went on to fight Ali) and Bruce beat Jack in six rounds. Then on the 17th May 1946 he fought Tami Mauriello in New York for the World Title, but in the fifth round he was hit by a massive right hand and Bruce was counted out. In his next fight he won the European Title and after that he went on to beat Freddie Mills but then he lost to Baksi, and also to Savold, and that ruined his title chances. Out of thirty-seven fights he lost only four. After retiring from boxing he went into the licensed business and on the 21st December 1997 he died aged seventy-six.

I suppose over the years I've thought of this man quite a lot and in one sense I'm kicking myself for not trying to meet him or to get in touch, one way or the other, but now I feel I know more about him than I ever have, so Bruce, thanks for those memories. And then, of course, these next events were very big talking points.

Let's see if I can stir something up in your old memory bank (as there could be a few cobwebs, eh?); the first person was John Christie, they say he murdered at least six women, he was originally from Yorkshire (not that there's anything wrong with that), he was hanged in Pentonville Prison in March 1950.

The second was Derek Bentley who, with Chris Craig, was doing a break-in when they were confronted by a policeman. They say Bentley was unarmed but he shouted to his partner in crime, "Let him have it, Chris." Craig shot and killed the policeman and was sent to jail (as he was only sixteen), while the nineteen year old Bentley was hanged in Wandsworth Prison in January 1953.

The third person was Ruth Ellis, she was the last woman to be executed and was hanged in Holloway Prison in July 1955, aged twenty-eight.

Now this will put a bit of pressure on you, can you remember the name of the hangman? To all those who said 'Albert Pierrepoint', well done, and to the ones who said 'Jack Robinson', you weren't within a bulls roar. Now, I haven't got the actual figures of how many people Pierrepoint hanged, but these three are the most memorable to me.

While we are around this time, here's some more trivia for you, I'll put them in this order and hope for the best; Hungary annihilated England 6-3 at Wembley (suffering soccertash); Mount Everest is conquered; Queen Elizabeth II is crowned; England beat Australia to regain The Ashes for the first time in twenty years (whoop dee do); and eggs, tea and sweets are taken off the ration.

That reminds me of the Co-op, I can still remember Grandma's divvy number (9058), I wonder if there's any way of checking on that, just out of curiosity. Sometimes us kids would meet at the Co-op. If it was only a couple of things you had to get you had no problem remembering them, but if there were a few things you'd write them down. But then you had to make sure you got there before that Jewish kid, you know the one I'm talking about, his name was Schindler, and boy, didn't he have a list.

Well, after getting away with that one, how's about you try this for size. I mentioned before about the Rosegrove Theatre Group, now I'm not 100% sure if it's a club or a group, but I'll plug for group. Now, there could be some saying it was definitely the other, so to those knockers out there I want photos (glossy ones). The RTG were always on the lookout for up and coming (Goons) actors. Half of the lads used to dare you to give it a bash, and I thought yeah, why not? After all, it can't be that hard, can it?

I made a few inquiries and was told to report behind the stage after school, there were a couple of lads waiting besides me, we all said how nervous we were so it came to my turn and they asked me to pop up onto the stage for a quick audition and say just one line of only two words, which just happened to be 'IT IS'.

I came through with flying colours and they told me to say these at every given opportunity as IT IS quite easy on the night to get stage fright and I thought that's a lot of rot IT IS but I'll play their silly game. So when I got chance I'd say IT IS, when I sat on the throne someone would sing out, "Is that you in there, Michael?"

And I replied, "IT IS."

Even on the bus the Conductor would shout out, "Lowerhouse Fold."

Quick as a flash I'd nod at him and say, "IT IS," and the last thing I'd say before going to sleep, then the first when I opened my peepers was IT IS.

Mum would say, "It's time for school, young man."

I'd get confident and say, "Yes, IT IS."

Then came the night of the play and the next thing I knew there was my cue, with arms outstretched and inhaling a deep breath so that my voice would carry those words around the school hall, I said, "IS IT." No sooner had the words left my north and south (mouth) and you all know that big hook they used in Vaudeville to drag those bad acts off, well need I say, but that was around my neck before I had the chance to take a bow.

Once I got into the wings (I thought, whatever's up?), they were on me like a ton of bricks saying, "How could you get it wrong?" and, "You'll never set foot on this stage again, you're fired!"

"So what have you got to say for yourself?"

I said, "I'm in the actors onion, I mean union, so you can't sack me and besides that I know my line backwards."

Now this is a ticklish situation but it's got to be dealt with and I'm going to try and cover it the best I can (as it happens to everyone) without making myself blush, but knowing me I'll wangle my way around it (so wish me luck).

There comes a time in a young mans life when changes start happening to ones body, most times it would occur on bath nights as many of the kids discovered, there would be movement (that seems to be the right word for it) and I don't mean from the Rubber Ducky, and the hardest part (if you'll pardon the pun) is you are well and truly snookered. Because you can't tell your parents or, worse still, confide in your brothers, you had to make sure the coast was clear, your ears were pricked (and that's as far as I'm going with that line), you then had to scramble outta the bath, yeah, you had to have your wits about you and be careful, as you could have someone's eye out with that.

I'll never forget my first sexual experience (oh, what a nightmare). I was frightened, confused and alone (ha), that's all I'm going to tell you about mine, so you just have to wait for the video to come out.

Most of the lads at school talked about it, when the teacher went out of the room there would always be some sort of a dare going on, this one kid, no name, no pack drill, so I will call him Portnoy, because he certainly had the complaint, you could say on one hand he knew what he was doing. It must have been through all the hands-on experience, I reckon there's a candidate for the Pullitzer Prize (if ever I saw one), he'd use either one, it didn't matter to him.

Now, in all seriousness I'd give my left hand to be ambidextrous. Back to the lad in question, this one day he got caught in the act (so to speak) under the showers. The teacher yelled at him, "What on earth are you doing?" (I thought it would be obvious).

Anyway, he never missed a beat (if you'll pardon another pun), leaning over he said, "Sir, look at it this way, it's mine and I'll wash it as fast as I like."

We'd say to him, "We knew you'd get caught with your pants down one day, and if you keep polishing it a Genie will pop out, and whatever you do, you better not rub him up the wrong way."

Then, of course, there was the Frustrated Robot, who pulled himself to pieces. Here's a proverb for you:

> *A woman, a dog and a walnut tree*
> *The more you beat 'em the better they be*

Now folks, can you imagine this, well I can, so let me write it. The housewife is on the plantation, and she shouts out to her husband, "Darling, what are you doing?"

He replies, "I won't be long sweetheart, as I'm just thrashing the old walnut tree." (That's a new name for it). Right, hands up those who noticed I put an extra 'L' in Pulitzer, just for the L of it.

> *Now for every Evil under the sun*
> *There is a remedy or there is none*
> *If there be one, try and find it*
> *If there be none, never mind it*

I think it's enough on the subject, as I managed to get a couple of jokes in that I didn't think I would. This next bit I'm going to share with you, at the time it took some clogging, all the kids were saying it, I don't think I knew then where it came from, but we had fun with it, so to anyone who doesn't know it I hope I can explain it properly, as it might not come across too good on paper.

For those of you who do remember, I wouldn't mind betting you haven't heard it for yonks and it will bring back some memories, so it goes something like this:

First person: "Do you know the man?"

Second person: "What man?"

FP: "The man with the power."

SP: "The power of what?"

FP: "The power of Hoo Doo."

SP: "Hoo Doo?"

FP: "Yes you do."

SP: "I do what?"

FP: "Know the man."

SP: "What man?"

FP: "The man with the power."

SP: "The power of what?"

And it just goes on and on till it dies a death, so with silly little things like that we kept ourselves occupied and as a last resort we could always watch the bacon slicer at Redman's (she was scrumptious).

Don't go away folks, I forgot to tell you after all those years how I managed to come up with that, on TV they did a Cary Grant marathon, or whatever they call them. This one night while I was reading plus writing and with the other eye on the telly (and that takes some doing), then you could have knocked me down with a feather, I couldn't believe my three ears, and I didn't have time to hit 'record' on the video, I was in a state of shock that I fluked this. I can tell you it made my day, when Cary Grant came out with those words, it was just as I'd remembered and it was from the 1947 film "The Bachelor And The Bobby Soxer". It also starred Shirley Temple and Rudy Vallee (which I always thought was a nudist colony).

Now, I've done some more research so, just for the record, did you know Cary Grant made 67 films, the first in 1932 and the last in 1966. He made "An Affair To Remember" in 1957, which you could say was remade into "Sleepless In Seattle" (1993). So there you go viewers, I can assure you I'm not trying to string you along. If that was the case there's a good chance by the time you get to the end of the book you could be very highly strung, meanwhile, back at the pen.

The hens were laying a lot (so we suggested they stand up, if only to stretch their legs). Now seeing as we had eggs to spare, Pop put up a sign outside 'Eggs For Sale. Apply Within'. Then a few days later I said to Pop, "There's a lady at the gate."

He said, "Would you go and ask her what she wants as I'm rolling a cigarette."

I forgot to tell you sometimes he rolls his own (do you know something, I don't think they ever came back), so I trotted up to the gate. The pig used his trotters and followed me, I said, "Yes Lady, can I help you?"

She said, "Yes Sonny, could I have six eggs please."

And I said, "I'm sorry, we forgot to take the sign down, there's no eggs left."

And she said, "Are you egging me on?"

I said, "Actually, I'm not egging anything as there are none."

"Well, can I just have two eggs," she said, "as I'm baking a birthday cake for my Granddaughter."

So I said, "Listen Lady, put it this way, take the 'F' out of Farm and what do you get?"

She said, "Arm."

"Now take the 'F' out of Fred."

And she said, "Red."

"Now take the 'Fugg' out of eggs."

She said, "There is no 'Fugg' in eggs."

And I said, "That's what I have been trying to tell you."

That's a very clever joke. I know it's been around a while but the old ones are the best and if I only make one person laugh that's enough for me.

Back: Pop, John, Bob, Uncle George, Aunty Mona
Middle: Mum, Grandma
Front: Me and Grandad

So with four men in the household there was always a chance of getting the underpants mixed up (when it came to the changing of the guards), especially if you had to grab them off the line at night when they had been forgotten to be brought in (most probably my fault), so I used to sing this (while I was out there) to the tune of "In The Misty Moonlight". I bet most of the readers know it, come on, join in…

> *Now in the Misty Moonlight*
> *Me undies don't feel right*
> *Also slightly off-white*
> *Besides down to the knee*
>
> *I'll have to get some new ones*
> *I could borrow our John's*
> *As long as they're not long johns*
> *Hopefully they'll fit me*

Well, that sounded like the cat's chorus, you know what, it looked good on paper, so I think I'll leave it there. Gee, there's a lot that happens in a young chaps life but wait, there's more. We'd go past a building and there would be a double extension ladder propped against the wall and a painter was on top of it, whistling away. He sounded as happy as 'a pig in poo' (I cleaned that up a bit). We shouted, "What yer doing mister, and why are you so happy?"

He sang back, "It's pay day and 'I'm Painting The Clouds With Sunshine'."

Then one kid said, "If I kick these two wedges from under this ladder you'll be brushing your bum with iodine."

Some of the lads would go into a chemist and say, "Do you handle Prophylactics?"

And the assistant said, "Of course we do." They'd tell her to wash her hands as they wanted two ounces of Liquorice Allsorts.

I don't know where this came from originally but Mum used to say it a lot and it's about, of all things, a shilling, though shilling itself isn't mentioned (if you know what I mean) so here it is:

> Now if your Bob doesn't give our Bob that bob, that your Bob owes our Bob, our Bob will give your Bob a bob on the nose, right, I'll see your Bob and raise you a Rupee.
>
> You know I always thought a Rupee was something a kangaroo had behind a tree. Honestly, I wouldn't have a clue where these thoughts come from, I just write them down.

Chapter
15

I didn't tell you before, Pop liked his music, actually, he had a good voice. A couple of his favourites were Nelson Eddy who sang with Jeanette McDonald. He would try and imitate Nelson Eddy, I said they can keep him because tonight Opportunity Knocks for our very own Bert from Brierfield, I don't think he chased me as that one hit the funny-bone. For those who didn't get this joke, 'Brierfield' is in between Burnley and Nelson.

There were some silly songs going around and I'll have to do some research to get the titles and artists right, so I'll come back to this a little bit later.

I told you Grandad liked his cards and when he and Uncle Ted got together they'd go back forty years or more, and they would talk about the war like it happened yesterday. Uncle Ted used to make me laugh saying he was, "Up to his neck in muck and bullets." Just like the English to find humour in anything. It would be years later that I saw the horrors of war.

I touched on radio comedy earlier in the piece, but now listeners, I'm going to clobber you to death with it. I mentioned Peter Brough and Archie Andrews, they were in "Educating Archie" and the other, of course, was "The Goons." There could be more later on those as there's a few ideas in the pipeline, so I'll see what comes to the surface. I'll name a few of the other programs, there's no charge, it's all part of the service, just see how many you can remember. We'll start with…

I.T.M.A. (It's That Man Again)
Ignorance Is Bliss
Variety Bandbox
Stand Easy
Workers Playtime
Band Wagon
Much Binding In The Marsh
Life With The Lyons
Take It From Here
Ray's A Laugh
Have A Go

The Crazy Gang

Hancock's Half Hour

Ray Galton and Alan Simpson were only in their twenties when they first met Hancock, "Not Many People Know That" (there's my Michael Cain impersonation for you), anyway let's go back to the list…

The Clitheroe Kid

Henry Hall's Guest Night

The Al Reid Show

Beyond Our Ken (later became Round The Horne)

Happy Go Lucky

A Life Of Bliss

The Billy Cotton Band Show

I'm Sorry I'll Read That Again (you can if you want)

The Navy Lark

It ran for eighteen years and became the longest running show on the Beeb. There's a lot of people who got their starts on Worker's Playtime, I wouldn't go as far to say that they had jugglers on the show, it wouldn't be very entertaining for radio viewers. And who could forget Dick Barton and his off-siders, Jock and Snowy, on radio from 1946-51.

Bonfire nights were great. There were always plenty of adults to supervise. Now the fires themselves would be (at a rough guess) only a couple of miles apart. Any spare ground was the ideal place, providing someone could keep an eye on the wood that was stacked there. Mums would keep guard during the day with a rolling pin in their apron pockets, any shifty looking kids were told to clear off.

Some days at school, if there were a couple of kids missing, you knew that (the little angels) they were up to no good as they would be planning a raid. After school we'd always be out looking for wood, Tommy used to tell us where to get some as he'd seen it on his travels so we would take a Mia Farrow (barrow), which seemed like a good idea at the time, but nine times outta ten it was more trouble than it was worth if it happened to be down Molly Brook, then at night when we were half inching (pinching) from the other gang's stacks they'd be thieving from ours (there should be a law against that).

Other times we went collecting a penny for the guy (for the bonfire) and if we hadn't had the chance to make him yet the scruffiest kid got the job. We'd sit him outside the canteen, put his balaclava on backwards, making sure one of his ears wouldn't be sticking through the eye holes, then make him as limp as possible, not to give the game away. Half the time would be spent trying to shoo off the stray dogs, but some managed to cock their legs and give him a quick squirt. One dog was right on target (I suppose you could call him 'a dead eyed dick') to which a muffled voice enquired, "Is it raining?"

We'd say, "No, it's just a couple of spots," (but we didn't dare tell him it was Spot that was a pot shot).

There was one dog who wanted to mate with the young lad's shoulder and he sang out, "What's that dog up to?"

And we said, "He's trying to find a hole in your balaclava, we're not sure if he's going to lick your lug hole or if he's about to knock some sense into yer. It's a good thing you didn't wear your Granny's tea cosy or you could have got one up the spout."

He said, "Disguised like this I know how Claude Rains felt in 'Phantom Of The Opera'."

"Well, we'd better keep that dirty great big Alsatian across the road away or you'll be 'clawed balls'."

Then a drunk came staggering out of the club saying, "Howdy lads, did you know my missus is a musician and I'm going home to face the music. She'll hit the roof when I get in, yeah, she's a dreadful shot."

Then glancing at the guy he did a double take and he tried to alter our young friends headgear and we quickly shouted, "No mister, don't twist his head around or his eyes will stick out like Chapel hat pegs."

He didn't know which way to take that, then he threw some loose change into the guys lap, we had to stop the young bloke from grabbing the dosh, or the drunk would have sobered up PDQ.

Then going one step forward and two back he approached the coal chap's horse and cart. At that moment the coal man was just putting the feedbag on his horse, and the horse seemed to be playing up a bit, the Molly the Monk (drunk) said, "'It's Impossible', you'll never do it mate."

The coal fella looked him up and down then said, "I won't do what?"

Then MM patted the horse saying, "Get Dobbin into that little sack."

Then he weaved his way across the road to Mary's shop while singing, "Sugar In The Morning."

He disappeared inside, then after a couple of minutes he staggered out munching on a pie and smacked right into a woman and her small yapping dog (one of those peckatyerknees). Being the perfect gentleman, while raising his titfer tat (hat), he said, "Sorry Ma'am."

And she replied, "That's alright. By the way, my little Fido likes pies."

He said, "Do you mind if I sling him a bit?"

And she replied, "Certainly not."

With that he picked the mutt up and slung him a few feet down Fox Street.

Gee, there were some old ones in amongst that lot, and I think I managed to get 'em all in. Er, hold your horses folks, I'm getting ahead of myself here, I almost forgot to tell you about singing for the guy which we did at night, we'd go knocking on doors, let's see if I've got it right…

> *Remember, remember the 5th of November*
> *It's gunpowder plot*
> *And we never forgot*
> *Put your hand in your pocket*
> *And pull out your purse*
> *A penny or ha'penny will do you no worse*
> *If you haven't a penny a ha'penny will do*
> *If you haven't a ha'penny well God bless you*

If there was no movement or lights going on, some kid would shout through the letter box, "Are you deaf in there or what? As we're singing in the rain out here."

So what we had to do was sing it once more with feeling then saying to each other, "Don't forget to change the last line," we rattled it all off, then of course we came to the line in question and it was changed to, "If you haven't a ha'penny your windows go through," (I don't know who came up with that, but it was very clever).

After singing that line you would be amazed the number of people who heard you, whereas before there was no sign of life. But if it was the upstairs window that opened first you had to have your wits about you (or a brolly). Especially if you saw the shape of a po, it's a wonder somebody wasn't trampled to death in the rush. I don't mind chamber music, but I'm not keen on its contents, when they came to the door and asked, "How long have you been there?" We knew we'd get a few coppers for our effort.

I don't know if you noticed or not when I mentioned about "Singing In The Rain" and "Once More With Feeling", I didn't realise till after I'd written them down that they were both films, so subconsciously they were there and just fitted into that tale. And you might have twigged somewhere along the way that I love films and music, which will all be explained at a later date (if I remember).

Now c'mon Mick, get back to this enthralling story before you forget what you were waffling on about. Okey-dokey, when "Singing In The Rain" came out, no matter how many times we saw it we'd come waltzing out of the Coli. Then pushing and shoving each other out of the way to see who'd be first into the nearest puddle, swinging around lamp-posts or trying to run up a wall just like Donald O'Connor had done. So people didn't have to ask which film we'd seen.

So getting onto the other one (that's if you haven't nodded off yet), "Once More With Feeling" starred Yul Brynner and Kay Kendall. She was from "Genevieve" fame, oh, how I loved that film, and if you remember the musical score was done by Larry Adler and for a small bloke like me I thought Max Geldray, who also played the harmonica, was just as good (we called it the mouth organ).

Now I'll tell you something and this is for your ears only (no, that's not a James Bond film), I had a lot of trouble telling Larry and Max apart on radio, and by the way, OMWF was in fact Kay Kendall's last film. I bet the film buffs are checking to see if that's true, I can assure you it is.

This little mouse went into a music store, I'm not sure if it was Pollards (in Burnley), and said to the rodent behind the counter, in his best James Cagney impersonation, "You, you dirty rat, give me a mouth organ."

And the rat, in his best WC Fields voice said, "Listen, my little chickadee, I sold the last one about an hour ago to a pretty thing who had a look of you, would it have been your sister?" The little mouse said, "Yeah, it sounds like ar Monica."

Now, we haven't had one of these yet, so, "I say, I say, I say, what's the difference between a post box and an elephants backside?"

"Well, for those of you who don't know, I wouldn't like to send you to post a letter."

I should have thrown this one in before when I was on about eggs, but the truth is, it's only just come to me now. There were two eggs boiling away in a pan, one said, "It ain't half hot in here."

The other said to him, "That's nothing, wait till you're taken out, then they smash your head in."

Chapter
16

Well look at that time, I was so busy writing and didn't realise how dark it was getting, so I suppose we should ask one of the adults to put a match to the bonfire.

Pretty soon the bonfire was blazing away, someone in the background whistled "Fireworks Music" by Handel, how appropriate I thought, and we had our fireworks at the ready, which we'd bought with the money collected. Bangers (not sausages) were number one on the list with the lads as it gave them a power (of Hoo Doo).

Rockets were great fired from a milk bottle, that seemed the best and safest way to set them off, because if you stuck them into the ground, sometimes if they were in too deep they'd be firing on all cylinders (so to speak) till they just burnt themselves out, and that happened quite a bit, which of course was a waste of good money.

> *Those skyrockets in flight*
> *Zooming off into the night*
> *Cats and dogs getting a scare*
> *This was fun, what did we care*

And you will remember the other ones, we used to nail them on a fence (Catherine Wheels), they were always very colourful, but there would be barrels of laughter when they used to spin off the fence (which happened often) and it actually seemed like they had a mind of their own, as they'd chase a kid, little chaps were crying and running everywhere, "Mum, Mum, it's following me," and he'd be hiding behind her.

Then she would yell at him, "Don't be silly, you just think it is."

And he said, "It's behind me and I'm in front of it, as far as I'm concerned that's being followed."

He'd get a clip round the ear hole for his cheek, she'd say, "Go and hide behind your Dad."

"I can't, he's in the canteen and kalied."

So if the lad wasn't quick enough he'd get another clip to match the first one. Then someone would bring along a bag full of toffee from Sabden Treacle Mines. I bet you're thinking we've got a right one here, this bloke's off his rocker (correct, I'm on the couch) which reminds me of the young chap who went to see the Psychiatrist, the place was full of plants and he says, "I keep thinking I'm a dog."

While sniffing the ferns he was asked, "How long have you been like this?"

And he growled, "Ever since I was a puppy."

The head man sang, in his best Al Jolson voice, "Climb upon my settee, sonny boy, and you can tell me all about it."

He barked, "I can't do that, I'm not allowed on the furniture. But really, my brother is worse than me, he thinks he's a chicken. Mum won't let him see you, we need the eggs and I'm not eggsagerating as me Dad always goes to work on an egg," (unless he runs outta Shell), and with that he scratched at the door, so the receptionist would let him out.

While waiting he cocked his leg and watered "The Biggest Aspidistra In The World". Then once through the door he bit the postman on the ankle, who just happened to be coming up the stairs. The moggy, who was having a scratch on the bottom step, hit the accelerator and took off when he heard the woof and the chase was on.

Did I hear someone say, "Strike a light, he's forgotten all about the bonfire." No, I haven't and I'm surprised at you lot playing with matches (how many times do you need to be told!) In fact, I've got a good mind to read you the riot act, unless of course you've already read it, so let's move nearer to the fire as it's getting a bit cold.

There were always plenty of spuds on hand after everybody had let their fireworks off, this would have to be the best part of the night, seeing as the ankle biters had been dragged away. Now it was time to get out the potatoes that had been put in earlier, but here's where the fun and games started, even though the fire had died down it still gave out a lot of heat. One of the best things to use was a toasting fork, which would be, at a guess, twelve to fourteen inches long. Other than that, a stick came in handy, but half the time you'd set fire to it before you could jab your (spud) grub.

Another idea was to have a glove, then when you did get it out it was easier to handle. The laughs we had when the object was thrown to someone as they tried to juggle the proverbial 'hot potato' and we'd sing, "One potato, two potato, three potato, four," or another way we had some fun was to lob them in the air and then belt them with a cricket bat, that way everybody got a bit.

We would stay out as long as we could, it was great if the 5th fell on a Friday or Saturday, but if it was school the next day you were dreading your Mum shouting, once you heard her you knew that it was late, then when you did get in you'd stink from all the smoke, so you had to do the bath at the sink trick, which really was no big deal, I just didn't like the idea of doing a balancing act at that time of night.

Next morning all the lads would turn up at the site, the fire would still be giving out some heat, sometimes there would be a few spuds that had been missed, they were like charcoal. I was always amazed at the number of springs we'd find, with a bit of luck you'd put your feet in them but you had to be careful or you could break your neck, being rough nuts we'd have a bash at anything once, and then try to bounce around like a kangaroo (what's that Skip, some clowns fell down the well).

Ah well, enough of that, now I don't mind telling you I do spring clean once in a while, but not necessarily in the right season. I've just been cleaning out the old think tank. These names were scribbled on the walls, and as this is my life story these people have been a part of it somewhere along the line. I think it will be virtually impossible to mention everyone. And this has just occurred to me, seeing as I'm the one with the talking biro, when you get on in years there's really not much difference between say, a sixty year old and someone who's fifty-five, but when you were younger, if one was ten and the other five that was a big gap.

If there's any spelt wrong, that's the way the cookie crumbles. I can hear some of you saying, "I hope he mentions me this time…"

You can read my reply
For your sake so do I
R U sitting comfy
Right then I'll begin
And it's eyes down
Yes folks, look in

There were; the Barretts, Bensons, Capsticks, Heaps, Pickups, Scotts, Whittakers; Malcolm Beckett; Jim and Keith Bradshaw; Jim Bowden; Peter Butterworth; Derek Castree; Mick and Tom Crabtree; and Bram Etherington. At first all the names were there in order until the rest of them started yelling and screaming, "Pick me, Mickey Plum, pick me," and I almost lost my concentration so you'll have to wait for your name being called.

Here we go again; Ken and Florence Knight; Jeff and Sheila Foy; Ken and Eileen Billington; Jack and Joan Clancy; Michael and Lilian Green (I think they were brother and sister); Brian and Beryl Finnigan; Neil and Dougie Allen; Keith Maudsley; Eddie, Florence and John Fisk; Edmond Heaton; John Turkington; Tony Pickering; Bobby Longbottom; Peter Outhwaite; Kenny Waterworth; Bobby Kershaw; Jack Preston; Derek Pye; Mick Widdup; Bernard Heys; Bobby Clegg; Jim Davis; Bruce Tomkinson (he lived on

Mersey Street, he died young).

David Dewhurst; Brian Tillotson; Jeff Lomax; Jim Graham; Peter Drabble; Peter Knowles; Keith Nun; Gordon Salkeld; Brian Walton; Tony and Sylvia Lord; Barry Vernon; Colin and Keith Brown; Alan Jones; David Graham; Dougie Chapman; Stephen Allock; Malcolm Stringer; Doreen and Betty Iverson; Irene and Maureen Isherwood; Jean and Margaret Baker and their parents, Albert and Margaret; Sheila and Maureen Moore; Patsy Lunt; May Smith; Gwen Towers; Marion Brily; Doreen Harrison; Sylvia Ormerod; Joan Tattersall; Vera Pickard; and Pauline Hastie.

Can you find yourself here?

Rosegrove Primary School, BURNLEY. 1950

1950 School Photo

There were two families of Blands, the ones who lived on Accrington Road were (I think) Alan, Geoff and Bob, and those who used to live on Liverpool Road were Barbara, Alan and Raymond, I hope that's the right way round. Now, these other people I think they were just friends of Mums; Bob and Cherry; Eric and Elsie; Sheila and her brother John Brennan; Bill and Florrie Stringer, they have a daughter, Sylvia, who married Harold (it's a lot to remember for a little chap). Sylvia's parents used to run the shop near Coal Clough School. I used to go and help sometimes and chat the girls up, I never got many telephone numbers. Mind you, phones were scarce in those days, you were well off if you owned one.

That was a lot of names and I'm still counting, as all the postal votes aren't in yet.

Chapter
17

Now after all that, it's my turn, so what I want from youse is to write me fifty lines (why, you say) because I am running out of writing paper (one to me).

Now those songs I told you about a few pages ago, they've been given some thought and this is what I've come up with, lets see if you remember these; "Sound Off (1.2.3.4.)"; "Quartermasters Store"; "There's A Hole In My Bucket" (Dear Liza); "Close The Door?" (those so and so's are everywhere), I'm having trouble locating the title and artist on that one; "The Happy Wanderer"(Valdarah ha ha hah hah ha) was sung by The Obenkirchens Childrens Choir, the whole town would be singing that one (even when Burnley got beat); then the Max Bygraves song that went (deep breath) "Gilly Gilly Ossenfeffer Katzenellen Bogen By The Sea" (it sounds like a Welsh railway station); and of course you'll remember those Stanley Holloway ones (which I have on record), "The Lion And Albert", "Albert Comes Back", "Albert And The Eadsman" and "Albert Evacuated".

And for those of you who are interested, I managed to pick up a great comedy record and most of these were recorded between 1926 and 1944. Here's a sample to whet your appetite; "The Bee Song" by Arthur Askey (hello playmates), recorded January 1938; "The Woman Improver" Max Miller (the cheeky chappie), November 1936; "Yorkshire Pudding", Stanley Holloway, November 1940; "Cocktails For Two", Spike Jones And His City Slickers, November 1944; "When I'm Cleaning Windows", George Formby (it's turned out nice again), September 1946; "My Mother Doesn't Know I'm On The Stage", Billy Bennett, August 1929; "The Battle Of Hastings 1066", Marriot Edgar, October 1935.

When I was reading the back of the Stanley Holloway LP cover I noticed that the 'Albert' monologues were written by someone called Edgar. Now I don't know if he is the one and the same that did 1066, I don't really have the time to go into that just now. I might check it out later (I'll probably have to do it for my own curiosity).

Back to the remainder of the others; "There's No One With Endurance Like The Man Who Sells Insurance", Frank Crumit, May 1935; "Everything Is

Fresh Today", Jack Hodges (the raspberry king), September 1933; "Gardening - What To Do With Your Aspidistra", Oliver Wakefield (the voice of experience), October 1936, I have a few suggestions but at this stage I'll keep them to meself; "Joe Ramsbottom Buys A Piano", Norman Evans (over the garden wall), December 1934; "Mad Dogs And Englishmen", Noel Coward, September 1932; "I Should Say So", Rob Wilton (the day war broke out), September 1931; "Joe Goes Up – I Come Down", Jimmy Durante, October 1944; "What Should We Give A Nudist For His Birthday?", Gracie Fields, October 1934 (well I think clothes are out of the question).

Now folks, I've saved the best for last. I couldn't believe my luck when I saw it on the LP so I bought it for this one track. I've always loved it since I was a little tacker as it got plenty of air play on Children's Favourites, and putting on my Maxwell Smart voice, would you believe, it was "The Laughing Policeman". It was done by a fella called Charles Penrose, recorded on the 22nd of April 1926 (that's old) and actually, I played it yesterday. I had a good old-fashioned belly laugh as it's been a fair time since I've heard it. There might be just one amongst those that you haven't heard for a while, so I thought I'd share that with you.

I can't remember the exact date (year) this happened (not that it's going to stop me) but I'll fit it in about here. We started going to the Chapel as somebody had told me that they played kiss chase. I thought I'll be in this, it sounds like my kinda sport. There were some people who went mornings only, while others would go at night.

There were a few that you'd see once every Preston Guild (as they used to say) so in a sense this is my way of saying I might find it hard to name them all but it's not the first time I've attempted something like this (and you can vouch for that), of course the same applies with the spellings, so if you'll pull up a pew then I'll read the first lesson.

There was; Albert and Florence Riley and their daughter, Joan; Tom and Edith Tattersall and their son, Keith; Charlie and Nellie Tomlinson and son, Gordon; Frank and Edna Brown and their boys were Ian, Phillip and Steven; Charlie and Eva Greenwood and they had Linda and Andrew; Jim and Peggy Reid, their sons Maurice and Ken; Tom and Annie Taylor, they had Vivian and Derek; Cyril and Nora Price, their son Alan; Denis and his sister, Sheila Brayshaw (Denis died young); Fred Hunt; Ernie Marsden; Peter Bennett; Barbara and Carole Greenwood (sisters); Jean and Rita Blackledge (sisters); Jessie Bolton; Margaret Craig; Jean Bailey; Margaret Dinsdale; Marlene Thornber; Rita Stevens; Jean Clarke; Jackie Watson; Enid Demaine; Susan Farrow; Margaret Newlands; and Mavis Redman.

There were some people who came from Hapton and they were; Ivan Dean; Mick Smith; Roland Pate; Paul and his sister, Pauline Rumble; Joe Barker;

and Dorothy Porter. In fact, Dorothy and Bob courted for a while and I liked Dorothy as she had a brand-new bike, of course it was a girls but that didn't stop me, I just put some curlers in and a turban on and I'd say to people that I was the new girl in the village (and my name), Michelle Plum (I didn't really), I just thought I'd throw that in for a bit of a laugh, but I did borrow the bike a lot.

Now I know I'm getting ahead of myself here but seeing as I mentioned the Chapel I'll talk about these people. I don't think there will be any objections, Bob met Brian Bury through work and Brian went to the Church in Whittlefield, so of course I got to know Brian and his brothers, George and Malcolm.

Then some of the others were; Barry and his sister, Barbara Castle; Ronnie Clarke; Peter Glynn; Roland Kay; John Hunter and his sister, Irene, who married Jack Barrett. Quite a few of the young lads used to hang out at Jack and Irene's, they lived on Poets Road which ran off Scott Street. We had some great times there.

Right, would anyone have a clue where we are, you know what we could do with, one of those boards, you've seen them, if you look right in the middle it shows an arrow pointing boldly to this spot and the words read 'You Are Here'. In fact, I've just had a great idea, I shall draw my very own board then it might read 'You are here, but your poor readers are bored senseless'.

Oh well, back to the drawing board, yes, this is a lot of fun and now I'm at that age where I don't want to grow up (I promise I'll tell you more about that later), then out of the blue Mum and Pop had some news to announce, they were expecting a happy event. There was talk it could be a boy. I think Pop wanted a boy as he'd had a girl with his first marriage, of course Mum wanted a girl as she'd had six boys (and managed to drown three) so nearly everybody's choice was for a girl (except me, I was keeping everything crossed for a donkey) and as the months went by Mum got bigger, and one day she got these pains and said to Pop, "Just feel my stomach," which he did, then she took hold of my hand and placed it there and said, "can you feel it kicking?"

I said, "Yes (my prayers have been answered), it must be a donkey."

Mum said, "I'll go in Towneley Museum if it is."

And Pop, not to be outdone said, "If that's the case, I'm racing in the Queen Elizabeth Stakes on Saturday."

Now we were all born at home (I wanted to be near me Mum), as most kids were in those days, but Mum went into Bank Hall, I suppose as a safety precaution more than anything, then the news came through and it was a bouncing baby boy. I thought as soon as I get chance I'd try that out to see if he really does bounce. In the meantime, the saddle and all that hay I got from

Collinge's Farm will definitely have to go back, then we couldn't wait for them to come home and life was different there for a while as James was the new kid on the block and I loved taking him out.

Do you remember those big prams (Silver Cross, I think), they certainly took some manoeuvring, especially if you had a vestibule. I'd heard people talk about Judas Iscariot, but now they say 'there goes Mickey Plum with his chariot'.

By the way folks, I'd hit onto something with this and I would have to say it was a real chick magnet. Honestly, they were all over me, I had to say, "Steady on girls, there's enough to go round, you'll just have to be patient, that's all there is to it," then I said, "go on then, you can give him a quick coochie coo, as long as I get a kiss in exchange and if you want to bounce him that'll cost you a kuddle."

> *They bounced him every which way*
> *And of course, on the Ash Pad*
> *But Pop wasn't that pleased*
> *Saying stop bouncing me lad*

And so by this time…

> *The girls were in hysterics*
> *While carrying on like dags*
> *I said bounce him on your knee*
> *Then you won't crack the flags*

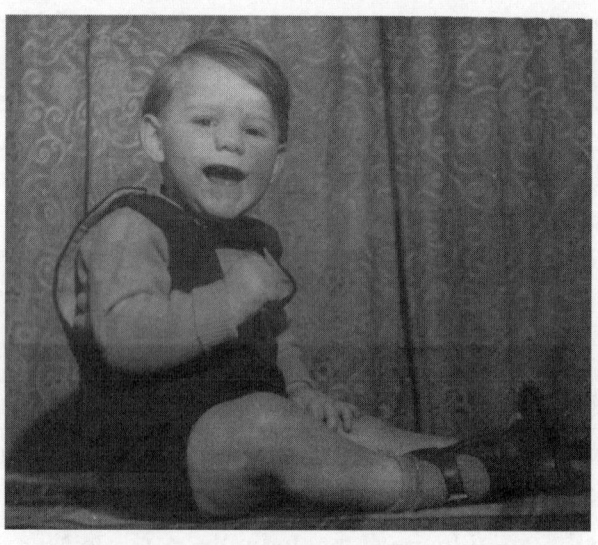

Jim, my earliest photo

I don't think Jim will mind when he reads this (as it's only a bit of fun). He has a great sense of humour, well, he did have before this went to press. I might have to butter him up (most probably on both sides) just for good measure.

Here's one for the boys, did you notice how teenage girls seemed to be tittering all the time (I was forever checking my attire, sometimes I wasn't wearing a tyre). In fact, some of them had nice titters (Michael, you're being cheeky now), but there was this one girl, we used to call her the Pirates Daughter, as she had a sunken chest.

There could be some viewers that've fallen by the wayside but to the remainder of you, if the slightest thing makes me chuckle, I'll use it. That's the best thing I love about this writing caper, you can ad-lib at the drop of a hat. Oh, that's very clever you lot, well seeing as nobody's dropped their hat I won't ad-lib then, so that takes us halfway through the fifties.

Chapter
18

Then 1956 came and John went into the Forces (REME), Royal Electrical Mechanical Engineers, and he came out in December 1958. I'm just covering myself there in case I forget when I do get to 1958. Now I really want you, the readers, to hear this so I'll turn the volume up a notch. Something else had happened and I think you'll agree it changed a lot of lads lives (and I suppose girls for that matter), I'll be doing three to four years with this next bit rather than going backwards and forwards over the coming pages. If that suits you (I'll carry on regardless), it's still January 1956, Bill Haley and his Comets' "Rock Around The Clock" had gone to number one in the UK after being featured in "Blackboard Jungle", which, if you remember, caused quite a stir. I've never thought of this before but it's just come to mind, I wonder what would have happened if Bill Haley (and his Comets) went into the Forces and our John recorded "Rock Around The Clock', there would have been an instrument over his shoulder instead of a rifle…

> *He'd be Johnny Guitar*
> *Or even "Johnny B Goode"*
> *The village would be on the map*
> *And not forgetting Molly Wood*

Now back to the serious side of things, then in May (of the same year) Elvis is number one with "Heartbreak Hotel" and we thought he was the greatest thing since sliced bread, then late in 1958 our very own rock'n'roller came along, he was Cliff Richard, and he hit the charts with "Move It" (great number). Then in February 1959 came a terrible tragedy that not only knocked but shocked the rock'n'roll world, a plane had crashed claiming the lives of Buddy Holly, who's to say how big he would have been (we'll never know), young Ritchie Valens, and of course JP Richardson (The Big Bopper).

We shall move onto something entirely different, it is, of course, football, which as you might remember is one of my great loves. By a strange coincidence this also happened in January 1956, now myself at this stage, I hadn't started going on The Turf but always took an interest in their results, either via paper or radio, so on the 28th of January Burnley played Chelsea at Turf Moor and drew 1-1. They went to Stamford Bridge on the 1st of February and after extra time they were still locked together 1-1. They played on the 6th at St Andrews, again extra time was needed but they were tied at 2 each.

The next meeting was at Highbury on the 13th, there was no score after extra time (again), then White Hart Lane was the venue on the 15th of February but Burnley were beaten 2-0 so I suppose they had a good run for their money. Just picking up on those last two grounds, I wouldn't say Highbury or, for that matter, White Hart Lane were neutral grounds, there was talk about playing behind closed doors if they had met again but I don't know how true that was and I'm not sure if the times that they did meet was some sort of a record. I know they weren't earth-shattering events but those three things did all take place in January 1956.

Here's one that maybe should have gone in a fraction earlier, but I'm not all that far out, James Dean had died in a car crash in September 1955, "East of Eden" was doing the rounds, but "Rebel Without A Cause" and, of course, "Giant" were not released till 1956 and that made JD bigger in death than he was in life, having been born in 1931, that made him only twenty-four. In fact, I read somewhere not long ago that even thirty years after his death, fan mail was still being sent to the studio. I made a joke before about John and Bill Haley swapping roles, are you ready for this one, I wonder what would have happened if John had played for Burnley. They might have gone to Wembley and even won the cup, would that have kept Jimmy Mac in the reserves?

Seriously though folks, I know they both have a sense of humour and I'm sure they'll have a laugh about that (I did). There will be more stories about JM later. Now, as far as my notes show, I don't think a great deal happened (well, nothing to write home about) but I'd better have a quick check to be on the safe side so I'll just hit you with these until I get onto the next story.

What's the difference between a violinist and the back end of a Dromedary? I don't know either, I've been trying to get rid of that one for yonks, now you can worry about it. And what do you get if you cross a Jehovah's Witness with an Atheist? A person who knocks on your door for no reason. And what goes ha, ha, ha, clunk? Someone laughing their head off.

Which is more than what's happening here, you know I don't write them so I shouldn't be held responsible for digging 'em up, and you'll have to watch that I don't repeat a joke. But there again, if I can't remember, well things aren't looking too good for the rest of the book, and just now my mind is going fifty to the dozen, there's that many ideas flying around in there and I promise you I'll try to keep them in some sort of order.

Well, once again we're up and running, actually I'm sat down writing (but you know what I mean). 1956 went out and 1957 came in saying there could be a variety of things you'll be taking on board this year but going to work will be the biggest one, and not just for me, but hundreds of laddies and lassies.

I can honestly say I was counting those days, yeah, for the last three or four months, I just couldn't wait to get outta there but looking back I wish I knew then what I know now, I think we all say that somewhere down the line, there's not a thing we can do about it. I don't know if you read into that, in 'That's My Rosegrove', which from memory, the two lines I'm referring to are on page 17, verse 6, unless someone has been mucking about with the page numbers, so you can go back and check it out if you like, but for those who don't want to let their fingers do the walking, I'll read it for you 'Rosegrove Junior School, the Secondary Modern next door' and the line underneath was 'All that education, who could ask for more?'

So that was a deliberate shot at myself (for being a dunce) and I'll have you know I'm allowed to do that. And just as long as you lot don't line up to have a go, a few lads that were a bit older had already left school and they said it was great because you got paid. I thought, it's a good thing you don't get a wage for what you know or I'd owe them something. You couldn't go wrong on the job front (not like today) and I can tell you there was plenty of excitement amongst the boys as to where they were going to work, the saddest part about leaving school was that you lost many a good friend.

So I suppose, in one sense, we took it in our stride and we all seemed to go down different roads in life, never knowing if our paths were ever going to cross again. Michael, how on earth did you get onto that, and if you dwell on it any longer, before you know it you'll have to get the tissues out.

Now there are a few loose ends to tie up before we leave school, so if you're ready, we'll see the last term out and maybe then I'll start to grow up (at last). Do you remember when I was telling you about the art teacher? I said there would be more later. So true to my word here is my version of what used to take place in the art class, as you know Elvis was in our lives and a lot of the lads tried to style their hair like his (yours truly was no exception), sometimes you'd get compliments on the sideboards, then you would put on your Elvis voice saying, "Yeah, I'm growing a chest of drawers next week."

By the way, where would you find a homosexual woodworm? In the bottom of a tallboy.

I've done my homework on this and according to one dictionary, sideboards and sideburns, or side levers (I hadn't heard them called that before) are whiskers from the hairline down to below one's ears, the name was taken from AE Burnside, who was a General in the American Civil War 1824-1881. You've got to admit folks, with this story book it might not be great reading but at least you're learning something.

So there I was, day dreaming, when out of the blue 'Spencer' was the name I heard screamed by you know who. I thought that name rings a bell, it's what they normally yell when the grubs ready, the next thing you knew his finger and thumb were on that piece of hair in question, while he had sneakingly laid his beady eyes on the paper I'd been doodling on, which was supposed to be a masterpiece, he said, "What on earth is this?"

"It's the houses across the road," I said, anyone who went to The Grove will know that his windows looked onto Dorset Street.

"Spencer!" rang out (I should have changed my name to Quasimodo), "do you know I'm sick and tired of shouting at you."

I thought, feel free to yell at the other lads, I don't mind, I'm not the jealous type.

Then you would be yanked out of your seat, it wasn't funny, but the rest of the class thought so. He would pull your hair so hard you were virtually on your tiptoes, he'd say, "You are just a little grub."

I'd say under my breath, "Well, from where I'm standing you're shorter than me."

He had this smirk on his clock, he would turn to the class and say, "What is he boys?"

And they chorused back, "Just a little grubby bugger."

"Hey, c'mon lads, he didn't say that."

Then I was told to be quiet and speak only when I was spoken to, "Yes Sir, no Sir, three bags full Sir," is what was mumbled so that he couldn't hear. I'd look skyward while still nattering to myself, "if there is anyone up there can you send a flash of lightening to his groin region and if that's asking too much, what about a clap of thunder just so he'd release his grip, and I promise not to put any more washers or safety pins in the collection plate."

When I was on about the sideboards before, you had to be very careful when you went for a haircut or you could finish up with short back and sides, as in those days it was all the go, and barbers were notorious for this, and if you didn't speak up straight away and tell them what you wanted, all that hard work you had put into your hair was (whoosh) gone in a couple of seconds, it was click go the shears. I think that must be why Teddy Boys carried knives, just in case the barber over-stepped his mark and got within a whisker of their sideboards (so to speak).

What I'm going to do is attempt to name most of the teachers, all these names are in my mind. One thing I can't remember clearly (and that's unusual for me), if they were all full-time teachers, maybe some were fill-in ones. I'll put Mister in front of the first teacher then you can do the same with the rest, here goes; there was Mr Branson, Clegg, Duerden, Foster; there were two Greens, Joe and John; then Hindle, McCall, Morris (Headmaster), Pollard, Porter, Proctor, Riding, Tomlinson and Wharton.

I'm not sure who the Deputy Headmaster was, but I do know Mr Morris used to take us for the music class. I still remember how he'd belt out "Fingal's Cave" by Mendelssohn, it must have been his favourite piece, I was a bit too young then to appreciate classical music, but I'd close my eyes and pretend I was right there in Fingal's cave.

I think Fingal was down at the Co-op chinwagging to Schindler, they used to get on like a house on fire those two, in fact, one day the Fire Brigade had to put them out (but that's another story). Even in those early days I'd listen to anything once, but hoping he'd put the latest Elvis one on the turntable for a change, which was "I Don't Care If The Sun Don't Shine" (I carries me brolly all the time).

Chapter
19

Right, I'm game if you are, let's play truant and shoot off into the future for a while, we could get into trouble when we get back into the past but we'll cross that bridge when we come to it.

I was trying to find out more about Mendelssohn, you know I thought I had a cassette somewhere, but I couldn't find it, I've most probably lent it to someone over the years (I think we all do that). So that was a great excuse to treat myself (which I don't do often) to a CD of the man in question. I'd checked out a few shops that I normally go into, in fact, there were a lot of CD's on Mister M, but not what I was looking for and, to tell you the truth, I was feeling a little disappointed, with only one shop left, I had everything crossed, including my eyes.

Have you ever tried to walk with your legs crossed? It ain't easy, and I was walking into things. It's alright if you bump into those gorgeous girlie assistants once, but after three times they get a little suspicious. I found the classical section, then went to the M's. There were only three (in the rack), the first two were the same ones I'd checked on in the other shops, but what's that saying 'third time lucky', because there it was, titled "The Best Of Mendelssohn".

I couldn't see what I wanted on the front of the CD, so I thought I'd just check out the back, and number 1 was The Hebrides-Overture, "Fingal's Cave". Well, I'd always known it as FC (I'm not being rude) but it didn't matter, I was over the moon (I thought, how on earth am I going to get home from here, I only have a zone 1-2-3 ticket). It was like my Birthday's all came at once (where would you put all those presents). That's another one of those clichés, there will be more thrown in later, which reminds me of that song title "Give Me A Home Where The Buffalos Roam" and I'll show you a house full of broken furniture.

I came out of the store feeling quite pleased with myself, I stuck a few bets on, and I couldn't wait to get home to play the CD. The first thing I did when I got in was to make a brew, then I put the headphones on (no, not Uncle George's), as soon as I pressed 'play' I closed my eyes and it took me right back, I pictured those waves crashing over the rocks. It's ages since I'd heard that piece, and no wonder Mr Morris liked it, I'd forgotten how nice it was.

Now, just at this moment of my life it's opened up a new world, so as from this day forward I'm going to collect all the classical composers, I'll make a list and tick 'em off as I go. I did notice in one store they had a big section under the title 'The Best Of', so now I know where to get them from.

Back to the story and, of course, school. As you know it'll be 'please explain' when we are in the class and I've got this great alibi which goes like this: "Sir, the boys and I have been working on a project, this is what we've made, it's a CD and a new concept in music. In fact, we believe it's that far ahead of its time we've got nothing to play it on but we're working on that. So we would like you to accept this gift and it's 'The Best Of Mendelssohn' as we know you like him."

Then he'll say, "I was talking to the art teacher the other day and he called you a little grub, I think you're a genius and you'll go far, even if it's only Australia."

"Thank-you, Sir."

So folks, it don't hurt to dream once in a while.

Another you'll remember was "Widecombe Fair" and all those characters trying to ride that grey mare (I thought it was a pub on Gannow Lane), no wonder the old grey mare ain't what she used to be…

> *So let's name those blokes*
> *That went to Widecombe Fair*
> *Please Tom Pearse, Tom Pearse*
> *Lend us your grey mare*

Said Bill Brewer, Jan Stewer, Peter Gurney, Peter Davey, Daniel Whiddon, Harry Hawk and Uncle Tom Cobley and all. I wonder if one of them had a stutter or was it Tom Pearse, Tom Pearse that was deaf, as his name was said twice by BB, JS, PG, PD, DW, HH and UTC and all. There was no way I was going to write those names again, so it's up to you to sort that lot out.

Some of the lads who used to go on The Turf would make up their own song to the tune of "Widecombe Fair" and with a combination of players at the time they would sing:

> *Angus, Seith, Winton, Adamson*
> *Miller, Shannon, Newlands, McKay*
> *McIlroy, Cheesebrough, Pilkington*
> *We just love to watch you play*
> *Then we asked who was in goal*
> *They sang, Uncle Tom Cobley and all*

No they didn't, I just threw it in to help me with that rhyme. The goalkeeper was, of course, Colin McDonald who, at the time, was England's goalie. But then a broken leg cut short his career, who's to say how good he would have been. And just singling out one of the others, and he was Albert Cheesebrough, a lad from The Grove.

Now, just hang on a second folks, as I put my biro into reverse and I'll talk about composers. Over the years, while reading (or hearing) bits here and there (mostly from here, as it's a long time since I've been there) and a word of warning, it'll be in my style (as usual). I'm not really having a go at anyone, I just seem to write this way (confused, so am I). If you want to bail out, that's fine by me, but you've come so far you might as well stay. I've got some ideas, as it works out, that I can't tell you till the end.

Now, I'll just stick a piece of musak on the stereo, then put my feet up, but not from a standing position as I tried that once and it was quite painful. Let's get onto those in question, I noticed a few of them died young (they say only the good do), so I thought I'd look into this and see just how many were younger than me at the age I'm at now, late fifties, in fact very late, my alarm didn't go off.

Paganini died at 58, talk about naive, it was years before I found out his name wasn't pronounced 'page-nine'. Beethoven was 57, Debussy 56, Grieg 54, Tchaikovsky 53, Boccherini 52, Schumann 46, Weber 40, Chopin 39, Mendelssohn 38, Bizet 37 and Mozart died at 35, but Schubert was the youngest at only 31. Stravinsky lived the longest, 1882-1971, and if my figures are right from the list I've got, Vivaldi was the first to be born, 1678-1741 and Shostakovich, 1906-1975, was the last to be born.

I could have put the Tattslotto numbers there and you wouldn't have known the difference. In fact, I might put those on the Pools and perm any 8 from 11. You'll notice I've never mentioned Brahms and Liszt, most of us have been there and done that. And I didn't put them in alphabetical order for the simple reason they probably didn't die that way. There shall be more on this subject in about four years, give or take a page or three. If, by chance, you are having trouble reading this, you should have a crack at a Goon Show script, that's harder than Chinese mathematics unless, of course, you're Chinese, or a mathematician.

Chapter
20

I told you earlier, when we were at the Junior School, about the (house) colours, and the same applied to the big school, which were Athens (red), Rome (green), Sparta (yellow) and Troy (blue).

Now I'm coming to the end of my school days, as did Tom Brown (but they made a film about his), so it was "Time To Say Goodbye". Most of the teachers shook me by my hand and wished me all the best, while the art teacher wrung my neck and wished me more of the worst, so I closed the door behind me, I could hear him crying, because I made sure that his fingers were in there (nice one, Mickey).

Then I popped in to the Headmaster's Office and, in my best Vera Lynn voice, sang, "Auf Wiedersehen."

Then Mr Morris said, "Good luck, Genius, don't forget when you make those CD players to put me down for one and who knows what lies ahead, you might write a book about your life, I'll give you a good title, you can call it 'Rosegrove Lad Makes Good'."

I said, "Just like Albert Cheesebrough, Sir, but then again, I don't think I've got a book in me, only the one I used to shove down me britches while you were giving me six of the best."

Right lads, let's show the teachers that we can respect our elders (when we want to), so their work wasn't all in vain. With our heads held high, we'll march out in single file (that's the way they taught us) for the very last time while singing…

Sparta's strength and Athens glory
Zeal of Troy and Roman right
May they stand forth in their glory
Of our school to prove its might

May the name of Rosegrove stand forever
And for honour and esteem
Cheerfulness and endeavour
Make us evermore supreme

So once out of the school, oh boy, did I kick my heels up (I knew I shouldn't have done that as it was a while before they came back down again). Now you know what, that diary would have come in nice and handy, as this part seems a little bit vague, it was July holidays when I left school as I turned fifteen that month, I think Bob and Pop pulled a few strings at Drew's, the exact date I started work escapes me. And as I said earlier, it was the nearest place, being only a hop, skip and a jump away. There were a few of the lads that took on an apprenticeship, but most of us went labouring as the dosh was much better.

So I hopped, skipped and jumped down the road to work. It wasn't a pretty sight but it got me there a lot quicker than the other workers. Pop was always an early bird, he would be there most mornings a good half hour before time. Mum used to make us laugh by saying, "He just loves swinging in on the gates," or another one was, "the place can't start till Bert gets there."

Pop said, "You know they call me the composer at work."

"Why?" I said.

"Because every night when I shout 'see you later fellas' they all sing out 'yeah, Shoobert'."

My first job was to clock on and I can tell you I was ready for a brew (phew) after that. I think in one sense I was lucky living so near and taking papers like I did because I'd gotten to know quite a few that worked there, but really, the size of the place amazed me, it was incredible. I remember saying to Pop, "How many people work here?"

He lifted his hat, scratched his head, "I reckon about half of 'em," as he disappeared into the Boiler House I heard him shout, "ATM," I thought, this chap's ahead of his time as they haven't been invented yet so what does that stand for?

He said, "Another to me."

Now then, here comes a tricky part (or a challenge) and that's to name as many as possible, and I can assure you there was a lot, I'll put them in alphabetical order and to heck with the expense, so let's have a go, Joe; there was B Airy, C Anderson, H Andrew, G Ashton, E and R Barker (brothers), J Barker; there was Frank Berry, his dad and his uncle, who I mentioned earlier; H Boothman (Pop), B Boswell, D Bryan, G Canty, W Clough, K Cockshutt, J Conlan, A Coward, A Derbyshire, B Dillworth, P Dillworth, L Drabble, Alexander Drew, Gordon Drew, G Duckworth, J Dyer, G Feather, K Flannigan, A Glassgow, M Gorton, R Hardacre, J Hartshawn, B Heys, A Heaton, C Hobbley, J and A Howarth (brothers), A Howarth, B Hughes, F Killgallon, A Langhard, B Lightfoot, C Lofthouse, Kit Lofthouse, A Lum, T Lynch, H Macartney, L MacDonald, J Maguire, E Marsden, G and J Marsden (brothers), J Mather, F Mellor, A Moolgoaker, J Moss, M Noon and J Nuttal.

Well, I think it's time for a breather as I'm about half way through, then the ladies will be next. Yes, I know it was supposed to be the ladies first but the devil made me do it. I shouldn't imagine anyone will sue me, there again, you never know these days.

Now folks, I can see a lot of blokes plain as day (what day is it?) but it's hard to put names to some of them so back to the list; R O'Connor, R Pate, H Peel, J Pinder; Edgar Poole and his sons, Fred and Harry; H Ramsbottom, A Riley, F Savage, B Scholes, T Scott, F Simpson, FP Smith, A Smith (Acko), F Smith, H Smith; B and J Spencer (me brothers), John had joined us later and it was our attempt at a takeover.

In one sense I'm glad we didn't become shareholders as I would've copped the smallest share, I'll wrap this up with these names; B Starkie, F Sutcliffe, J and A Tattersall (brothers), A Thompson, S Vitton, J Waddington, E Ware; B Wightman and his son, Eddie; L Wilkinson, E Westwell, T Whalley and Richard the joiner (can't remember his surname). There's one left so let's have a fanfare for me, it wouldn't do if I forgot myself.

Right, I think that the ladies are outta the powder room at long last, so here is what I've come up with; A Astin, P Berry, H Boult, B Coupe, A Gorton, E Mather, F Riley, J Scott, E Steel, J Sutcliffe, B Tattersall, C Ward and A Widdup.

There's got to be more but at the minute they won't come to mind. So I shall leave a mental note for myself and I'll get back to it before the end. I have this idea that might just pay off, so while you've been reading that I've been double-checking on the men and I reckon there was about thirty that I knew before I started working there, and it didn't matter which department they put me in I was shown the ropes by someone I knew, which made the job a lot easier.

And like every young lad that went into the workforce, of course, I was sent for a long stand (but I fooled 'em and sat down for quite a while), when I first got back they would say, "Where the bloody hell have you been?"

I'd say, "I went into the Mechanics Shop for a long stand, but nobody seemed to know where it was so I had a word to Bill, the blacksmith, and he said if I come back in an hour he'll have one made for me by then." They had a good laugh at my expense (so they thought), from then on, every time I went to work in a different place and was sent for the old LS, I'd just disappear for an hour or more (it was a good lurk).

My first pay was 4 £ound 7 and 6 pence, which I thought was a lot of money. Now the thing that surprised me most was the swearing, I'd never heard language like it, that was only from the women, and the men weren't far behind. Still, I suppose it's a part of growing up and it's their way of saying 'welcome to the big wide world'.

It was so funny when I came home from work, there would be a race to get up the pen first. If Pop beat me I would sing out to Mum, "Pop's going out!"

Quick as a flash, Mum said, "Throw some more petrol on him, one to me," then said, "by the way, before you go, bring that washing in, it looks black at the back of Bill's mother's."

Now back to work, this brings me to my boss, Allan Thompson, you know he was telling everybody what a little cheeky bugger I was, and he swore (did he ever) that somehow I always seemed to be one step ahead of him. Now the truth can be told, I was a couple of paces behind, that's the reason he could never find me.

The Electroplating Shop was a good place for a smoke and a chat about Burnley's performance or their chances for the next game. The only snag was, Allan used to go in there, so I had to be sneaky and make sure he'd been in. Most times I'd shout, "Is the coast clear?"

And a voice would yell, "Aye, c'mon in lad."

Till this one day I just said, "Is it okay?"

"Yeah."

Little did I know it wasn't Jimmy, but Allan, and he said, "Gotcha!"

Curses, I thought, caught at me own game, so I took my hat off to him then put it back on and whoosh, I vanished. The next time he saw me I was actually working. I think the shock was too much for him, he had to sit down for a couple of mins, one thing I do remember is that he used to ride a motorbike, and I said one day, "You'd be better riding that, it'll save you a lot of shoe leather."

He said, "Listen, you cheeky little bugger," I thought to myself, he's getting confused because he called me a little cheeky bugger, he must be weakening under my power (of Hoo Doo).

He read my thoughts and said, "No, I'm not, but I was thinking of putting up wanted posters," then he said, "knowing you like I do you wouldn't be all that far behind me pulling 'em down," (how right he was).

Chapter
21

Now, has anybody out there got a clue what year we're up to, I think we'll settle for 1958, yeah, that sounds like a good number. So in it came and guess what? We were flitting again.

Grandad had become sick and the idea was to live with them at number 7 Saltburn Street. How on earth were we going to manage as it was only two up and the same number down, but it was all worked out by Grandad and Grandma moving their bed into the parlour. Then us lads had the back bedroom while Mum and Pop went into the front. It wasn't long after this that Bob went to Cliff College for nearly twelve months but when he came home for holidays, and the same applied when John was on leave, I don't think that happened at the same time, but elbows had to be kept to yourself, and it was my turn to breathe in on Pancake Tuesday.

I don't know how this bit came about, Bob must have written (because we didn't have the phone on) asking if he could bring a friend home for a couple of days and, of course, Mum, in her typical way said, "Yep, the more the merrier, there won't be room to sit down till Sunday," and left it at that.

The day arrived, I think Jim and I (and Gemini) were more excited than anyone, that this person was staying with us, plus not knowing anything about the lad. Bob had said he was male, so that's all we were told, but there would be all sorts to ask him. Bob walked in with this coloured man and said, "I would like you to meet my friend, Horace."

Well, straight away Jim hid behind me and it took him about an hour to come out of his shell, I told him never to go in there again when we had company. Then Jim said, "Did you shake hands with him?"

And I said, "Of course I did."

He made me laugh by saying, "Give us a look at your hands then."

Once Jim got to know Horace he followed him around like a lap dog, but there was one day he couldn't believe it after Horace had a wash and that there were no marks on the towel (that's a true story folks).

Now I'm going to talk about something I love and it's humour (you might have already picked up on that) and being amongst all those blokes (at work) believe me, there were some great comedians, and also singers. Those days in factories there was tons of talent, I think it was a case that most of them didn't know how to pursue it, or for some of them they couldn't be bothered (what a waste). Now you can believe this or not, and that is I heard these the first week at work, that shows how old they are (it happens to the best of us). There may be a couple of viewers who haven't heard them so here goes:

> *There was a Scotsman named Andy*
> *Who walked into a bar for a shandy*
> *He lifted his kilt to wipe what he'd spilt*
> *The barmaid said, "Eee aye, that's handy"*

Tarzan is sitting at the dinner table and he sings out to Jane, "What's to eat, dear?"

She says, "Pygmy, and I'll do you some chips and mushy peas."

No folks, there was only pygmy, I couldn't help myself, I had to throw that it to make it a better meal for poor old Tarzan. After all, he'd had a hard day gathering gossip off the grapevine. And in his spare time he'd been wrestling with crocogators or allidiles, I always get them mixed up (I think the crocs are the ones with the nicest shoes).

He said, "Pygmy, that's all we ever have."

She looked him in the eye and said, "Why don't you catch something different tomorrow?"

He said, "I might just do that."

Of course, he came home empty handed, she asked him, "What happened?"

"I almost caught a python, but it got away."

And Jane said, "What a pity, with all those leftovers I could have made you a nice snake and pygmy pie."

While on the subject of Tarzan, and how all of us lads loved him, most probably so did the girls and, to tell you the truth, I always took an interest in what Jane was wearing, which was next to nothing (I wouldn't mind being next to nothing), I couldn't wait for autumn, hoping she'd turn over a new leaf.

Now, I thought I'd try and get some facts for myself, if you would like to read along, be my guest. So, according to the film guide there were over 39 films, to save me writing 'Tarzan' a lot of times there will be just a T (which you can pay for later, the biscuits are extra). So here's a list of men that played the part and I'll start with; Elmo Lincoln, he was "T Of The Apes" in 1918; Johnny Weissmuller would have to be the most popular, he was the first "T The Ape Man" in 1932, which was remade in 1959 with Dennis Miller in the lead role;

and would you believe it was done again in 1981, Miles O'Keeffe was the man with support from Bo Derek, Richard Harris and Wilfred Hyde-White; back to JW, he made twelve films then after making "T And The Mermaids" in 1948 he quit, at the press conference later they asked him why, his reply was he'd, "Gotten sick and tired of the same old, same old, in fact, it smelt fishy," with that he left, so you could say he went out on a limb.

Lex Barker took over and in 1949 made "T's Magic Mountain", he went on to do five films, his last in 1953 was "T And The She Devil" with Raymond Burr; Gordon Scott was in the jungle for a while, he played the part six times; Mike Henry wore the old loin cloth on three occasions; Ron Ely swung by twice; Joe Lara was the last when he made "T In Manhattan" in 1989, which also starred Tony Curtis. By the way, JL was the eighteenth used; even Buster Crabbe (Flash Gordon) got in on the act in "T The Fearless", 1933; and here's a 'did you know' that Sean Connery was in "T's Greatest Adventure" in 1959.

And being a gambler, I bet you didn't know there had been so many Mr T's, neither did I, till I looked into it, maybe I shouldn't have gone so deep but what the heck, I enjoyed it. And here's a PS, if there is such a thing in a book (if not, you heard it here first). Johnny Weissmuller made films under the name 'Jungle Jim'.

I must own up here and now, those people who thought I was a little cheeky bugger, you were spot on, but when they used to say I couldn't be found anywhere (well, everybody's got to be somewhere), and little did you know I was storing information for the book. That's my story and I'm sticking to it.

Any of you reading this that worked at Drew's would remember the football (soccer) pitch, which you got to near the Mechanics Shop. I don't know whether there was a gate or if we jumped over the fence. Most of the factories had teams in the comp, Drew's had a good side and they were right up there with 'em, so at lunchtime we'd go up. There wouldn't be enough for two full teams but if we got say, a dozen, we'd have six-a-side. Of course, the pitch would have to be brought back to size, it was so funny, there would be goal posts at one end and where we had made it shorter a couple of coats had been placed at half the width of the right size. If someone fired in a low shot and the ball hit a sleeve there were cries of, "It went in off the post."

It was great playing against the blokes, they knew so much and they didn't hold back either, they'd give you a hard time, just to see how you would react. I can assure you I gave as good as I got but still came away pretty sore.

I bet you're a bit dubious when I start to tell a tale, well I shouldn't go into it with my "Eyes Wide Shut", but I think that's the only way to travel. And it amazes me what comes to mind, like this next bit, it was just a small thought at first and then I knuckled down and tried to get as much out of it as I could. I think you'll find it interesting, and hopefully it'll take you right back, but then

I suppose it'll be up to me to bring you to the present time.

I was growing up but still "Young At Heart" (I wonder if fairytales do come true). I used to read the comics every chance I got, there was a second-hand shop just a bit further down than Granville Dairies, I think the lady that ran it was called Mrs Wilkinson and she always had plenty of comics in stock. I loved looking around in there, sometimes you could read a couple while your mate kept her talking, that way you never had to buy any, here's what I found out about my two favourite comics, The Beano and The Dandy.

So I'll get The B outta the way first, it hit the shops in 1938 (and it's still going), some of the characters were; Lord Snooty; Biffo The Bear; Dennis The Menace, didn't he get into trouble (and to think they called me a little cheeky bugger); there was Roger The Dodger; Minnie The Minx; The Bash Street Kids, they were Danny, Smiffy and Plug; and there was one called "When The Bell Rings".

Now for The D, and their mob consisted of; Desperate Dan (what a man), he used to shave with a blow lamp, there's tough for you; Beryl The Peril; Korky The Cat; Ginger; and not forgetting Keyhole Kate.

I had more luck with B
Than I ever had with D
Now folks, I'll let it B
Frankly, I don't give a D

You will no doubt remember there were other comics which included Rover, Hotspur and Wizard and then, of course, there was Film Fun and I'll tell you, I didn't mind that one but I preferred to see my idols up on the big screen. So listen, readers, I think you are getting terrific value for your folding material, but I'd better be getting back to work, or I could be served with my marching orders and, as you'll agree, I'm a bit too young to be on the Nat King Cole (dole).

One night I came home from work and Pop said, "How did you go today?"

"It wasn't that bad."

"Where were you working?" he asked.

"In the Grey Room," I replied, while slapping a dollop of best marge (you know what I mean) onto a big (yummy) crust and I slipped into my serious face (always like to get comfy when I come home from work), "geez, he's got a big head that geezer."

"Who's that?" he queried.

"Humpty Dumpty," said I, then doing a lap of honour around the kitchen table after blasting one home from the penalty spot and singing, "We Are The Champions."

He said, "Very good that, and it's about time you got one back."

Now folks, speaking of old Dumpty…

> *There he was, sat on the wall*
> *When HD had that great fall*
> *And, of course, all the Kings men*
> *Said, "Bugger him, he's only an egg"*

So now people…

> *By putting that in rhyme*
> *Surely it must be time*
> *For a tribute of mine*
> *Which follows this line*

And it's about…

Mr Football

> *I've written a rhyming tribute*
> *About a man that stood so tall*
> *He was known to many people as EJ*
> *But to most he was Mr Football*
>
> *I came to Australia in the sixties*
> *Didn't know much about your game*
> *I'd been told to watch EJ*
> *I thought, that's a funny name!*
>
> *This I'm writing is near to the truth*
> *Now, as you know, he was no bunny*
> *When Teddy put those boots on*
> *He gave you value for money*
>
> *He loved those Adidas boots*
> *He'd flash that unmistakeable smile*
> *And put some oomph into that pigskin*
> *It would travel the proverbial mile*
>
> *He was a Western suburbs battler*
> *A lot of them were really poor*
> *Ted said, "If it was raining palaces*
> *He'd get hit by the dunny door"*
>
> *A larrikin who never forgot his background*
> *He'd always kept that common touch*
> *The impression he made on football*
> *For the game he loved so much*
>
> *Teddy could pull the crowds in*

They'd arrive early to avoid the rush
They cheered this gutsy player
Who gave the fullback one in the mush

He ate, breathed and slept footy
Whether for Footscray or the Big V
They'd call him Captain Courageous
When proudly wearing that number 3

There would be a precision chip
Or a centimetre perfect pass
It was like watching a Flymo
Mowing in a paddock of grass

He'd zoom through the defence
Leaving the defender like a stunned mullet
Teddy was just the right calibre
Likened to a speeding bullet

Now this bloke he could shepherd
I don't mean look after the sheep!
When the opposition was 'King Hit'
You never heard another peep

I once met Ron Barassi
I've even seen 'The Big Dipper'
But that last game of yours, EJ
That was a bloody ripper

Ted said, "You can do it for me
Tell me that you are ready"
Yes, the lads were really fired up
And pulled off a great win for Teddy

One thing for sure about him
He was steadfast, loyal and true
He'd paint the town after a victory
In the colours of red, white and blue

He played his guts out every week
Himself and Footscray went hand in hand
Then after he hung his boots up
They honoured him with the EJ Whitten stand

He never won the elusive Brownlow
Looking back it seems a great pity
He was Footscray's favourite son
So they gave him the key to the city

Ted gave his heart and soul to football
321, that's the record he made
He was an outspoken character
Who certainly called a spade a spade

After football, he became a commentator
His comments are too many to mention
I'm sure this one you'll remember
That's just come to my attention...

With St Kilda one point in front
Collingwood were running out of time
Ted came out with the classic
'Hit the boundary line'

They say Elvis was the greatest
He could make that pelvis swing
What about cool rocking Teddy?
To Footscray he was their King

Ted Junior played for Footscray
Having followed his famous Dad
He didn't wear the number 3 jumper
But Teddy was still proud of his lad

I used to like Sunday lunchtime
Watching Ted on the 'Footy Show'
Especially the run-ins with Sammy
Were they fair dinkum? I don't think so

Then when greeting Peter Keenan
He'd say "How ya going, Crackers?"
When meeting someone for the first time
They'd get that handshake and "G'day, Knackers"

The news broke that he had cancer
It was to be the biggest fight of his life
His colleagues gave him support
As well as his family and wife

How did he ascertain that strength
For the lap of honour at the MCG?
He brought a lump to the throat
And a tear to the eye, you'll agree

Then on Thursday the 17th of August
It was indeed a very sad day
For thousands of footy fans
Had witnessed the passing of EJ

It was 7.25pm in his home
When the angels called for Teddy
He then went via The Western Oval
Said bye Doggies, right, I'm ready

Now those steely blue eyes
Have seen the coming of the Lord
Some say he should have got a Knighthood
And been dubbed by the Regal sword

Dougie Hawkins said "I loved that guy
He was the inspiration of my life
Ted was like a father to me
In times of celebration or strife"

And Ernie Sigley, a Footscray boy
Said Teddy was like a hero to men
If you live in the Western suburbs
You need heroes and EJ was one of them

The Church was packed to the rafters
This would have been beyond Ted's wildest dreams
With representatives from sporting clubs
And most of the AFL teams

Some words from his friend Bob Skilton
He said Ted gave so much to us all
He epitomised what sport was all about
With his contribution to football

Bob said, kapow, a nose was out of joint
Ted would say, "Sorry, I didn't think"
Then he would drive them to hospital
And after, he'd buy them a drink

It was up to Ted Junior to say goodbye
With his eulogy and wasn't it great?
He brought tears to my eyes
When he said "Dad, I love you mate"

Colleen Hewitt sang "Wind Beneath My Wings"
Then Lisa Edwards gave us "Hero"
If Teddy had passed this way before
I'm sure he would have shirt fronted Nero!

As the procession left the Church
The cortege went along Victoria Street
Onlookers were unashamedly weeping
Also the children at their feet

The flags at Footscray and the MCG
Were flying at half-mast
Fans from rival clubs said a prayer
As the hearse made its way past

Girls were crying in the street
Their faces awash with tears
They chorused "We love you, Teddy
You've been our hero for years"

Placards read 'Farewell Mr Football'
Also 'Edward James Whitten RIP'
While one said 'On ya EJ'
Another was simply 'Hooroo number 3'

He was proud of his heritage
A great man amongst men
He was a working class hero
Who stuck it right up them

Now I've always barracked for the Dees
The way they are playing I shouldn't brag
Right now I wouldn't mind one bit
If Teddy's beloved Bulldogs won the flag

Ted gave his all for football
Whether Footscray or the State
Accolades have been bestowed upon him
To sum him up in one word 'Great'

His spirit has soared so high
Higher than a white dove
Teddy would have been moved
By this extraordinary outpouring of love

His family and friends have said goodbye
And now he is laid to rest
Edward James Whitten, alias Mr Football
Yes, you were simply the best

So now somewhere over the rainbow
Way up in that football sky
Teddy's now amongst them
Where those great big men fly

He's marched with those Christian soldiers
To achieve his lifelong dream
Now he'll be Captain and Coach
In that great angelic team

EJ loved being in the limelight
Now he has travelled further along
You can bet if there's a newspaper in heaven
He's sure to make page one

Mr Football they christened him
No name could ever be more apt
I'm sure if he's looking down now
He would be absobloominglutely rapt!

So now he's in that heavenly abode
He's left us after serving his time
I never had the pleasure to meet him
But I feel I know him through my rhyme

EJ ascended that golden staircase
Waiting for him was Alan Gale
Teddy said "It was a sell-out down there
By the way Butch, where's the ale?

He'll be the number one ticket holder
Inside those Pearly Gates
Now the final siren has sounded
He'll be reminiscing with his mates

They've named a bridge after EJ Whitten
Motorists beep as they go along the freeway
I was inspired to write this
And for you Ted, I did it my way

I'll go on barracking for the Demons
Garry Lyon, he's the greatest to me
I call him Mr Football Junior
Plus he wears the infamous number 3

So every year from now on
On that one day in September
Footy fans will be silent for a minute
For they will always remember

Well, I'm near the end of my rhyme
Dedicated to the memory of EJ Whitten
I've really enjoyed writing this
So now the tribute is written

I didn't want to tell you too much beforehand, but now I will. I never had the pleasure to meet the great man, then after his death, all that I'd seen of his career and had read about him, it was somehow stored in my noggin, so a couple of lines were jotted down on scraps of paper, then it was time to get those notes while stirring in more thoughts and I can assure you nobody was more surprised than me with the end result.

You would have noticed, Aussies, that I mentioned Ernie Sigley, now as it works out, he was a very close friend of Ted's and the reason I'm telling you about Ernie, he was a Disc Jockey on Radio Luxembourg, and I most probably used to listen to him all those years ago. Also, in one of those verses there was a bit about the Demons (go Dees), Melbourne Football Club. I chose them as my team because their colours were red and blue, which is near enough to the same that Burnley wears (go Burnley). Now, back to MFC, they had a great side in the fifties and sixties but, of course, once I started following them (or barracking), I think I put the mockers on 'em (as they say) because they haven't won a Premiership on that 'One Day In September' (they've knocked off a few night cups).

I put Ron Barassi in as he played and coached them over the years, not forgetting Garry Lyon, who went on to Captain Melbourne and he's since retired but he's very big in the media (6ft 4, I think). Back to the tribute, after reading it through and thinking, hey, that's a bit of alright, I then tried a few avenues, unfortunately they turned out to be cul-de-sacs. One thing that really annoyed me (and it takes a lot, I can tell you), after getting photocopies made, plus postage and handling (which is not cheap) and not to hear from them again (it hurts). Copies were also sent to a couple of influential people who, at this stage, shall remain nameless, just in case I get a libel suit thrown at me (it would be my luck that the pants are too long, but I could have 'em altered, eh?).

Now folks, here's a thought, maybe I should have written on the envelope 'this is a boomerang, make sure you "Return To Sender"'. It was like, here's another hurdle for you to tackle, I'm not an athlete but it keeps me in shape, yes folks, I'm as fit as a Mallee bull (and twice as dangerous). So I said to myself, just take it in your stride, that's all you can do, the main thing is it's finished and you've achieved what you set out to do, call it another piece of the jigsaw and for now keep writing the other tributes (those you have the ideas on), and who knows, one day it could all "Come Together".

I think anybody that's ever been employed (male or female) would have said this, or been asked it by their workmates over the years, the object in question is the factory whistle, hooter or siren. Let's call it the siren, not that I have anything against whistles or hooters, in fact, I like both, but I do tend to lean more to hooters, especially if they're leaning towards me.

There were normally a couple of questions about this thing, one would be, "Don't you know the sirens gone?"

Answer, "Who took it?"

Or the other one was, "Has the siren gone yet?"

Answer, "No, it's still there."

So if Allan asked me either of those, nine times out of ten he'd get a clever reply, plus a raspberry thrown in for good measure and I'd be called a little cheeky bugger again (so what's new). So just take notice next time you're at work (that's if you have a job), if anyone says about the sirens going, you can say to yourself, "By gum, that Mickey Plum, he's a genius, even the Headmaster told him that." A word of warning, be careful of your replies, as you could finish up with a knuckle butty but, then again, I suppose you could always say, "Is zee bread Helga's?" (Melbourne TV commercial).

Well, seeing as the whistle hasn't gone yet, we've got a few more minutes, I just didn't know where this would fit so I suppose here is as good a place as any. Like a lot of young men my age we'd had a bash at shaving, it's funny looking back now but I can assure you it wasn't at the time. On my first occasion I wanted privacy, as it was a personal matter between man and steel, which turned out to be cutthroat stuff, now just sit there while I glissade (look it up, I had to) around the zits.

Mum told people and made an episode out of it (like Mum's do), it's a wonder she never dropped the Express a few lines then all the town would have known, I reckon she could have made it into a script, I wouldn't mind betting an Oxford Scholar (dollar) each way if my Mum had been musically minded she would have written an Opera around it. No, not "The Barber Of Seville", that's been done already. Her first words when she saw me were, "You've had a close shave, who did it, Captain Hook?" or, "are you something that the cat's dragged in?"

Then she said, "With all those bits of paper stuck everywhere you could be mistaken for a walking newsagency."

I said, "Is there no end to these cutting remarks?" (being very Schick, I might add).

She said, "But Mickey Dripping…" (and I was).

> *Now you should sit down and rest*
> *Because of the blood you've lost*
> *And next time go to Sweeney's*
> *It'll be quick and half the cost*

"You know, we're so proud you want to be a blood donor, but if you had gone to the (Vic) hospital they would have taken it out of your arm."

"Alright, keep 'em coming," I said, "I'm thick skinned."

"Not from where we're standing," they said.

Talk about being bombarded, I was getting my share, I thought, when it rains it pores and there was blood coming out of mine. Then Pop came a bit closer and he had this serious look on his dial (but his eyes gave the game away), I knew there would be a good one coming, he sang out, "Should I wallpaper him, Margaret?"

"You can do whatever you think's right if it'll stop the bleeding, but don't blame me if your tea goes cold."

> *I'll give credit where it's due*
> *Yes indeed, he got me good*
> *I'd gone a "Whiter Shade Of Pale"*
> *After losing so much blood*

Then he said, "Here's a bit of advice for you, so can I have a word in your shell-like?"

I said, "You'd better make it the left one, I'm not sure what's happened to the other, I think the cat's under the sideboard with it. So let's hear from you."

Then he goes into, "Did you use a mirror?"

"Of course I did, do you think I'm silly," while quickly adding, "don't answer that," then I couldn't help myself as he'd used just enough bait to get me in, "why do you ask that then?"

He could hardly keep a straight face but he managed to say, "You would have been better using a razor, or it would have helped if you were in the same room as one," while still chuckling he said, "you crack me up."

I said, "Listen, Humpty Dumpty, I'm not putting you back together again."

Chapter
22

Now, a few weeks ago I was walking down Bourke Street (Melborn, as the Americans say) and actually passing The Southern Cross Hotel (where The Beatles stayed), they are redeveloping it at the moment. I stood there for a while because I used to have a gargle in the saloon bar and the TAB was only a couple of shops away in another part of the complex, so all in all it was a great place for a stopover where I could kill two birds with a "Fist Full Of Dollars". I closed my eyes for a couple of seconds and I could see the bar plain as anything, but then when I opened them it was hard to picture with all the cranes being there, plus the trucks whizzing around. There wasn't a shortage of workers on the site, and standing quite near to me were two strapping blokes (who just happened to be giving each other the strap) built like brick outhouses, then one said, "Ben?"

And Ben replied, "What is it, Bill?"

To which Bill said, "Has the whistle gone?"

Straight away I thought, Michael, me boy, whatever you do don't you dare say a word, you know that you can't run as fast as you could fifty years ago, and at this stage of your life didn't you say you'd like to finish the book before you climb that golden staircase. Then I laughed to myself, 'Bill and Ben, the Flower Pot Men' (more like a couple of pansies if you ask me).

Now, you know what viewers, I reckon you lot are on a good thing with this book (it's like TV), you're seeing everything, you don't have to go to the cinema or rent a film (movies, videos or DVD's, whatever they call 'em these days). In fact, your past is right here between these pages, the only problem with that is, I'm the one that's digging it up (and loving it).

Seeing as the siren's blown (and that's how it should be said), over a period of time I'd had quite a few jobs, and excelled in them all, I might add (ha ha). And if you'd like to come a little bit closer and fill out this union card, that's for those people who didn't work there, Drew's I mean (otherwise you could be in diabolical). In those days everybody had to be a paid up member (I'm not saying it's changed) but there was never any talk of striking, in fact, I wouldn't mind betting that during the time I was there, which was a few years, we never went out once. I can't even remember us having a stop work meeting, if they did I was most probably on me travels collecting stuff for the book (good one). I think the dues (at a guess) were only a tanner (not Elsie) and had to be paid weekly, even the mice were in the union, as one of the comedians there said...

Hickory dickory dock
A mouse ran up the clock
The clock struck one
The rest went out in sympathy

There were a few jobs that I liked so I'll tell you about those, and just for the record there is no guarantee that I won't get sidetracked somewhere along the way, I honestly don't know why I told you that as you should be used to me by now.

I'd worked in the Lab right under Allan's nose, so to speak, he thought that way he knew where I was (I'd do my disappearing act at least once a day to make it interesting). The job itself was good, mixing up portions (as I called it) or bleaching things and then taking samples out to the Colouring Shop. People rang to see if you'd go and pick things up, one good thing about it, you got to go to a lot of different places so you'd cover a few miles with some fabric or even just a piece of paper in your mitt. And then you just looked busy so no one asked any questions and, of course, answers weren't given (simple as that).

You know, I haven't thought of this part of my life in years (and I like it, I might even get paid again, I'll pencil it in as overtime and see what happens). Meanwhile, back at the Lab and if my memory serves me right (it normally does) next to the telephone was a list of numbers for the Gaffers, as the phones were in their offices, but if you knew that a boss had just left the Lab then it was okay to ring his number, because no way known he'd be back in time. Are you with me folks, as I don't know where I'm going with this but I'll come up with something. Unless, of course, you want to finish the tale for me, there wasn't many hands went up so I'll carry on for now. I'd take a punt and ring, hoping some worker would pick it up, then once you heard the blokes voice and you knew it wasn't the boss, you'd say, "Is Walls there?"

"Sorry, there's no Walls here, lad."

Then quickly you would say, "Well what the bloody hell is holding your ceiling up?" and slamming the phone down right away in case they picked your voice.

Some blokes were in their element (yeah, that's what I said I meant), as they would tell the person in question, "It'll be that little cheeky bugger, you know, the one that works in the Lab," (curses, they were on to me). It was time for Plan B to be worked out.

Plan A was always there
It didn't hurt to keep a spare
You'd pass 'em onto a mate
If headed for the same fate

The next day I'd be doing the rounds and flicking bits of paper at lads, then without warning someone had "Cast A Giant Shadow", most probably Kirk Douglas, John Wayne, Frank Sinatra, Yul Brynner and Angie Dickinson, as they were in the film of the same name (film buffs will know this), for those of you who are not FB's I thought I'd fill you in (no, not with cement, but it's an idea).

So this hand had me by the scruff of my neck, then it was like, "I gotcha! You're the little cheeky bugger that rang me the other day."

Me first thoughts were, if your name is Walls you're spot on, or blinking heck, you didn't seem that big on the Eau De Cologne (phone). At this stage I was on my tiptoes (it was a good view from there) but I didn't know if my nose was bleeding by being so high or the shaving wounds had opened up. In the blink of an eye I wiped whatever it was on his sleeve, then the Plan B I'd decided to use came out, "Oh nnno, it wwwas not mmme, I have a ststammerrr," and then I was off like a pork chop in the sun.

By the way, it got me thinking when I mentioned that film before and like all the other kids we used to go to the matinee (at the Coli) but now we were a lot bigger we could get into the big pictures (as I called them) without being taken in (what a joke). As most of you will remember you had to ask a couple, or a bloke, to take you in, then once inside you could sit where you liked, most times you'd go and join up with your buddies. It seems so funny looking back now how you'd trust people, I mean, for heavens sake, imagine asking a total stranger to take you in, the chap could have been the Boston Dangler for all we knew.

Here are some films that were around (most of these were my favourites) and a few of them were a bit earlier so they'll all go in together. Now, lights, camera, action! Get your teeth into this lot (no, I promise not to look if you want to whack 'em in)…

Abbot and Costello made over thirty-odd films and who could forget that brilliant "Who's On First" routine. Laurel and Hardy starred in 29 films together, I bet you haven't thought about these in years so here they are, The Bowery Boys first appeared in "The Dead End Kids" and made 7 films from 1937 to 1939, they made "Angels With Dirty Faces" 1938 with Jimmy Cagney and "Crime School" 1938 with Humphrey Bogart, then they did "Dead End Kids And Little Tough Guys", 9 films from 1940-45, then The Bowery Boys knocked out 48 films from 1946-58. So from 1937 to 1958 the total was 86, whoever said 'Bingo', that house is correct.

Right, eyes down for the next lot. By the way, if it's not your cup of tea, put it down, it must be mine. That brings us to Blondie, she starred in a comic strip in 1930 but it wasn't till 1938 that it hit the screen and they made 28 films in twelve years, even to this day I read them in the daily papers. Mickey Rooney and Judy Garland (Judy, Judy, Judy, that was my Cary Grant voice, not bad eh?) made a few films together. Mickey did 16 "Andy Hardy" films from 1937-58. Some of his other girlfriends were Kathryn Grayson, Donna Reed, Lana Turner and Esther Williams (Dangerous When Wet), she could have done water aerobics in my bed, and still on the subject of teams…

> *Hope and Crosby made road films*
> *About seven according to my list*
> *I was bitterly disappointed*
> *The road to The Grove was missed*

The Marx Brothers made 21 films from 1929-68. There were the "Charlie Chan" ones, 41 in all from 1929-49. 'Sherlock Holmes', Basil Rathbone and 'Dr Watson', Nigel Bruce, chipped in with 14 from 1939-46. Who could forget 'Francis' (the talking mule) 1949-56 with Donald O'Connor, there were 7 made, the last in 1956 was done by Mickey Rooney and 6 outta the 7 were directed by Arthur Lubin, after those he produced "Mr Ed". Then 11 films of Bomba "The Jungle Boy" were made between 1949 and 1955, Johnny Sheffield played the part, he was the boy in some "Tarzan" films. Martin and Lewis did 17 from 1949 to 1954 then Jerry went on to do 35 and Dean 38.

There were 9 "Ma And Pa Kettle" ones made from 1949 to 1957 with Marjorie Main and Percy Kilbride, in the films they had fifteen kids, every night when the tribe were all tucked in and Ma and Pa were in their bedchamber, Pa would say, "Do you want to go to sleep or what?" and, of course, Ma would reply, "Or what." Their last film in 1957 was "The Kettles On Old McDonald's Farm" or do you want fries with that? You can trust me to slip some humour in, my jokes are like buses, if one gets past you (or you don't like the colour) then another one will be along shortly. I bet you're thinking he's forgotten about The Stooges (how could I forget, you lot). I'm having a bit of trouble with them at the minute, there's not much in my book, so I think I'll have to upgrade next time I go to the bookstore…

> *Soon as I walk through the door*
> *Oh, that bloody Pom's here again*
> *He's armed with his briefcase*
> *Writing paper and Shaeffer pen*

Chapter
23

I'll name a few of the stars now, so anyone not all that keen I suggest you go to the flicks, if you'll pardon the pun, and flick through till you come to a part you like, as this'll go on for a while and I'll be covering the films after this.

One of my favourites would have to be WC Fields, he made 25 films from 1925-45 (he was a genius) but did you know he died on Christmas Day 1946? Then there was Mae West, she did 12 films (and most of her own writing) which ran from 1932-78, she was one clever lady. I'll go with this gang first and see what happens; Frederic March made 58 from 1929-73; Jimmy Cagney made 65 from 1930-84; George Raft made 69 from 1931-80; Humphrey Bogart did 72 from 1930-56.

I just thought, it'll be interesting to find out how many they made together, I reckon there would be a lot of work involved, at the moment I've got enough on me plate. I've just had a large pizza delivered and a Diet Coke, yes, I'm watching my weight, when I rang the order through they said, "Would you like it cut into four or six pieces?"

"You'd better make it four, I honestly don't think I could get through six."

The next lot that's lining up for a mention are; Boris Karloff, he made 81 films from 1920-85; Basil Rathbone, or Bathbun as they called him, did 62 from 1930-67; Edward G Robinson made 89 from 1930-73; Vincent Price starred in 93 from 1938-95; Peter Cushing made 86 from 1939-82; then Christopher Lee did a whopping 126 from 1948-93. So, according to my calculations, Vincent Price and Christopher Lee will (Frederic) March into the final. I'll get that result to you as soon as it comes through, in the meantime, cast your peepers over these and the ones that have an asterisk means I never get tired of watching them.

Let's get "The Greatest Show On Earth" (1952) moving with some of the earlier ones; "Scarface" 1932; "King Kong" 1933; "Mighty Joe Young" 1949, the gorilla is back and he's mad, both good for their day; three in 1935 were "Top Hat", "Mutiny On The Bounty" and "The Scarlet Pimpernel"; then "Petrified Forest", "Rose Marie" and "Pennies From Heaven" all 1936; "Prince And The Pauper" and "Lost Horizons" both 1937; "The Adventures Of Robin

Hood" 1938 and wasn't he in like Flynn; "Boys Town"; "The Lady Vanishes", Orson Wells, we knew him when he was Orson Cart; "The Hunchback Of Notre Dame" 1939, that's the Charles Laughton classic, Lon Chaney played the part in 1923, it was done again in 1957 with Anthony Quinn taking the lead and his co-star was Gina Wollabridgeider (huba huba). But wait, there's more, in 1982 it surfaced again, Anthony Hopkins was the star, the video title is "Hunchback", I haven't seen that one, must give it a Captain Cook (look).

These were 1939; "Gunga Din", so he was responsible for all that racket; "Wuthering Heights"; "The Wizard Of Oz"*; "Gone With The Wind" (I was like that last night, must have been the pizza); "Stanley And Livingston"; "The Four Feathers"; "The Man In The Iron Mask", it would be hard to munch anything with that on. These next six were made in 1940, "Citizen Kane" (used to walk with a stick), "Grapes Of Wrath", "Young Tom Edison", "Rebecca", "Pride And Prejudice" and "Waterloo Bridge".

"Dr Jekyll And Mr Hyde"* 1941 with Spencer Tracy; "They Died With Their Boots On" and "How Green Was My Valley" both 1941; these six were made in 1942 (and for me it was a very good year), "Casablanca", "Gentleman Jim", "In Which We Serve", "The Turtles Of Tahiti", "Yankee Doodle Dandy"* and "There's One Born Every Minute" with ten year old Liz Taylor; "Jane Eyre" 1944 (Liz again); "National Velvet" 1944 (and again); "Buffalo Bill"; "Fanny By Gaslight" retitled "Man Of Evil" and he said, 'I'll be glad when the electricity gets connected.'

"The Phantom Of The Opera"* 1944; "Henry V" in 1945 plus "Rhapsody In Blue" and "A Tree Grows In Brooklyn"; "The Jolson Story"*, "These Three", "The Yearling", "Ziegfield Follies" and "The Postman Always Rings Twice" all 1946; "The Canterville Ghost"* 1947; "Annie Get Your Gun"; "Miracle On 34th Street"* (still holds up well today); "The Fabulous Dorseys"; "The Egg And I" (Ma and Pa made their first appearance); "Sorry, Wrong Number"; "Call Northside 777"* 1948.

The next nine were made in that year, "Easter Parade", "Mr Blanding Builds His Dream House", "Give My Regards To Broadway", "Oliver Twist"*, "The Paleface", "The Return Of Rin Tin Tin". Here's one that was doing the rounds, you'd say, "Have you seen the tin?"

And they would say, "What tin?"

Then here was your chance to hit them with, "The tin that Rin Tin Tin poo'd in," (that was cleaned up a bit). "The Babe Ruth Story", "Kidnapped" and "Hamlet".

If Humpty Dumpty had made a film, would it have been called "Omelette"? "Take Me Out To The Ball Game" was made in 1949; also "Twelve O'Clock High" and "Tight Little Island", original title "Whiskey Galore"; "Jolson

Sings Again"*, "The Third Man", "Samson And Delightful (sorry, Delilah)", "The Blue Lagoon", "White Heat", "The Champions" still on 1949, they made "Down To The Sea In Ships" with Richard Widmark and Neil Down, Bob Down, Ben Down and their sister, Ida. There was a younger sister, they called her Periscope because she went down on a submarine, there were no survivors. Now, her father was well and truly devastated as he had lost his own mother, who years earlier had gone down on the Titanic.

Along came the fifties with these; "The Wooden Horse"; "Young Man With A Horn" (he should be careful, he could have someone's eye out with that); "The Mudlark"; "The Miniver Story"; "Fancy Pants"*; "Treasure Island"*; "The Asphalt Jungle"; "Cinderella"; "The Happiest Days Of Your Life" (and they certainly were for me); "Harvey" that was a 6ft 3ins wabbit, Tommy would have had trouble trying to get that wascal in his sack; "The Blue Lamp"; "King Solomons Mines".

I read somewhere that when Elvis met Stewart Granger, he told him he'd seen "King Solomons Mines" sixteen times, so naturally SG thought that EP was a big fan of his but said, "Why did you see it so many times?"

Elvis laughed then said, "I worked as an usher for a short while and it was showing then."

There were these made in 1951, so read on; "The Detective Story"; "No Highway In The Sky"; "The Day The Earth Stood Still"; "Desert Fox"*; "Strangers On A Train"; "Kon Tiki"; "Tom Browns School Days" (Max Bygraves had a part in that); "The Lady With The Lamp"; "Valentino"; "Man In The White Suit"; "David And Bathsheba" I don't mind David but I'd sooner give Sheba a bath; "The Lavender Hill Mob"; "Distant Drums"; "Captain Horatio Hornblower"; "African Queen"*; "Superman", George Reeves, he managed to do what no man could, he killed Superman by shooting himself, he should have bit the bullet, or wasn't he supposed to be faster than one?; "Two Tickets To Broadway"; "Lorna Doone"* I knew her sister, Nuttin Doon; "Cheaper By The Dozen"* about a couple who have twelve children (hence the title). The kids put Mum on a pedestal, yeah, so Dad couldn't get his hands on her.

Now, here's a few from 1952; "Ivanhoe"; "Scaramouche" and "Prisoner Of Zenda", both Stewart Granger; "The Sound Barrier"*; "High Noon"; "Down Among The Z Men" (The Goons); "Singing In The Rain"*; "Jack And The Beanstalk"*, Abbot and Costello, very good for its time and changes to colour, or if you're an American, color; "A Farewell To Arms"; "The Crimson Pirate"*; "Hans Christian Anderson"; "The Story Of Robin Hood And His Merry Men" (Richard Todd); "Snows Of Kilimanjaro"; "The Story Of Will Rogers"; "Limelight".

Now you'll see the ones of 1953; "Niagara"; "Botany Bay"; "The War Of

The Worlds; "Shane"; "Lady And The Tramp"*; "Adventures Of Robinson Crusoe", do you know he was the first man to invent the four day week, because he had all his work done by Friday; "The Robe"* and "The Desert Rats"*, Richard Burton was in both of them; "Around The World In 80 Days", that's what I set out to do on page one (I'm getting there).

We're still on 1953; "By The Light Of The Silvery Moon" as a follow-up to "On Moonlight Bay" in 1951, both Doris Day and Gordon MacRae; "The Eddie Cantor Story"; "Knights Of The Round Table"; "The Joe Louis Story"; "House Of Wax"*; "The Naked Spur"; "The Jazz Singer"; "Titanic"* (classic); "Peter Pan"*; "The Cruel Sea"; "From Here To Eternity"; "Botany Bay"; "The Titfield Thunderbolt"; "Stalag 17"; "Act Of Love", Brigitte Bardots first film (hurly-burly, what a girlie); "Genevieve"*; "Calamity Jane"*; "Gentlemen Prefer Blondes" with Jane Russell and Marilyn Monroe (well there's a nice pair that don't lose their shape); Tony Curtis was great in "Houdini"*.

Now here's more, and they were made in 1954; "Rififi"; "On The Waterfront"; "Magnificent Obsession"; "20,000 Leagues Under The Sea"; "Young At Heart"; "Runaway Bus"; "The Seven Year Itch"; "The Belles Of St Trinians"; and "Lady Godiva".

Onto 1955; "The Cockleshell Heroes"; "The Harder They Fall" (Bogies last film); "The Ten Commandments"; "The Girl Can't Help It" with Tom Ewell, Jayne Mansfield, Edmond O'Brian, Julie London and the musical cast of Fats Domino "Blue Monday", The Platters "You'll Never Never Know", Gene Vincent "Be Bop A Lula" and Little Richard belts out "She's Got It", "Ready Teddy" and "The Girl Can't Help It".

"Hobsons Choice"; "Demetrius And The Gladiators"; "Knock On Wood"; "The Caine Mutiny"; "The Student Prince"; "There's No Business Like Show Business"; "Suddenly"; "A Star Is Born"; "White Christmas"; "Seven Brides For Seven Brothers"*; "The Dam Busters"; "The Glen Miller Story"; "The Sea Shall Not Have Them"; "Dial M For Murder"*. It looks like the interval is getting near, so off you go, I'll have a creamy soda, a packet of crisps and if they have a small tub of ice-cream, just one please. You can foot the bill as I paid for you lot to come in, I'll make sure the pictures don't start till you get back, toodle pip.

Well done folks, you're back early, I was just checking my notes, while looking for a dog-end, and I found a list with titles on, so here they are; "Snow White" 1937; "Great Expectations" 1946; "The Three Musketeers" 1948, how on earth could I have missed that one, it deserves a slap on the wrist, thwack, ouch! Thank-you D'Artagnan, I needed that.

Right, there's only a couple left and they are; "Tea For Two" 1950; "Quo Vadis"* 1951, good for its time. At this stage I'll only go up to 1957 because that's near enough to where we are (I think?). Let's look at those that came out in 1955; "Lady And The Tramp"*; "Love Is A Many Splendoured Thing"; "Love Me Or Leave Me"; "Pete Kelly's Blues"; "We're No Angels"; "Helen Of Troy"; "A Kid For Two Farthings"; "The Benny Goodman Story"; "The Lady Killers".

As you might have picked up on a lot of these films, I loved musicals, so in 1956 we got music in the form of rock'n'roll and wasn't it great, with films like; "Rock, Rock, Rock", Tuesday Weld played the lead (Connie Francis sang her songs), Chuck Berry was there and Frankie Lymon And The Teenagers sang "I'm Not A Juvenile Delingquent"; Bill Haley's film was "Rock Around The Clock", BH does "Razzle Dazzle", the title song and "See You Later Alligator", The Platters sing "The Great Pretender" and, of course, (the beautiful) "Only You"; then Bill is back in town with "Don't Knock The Rock" and making an appearance is Little Richard and he sings "Tutti Frutti" and "Long Tall Sally".

Here's some others I liked in 1956; "The King And I"; "High Society"; "Above Us The Waves"; "The Court Jester"* with Danny Kaye, just where was that poisonous pellet, did you think it was in the vessel with the pestle, very clever routine (between you and me, folks, I'm still trying to work out who's on first).

"A Town Like Alice"; "Somebody Up There Likes Me"; "Reach For The Sky"*; "The Mountain"; "The Lone Ranger" with Clayton Moore and Tonto, Jay Silverheels. So one day they rode into town and LR said to Tonto, "Silver seems to be a bit hot, will you fan him while I have a quick beer then I'll take him to the vet?"

So off he goes and our Indian hero tries to keep the horse cool. Honestly folks, I think that's why he was shoved in the film, as no other muggins would have done that. Then he had this idea, so he grabbed the blanket off his horse, to which the horse whinnied then said, "Neigh, you're nothing but an Indian giver."

Then Tonto said, "I've a squaw and five papooses to support, that's why I need the Bugs Bunny (money)."

He started circling Silver, while wafting him, and the big fella across the street had noticed what was going on, so he went into the saloon and said to the masked man, "Are you The Lone Ranger?"

To which Mr R said, "Yes, why?"

The bloke said, "Well, you've left your Injun running."

There's six left in this year and they were; "Trapeze"; "The Good Die Young"; "Three Men In A Boat"* (great to see Laurence Harvey doing comedy); "Privates Progress"; "Moby Dick"*; and "Giant". Talking of giants, what is twelve foot long, red, and lies on the bottom of the ocean? Moby's dick. Hey, like I told you before and I'll go on record (or CD) as saying, "I don't make 'em up, I just remember 'em."

So that brings us to 1957 and these ones have stuck in my memory; "The Shiralee"*; "Twelve Angry Men"; "The Buster Keaton Story"; "Funny Face"; "Witness For The Prosecution"*; "An Affair To Remember"; "The Rainmaker"; "Island In The Sun"; "The Joker Is Wild"; "Old Yeller"; "The Colditz Story"; "The Bridge On The River Kwai". Which reminds me, what happened when the onion fell into the water? It made "The Bridge On The River Cry".

That brings us to; "The True Story Of Jessie James"; "The Tommy Steele Story" retitled "Rock Around The World", just thought you'd like to know that; and the last one is "Mr Rock And Roll" with Little Richard, Chuck Berry, Frankie Lymon and The Teenagers, plus Brook Benton.

By the way, I forgot to tell you, as they announced it at the interval before you got back…

> *About the big game between*
> *Vincent Price and Chris Lee*
> *No score after extra time*
> *But Lee won the replay 4-3*

Well, I hope you lot realise we've got to get back to work or some of the bosses will be having kittens. So here we are, then came a change of jobs, I was asked to go into the Mechanics Shop. I'm not sure if I'd got a promotion or demotion, I knew a lot of blokes that worked in there and half of them said, "You're the little cheeky bugger from the Lab, we've been expecting you."

"Well you can thank your lucky stars because now I'm here in living colour, but it's too late to start, as it's nearly morning tea, so I'll see you shortly," then I was off and I'd make a beeline for the canteen.

Now, with living in The Grove I would take sandwiches for lunch, Mary's Pie Shop used to be a good hang out or Scott Street Chippy, the only trouble with that was, blokes found out you were going and before you knew it you were getting orders. Mind you, I wasn't against canteen food, I believe they put some good meals on (but not for me). I remember in the mornings they'd do these great bacon butties, the bread was cut so thick, then toasted, buttered (or marged), then the bacon was plonked on. I would be stood there tapping my fingers on the counter while slavering (whistling was out of the question), upon seeing this, extra bacon would be added, plus a wink, and that's all that was said. One was great but if you were greedy, need I say more. You know something, I'm licking my lips at this moment just thinking about them, right, that's enough about food.

So working with the mechanics (maniacs, I called them, while quickly ducking to avoid a swipe) was really good, always something different to do whether you worked on-site, as I called it, or in the Shop. If you were working out, many a time you'd get to the job and find out something had been forgotten, so that was the task for me to gofer a certain spanner or hammer. If I remember right, all the mechanics had cupboards under their bench where tools were kept, so if you were sent back for anything, you could put your hands on it, so to speak.

But this one day I was given strict instructions to go back and get some string which was supposedly on a certain bench, well, I looked high and low, I don't know why I looked high, I knew it wouldn't be up there and, of course, it wasn't in the cupboard. Quick as a flash I thought, I'm not going back without it or there's a chance it could be 'sock it to me' time, then I realised there was nobody downstairs, but I heard a noise from above, yes, good thinking Mick, as I raced up to see Richard (the joiner). When I got there, being cheeky (if you know what's coming, skip a few lines) I said, "Have you got a piece of string on yer, Dick?"

He said, "What do you think it is, a roll of bacon?"

I found out later someone said he had used that line before (I thought it was very clever, just the same).

Now, I know I'm a pain in the back of beyond (but a likeable one), here's a couple of films I had to check on, in fact, I had trouble finding them as they both had their titles changed (I don't know why they do that). It's so annoying when you know the original title, but don't know it under its other one. The first is "All Mine To Give" and it's based on the book "The Day They Gave Babies Away" and that's the title I remembered. It starred Glynis Johns and, as it suggests, the family was given away, Mum would most probably have drowned half of 'em. And the next one, I am sure you'll be interested in these facts (well, the lads will), about "Albert RN", Anthony Steel played the lead, those other titles it went under were "Break To Freedom", "Marlag 'O' Prison Camp" and "The Spare Man". Now you know why I had Barney Rubble (trouble) with it, as it was like looking for a needle in a haystack and, of course, you'll remember Anton Diffring who was in a lot of war films, it's a good job he wasn't an Indian or he might have been galloping around a horse with a blanket.

Now, the blacksmith always worked on his own, except when he had a big job, so odd times I was sent down to help him. When he saw me I bet he thought 'what have I done to deserve this'. Anybody who has been in a Blacksmith Shop (or worked in), would know that coke (not Pepsi) was used on the fire and didn't it pen and ink (stink). Many a time he said, "Is that you or the fire? If it's you, with wind like that who needs bellows." I used to love watching him make things, he made it look so easy and, apparently, he made a lot of the ironwork (if that's the right word) outside the Tin Bobbin. The pub is still there but I'm not sure about his work.

Now, I know this happened in 1958 and it was a terrible accident (or some said sabotage) and I'm talking about the day a team died, which was the Munich air disaster. Forty-three passengers were on the flight and twenty-three of them died, the Club Secretary, the Chief Coach and the Trainer, there were eight journalists, including Henry Rose (Daily Express) and Frank Swift (News Of The World), who was one of Manchester City's great players. The other four who lost their lives were the Co-Pilot plus a Steward, and there was a supporter and a Travel Agent. And, of course, the eight players; Roger Byrne (Captain) aged 28; Tommy Taylor 26; Geoff Bent 25; Mark Jones 24; David Peg 22; Liam Whelan 22; Eddie Colman 21; and the great Duncan Edwards 21 (my favourite). He'd already been capped eighteen times for England, I remember reading somewhere (and never thinking I'd ever write about it) that he fought for fifteen days but, sadly, he died. There were nine players that survived and their Manager, Matt Busby, I think it was a few years later that he was Knighted.

So where were we, yes, with the blacksmith, and one thing I do know is he liked a bit of classical stuff, in fact, one day we belted out "The Anvil Chorus" from "Il Trovatore" by Verdi. Then for an encore we went into "Clang, Clang, Clang Goes The Trolley", then I gave 'em a couple of lines of now "If I Had A Hammer" (I'd smash your bloody head in). Then some wally said, "Less of the din, Gunga, unless you can play 'Silent Night'."

"Yeah," I replied, "we'll make it the last."

Those that worked at Drew's would remember, with it being quite an old building, that a lot of the doors had snecks, now we'd done this trick or prank, call it what you like, loads of times but in the workforce it went down better and, of course, the blokes would roar with laughter when they saw their mates being had (so to speak).

Now, I hope it comes across on paper, here goes; the idea being you'd put a drawing pin on the sneck with the point end up, then it was covered by anything that tasted bad, for example, dog droppings. Sometimes that was hard to find, but there were plenty of cats. The trouble was their deposits seemed to be runnier but it did the trick, so you covered the pin with it. Now, if you've ever jabbed or stabbed yourself with a sharp object you know that the digit in question goes directly into the Lee J Cobb (gob), don't ask me why, as it's baffled scientists for years. You would then watch from a distance and some chap would come along, press the sneck, then a few choice words and, of course, the thumb went straight into the mouth, followed by a coughing and spitting fit. It's funny to see someone copping it, but it's not very nice to be on the receiving end.

Did you ever notice how some people could peel an apple with a knife and the peel stayed intact? Well, Pop could do this, then the idea was you threw it over your shoulder and sometimes it would make a couple of initials. So if you were having an apple, Pop would peel it and sling it over his shoulder, this one time he said, "Look, it's HJ."

I said, "Who's HJ?"

He said, "Herbert and John."

I said, "More like Heckle and Jeckle, if you ask me, and next time I'll have a go as I've been practising at work."

So when the time came I said, "Let's have a bash then," and with quite a bit of patience I managed to do the deed, then I slung it over the shoulder, "Mum, Pop, come here quick and see what it's spelt."

Mum said, "Read it to us."

"Xylophone," I said, "and that's one to me," and they both shook their heads and looked at the ceiling, I said, "what are you looking up there for, does it want papering? And that's another one to me."

Mum said, "'Some Mothers Do 'Ave 'Em', and occasionally they survive, where's that dolly tub, Bert? He might still fit in it, or better still, when he comes home from work tomorrow we'll have moved, I'll put his bait up in a road map."

"Well, I haven't got time for this, I'm off to the flicks so I'll have a shave, if you hear screaming don't panic."

"Pop said it might help you by standing a bit closer to the blade."

"By the way, Pop," I said, "there's a new kid started at work, we call him Harpic." (I didn't even need a rod).

He said, "Why do they call him that?"

"Because he's clean around the bend! So this is zee Ceesco Kid saying so long, Pancho."

Then Mum shouted, "How do you keep an idiot in suspense?"

"I don't know," I replied.

"I'll tell you tomorrow. By the way, what's the film you're going to see, Michael?"

She always gave me my Sunday name (maybe because it was the Sabbath), I sang back, "The Boy Who Killed His Parents, So He Could Go To The Orphans Picnic."

There was one bloke at work, trouble seemed to follow him, he was always in the wars, so you gave him a wide berth when he had an implement like a screwdriver (he could have someone's eye out with that), or worse still, when he wanted me to give an object a belt, for a bit of fun I'd say, "You nod your head and I'll hit it."

He took me quite seriously then shouted, "Hang on a tick, that's not right!"

Then he'd see the funny side of it and say, "Oh yeah, you're a little bugger."

But he was forever hitting himself, either on his hand or shin, whichever was the nearest at the moment of impact. This one day it was hilarious, he'd dropped the hammer on his foot, then he was effing and blinding, sat on the wheelbarrow while telling God all about it. After that he said, "Make us a brew, there's a good lad."

I couldn't resist throwing in, "Will that be one lump or two?"

Then next time I was told to go and work with him I thought, this'll be fun, as by now I could read him like a book, you know, I was just thinking, he should be available on video soon.

That brings us near enough to 1959, give or take a couple of months. I remember this like it was yesterday; we were into February, then on the 3rd (like I mentioned earlier) the plane crashed killing Buddy Holly (22), Ritchie Valens (18) and The Big Bopper (29). Of course, it was a big talking point at work and I know I was really annoyed at one bloke's remarks (I won't name him), which were 'good bloody riddance'. I know when all's said and done that he's entitled to his own opinion but, I thought, how on earth could you say anything like that. He was a big un and you know what they say, the bigger they are the harder they fall, it would take me a while, that's all. He was very lucky there was nobody about to lift me up or I would have snotted him good and proper. You know, in all honesty, I feel better for getting rid of that, as it's been stored in there for a lot of years, I don't think I've told that story to anyone before.

Now folks, I can't guarantee you'll find any of these stories interesting but it's doing me a power of good. I also remember this like it was yesterday, John had come out of the Army (see, I did remember). Now, he and Pauline had been going out together, or as we used to call it, courting. But you take these days, the baby comes along, then it's setting up house together and finally they get married. So the date was set and Bob was Best Man, Frank (Pauline's brother) and I were Ushers, we'd go around saying, "'Hush, Hush, Sweet Charlotte', and if I have to tell you again I'll repeat it." Mum used to say that a lot, so I thought I'd throw it in.

The ceremony was performed and they settled down to married life, then their family came along over a period of time. Paul is the eldest, then David followed by Adam and Peter. I reckon I got through that reasonably well as sometimes it's a bit of a worry how I'm going to get the old pen around some things, so I think I've cracked it for later (we shall see).

Now, hang on folks, I've lost my running sheet (it could have been while I was out running) and on the table there are about twenty-odd pages and it's not amongst those, I might paper the coffee table, I know I won't find the sheet in question but it'll take my mind off it.

A lot of time, after work, we'd play football on the Loco. There were no goals so we made makeshift ones which would budge at the slightest touch, the two posts managed to stay upright but the crossbar hung there by the skin of its teeth (so to speak). If someone fired in a rocket that went in off the post (or bar) there wouldn't be shouts of, "Goal!" It was more like, "Timberrr!"

There's a few names coming your way now so that will make some of you sit up and take notice. This weeks team shall be picked from: Malcolm Allen, Jim Bowden, Alan Bushby, Mick Crabtree, Tom Crabtree, Bram Etherington, Jim Graham, Bob Markham, Keith Maudsley, Jimmy Miller, Bernard Platt and Dave Scott. They went on to form Rosegrove United and I think they had quite a bit of success.

Sometimes, after leaving the Loco, a few of us would go down to the selling out shop for a couple of bottles of 'you know what' (hic). It wasn't long after that I bucked up courage to try the Real McCoy. So this one night we'd gone down town, picked out a pub, which was the Craven Heifer (I think that's how it was spelt, it's still there but had a change of name since). We stood outside for what seemed like ages (while trembling) and saying to each other, "After you."

"No," I said, "after you chaps, and just walk up to the bar and say 'Landlord, your finest ales for my friends'."

Then, drinkers, there I was with a pint (what a whopper) in me mitt, I could've soaked my feet in it. The regulars who were drinking there, they could tell you were first-timers and would be encouraging you, saying, "Get it down thee lad, it'll do yer good."

Now I must tell you this, I think the Hollands pie and chips, not forgetting the mushy peas, that had been consumed earlier weren't too pleased with all this liquid that was raining on their parade. So something had to give, well, instead of going the natural way it had a mind of its own saying, "We know a quick way out, it's an express elevator and we'll keep going till we get to the top!" My eyes were sticking out like organ stops while the cheeks were bulging. I could feel it coming up and I thought, it's ages since I've been sick, then I said to myself, "It's no good thinking about that now as you've got to get out of here before you whitewash some poor bugger."

It was touch and go if I made it or not but a quick shout of, "Gangway!" seemed to do the trick and the path was cleared. I just got there with seconds to spare then whoosh, the biggest technicolour yawn you've ever seen and now I was on my tiptoes and spraying from a great height, I never thought so much stuff could come up, I swear blind I saw a sock, goodness knows where that came from. But suddenly, one foot was colder than the other, there were even carrots and I hadn't had them since Jim was born because, if you remember, I wanted a donkey and I just happened to have a sack full at the ready and, as you know, I didn't get the D but I had to eat all the blinking carrots.

There were a couple of blokes out there, one said, "Get it up young un, it'll do thee good."

And the other chap, he'd been giving me a hard time all night, he said sarcastically, "Thars got a weak stomach."

I came back with, "I don't know so much, I'm spewing as far as him," pointing with my winkle-pickers to the chap next to me who just happened to be the Landlord, then I just had enough in the reserve tank to which I yelled, "look out!" and I heaved, making sure it went all over his drainpipes. That'll keep him quiet for a bit, so I said to the lads, "That's it, I'm never drinking again, till the next time, who's round is it?"

So next day at work, I don't know about a bear with a sore head, but the old comic cuts (guts) weren't too good. Some of the lads were quick to offer advice, saying, "Hair of the dog, that's the best bet." Then I thought, I know what'll fix me up and that's a couple of King-sized bacon butties and to heck with the expense.

Now, there were a lot of times when it rained during the lunch break, so football was out of the question, but here's some of the other things we used to do; there was always a few bob to be won (or lost) by playing cards, which took place in the storeroom and that was upstairs in the Mechanics Shop; and then near the offices there were some rooms, in one of those they used to keep all the football (and cricket) gear, then there was a big room which contained a full-sized snooker (or billiard) table.

And those of you that worked there (or were employed) would remember they had a radio in there and we always made sure we'd be in and listened with interest when they made the draw for whatever round the FA Cup was (providing Burnley were still in) and hoping they'd get a big name, especially if the venue was Turf Moor. Other teams in the comp from Lancashire were, of course, Man U and City, Blackburn, Blackpool, Bolton, Everton and Preston. So any one of those would be a good gate.

Then there was a room which we used for table tennis (great times and a lot of fun), either singles or doubles. It was nowhere near as energetic as football but, I can assure you, after a good session we were ready to go back to work, yeah, for a well earned rest. Sometimes I'd say to Allan, "Let's have a quick game."

He said, "You'll get me shot."

"Well," I said, "as long as it's you they shoot, that's alright then."

"You little cheeky bugger," he said, "okay, but just up to eleven."

I thought that was a very clever plan because if he was late back then I was covered.

Let's see if I can work this little bit in somewhere around here, one of the printers who worked there used to run what I suppose you'd call a Bookmakers Bag. If I remember right (as I haven't thought about this in years) it was something like what a Doctor used or a Gladstone bag, which was named after William Ewart Gladstone (1809-1898), he most probably kept his Gunga Din (gin) in there.

You got all that thrown in for nothing, now read on, let me try to explain it this way, anybody wanting a bet (on the gee-gees) would write their selections on a piece of paper, you then gave it to Bernard, then a time was stamped on it and it was put in the bag. Say, for instance, the first race was 1 o'clock, if you weren't in on time (hard luck mate) the bag was locked. Blokes would write their bets out and I would put them on for those who couldn't leave their machines, if they had a win I'd get maybe a thrupny bit or a tanner.

Pop liked the tomato sauces (horses), I think that was written on the page that went missing, now it doesn't matter as all roads lead to the Bookies Bag. That's how I became interested as it got me right in and I've been following them ever since, yeah, with a shovel. Then I was on the move again and this time I was sent to the (sweat box) Boiler House and, believe me, it sure was hot in there, even in winter…

> *They were all big blokes*
> *And of course there was me*
> *Hey c'mon, don't titter*
> *Someone had to brew the tea*

I can tell you, they had lots of laughs at my expense (I didn't mind one bit as it was all good fun), anyone who knew the Boiler House would remember at one end was a room with a table and a couple of benches, which doubled for a morning tea and lunch place or just somewhere to park your carcass while waiting for the boilers to be stoked again or, in my case, taking the ashes out. And then at the other end there were (about) six steps, but seeing as the ashes had to be taken out that way (in a barrow) there was a long plank, which was roughly twelve to fourteen feet.

To the right of this, on the way up, was where they kept a lot of scrap wood and old newspapers, plus comics, need I say more, but I will and that is yours truly would be in there, head first, at any given opportunity, even though I was getting a bit old to buy them I still liked to read about those characters and what they were up to. The blokes gave me a few trial runs to get used to the size of the barrow (in fact, it was quite big) then one of them said, "Go and make us a cuppa, that's a good lad, and I'll fill the barrow for you then when you come back you can have a go."

So the tea was made, then I said, "Right chaps, I'm off."

They said, "We wondered where that smell was coming from."

I grabbed the handles and sang out, "Hi ho, hi ho, it's off to work I go."

Half way up the plank it became too much, so overboard I went, straight into the rubbish, to the cheers and jeers of the blokes behind me who were eagerly watching my departure. Then, of course, the hot ashes went every which way and you had to be quick or you would have set fire to the rubbish, you'd clean it up the best you could but it didn't really matter that much once the ashes had gone cold and what I remember is it was a really dirty place anyway. They say where there's muck there's money, I never found any, but what I did find were the house bricks that had been planted in the bottom of the barrow, no wonder it was heavy and I thought, my arms are long, as I can touch my toes without bending down, so then I copped 'Mickey The Monkey'.

But I watched them like a hawk after that, other blokes would still try to play tricks though, I'm sure there was a sliding door and I would be half way up the plank and some joker would slide the door shut (from the outside) then I shouted, "Open the bloody door!"

And a voice said, "What's the password?"

I'd say, "Please."

Then he said, "That's near enough," and the door was opened by Pop saying, "one to me," with a grin from ear to ear, then adding, "that's enough of the bloody language."

"Well, you'd make a Parson swear," I said, and we both started laughing.

There were other times I'd be left stranded and then trying to do a balancing act while walking back down the plank, but they did get me another time and, I must admit, it was a good one. I think I got back from the bog and, of course, the barrow was full of smoking ashes so I said, "Okay chaps, what's the joke?"

They all managed to keep their faces straight, "No joke," was the reply, "if you don't believe us, feel the weight."

They were right, it didn't feel any heavier but, unbeknown to me, cardboard and paper had been placed in there, so half way up the plank I was nonchalantly singing, "I Walk The Line," but with the shaking and the waft (or draught), what had been smouldering suddenly burst into flames, I think I screamed then filled me pants and fainted, in that order.

The comedians had a field day with, "It's Mickey and his barrow in (Furness) furnace, and for his next trick he'll make smoke rings come down his nostrils."

I said, "As far as I'm concerned you can blow it outta your ar… here's the Gaffer, I'll tell him it wasn't my fault. And if that was an attempt at humour, for goodness sake, don't give up your day job, and if comedy has to be added to the story let me be the judge of that," (yeah Mickey, you tell em).

Now, girls had been on the scene for a while but, at this stage, nothing serious. The blokes from work had lined me up with a girl, I think her name was Bertha, she was so big she kept getting knocked down, the reason being the motorists didn't have enough petrol to go around her, so I thought I'd go and see her in hospital and cheer her up (she was in Wards 2 and 3). She thanked me for that then squeezed my hand and said, "I could go for you."

I said, "I could go for meself, ta very much," then it was almost time to leave and I said, "do you fancy going to the Odeon on Saturday night?"

She said, "That would be nice, I'll see you outside then."

Curses, I thought, I'd rather meet you inside (plus it works out a lot cheaper) but what the heck, in those days I used to have more money than sense, in fact, I'd cob it about like a chap with no arms (as Mum would say).

The night came and I didn't bother having a swill, I thought with all the necking going on she'll get rid of me tidemark. We went on the back row, she said there was more room, I didn't know if she wanted to dance or watch the film. So by the time we danced, in the old-fashioned way, the film was finished and I said, "Do you like Chinese food?"

She said, "I like any type of grub, so let's have a good nosh-up."

Once inside the restaurant the waiter said, "Would you like a table for three?"

She said, "Should I hit him with me handbag?"

I thought, it's more like a Portmanteau and if you'd have hit him with that you would have knocked him into the middle of next week. The waiter gave us a menu each, then pointing to something I couldn't pronounce, I said, "I'll have this, please."

He said, "You can't, that's the Manager."

I said to Bertha, "You pick yours (not your nose), while I choose something else."

She sang out more numbers than a bingo caller, then I ordered the steak and blackbean sauce, he said, "Would you like chips with that or veggies?"

I said, "Make it chips, Rafferty," but it went through to the keeper.

Then they brought out this humongous meal, "Yummy," I said.

The food's here but it was Bertha's entrée and it was on a tray, not a plate, the waiter said to Bertha (while keeping his distance) as she was rolling her sleeves up and also her jeans, which just happened to be conductors ones, yeah, room for two inside, "Will that be a knife and fork or chopsticks, Miss?"

She said, "Bring me both, and bring me a large spoon while you're at it." I thought, he shouldn't be at it, well not when he's working, and in no time she had cleaned her plate.

Another thought came to mind and that was she'd eat a potato more than Farmer Collinge's pig, and that could shift some spuds. Charlie Chan came over and asked if the meal was to our liking, I said, "Yes it was, thank-you very much."

He then said, "How did you find your steak, Sir?"

"I lifted up me chips and there it were."

So we left there and I took her home, we got to the door and I noticed she couldn't stop looking at the bulge in my pants, she said, "Would you like to come in for a bit?"

I don't know why she was so excited by what she'd seen, I always keep my wallet there, but quick as a flash I thought, who wants a bit, I'd like a lot if it was food and it's a well known fact that after Chinese you always want more (or is it just me?). So we were sitting on the couch, swapping spit, and it was then I noticed that hers was greener than mine, and lumpier too. Then she frightened me by saying, "I'll sit on your knee and we'll talk about the first thing that pops up."

All of a sudden my wallet moved, she must have known the combination, then she said, "What about Oompaloompa?"

I said, "It wasn't a bad run last start, so I suppose it has a chance in the Grand National, my money will be on it."

She said, "Now we've got over that hurdle, let's get down to it."

"Hold your horses girlie, I've got to go to the loo, so can I use your toilet?"

She said, "No, because it's next to Mum and Dad's room and they don't like being disturbed by the toilet flushing."

"Well," I said, "I'm bursting to go, so what am I supposed to do?"

"Can you do it in the sink?"

I said, "As long as the dishes aren't in there, I think I'll manage."

After being in there for about ten minutes she popped her head in and said, "Are you alright?"

I said, "Yeah, I'm just looking for some paper to wipe me bum."

Well, viewers, didn't she go berserk and I'll tell you something, it ain't easy running with your pants around your ankles. That was a good chance to get some old gags in.

Chapter
24

Now here's a fact, any building with space (or a place) to write something on then the deed would be done. Do you remember those 'Wilful Damage' posters that were plastered everywhere telling people not to cause damage, and that included graffiti (we didn't call it that in those days) but it was still an offence and no matter how hard they tried no one could stop those idiots from writing (especially) 'Kilroy Was Here', and I would scribble underneath 'So Was Mickey Plum' because, all in all, it was just another brick in the wall. I bet you didn't know KWH was a film (made in 1947) about "Kilroy Was Here" (there and everywhere), it starred Jackie Cooper and Jackie Coogan. You know, over the years I always wondered who Mister K was so I found out by reading about all those films earlier (who said you can't teach an old dog new tricks), and now I've learned something, mind you, I had a good teacher (and I like the boy).

Now, I'm not really sure in what month this happened but Errol Flynn died, he was fifty, and at our age we thought that was ancient, so here's what I found out; he made his first film in 1935 and went on to do fifty in total; his last was entitled "Cuban Rebel Girls" which didn't do too well, his co-star was sixteen year-old Beverly Aadland who, by the way, was his last girlfriend, his mates had told him it could be fatal, he said, "I'll drink to that!" As you may well know he had quite a few run-ins with his enemy, Aristotle (bottle) in his time, so the swashbuckler buckled his swash for one more fight, but none of his sparring (drinking) pardners would throw in the William Powell (towel), pretty soon he was on the canvas, down and out for the count, and that last round was a killer.

Now at work, things were plodding along (just nicely, thank-you) as they tend to do, it was still hard graft but when you're doing something you enjoy, well it seems easy peasy, and there's a couple of words to pick the bones out of, which weren't around when Adam was a lad (as the saying goes).

I can't actually remember how this happened and, to be perfectly honest with you, it's not something I lose sleep over. Tommy used to drive the truck to Manchester and he had an off-sider who left, or was sacked, so my name was mentioned to replace him. I do know it was about this time that I'd started watching Burnley with John, they were always good days and it was a bonus if The Clarets won. I'd meet John under the culvert (just in case of rain) then once on The Turf we made for the corner at the cricket field end, as a few blokes from work used to stand there and it was a great view. Then when they played away one of the newsagents in The Grove ran coach trips so I went on a few of those.

Then it was time to say goodbye to the blokes in the Boiler Room. They wished me luck and said, "Pop in and see us anytime, even on Ash Wednesday." I liked that and I thought it was clever. I reported to Tommy, I bet he was thinking, I'm going to be stuck with this little cheeky bugger all the flipping way to Manchester, but that doesn't mean to say I've got to bring him back. Did you ever notice how a lot of people used to say 'flipping', I suppose it was their way of swearing but I can't understand why they didn't just come out with it as every Tom, Dick and Harry knew what they meant anyway.

I'd say the hardest part of the job was loading the truck, Tommy made sure it was stacked just where he wanted it, not for safety reasons, so that the exact amount of cloth could be dropped at the right warehouse then we just had to double-check to make sure the hatches were battened down. Once in the cab I'd shout, "Wagons roll."

One thing I noticed, you had to yell at each other, as it was so noisy. Tommy said, "I've heard about you, you're the young chap that throws his voice in the battle cruiser (boozer) and a mate of mine saw you in the Rams Head on Friday night."

I knew most of the pubs but I hadn't heard of this one so, of course, I said, "Where the hell's that?"

He almost had a laughing convulsion then said, "Three foot from its bum."

I thought, if this fella wants a battle of wits he'd better watch out, I'm full of it (wit, I mean). Most of the places that we delivered to, you got as close as you could (which saved a lot of carrying), and a plank would be used from the truck to the basement (that's a good idea, Son). Tommy did all the paperwork while I quickly threw down the plank what had to be dropped there (and making sure I let go or I'd be down the chute with it).

If we made good time we'd grab a cuppa and have a natter with the blokes and we would give them a serve if Burnley had beaten Man U or City, and gave 'em heaps more, especially if they'd been clobbered at Old Trafford or Maine Road. Then for lunch, sandwiches were the order of the day, Tommy used to take a flask (thermos), he gave me a brew and he also knew places "Far From The Madding Crowd", so we would go there for half an hour and have lunch.

This one day he said, "I know this area like the back of my hand."

"For goodness sake, don't turn it over or we'll be lost."

He said, "The last time I was here a bloke came down the gangplank with a sack over his shoulder, a policeman saw this and shouted 'Hoy'..."

So the chase was on and the copper caught the culprit and said, "What's in the sack?"

The bloke said, "Nowt."

To which the cop asked him, "Why the hell were you running?"

"I'm just timing you for tomorrow."

Tom thought, I've got to see this, so he was there at the same time and place, the scene was set, the crim waddled down the plank but now the sack was bulging and right on cue the long arm of the law grabbed him saying, "Okay, the game's up, what's in thee sack?"

And the crim said, "Belly buttons."

The Officer spluttered, "Where on earth did you get those?"

"From the Navel Stores."

Well, he certainly pulled my leg just like I tugged at yours.

Now, I don't know how many of you noticed when I used the word 'okay' before it got me thinking, as I've seen it spelt all sorts of ways like okay, okey, oke and, of course, OK. I did a bit of checking and it's (if you'll pardon the pun) okay to use it any which way. So when Martin Van Buren was running for President in 1840 (I don't know why he couldn't run for himself), his party used the slogan O(ld) K(inderkook), as Kinderhook was where MVB was born, which is near Albany, in the New York State.

I don't seem to have trouble with the years, it's the months I struggle with (but it's no big deal), so if you don't tell anybody, that's all that matters. Now, I think it goes something like this, the sixties had arrived (we didn't know what we were in for, music-wise, I mean) and being a little bit crowded where we were, we got a house on Rosegrove Lane (76), almost opposite Bob Birds Chippy (good one).

Now, it's back to the round ball game and Burnley were playing well this season, then they were drawn to play Lincoln (away) in the FA Cup, so Roy Hardacre and Eric Barker, who both worked at Drew's, were going. I don't know how it came about (maybe with me being cheeky) but John and myself managed to go with them, I think we all chipped in towards the petrol. I know one thing for sure, that Pointer scored for Burnley, so after we'd stopped jumping up and down (I used to do that when they won a throw-in), it was then that I remembered I had 10 goals in the pontoon at work and as it hadn't gone off for a few weeks it was over nine quid. I thought, that'll keep me in beer and smokes for a while, as that was more than a couple of weeks wages. So Burnley came away with a draw and I was singing, "I'm In The Money".

Burnley won the replay 2-0. The next round was Swansea away, the result was a no-score draw, back at Turf Moor Burnley won 2-1, then it was Bradford away and a 2-all draw. Some of the lads who went (I didn't) said Bradford was the better side, but Burnley really turned it on when they met again with a convincing 5-0 win in front of 52,000. Then Blackburn Rovers were the visitors and over 51,000 saw Burnley squander a 3-0 lead and Rovers went home with a draw, so John and I went to Ewood Park but came home disappointed after losing 2-0. In fact, I think that year BR went on to play Wolves in the final but lost 3-0. I shall come back to football shortly.

Now, on the home front, Grandad got worse so they came to live with us this time. I think that's the reason we hadn't moved too far away (just in case), I know I had to stop smoking, there was no room to breathe in. Now, I've got to try and think of where I was at work, yeah, that's it, we were at the docks watching the sack race. Meanwhile, rumours were doing the rounds at Drew's that the place could be folding, I thought, I'll worry about that when it happens.

This one day, Tommy was changing one of the wheels and I just happened to be busy watching all the girls go by (as it was a pastime I enjoyed), while whistling and winking at them, in that order. I had been known to wink and whistle, it just needed a bit more concentration that's all, then before I had chance to whistle at Tommy to warn him (well, it was no good winking) the object in question had fallen on his leg and he was like a bear with a sore head (or leg) and I thought, I'd better stay clear for a while as I could see he was hopping mad.

Now, I don't know about you lot but over the years I've noticed people get so angry in situations like this and they just can't seem to see the funny side of it. Now, before you moan and groan, I know this gag is as old as them thar hills but I'm going to use it to prove that laughter is, without doubt, the best tonic. So here's the scene, it's a building site (no, not on Bourke Street) and this entrepreneur just happens to be walking past when he sees this blur, at a closer look it's a bloke doing somersaults and back flips then landing on his feet, so the showbiz bloke (who wasn't one to let an opportunity go begging) said, "Here's a contract, sign on the dotted line."

The fella said, "You'd better get me mate signed up as he's the one who hit me on the foot with the sledgehammer."

After I'd told that one to Tommy I said, "I'm not playing hopscotch with you, you'd win hands down, or with a leg in the air and another thing, I think you should stop drinking or at least cut down on the hops, otherwise you'll have to re-tyre."

He said, "You've been very sharp these last few days."

I told him, "With the Grandparents being there I have to kip in the knife drawer."

Not long after that Tommy finished, he retired I think. Now, I don't know where Wilf came from, I'm having a little bit of trouble with this one as I don't think he came from inside, meaning the factory (and not clink). Or if they advertised for a driver, but I do know that he took over and I was to show him the ropes, which I did. He said, "Oh yeah, they're nice ones," then I coiled them up, cobbed them in the cab and we were on the road.

I said, "Did you hear about the little Polar Bear who went up to his Mum and shouted, 'Mum, am I a real Polar Bear?' She said, 'I'm busy cleaning this fish for your old mans tea, go and ask him.' So he sings out, 'Papa, am I a real Polar Bear?' Dad said, 'Of course you are.' The cub said, 'There's no Black or Brown Bear in me then?' 'Nah,' Dad asked, 'why?' The little Polar Bear said, through chattering teeth, 'I'm bloody freezing!'"

So, as the days rolled on we became close friends and Wilf had a good voice, he used to go singing in the clubs (like a lot of blokes did). I went with him a few times and one thing I noticed, he'd always get a fair share of ale bought by the audience, I think that's why he took me along and they were terrific nights but most times we both looked worse for wear. Then this one morning I told him I woke up in the fireplace, he said, "How did you sleep?"

"Like a log," I said, and then once we got on the road we started singing and we sang every song that truckie knew.

Now I said I'll be back talking about Burnley, well here I am, and as you know this is an autobiography and they really were a big part of my life, so after their good cup run a lot of the lads reckoned they'd have a chance for the Championship. It came down to the last match and they had to win against Man City (away). By the time we got there the gates were already locked, they say first in best dressed, I thought I looked smart with my azure shirt and blood spots (from shaving) but I couldn't get in. A lot of people asked me where I got my Claret and Blue shirt, I just told them it was a one off, like my left ear. It's a good job I didn't shave me feet or "My Left Foot" would have been in the wars.

Right, where are we, stood outside Maine Road, of course, and demanding to know why. We found out later there was a crowd of over 65,000 because a lot of Wolves fans had gone hoping that Burnley would lose, then they (Wolves) would win the title. To anyone who hasn't done this, I can tell you, it's a strange feeling listening to a game outside the ground, we wondered why it had gone so quiet, Burnley had scored in the first five minutes, we were shouting, "Blow your little wooden whistle, Ref." I don't think he heard us, then by the noise we knew that City had equalised, but after half an hour Burnley were back in front. Half-time came, they went in on the score, and then with forty-five minutes to go, could Burnley hang on?

With the ooh's and ah's it sounded like City were throwing everything at Burnley, including the kitchen sink. Then it was all over (Red Rover) and Burnley (our team) were the Champions of England. So there we were all hugging and kissing while wishing there were some girls. In fact, there was a couple of crackers but they were Wolves fans and by the look on their faces you could tell they were in no mood for any huggin' or kissin'.

Back row: Elder, Robson, Cummings, Blacklaw, Miller, Angus, Pointer
Front row: Connelly, McIlroy, Adamson, Pilkington, Meredith

On the way home we weren't sure whether to head for Turf Moor but once we got halfway down Manchester Road it was evident that the Town Hall was the venue, the police were out in force (so to speak) as there were thousands of fans who had turned up. Some of the lads I talked to hadn't been to the game but when they heard the result they came down to join in the celebrations. Plus there were plenty of chicks who, by the way, didn't mind being hugged and kissed. The chant went up for our heroes and, as if on cue, they appeared, but there was one missing. Then it was, "We want Mac, we want Mac!" But it turned out nobody expected such a big reception and the team coach had dropped him off near his home.

Now, seeing as we were into the wee small hours of the morning it was time to hit the road, otherwise I'd be going straight to work. By the way, winning the title, that meant Burnley would be playing in Europe next season, anyone who can't get to the return leg (at Turf Moor) these results will be broadcast on IMR (my radio), stay tuned. The semi-finals had been decided in the European Cup, Real Madrid had accounted for Barcelona 6-2 (on aggregate) and Eintracht Frankfurt had given Rangers a thump 12-4 (on agg), so the scene was set for a great final. I stayed home that night as it was being shown live, I said to Pop. "Are you going to watch the match tonight? It should be a good showdown."

"I wouldn't look at that foreign rubbish if you paid me."

After I'd given him the ten bob note we sat down to watch the game, he said, "Who are you going for?"

"Real Madrid 2-1, what about you?" I asked.

"The other mob 1-0."

Then the game was underway, Eintracht scored first, Pop said, "I told you 1-0."

I said, "It's not over yet."

Then Real Madrid equalised, three minutes later they added another, I was jumping up and down shouting, "That's it, 2-1, and it'll stay that way!"

But RM had other ideas and they scored again right on half-time. Pop said, "If Eintracht can come out and get a quick goal then the other lot will have a game on their hands, you mark my words."

His words were marked accordingly and I told him he passed the test, then it was time for the second half and RM quickly sorted the men out from the boys by scoring three goals in fifteen minutes. Then after seventy-odd minutes E got one back, but not long after that RM banged in a quick one then E managed another. I said, "The writing's on the wall, it's not your words then."

Pop said, "Certainly not, but you'll find a cloth under the sink, go and wipe 'em off, there's a good lad."

I said, "Can't you wallpaper it?"

"Not before your mother gets back and if she sees that she'll go up the wall."

"Well, can't we just get her to do it while she's up there?" Then adding, "Okay, I'll do it, and you better give us a shout if anybody scores."

But they didn't and it finished 7-3, what a game! Now, Puskas (RM) slotted in four, one from the spot, and Distefano had a stroll in the park picking up a hat trick. By the way, it was played at Hamden Park, Glasgow, in front of 135,000 (that's a lot). For those of you who thought I had all that in me noggin, I only had a few details, like the venue plus teams and, of course, the score, the rest I had to check on and I thoroughly enjoyed it as it brought back good memories.

Now, at this stage Grandads condition has worsened. In those days most people seemed to keep their parents at home, rather than put them in hospital. Looking back now it must have been very hard for them, as in bathing, changing and feeding, there was not a lot anyone else could do but you just made sure they were comfy. I'd go in to say hello to him but half the time he was drifting in and out. I came home from the flicks this night, I couldn't tell you which film I saw (it's a wonder), and I knew as soon as I walked in that something was wrong because their door was closed and Uncle George and Aunty Mona were there and looking at dear Grandma's face… they say every picture tells a story.

She was sat there, not knowing how to accept it, but there again, it must have been a big relief as she looked worn out. I think the kettle was put on for the umpteenth time then before long Grandma was telling us all those stories that we'd heard lots of times and, now with Grandad gone, it was like they had a special meaning and were written into our minds for ever and I can bring them out whenever I want to remember him and have a good laugh.

So this one day, Grandma was coming home and she kicked this piece of paper, she later realised it was a ten bob note, Grandad said, "Why didn't you kick it into Saltburn Street?"

Now, Grandma would always seem to upset him by giving him a kiss. Even when people were there she'd go up to him and give him a big smooch, just when he was into a cowboy book, and he'd say, "Stop fussing."

Other times he would have a ciggy dangling from his lips, she'd plonk one on his forehead, he'd say, "What's wrong with you woman?" And as a lot of the family knew, he didn't like wearing his false teeth, in fact, he used to hide them.

They were going on holidays and she'd found his choppers and shoved them in the case, when they were on the train she said, "You'll have to wear your teeth when we get to the digs," but unbeknown to Grandma, while he'd been putting some hankies in, he'd spotted the dentures and out they came! So poor Grandma, she couldn't win.

I went into the front room to say goodbye to Grandad, which wasn't easy, but I thanked him for being there in the early days (after Dad left) and for trying to keep me under control and a couple of days later the service was held at Lowerhouse and then he was buried at Habergham. It was a sad day, but like families do, they get through them, and then life went on as it does. Later in the year Burnley, of course, were in the European Cup. Their visitors were the French team Reims, Burnley showed the fans they were in control with a 2-0 win, I sang out:

They seek him here and also there
Those Frenchies search everywhere
Is he in the defence or the attack
That damned elusive Jimmy Mac

A few of us had made enquiries (just for a laugh) at the newsagents to see if they were running a charabanc to France for the second leg, he said, "I don't think so, as I've got to be up early in a morning to get the paper lads sorted," as we were leaving the shop he said, "just for a matter of interest, which way would you go?"

One of the lads shouted back, "Most probably through Hapton."

So the second leg came, we lost 3-2 but won 4-3 on agg. Before we knew it Christmas was upon us, we made the best of it as it wasn't the same being the first one without Grandad. Not long after the New Year, Hamburg came to Turf Moor, The Clarets turned it on again (did they ever) in front of 47,000 they won 3-1 then in the second leg Hamburg went to town and when they came back they won 4-1, winning 5-4 on agg.

Now, I'm not sure if I've got my facts right but I think they're near enough so hopefully nobody will have me up before the Tribunal. Grandma moved out and went to live in Padiham, Mum said, "I'd make sure your passport is in order or they won't let you in!"

Bob, Jim and Brian

Brian (who I told you about earlier), Bob's friend, came to live with us (what a character) and the best thing about it (from my point of view) he was a Burnley fan, whereas Bob and Pop didn't go on, I think they followed their results via TV or papers and, of course, Jim was too young so that was out of the question to take him.

Chapter
25

I mentioned before about classical music, well, I reckon there's a few pages gone under the bridge but at least I'm back to it now (I suppose that's the main thing). Bob and Brian loved the classical stuff, as I said, I didn't mind it but not as keen as them, they'd sit there listening while staring at the ceiling, I thought it must want papering, but I'm not the one that's going to tell Pop as he could hit the roof (so to speak).

One of their favourite pieces was "Capriccio Italien" by Tchaikovsky, well I can tell you, when music like that is placed on the turntable at every opportunity, it tends to seep into your mind, so folks, before I knew it I'd been brainwashed and I'm glad I was. If you've heard it you'll know what I'm talking about, if you haven't had the pleasure, do yourselves a favour, go out and get it right now (if not sooner), as it should still be available in most record (CD) shops.

Now, this one day I'd been reading the Express (see folks, I did learn something at school) and I saw this advertisement which read 'Fancy Living Down Under? As soccer (that's what they called it) players are wanted in Australia. If you are interested you can write to the Manager at…such and such' I thought, that must be near Woy Woy or Woop Woop and he could be Chinese as his name was E Mu. I said to Mum, "Can I go?"

She nodded her head and said, "No."

"Why not?"

She came back with, "Who's going to help Pop with the wallpapering?"

Quick as a flash I said, "I'll ask 'em if I can come back when he's got a big job on, so please can I go?"

She said, "No," again, I demanded to know why and she said, "I'll tell you, because your tea's ready, that's why."

"Put it in the microwave."

She said, "What on earth is a microwhatchamacallit?"

"It's something to put your grub in to heat it up," I said.

"And what sort of food would you put in one of them?" she asked.

"Most probably microchips," I said, "and that's one to me."

Now that story, like most of the others I've told you, I had a bit of fun with it. You know something, I always wondered what would have happened if I'd have made that move. I realise I can't turn back time (luckily I can in the book) but maybe if Mum and Pop had encouraged me I could have got cold feet anyway.

Back at work things went along as they tend to do and by this time we'd formed a good friendship, we were always cracking jokes and having plenty of laughs and half the time playing tricks on each other. Now with Wilf being a singer, I think "Frankie Baby" was the number one for him, here's a few that he used to sing which I liked: "Come Fly With Me", "I Could Have Danced All Night", "I've Got You Under My Skin", "Up A Lazy River", "You Make Me Feel So Young" and one I loved to listen to, "Zing Went The Strings Of My Heart". I don't think it was a big record for Frank (there was just something about it for me), in fact, I haven't heard it for a while, I must dig it out (or up). I said to him, "You've got a real gift being able to sing like that."

He said, "Everybody's got a gift."

I said, "I don't know, when I belt a song out it sounds like someone's throttling next doors ginger Tom, so I must have the gift of wit."

He said, "Would you spell that?"

I said, "Just keep driving and sing me another song."

"Certainly," he said, "which one?"

"All The Way (to Manchester)."

Now, along the line a few blokes had told us about this great transport café where you could get plenty of grub and a brew for reasonable prices. You'd see a lot of the drivers getting stuck into steak pudding, chips and not forgetting mushy peas, but my favourite at the time would have to be egg and bacon toasted butties (yum), I'm slavering at the minute just thinking about 'em, in fact, they could be requested for lunch, I'll have a word with the chef.

So we would take turns in who'd pay for the meals, this one day we went in and Wilf said, "I'll get these, so what do you want, Mickey me boy?"

I said, "I haven't made my mind up yet, what are you having?"

"I'll try the rollmop and salad."

My first thought was this is no time to be cleaning the floors, then I said, "What on earth is that?"

He gave me a sideways glance and said, "Look it up."

So right there and then, in front of all those people, to heck with the embarrassment I said, and I quickly whipped it out, my dictionary I mean. Now, I don't know if you've ever looked up rollmop (it's not a pretty sight), I wouldn't recommend it to anyone. For those of you who don't know, it's an uncooked herring fillet rolled around onion slices, you can also use gherkin or pickled cucumber and then serve it as a hors d'oeuvre and if you've ever sneaked a peek at a horses doofah, that's not a pretty sight either. So I said to him, "How do you know all these things?"

He said, "By reading and travelling, as that broadens the mind and even when you get married you'll soon learn what's what. Anyway, enough of that, what do you want to eat?"

"I think I'll try that four-course special meal deal."

He said, "What in blue blazers is that?"

I said, "It's baked, mashed and roasted potatoes plus chips."

"No doubt about it, you're a nutter."

"So it's you that's spreading all those vicious rumours is it?" I said, "but a word of warning, don't call me Alice."

For those amongst you who don't know, Alice Nutter was one of the Pendle Witches who was lynched, the angry mob showed her the rope while shouting, "We got noose for you."

She sang back, "Can you put it around my waist as I have a boil on me neck."

So back to the diner, we were sat there letting the meal digest and finishing off a pot of tea when in walked a gang of motorcyclists. They went up to this blokes table, who just happened to be sat there having his soup and dumplings, they poured the soup over his head and stuck the dumplings in his pocket, the bloke got up from his table, walked over to the cash register, paid for the meal, went outside, got into his truck and then drove off. One of the bikies said to the chap behind the counter, "He wasn't much of a man."

"You're right," said the chap, "and he's not much of a driver either because he just ran over six motorbikes."

You would have noticed before that I mentioned The Chairman Of The Board, there was a reason for that, now just give me a couple of seconds and I'll try to remember what it was, yes folks, I've got it, I'd been trying for a while to put something together on Old Blue Eyes. Then John gave me a couple of books about Frank, and also a list of songs that he sang during his career and, would you believe, there's over 1,500. I thought, "Jeepers Creepers" I can't wait to give these the once-over with me peepers and I can really go to town with this lot (I don't know what I'll do when I get there but knowing me, I'd think of something). Now, with all those titles it was possible to put three or four and sometimes more into a verse, like I'd done with 'Beatlemaniac'…

> *So it was head down and bum up*
> *And then to give it all I've got*
> *But a few mins in that position*
> *I know what I gave was not a lot*
>
> *I shouldn't have tried it*
> *As I'm no longer a scamp*
> *Then I was stuck there*
> *Yeah, with writers cramp*

Once things got back to normal it didn't take all that long to get it into some sort of a story. Then, of course, the same applied as with the others, that the challenge was to make it rhyme, well folks, the kettle's just boiled so I'll go and make a brew and you can read…

The September Of My Years

> *Let's take a musical mystery tour*
> *Along the corridor into my mind*
> *The spotlight's on a man and his music*
> *His songs that I name I'll underline*
>
> *First <u>I'm Gonna Sit Right Down</u>*
> *<u>And Write Myself A Letter</u>*
> *<u>Looking At The World Through</u> *RCG's*
> *I must admit it's 'Getting Better'   *B*
>
> *<u>Oh What A Beautiful Mornin'</u>*
> *All around me are <u>Blue Skies</u>*
> *We'll go on a <u>Sentimental Journey</u>*
> *And you can travel through my eyes*
>
> *Now that I'm <u>Getting To Know You</u>*
> *And <u>I've Got You Under My Skin</u>*
> *<u>Somewhere A Voice Is Calling</u>*
> *<u>You And I</u> can <u>Begin The Beguine</u>*
>
> *<u>Let's Take An Old Fashioned Walk</u>*
> *Go <u>Down By The Old Millstream</u>*
> *<u>Let's Get Away From It All</u>*
> *And pretend we're <u>Deep In A Dream</u>*
>
> *We'll sprinkle in some <u>Stardust</u>*
> *Take <u>Something Old, Something New</u>*
> *Stir in <u>That Old Black Magic</u>*
> *Then add <u>Soliloquy</u> parts 1 and 2*

He was <u>Born Free</u>, <u>Strictly USA</u>
His blood was <u>Red White And Blue</u>
He would become a great singer
He'd have <u>All This And Heaven Too</u>

The teenager was nicknamed Slacksy
He liked physical training and swimmin'
When he hit a <u>Wave</u> down <u>By The Sea</u>
The young lion was swimmin' with women

Frank got interested in music quite young
He said it soothed the savage breast
He'd sing <u>Downtown</u> on <u>Saturday Night</u>
And his audience was very impressed

He was building himself a career
The construction was on the way
By using the old <u>Cement Mixer</u>
He made himself <u>Feet Of Clay</u>

<u>Let's Do It</u>, name the <u>Good Old Songs</u>
But fair dinkum, where do I start?
I like <u>Summer Wind</u> and <u>Granada</u>
Plus the 'Unforgettable' <u>Young At Heart</u>   *NKC

He'd sing <u>A Dream Is A Wish</u>
And you are just a <u>Dream Away</u>
<u>Meet Me Tonight In Dreamland</u>
Then we'll take a <u>Dreamer's Holiday</u>

He sang <u>I Couldn't Sleep A Wink Last Night</u>
When I do <u>It's The Same Old Dream</u>
<u>You'll Always Be The One I Love</u>
<u>If You Are But A Dream</u>

<u>Call Me Irresponsible</u> he sang to Nancy
Or <u>Call Me Up Some Rainy Afternoon</u>
Later <u>Can I Steal A Little Love</u>
<u>By The Light Of The Silvery Moon</u>?

<u>Yes Indeed</u>, <u>Come Fly With Me</u>
Let's <u>Take A Chance</u> on love
He sang <u>From Here To Eternity</u>
You're <u>My One And Only Love</u>

Singing I'm <u>A Fella With An Umbrella</u>
And not a sign of <u>Stormy Weather</u>
<u>The Night Is Young</u> and <u>You're So Beautiful</u>
It's <u>A Lovely Way To Spend An Evening</u> together

He joined Skelly, Patty Prince and Tamby
They'd sing <u>Tenderly</u> <u>More And More</u>
The group sang in <u>The Hungry Years</u>
Known simply as The Hoboken Four

Nancy and Frank were more than <u>Just Friends</u>
They exchanged vows in <u>Love And Marriage</u>
He'd purchase <u>A Cottage For Sale</u>
They drove there in a horseless carriage

He cut a disc with Dorsey
It was called <u>The Sky Fell Down</u>
Now his <u>Nice'n'Easy</u> technique
Is the talking point in Shanty Town

TD said you could feel the excitement
As soon as the kid got up to sing
When he sang <u>For Me And My Gal</u>
They crowned him the King of Swing

He'd sing <u>People Will Say We're In Love</u>
He was liked by Presidents and boxers
Then while singing <u>Close To You</u>
He was deafened by those bobby soxers

He sang <u>Let Us Break Bread Together</u>
He was getting known from coast to coast
Women would drool about <u>Paradise</u>
While most preferred him with toast

He said you gotta <u>Accentuate The Positive</u>
As he did with <u>The Birth Of The Blues</u>
<u>Blame It On My Youth</u> he sang
I just love to <u>Ad-Lib-Blues</u>

Referred to as a pipe-cleaner in suspenders
And as far through as a tram ticket
Nevertheless he sang <u>Embraceable You</u>
He showed those critics where to stick it

In 1940 their first child is born
She is <u>Nancy</u> with the laughing face
He's the proudest dad in <u>Watertown</u>
When <u>Little Girl Blue</u> wears <u>Blue Lace</u>

He was the Pied Piper of Hoboken
When singing <u>Alexander's Rag Time Band</u>
And while <u>April Played The Fiddle</u>
He was <u>The Number One Guy In The Land</u>

In '42 he recorded four songs
The Song Is You and Night And Day
Another was The Lamplighter's Serenade
And The Night We Called It A Day

Then in July of the same year
He sang Light A Candle In The Chapel
As well as There Are Such Things
Which was a hit in the Big Apple

There were many songs about L.O.V.E.
He'd sing Love Is Here To Stay
Everybody Loves Somebody sometime
So Love Me As I Am today

Love Isn't Just For The Young
And Love Looks So Well On You
Now Love Is Sweeping The Country
Love Me 'As I Love You'   *SB

In '44 a second child is born
Named Franklin after President Roosevelt
He sang to his son The Cradle Song
As he gave that Jack Daniels a belt

People would call him Mr Success
Yes, he was That Lucky Old Sun
Bang Bang, he sang I'm the right calibre
And not just another son of a gun

He'd sing somewhere Over The Rainbow
Every cloud contains a silver lining
Once Upon A Time he was unknown
But now the Star is brightly shining

He made Anchors Aweigh with Gene Kelly
They wore those Bell Bottom Trousers
Then they sang We Hate To Leave
While playing to capacity packed houses

He then sang with Jimmy Durante
The Song's Gotta Come From The Heart
Snozzle had been going For A While
Now Frank was off to a flying start

He'd sing Well Did You Evah with Bing
Who was known to us all as 'The Crooner'
When Frank sang The One I Love
His nom de plume became 'The Swooner'

With Pearl Bailey he sang the song
A Little Learnin' Is A Dangerous Thing
He said, you know Crosby's Worried Now
I've started to Learn To Croon like Bing

In '48 a third child arrives
She was christened Christina
All their friends said Ain't She Sweet?
Then gave her the nickname 'Tina'

Kisses And Tears he sang with Jane Russell
He was now in demand More than ever
He co-authored I'm A Fool To Want You
And in his hat went another feather

A White Christmas was always celebrated
Their home decorated with Mistletoe And Holly
Satchmo came over for a singalong
They'd sing Jingle Bells and Hello Dolly

There was Swinging On A Star
And Three Coins In The Fountain
Love Is A Many Splendoured Thing
So Go Tell It On The Mountain

Nancy said It's Over, It's Over, It's Over
So inevitably they parted
He was Bewitched, bothered and bewildered
Not to mention broken hearted

When it's The End Of A Love Affair
He sang It Could Happen To You
As Time Goes By you will know
I Only Have Eyes For You

You are My Kind Of Girl, Ava, he said
Cherry Pies Ought To Be You
You Brought A New Kind Of Love To Me
Just with The Charm Of You

He sang I'll Never Let A Day Pass By
I seem to be Looking For Yesterday
Also, The Things We Did Last Summer
Now I Fall In Love With You Every Day

He'd sing The Way You Look Tonight
So Aren't You Glad You're You?
You'd Be So Nice To Come Home To
Baby, I Get A Kick Out Of You

You know how he loved <u>Manhattan</u>
But sang <u>Chicago</u>, it's <u>My Kind Of Town</u>
I like <u>Just In Time, How About You?</u>
As well as <u>Bad, Bad Leroy Brown</u>

Now <u>I Got It Bad</u> and <u>That Ain't Good</u>
But I suppose it's for the best
Last night <u>I Had The Craziest Dream</u>
So <u>I Guess I'll Have To Dream The Rest</u>

I'm an easygoing fella
<u>Ask Anyone Who Knows</u>
I will resume with my story
So be prepared for <u>Anything Goes</u>

Frankie sang <u>Luck Be A Lady</u>
Along with <u>The Lady Is A Tramp</u>
She detested the <u>Rain</u> in <u>California</u>
Because it's cold and it's damp

He called Ava <u>My Funny Valentine</u>
Although they were starting to disagree
"I've still got my career, baby," he said
And <u>They Can't Take That Away From Me</u>

Along with Dean, Sammy, Peter and Joey
Their infamous 'Rat Pack' was born
If you ever needed their assistance
You only had to <u>Come Blow Your Horn</u>

They had that <u>Devil May Care</u> attitude
Those halcyon <u>Days Of Wine And Roses</u>
<u>The Best Is Yet To Come</u> they sang
To the hecklers they thumbed their noses

<u>We're Glad That We're Italians</u>
Sang Francis Albert and his old pal Dino
<u>I Will Drink The Wine</u>, toasted Frank
As Dino filled his glass with vino

The press hounded FS <u>Day By Day</u>
He said, "Reporters are parasites and boars"
<u>I'll Be Around</u> singing <u>Some Other Time</u>
But frankly speaking, <u>You'll Get Yours</u>

Frank was Chairman Of The Board
While young Elvis was Rock'n'Roll King
They sang <u>Witchcraft</u> and <u>Love Me Tender</u>
And produced a <u>Ring-A-Ding-Ding</u>

Duke Ellington had a great orchestra
So did Billy May and Nelson Riddle
Frank was in his element in the studio
When he was <u>Smack Dab In The Middle</u>

Not often did he sing <u>Off Key</u>
He was a perfectionist through and through
And <u>If</u> by chance <u>The Music Stopped</u>
He sang to the musos, <u>I Will Wait For You</u>

<u>Fly Me To The Moon</u> and <u>Pennies From Heaven</u>
He did with Count Basie and his band
It was <u>Nice Work If You Can Get It</u>
And the audience was at his command

Nice ones were <u>Charmaine</u> and <u>Clementine</u>
<u>Lost In The Stars</u> and <u>Ciribiribin</u>
He was <u>The Man In The Looking Glass</u>
And a better man than me <u>Gunga Din</u>

He serenaded <u>The Caretaker's Daughter</u>
With <u>Are You Lonesome Tonight</u>?
But for <u>Sweet Lorraine</u> and <u>Mrs Robinson</u>
Were they just <u>Strangers In The Night</u>?

He's <u>The Man With The Golden Arm</u>
He wore 'Cufflinks And A Tie Clip'   *NS
He'd sing I'm <u>Always Available</u>
Yes Ma'am, this cat was hip

Then of course there was <u>Monique</u>
<u>The Girl Who Stole The Eiffel Tower</u>
<u>Whispering</u> to himself <u>C'Est Magnifique</u>
As he sneaked a peek in the shower

He sang <u>September Song</u>, <u>Where Or When</u>
Also the <u>Evergreen</u>, <u>Hello Young Lovers</u>
<u>You Brought A New Kind Of Love To Me</u>
Was from the LP Songs For Swingin' Lovers

There was <u>Send In The Clowns</u>
<u>Winners</u> and <u>Here's That Rainy Day</u>
When under the <u>Moonlight In Vermont</u>
He'd sing <u>Put Your Dreams Away</u>

<u>Look To Your Heart</u> and <u>Our Town</u>
They were from <u>The Impatient Years</u>
<u>Five Minutes More</u> and <u>The Tender Trap</u>
Are now <u>Among My Souvenirs</u>

He sang *You Turned My World Around*
You Are The Sunshine Of My Life
Will your love *Satisfy Me One More Time*?
What Are You Doing The Rest Of Your Life?

And so he'd started *A Fine Romance*
He'd said, "When I'm with Mia *It's Magic*"
They tied the knot in July '66
It lasted two years, which was tragic

He sang about *New York, New York*
So good they named it twice
His 'True Love' was gambling at Vegas   *BC:GK
Just on the roll of the dice

She's The Right Girl For Me, he said
I know it's *The Right Kind Of Love*
Suddenly It's Spring, he confessed
And *I'm In The Mood For Love*

He sang the song *My Bride*
When he made *Barbara* his wife
The reception was a lavish affair
And the cake was cut by *Mack The Knife*

Once I visited *America The Beautiful*
I Left My Heart In San Francisco
You know these *Accidents Will Happen*
There in *The Oldest Established* disco

Then when I'm in a *Melancholy Mood*
Believe me *I Whistle A Happy Tune*
But when I sing *Something Stupid* happens
That's why I whistle better than I croon

I'll go on listening to his music
Most probably *Till The End Of Time*
His voice gets better when I hear it
Time After Time, after '*Time After Time*'   *CL

Yesterday he sang *Something* on the radio
I said, "*There Goes That Song Again*"
There'll Be Some Changes Made shortly
Nearly *Empty Is* this rhyming pen

Frank, Liza and Sammy came to Melbourne
And *Together* they sang *We Three*
What an entertaining experience
For John, Rhonda, Audrey and me

<u>*I Didn't Know What Time It Was*</u>
Yes, it's *'Funny How Time Slips Away'*   *WN*
You know <u>*I Could Write A Book*</u>
About <u>*All My Tomorrows*</u> *'Starting Today'*   *E*

Peter, Sammy and Dean have passed on
Frank said *'Arriverderci Roma'* to his mates   *DM*
The Lord's Prayer was spoken to <u>*Our Father*</u>
Then he sang <u>*Open Up Them Pearly Gates*</u>

Remember <u>*Violets For Your Furs*</u>
<u>*I'm Confessin'*</u> and <u>*Song Sung Blue*</u>
I won't <u>*Forget To Remember*</u>
It's <u>*Misty*</u> but <u>*I'll Be Seeing You*</u>

<u>*In The Wee Small Hours Of The Morning*</u>
Then, <u>*When Your Lover Has Gone*</u>
Just <u>*Wrap Your Trouble In Dreams*</u>
Let <u>*Frankie And Johnny*</u> sing a song

<u>*I Got The World On A String*</u>, he sang
While <u>*Cruising Down The River*</u>
Once he was <u>*Younger Than Springtime*</u>
Now he's the graceful <u>*Ol' Man River*</u>

During his lifetime he had <u>*High Hopes*</u>
Most importantly the ability to sell a song
He'd started with <u>*All Or Nothing At All*</u>
Then concluded with <u>*This Is My Song*</u>

Just think, if every day was like Christmas
So we could <u>*Buy A Piece Of The Peace*</u>
The bloodshed would be <u>*Gone With The Wind*</u>
The <u>*Feudin' Fussin' And Fightin'*</u> would cease

<u>*Yes Indeedy, It's A Lovely Day Today*</u>
I hope <u>*It's A Lovely Day Tomorrow*</u>
You know <u>*God's Country, It's A Wonderful World*</u>
But <u>*It Worries Me*</u>, the trouble and sorrow

Now <u>*You Can Take My Word For It Baby*</u>
With this research I was assisted by John
His knowledge of Ol' Blue Eyes is invaluable
<u>*After All, Two Hearts Are Better Than One*</u>

<u>*After You've Gone, One Hundred Years From Today*</u>
He'll be <u>*Comin' In On A Wing And A Prayer*</u>
We'll be able to <u>*See The Show Again*</u>
<u>*Anytime,*</u> on Patrick's supersonic video player

And now The Old Master Painter
Has finally painted his masterpiece
Pretty Colours depict this Golden Moment
And he calls it his golden fleece

I've read this From Both Sides Now
Also From The Bottom To The Top
As it reads It's All Right With Me
But my wife She Says Ya Better Stop

You know, If I Had Three Wishes
Yeah, my friends I'd Do It Again
But If It's The Last Thing I Do
I'll put Inka Dinka Do in my pen

As I put my Head On My Pillow
In my Imagination he's my friend
So From The Bottom Of My Heart
This is The Beginning Of The End

Yes, it's The September Of My Years
And There Will Never Be Another You
I think back When The World Was Young
As I cling to those Memories Of You

Well As Long As There's Music
It's time for Auld Lang Syne
But just Before The Music Ends
I'll awake from this Dream of mine

Then we'll sing Glory Glory Hallelujah
As we've travelled each and every highway
Now Is The Hour so Goodbye Old Buddy
Yes, For You I wrote this My Way

I hope you enjoyed my screwball Style
I Apologise for the corny jokes
So now this is My Shining Hour
Until next time, Sorry, That's All Folks
Amen

Now to me, most of the verses make sense but there are others that I just can't explain, there is one line amongst that lot I will tell you about and why I put it in. Can you remember when we were at school the art teacher came into the story once or twice, well he's back (but not by popular demand). I've got to talk about him here as one of his sayings was used in a verse so I'll go through that with you, he once said, "Do you know what, Spencer?"

Straight away I thought, 'I'm like an owl with laryngitis, frankly my man, I don't give a hoot.'

He continued, "I'll tell you right here and now you will never learn anything and if I've told you once I've said it time after time after time after time (that should be on page 215 verse 8), you'll never amount to much and just go through life wandering aimlessly," then adding, "am I wasting my breath?"

Under mine I said, "Most probably," but really, folks, he didn't waste his breath (he thought he did), I did remember what he said, then when it came time to try and work those seven words in, I knew Frank sang "Time After Time", and so did quite a few others but I was looking for something else I just couldn't put my finger on (it kept slipping off). Then, by the gow, it hit me, Cindy Lauper had a record out with the same title so what a stroke of luck, I thought, it's just a matter of sticking 'after' in between the two songs and Bob's your uncle, or in my case, me bruvver.

Now, throughout the book, while you've been reading most (or some) of the tributes, I was having a cuppa. Now, a lot of people in Lancs used to drink out of a pint pot (well, the men did), I don't know about the other Counties. And one thing I forgot to tell you when I mentioned Grandad, he loved a big pot and as a lot of you would remember in those days it wasn't worth the trouble to brew the teapot, as Grandads pot would take nearly all of it so the loose tea leaves were placed in his pot then brewed. But that way you got a lot of what we called 'floaters' so Grandad would take it over to the slopstone sink (at Saltburn Street) then while tilting the pot the flotsam and jetsam would be blown from the water, but what we thought was funny, he'd get back to the table with only three quarters of his tea left. So I think that's why I started to use one and Grandma used to say to me, "You're a real tay belly," and I still drink out of one, but the best thing about the pint pot is it just fits under the bed in case you're taken short during the night (only joking).

Just back to Burnley (football) for a minute or two, they'd finished off a good season and were fourth in the League, they also got to the semis of the League Cup after drawing twice to Aston Villa, they played on a neutral ground (Old Trafford) but went down 2-1, they met Spurs in the semi-final of the FA Cup (at Villa Park), I went to that match, they got belted 3-nil.

I don't think the score line did them justice and when you think back and realise what they had on their plate (so to speak) with being in the European Cup, the League Cup, the FA Cup, plus the League games, it wasn't a bad effort. And as a lot of Burnley fans would remember, when they took on Chelsea (who weren't a bad side at the time) at Turf Moor, during this period they more or less fielded their reserve side and in front of nearly 20,000 I thought they were a bit unlucky not to beat Chelsea and it finished in a 4-all draw.

So the new season started and they had some great gates (big green ones), their first game was a draw followed by two wins and a loss then they went berserk winning the next six. Now most of the lads like me had been to a few away grounds such as Sheffield (Wed & Utd), Birmingham and some of the Lancashire ones, so we thought, what about we go to London. We checked the fixture and Fulham were the next away side, just for a joke I asked Wilf to take us in the truck.

Now viewers, as you will have noticed I've kept it pretty clean up till now so I won't print his reply, anyway we went and had a great time and Burnley won (5-3), that was a bonus. Connelly got a hat trick, also Mac and Pointer got one each, well we thought this is a bit of alright, must do it again sometime, the next one away was West Ham.

We didn't fancy that. But then we couldn't believe who the opponents were, none other than Spurs, they were always good games when these two met, I thought if we get a point it won't be a bad result. There was a crowd of over 56,000 and quite a few from Burnley had made the trip but like me they were disappointed, Pointer had managed to get a couple, but Spurs said anything you can do we can do better and they certainly did by winning 4-2. I'll have a break from that but come back to it near the end of the season.

I'll tell you this story now, when I was reading up on Frank Sinatra, here's something that caught my eye but I visited the Doctors and he prescribed me some ointment and after a couple of days I was back to normal.

Yes, I'd read about the Dorsey boys, Jimmy was born in 1904 and died in June 1957, Tommy was born in 1905, he died in November 1956. Now you don't have to be a Rocket Scientist to work it out that they both died young (in their fifties). In 1934 they formed The Dorsey Brothers Orchestra, there were plenty of arguments as they always disagreed, so in 1935 Tommy walked out and Jimmy ran the band on his own. A lot of the big bands packed up in the late forties, the fifties came along and they were tough times then in 1953 the brothers were reunited and they started the band again. Now here's a little bit about Tommy, they said he was a very big eater and one night (or day) he choked to death in his sleep and as you would have noticed by the dates Jimmy died only eight months after his brother.

I don't know about you people but I thought that was very sad, mind you, they most probably crammed a lot more into their fifty-odd years than what an average person would and talking about brothers, did you hear the joke about the two that lived together? Now one of them, as they say, wasn't the full quid and his job in the household is to look after the place while the other lad is the breadwinner. There is a slight problem with this and that is the one who's been "Home Alone" can't wait to tell his brother all the news that's happened from around the world and as you can most probably gather his brother had heard it at work. But for the one who'd been at home the annoying part was, for instance, he'd say something like, "What about that train crash?"

And, of course, the worker would say, "Yeah, I know, I know."

Then he'd tell him, "There's hundreds of people feared drowned in those floods."

To which he'd reply, "I know, I know."

So this one day he'd changed the beds, done all the washing and hung it out, so he decided to go for a walk and get some fresh air into his lungs. Then he was about half way through the park when he noticed a few people were standing around looking at something, he couldn't quite make out what was going on, so he wandered over to see what all the commotion was about and there on the ground was a donkey who had carked it and the young chap who was with it was very upset and didn't know what to do. So our bloke in this story says to him, "Listen, if I can just borrow the donkey for a couple of hours, I'll help you to get rid of it later and even pay the expenses for you."

The sniffling boy said, "Thanks very much, Mister, but what are you going to do with it?"

Then he quickly told him what his brother was like and said, "I'll put it in the lav because every night when he gets home the first thing he does is he goes to the toilet, now can you imagine this, he'll come bolting out of there screaming there's a dead donkey in the karsi and then I'll say, 'I know, I know'."

Now readers, there's a few months (again) that I'm not sure about but I'll try to get it as near as I can, I'll call it the New Year. Now those rumours that had been circulating for a while at work were getting stronger and it looked like the end was nigh, a few of the blokes (and lads) had been looking for other jobs, I thought I'll cross that bridge when I come to it, besides, I didn't really want to take any time off work as I felt I'd be letting Wilf down, so we just kept turning up not knowing which day would be our last. So this one Friday night we'd got back and I was told to report to the office, yes folks, I put on a brave front (I couldn't see the back so I didn't worry about it), I wasn't inside all that long as they quickly gave me the DCM (don't come Monday).

I came out of that place in a daze, how could they do this (to me, those powers that be). I didn't want to accept it, then I realised there was a hell of a lot in the same boat, but as soon as Wilf saw me he knew straight away what had happened. I burst into tears asking him, "Why?"

He just said, "These things are sent to try you and they'll either make you or break you."

With that we shook hands and I sang out, "Wish Me Luck As You Wave Me Goodbye," which he did, then I was on my way.

I got home and told Mum, "I don't believe it."

She said, "What's that then?"

I said, "I've got my march(ing) orders, and it's only February," so I asked her, "can Feb March?"

"I don't know but April May," then Mum assured me it's not the end of the world and she added, "you'll be going to football tomorrow, that'll take your mind off it."

Yeah, I thought, there's a chance to let off some steam and then Monday, it's the start of a new chapter.

Chapter
26

Burnley were right on track in the chase for the title, in their last three games they had beaten Sheffield Wednesday 4-0, Manchester City 6-3 then drew with West Brom and today they were up against Birmingham City at Turf Moor. So a pint or three would hit the spot, then once on the pitch they ran amuck (I don't know what the muck was doing on the ground in the first place). The crowd would sing out, "2, 4, 6, 8, who do we appreciate, B-U-R-N-L-E-Y," then they would give it, "who for, why for, who the hell are we for?" and the crowd went up as one shouting, "Burnley," (they don't write 'em like that any more). They didn't let the fans down as they nearly kicked the sweep, the end result was 7-1 and even Jimmy Adamson got on the score sheet.

A few days later I got a start at a furniture store on Manchester Road, I had a bit of luck and made a sale on the first morning, the only problem was getting his purchase home for him that day, as they didn't deliver till Friday. He'd bought a smaller, lighter version of a Grandfather Clock so I assured him it wasn't all that heavy and with some good strong string we could strap it on his back and that should be enough to get him home. Once we'd done all that I held the door open for him but on his way through he lost his footing and went straight into a little old lady who was on her way in. There was such a crash, she picked herself up, dusted herself off and said, "Why don't you wear a wrist watch like anyone else?"

The Boss was out so he missed that, but then not long after I was called into the office, I thought, hey up, I could be in line for a promotion, but when the Boss said, "Spencer," I knew by the tone of his voice it wasn't good news week. He went on to say, "We've had a few complaints from some female customers about how you approach them and then when you go into your sales pitch. I've told you time after time after time after time, you are supposed to say 'excuse me Miss, may I be of some assistance' and not 'hi gorgeous, can I show you something new in a double bed'," (hang about, he sounds just like the Art Teacher with the time after time line).

I said, "Are you trying to say I won't be here tomorrow?"

He said, "It should be quite clear that you don't need to wait around until morning tea."

So, under my breath, I said, "Well, it looks like there won't be a gold watch presentation."

Then I thought, right monkey, just you wait till me Mum hears about this, I'll tell her not to make the hire purchase payments this week and to settle up with the coal chap instead as he'd been giving us black looks for the past fortnight. Now thinks, seeing as the wardrobes are all lined up in a row, Michael, if you use your noodle you can start a "Chain Reaction" (that would have a domino effect) and then making it look like an accidental trip I stumbled into the first one then it didn't take long for the rest to follow suit and go crash bang wallop. Half the staff watched in disbelief while the other half were taking bets to see if it would stop before going down into the storeroom and then out through the loading bay. While all this was happening I winked at the pretty blonde who made up the wages and said, "If you won't meet me on the mattress, I'll see you in the spring."

Now, this friend of mine worked at the Post Office and during the busy periods they would put casuals on. He said, "Come down, you'll get a days pay (or two)."

I thought, what the heck, I've got nothing to lose so I went this one day and he showed me around, he said, "You can watch for a while if you like," but from what I saw (it was nothing to write home about) it looked pretty boring as the workers were stood up most of the time (without having a break) just sorting through all the English letters and the American letters and, of course, the French mail.

Another mate had a job at Thompson Park (on the boating lake), he said, "The next time you're passing, drop in," (I think he meant to see him, not the lake). I knew it wasn't all that far from Prestige so I thought, seeing as I'm so close I could always pop in there as you never know your luck in a big town, Stewart Granger (stranger) things have happened.

Now, it had been a few years, in fact I couldn't remember the last time I was there and I'd forgotten how big the place was, it didn't take long to find him, then he gave me a run down.

"Here's what," he said, not word for word (but near enough), "it was built in the late 1920's, over fifty-odd men were given the job, it was finished half way through the following year, then wildlife had been introduced just to give it that extra effect. They reckoned it was so busy that thousands had gone there in the first few days."

He went on to say the attendants were out in full force and giving the rowers instructions, the main thing being they all should keep to the left, there would be shouts of, "For goodness sake, number 23, will you stop crashing into 7."

And, "42 don't rock the boat."

Some kids in boat 32 were flobbing at the flamingos, a couple of lads in 65 had catapults and were pinging pebbles at the pelicans, one of the attendants told them to sit down and "Row Row Row Your Boat", then he sang out, "Come in 99, your time's up."

But his mate quickly said, "Hoy Cyril, we only have 76 boats."

And with that he cupped his hands over his mouth and hollered, "66, are you in trouble?"

After spinning me a yarn like that I shook my head (it rattled) and said, "I'm off then," I thought, I'll nip into the rubbity dub (pub) for a swift one. So after downing the liquid lunch I made my way towards Prestige (or Platers & Stampers, as some people call it). I knew I was getting close as there was a fork in the road, which I quickly stepped over (anyone not knowing what Prestige did, they made cutlery).

After inquiring I found out where the office was, I polished me shoes on the back of my jeans then I whipped out a matchbox and rubbed it up and down on the ocker peringer (finger) to try and get rid of the nicotine (in the nick of time). I went through the door, the young girl in reception had been watching me through the window. Once I got inside I could see she was just my cuppa tea, yeah, with two lumps, she said, "What can I do for you?"

Then at that precise moment she sneezed and the lumps I just told you about turned out to be her shoulder pads. So once she patted and pushed everything back to where it should be (they have a knack of doing that), she fluttered her eyebrows at me then said, "Sorry about that, but where were we?"

I wasn't one to let a chance like this go begging, so quick as a flash I said, "On the back row of the Odeon."

She said, "I don't follow."

"You would if you were on the back row of the Odeon."

She sorta looked down her nose at me (I thought, that snot a nice thing to do). Then she flashed a weak smile, or it could have been wind, I wasn't game to ask, but after all that I said, "The main reason I'm here is to put my name down for the next vacancy that comes up."

She said, "Okay then, I'll take you through to see the Personnel Officer."

When I'd filled the forms in I said, "Right, I've finished."

"Good," she said, "so now if you'll walk this way," I thought, if I do I'll be frog-marched to the nearest lockup or if I had been German they would have goose-stepped me and said, "do not pass 'Go' and do not collect £200."

So there I was, watching her rear end go every which way, in fact I'm sure she had shares in British Rail, yeah, a waggin' bottom. She introduced me to the bloke who did the hiring and firing then handed him the papers. I noticed he was glancing at the back of my jeans plus the sandpapered digit, I said, "Don't ask, you wouldn't understand."

He checked out my details and said, "If you'll sign on the dotted line you can start on Monday." I thought, that's good, I've got the weekend off, should I ask him if I get paid for it, no, I'd better not. I skipped gaily back into reception, I can assure you I wasn't gay, I just used to skip that way, then I sang out...

Hymn Number 434
O Love Divine How Sweet Thou Art
I'll see thee on Monday
As that's when I start

Now, most of the Burnley people will remember this, so I'll share it with the rest of you, there was a film made in and around Lancashire (1961) but it wasn't released until 1962 (so that's why I'm putting it in here). The film in question was "Whistle Down The Wind", starring Hayley Mills and Alan Bates, it was adapted from a novel by Mary Hayley Bell (Hayley's Mum) and directed by Bryan Forbes. It was the talk of the town as Hayley stayed at the Keirby, which just happened to be Burnley's newest hotel.

This next event came as a real shock and it affected quite a lot of the close-knit community and it was the Hapton Valley Colliery disaster. It was in the morning (of March 22nd) and a very black day for the place called Happy Valley. When the tragedy happened we heard the news on the radio at work and everything seemed to stop as most people were in a state of shock. Many of them said they had goosebumps, you could feel the chill going through the building and, by the way, it just had the same effect on me now (all those years later) that I'm writing about it. We didn't know the full extent of the damage (or lives lost) as the details were still a bit sketchy and then an updated bulletin came through saying twelve men had perished already and it could go much higher as, at this stage, they didn't know how many more were down there.

Now, it was up to the rescuers to get out any survivors and as quickly as possible, relatives had raced there hoping their loved ones were safe but no names had been released. There was a bloke in the next section to me (at work), he was hysterical, they told him to go home as his brother worked at the pit, it came out later he wasn't on that shift. Then it was reported that sixteen had been killed and there were still quite a few on the serious list and three more died later from their injuries.

What seemed to hit me the hardest was to think those young lads lives had been snuffed out just like that, as there were about six of them younger than me. There was a couple of stories going around (how true they were, I don't know), one was that some bloke didn't go in on the fateful day, the chap that had replaced him had died, with something like that on your conscience it would torture you forever and a day. Then came all the funerals and as you would imagine the streets were packed, I've never witnessed anything like that before and I hope I don't ever have to again.

Now anyone who has worked with knives would know how dangerous they are, you could have someone's eye out! This one day a bloke lost two fingers while working and he didn't even realise till he was saying goodnight to the Guv'nor. I had a bit of trouble with the transport and, like everyone else, if you missed a certain bus or train you were late and my problem was that extra five minutes in the cot. Then this one day I was told to report to the wigwam, the Big Chief wanted a word. I thought, we could have gone down behind the toilets and had a chinwag, plus a smoke, and splattered two birds with one spatula but no, he wanted it this way. I knocked on the flap, which isn't easy, then I entered and zipped it up behind me, while thinking he should have an office like anyone else. Once inside I sat cross-legged on the floor as I was dying to go to the loo, see, I knew we should have met there. He put his peace pipe down and said, "Spencer, do you know what time we start?"

I said, "Nope, they're always working when I get here."

Then he said, "You should have been here at seven this morning."

"Why, what happened?" And by the look on his boat race (face) I shouldn't have said that, in fact, it wasn't long after I had to finish for health reasons, yeah, he got sick of me, so now I was in between jobs.

We'll have a break and, yes folks, it's back to football (and I bet you're glad). Burnley were up there in the League and enjoying a run in the Cup. They beat Aston Villa away (in the League) then they had a slump after that and out of their last ten games they only won one, drew five and lost four. One of these was against Man U at Burnley, going down 1-3 and then Blackburn where they lost 0-1 (and that hurt) but they still managed to finish second in the title chase, which I suppose wasn't a bad effort. So that brings me to the Cup where they beat Queens Park Rangers 6-1 at Burnley. They drew with Leyton Orient 1 each then beat them away 1-0, Everton were next and they beat them at Turf Moor 3-1 in front of fifty-odd thousand.

I'd been to all the home games then they played Sheffield United away, which John and I went to and Burnley won 1-0 so that meant they were in the semis and up against Fulham at Villa Park (I went), and it ended in a 1-all draw. The replay was to be at Filbert Street (Leicester) and, of course, I wanted to go but it worked out a bit expensive so I thought I'd stay home and watch it on the radio (which I did) and The Clarets won 2-1 and both goals were scored by Robson. Now they were through to the final and of all the teams to meet it had to be Spurs as they were the top two teams and it was billed as the match of the century and that's what a lot fans wanted.

Now, I remember Mum was doing part-time work at Bob Birds and, of course, Bob knew a lot of people, he told Mum about a fella that came in for fish and chips on Fridays and he worked at Brooke Bonds. Then he went on to say maybe he could get your Michael a job and Mum, never short of a reply said, "He's a real tay belly (Brooke Bonds was a tea factory) so he should be in his element (and that's what she said she meant)."

She asked Bob to point this chap out when he came in, then the man in question walked in and Bob said, "That's him, Margaret."

She asked him if there was any chance of a job for her son and he said, "Aye, send the lad up."

So when Mum came home it was the old 'guess what' routine, my first guess was that she'd bought me an electric razor to stop me getting blood on my good shirts, she said, "No, but what a very good guess, now try again."

I said, "I'm in no mood to be guessing as my fish, chips and mushy peas are going cold."

She replied, "You are a spoilsport, but I'll tell you the story."

I thought, this could take a while so I might as well make myself comfy, I grabbed a quick pot of tea then said, "Okay, let me have it."

Now I swear blind she told me word for word what was said (and by whom), she even threw in the one, if there were two flies in a chip shop, which one was the cowboy? The one on the range. So she wound it up by saying, "I suggest you go up there tomorrow or ASAP."

I did just that, then it didn't take long to find the office, once inside I was told to wait and someone would come and give me an interview. The man in question came in and introduced himself (as Mr Milne) to me, then he asked some questions, told me to sign a couple of papers and said, "Can you start on Monday?"

I said, "Fine, fine, fine," I bet he thought we've got a right Goon here. So there I was, not knowing what to do with myself, so I thought I'd nip in the New Inn and give it a nudge as I hadn't been in there before and it could turn out to be the local (being so close to work).

Now here came a tricky bit and I asked myself this, did I want to go to Wembley (yes), did I have a ticket (no), could I afford it (no) and from the three questions the two no's outdid the one yes. But I thought I'll go to the top and get Mum's opinion, she listened to what I had to say then she said, "Mickey Plum, you're a funny un and you've a face like a scallion onion."

"I know that, but what's it got to do with football?"

"Nothing, but I don't want you to go to Wembley, in fact, if you don't go I'll buy you a brand spanking new bike with drop handle bars and that will do for your birthday then you can even go to work on it, how's that grab you?"

Well, I couldn't believe my ears (and now the Cup Final was the last thing on my mind). I said, "I'll drink to that."

"Oh no," she said, "there won't be any drinking and driving."

On me bike with Jim

So for the next few days it was my pride and joy and then came the final. All week I'd been reading the lead up in the papers and I thought they were evenly matched then came the time for the kick-off and Spurs didn't muck about and they scored in the first five minutes. The score stayed that way till half-time, not long after that Burnley equalised but, as me and Pop were still jumping up and down, Spurs scored again (and that hurt) and then with about ten minutes left Cummings handled the ball and, of course, a penalty was given and Blanchflower slotted it home to put the game well and truly out of Burnley's reach. So I suppose, in one sense, I'm glad I didn't go all that way to see them lose, I think it would've been hard to swallow.

Then Monday came and it was off to work, now there were quite a lot of people worked at Brooke Bonds and I do remember most of them, which is good for me. Here is the list I've come up with, there could be a few spolling (spelling) mistakes (so what's new) so sit in your favourite chair and I'll read these names out, men first…

B Allen and his sons, Dave and Bill; M Ashworth; A Baker and his son, Brian; R and A Bannister, brothers; B Barker; W Bridges; B Brown and his son, Bill, it was Bill senior who got me the job; P Brown; E Burke; B Burnett and his son, George; G Callaghan; B Cockett; T Cole; A Cook; V Dolan; J Dunleavy (that could be spelt wrong, I'll check it later); J Eastwood; B Feenie;

J Firkin; D Firth; W Fisk; F Forest; A and J Gent, brothers; T Goad; B Gorton; D Hargraves; A Heaton; J Hiam; A Hibbert; B Howcroft; B Hoy; J Jones; B Leaming; B Lockyer; B Markham; Mr Milne; H Mitchell; D Newton; A Overy; H Parkinson; H Pert and his son, Carl; F and B Rothwell, brothers; Mr Rush; J Rushworth; J Sager; A Salisbury; H Sharples; K Shepherd; H Simpson; K Smith; J Southwell; G Speak; J Strother; A Taylor; B Thompson; B Towers; E Walker; T Wallace; B Walne; R Walsh; and A Woodvine.

I hope your name was amongst that lot, I know mine wasn't. Now for the girls turn and alphabetically they are…

Marie and Marion Ashcroft, sisters; E Ashworth; A Barker; A Bromley; Miss Browning; E Bullen; B Burrows; M and D Campion, sisters; A and M Cockett, sisters; J Cotterill; S Creswick; B Dean; M Digger; V Driver and her daughters, Hazel and Linda; J Duckworth; G Edwards; A Etherington; F Fort; A Garnet; A Gibson; E and M Graham, sisters; these next five all had the same surname, let's see if I can get it right (I hope so), B and P Green, sisters; Ruth, Mary and Maureen Green, who I think were sisters; A Harris; P, K and M Haynes, sisters; V Heaton; B Howcroft; M Hudson; K Jones; C Jordan; S Kershaw; D and J Lee, sisters-in-law; L Lee, who I think was Joan's daughter, I'll take a chance on that; M MacDonald; C Madden; A Markham; E Parkinson; A Pepper; E Riley; J Riley, I don't think they were related; M Rothwell; D Sharples; M Smith; M Sparks; I Stacey; L Stubbs; C Tarren; E Taylor; S Wallace; J Walmsley; M Zarba.

You would notice quite a few sisters (I hope I got them right), all in all that tested me but it was fun. Now let's stay with the girls (yes please) and, as you can imagine, it wasn't all that difficult to line up a date, plus there was always a couple of the girls who would play matchmakers and put in a good word for the lads. Just thinking back, quite a few of the girls were straight outta school, sometimes you'd walk past and smile at them or say good morning and boy, did they blush, it was so funny. But I must admit the overalls or clothing (call it what you like, the girls know what I mean) and the hats, they didn't do them justice.

My first job was in what they called the Reclamation Area, the tea chests would come hurtling down the chute from upstairs, as that's where the Blending Crew worked and one of the hardest jobs was cleaning them out. They were placed on a bench and they were tilted so that made it better to get in as you had to scrape the lining out, but you had to be very careful as you could get a splinter or there would be a nail lurking (and that could be painful), especially if you just happened to be talking about Saturday's game or the new record by Elvis, which was always a big talking point and at this time it was "Return To Sender". How can I be so sure, you ask? My reply is, I've just looked it up, it's all part of the service.

Now, back to the story, the first lining was like a white tracing paper and you got rid of that as quickly as you could and then, of course, there was silver paper, or more like aluminium foil, I think that sums it up. So next time you see a tea chest just stick your bonce inside, I'll guarantee you won't hear the sea but you will certainly smell tea. Sorry about that, it just came from nowhere so I thought I'd stick it in, then at the end of the day, with all those splinters and nails against you, I finished with more cuts than a Russian phone book.

The white and silver paper was kept separate and then, when there was enough of it, it was put into a big press and came out in the shape of a bale. Any damaged tea chests would be fixed up then sent on their way, good as new. Let's go back to the silver paper, as you will know, when it's scrunched up into a ball it makes a good missile, so when the Boss was away the lads would come out to play and just like the school days there would be a lookout and most times we'd bombard him (just for something to do). The only trouble with that was if he shouted, "The Boss is coming!" you just had to take his word for it, but then after a couple of seconds if the Boss hadn't turned up it was on again and this time he'd cop the lot till he shouted, "Uncle," but his uncle wouldn't help him, he just kept pelting more.

There was a big room down the end and the tea chests arrived there via a gantry, which ran the length of the place. Once they got into the (store) room they were stacked according to their sizes and the other side of the room, that lead through to the yard, that's where we would load the trucks. I can't remember if we worked to a roster or not, I think we were just given different jobs when we turned up each day.

When I mentioned the names of the people who worked at Brooke Bonds there were two that I knew before I started work there and they were Bob and Ann Markham and they only lived a few houses further up from us on Rosegrove Lane and, of course, we went to school together. The reason I'm telling you this is you would have noticed by the list that not many Christian names were given, only the ones like father and sons, or sisters, that had the same initial and, to be perfectly honest with you (and you must admit I have been) there are about eight that I can't remember (and it bothers me). I don't want to show favouritism as I made lots of good friends (male and female) and hopefully you'll all come into the story somewhere along the way.

You know sometimes I hate that, when I just can't seem to get my pen around what I'm trying to say. On the other side of the coin I love it when I get my teeth into a good story and I manage to get in everything that I set out to, plus adding a few jokes (which are always waiting in the wings), or ad-libs, it certainly gives me a kick and I'm sure you will if I don't get on with the story.

Now to all the readers and those watching on the radio, you should remember earlier (don't worry folks, it's not a test, just a question) when I was on about names, as in Alan (Allan) and Ann (Anne), I do seem to get into trouble with spelling, as when the name is spoken it sounds the same anyway, or is it just me? So, hopefully to bring this to an end for once and for all, there were seven Ann's or Anne's, so I hope I haven't offended Ann or Anne. Right people, I'm going to throw this at you, do you know the girl (or woman) that Frank Sinatra sings about in "My Way"? Well, of course, it's one and the same that we've just been talking about, which goes 'Ann now the end is near'. Well, I thought it was funny Anne you should be used to me by now.

I know I've got the year right but (what do you mean, there's heaps of room for 'em), it's just a case of putting them in the right order, and I shouldn't think too many viewers will pick me up on this. It might not all be true what I put down on paper (but I assure you it's near enough) as I'm trying to avoid telling little white fibs. So, if you're ready we're off again, by now I'd had a date or two and then I got to know June and we started courting (as the saying goes), we'd met each others parents and June's Mum and Dad, Nellie and Jim, were great people, they made me a brew in a pint pot.

Me with a pint pot

Now, I'm not saying this wouldn't have happened (I'm glad it did) but it's funny sometimes how friendships start and, of course, with going out together I got to know June's sister, Lillian, and her husband, Alan (there's that name again) and his best mate, Terry (as they were in the Forces) and Terry's brother, Bob. Then through that meeting, plus Terry starting at Brooke Bonds, we became very good friends. I might just be getting ahead of myself but I'll mention this while I'm here, Terry met Beryl and they started going together and then later they got married, come to think of it, there were quite a few marriages through work, it would be interesting to find out just how many, so I wonder, if possible, that in itself could be a challenge (which I would enjoy), we shall see.

Now, you will have to forgive me as I drifted off, it's been a long day, in fact it must be after ten, I've had 5 o'clock shadow twice. Now I don't know about most of the readers but I'm enjoying this, it's like trying to fit a jigsaw together (yeah, a thousand pieces) and, of course, I'd had a birthday in amongst all of this. So I'd gone from a teenager to a whatever by just going to bed one night and waking up the next morning, simple as that (there was nothing to it), in fact, boys my age all over England were doing it and then, like lads do, we'd wish our lives away as we couldn't wait to get to that magical twenty-one.

In August, Marilyn Monroe died from an overdose so they closed the case by saying the verdict was suicide and, like a lot of folk, I didn't believe that for one minute. The reason I put that in was because there used to be a young lass who thought she was it an' a bit and she would sashay through the canteen with one hand on her hip teasing the lads, as females tend to do (Mae West style), but this kid seemed to have her wires crossed as she asked, "What's Marilyn Monroe got that I haven't?"

And one quick wit quipped, "A coffin!"

You would have noticed how no names were used then, any excuse to get a line in, yep, you'll see I don't need them.

June had a younger brother, Anthony, so if her Mum and Dad wanted a night out we'd baby-sit, which a lot of couples did. I mentioned music earlier and we were always up to date with new releases and young uns like us would buy the singles, the record player sure copped a belting. Other times we went down to the nearest pub (The Griffin, which was not that far from Little Cornwall) for a few jars. About now Frank Ifield hits number one with "I Remember You" and it stayed there for a month, the whole town was yodelling (or trying to), it sounded like the cats chorus.

I suppose we had better go back to work, well just for a short time, eh, in the (tea) Machine Room was where most of the girls worked, I was amazed at the machines, how the tea was put into packets and the finished product shot out the other end where it was greeted by the girls who would put it into parcels. Now, on the machines were glue, or gum, troughs (we'll call them that), at the end of the day the girls would clean their machines down but on a Friday night all those troughs were dismantled and then taken into what they called the Gum Room. You know something readers, I've always wondered this, why doesn't glue stick to the inside of a tube, I'll leave that with you and maybe you can fathom it out.

Now, in the room I just told you about there was a couple of big sinks which were used for soaking then cleaning the troughs, so for a bit of overtime I'd go up there with Vinny and, of course, Bill Brown Jr. (who used to work in the Machine Room) and he used to go out with Marie, I don't think they were engaged at this stage but they later married and we became good friends. Then there was a vacancy in there so I was given the job and I can tell you they didn't have to ask me twice, I couldn't believe me luck, working with all those girls and I suppose it's fair to say they were just as lucky.

Looking back, it wasn't really hard work but it kept you busy. Now, a lot of you will remember the bakery across the road (Farrers), great pies and cheap too, I used to nick over there and come back with a few goodies. Another great place was the fish and chip shop on Accrington Road and you went through the back and there was a café (the name escapes me), the food was yummy, I can still taste it. Then other times I'd shoot home for lunch, it wasn't that far (on me bike) and it broke the day up unless, of course, it was raining and if it happened to be doing that the (New Inn) pub used to put pie and peas on, so we'd go in there but it was best to only have one drink or you got the taste (as they say) and that made it hard to go back. So seeing as we're still at work, June and I had decided to part company, and not long after that she went to live in the States and we lost contact, so that story ended and it makes way for this one.

I said there were a couple of responses (from two ladies), well I have got permission to use one (and it's an honour), but at the minute I'm having trouble with the other so I'll do everything I can to get it sorted. Now, I'll go and get a cuppa and you can read…

Treasured Memories

In response to "That's My Rosegrove" I would like to say to Mr Spencer, I wish I could shake his hand and walk with him down Liverpool Road. I walked up and down that road for many years as I worked at Edmondson's Mill, I went to Rosegrove School before I was four years old and my children and grandchildren followed.

All my shopping was done in Rosegrove as I lived in Little Cornwall, the little village with three streets, Griffin, Hapton and Valley. I was born at 17 Hapton Street and married from 8 and had my children at 7, my eldest daughter was married from there and she had three children there.

I also left there in 1968 to come to Australia. I remember Rosegrove as he wrote it and, Mr Spencer, I still make potato pie and sad cakes. Those were the good old days, no murders, rapes or violence, we would enjoy ourselves without any money. We weren't always little angels, we would drive our parents round the bend, which always ended up with hard bare hands on bare flesh, still, it was all good fun. One thing we always kept was respect for our parents and elderly.

Thank-you again, Mr Spencer, for those Treasured Memories.

And I'd like to thank May (Hoyle) Feathers for that and it's nice when someone thanks you in print and, not only that, but I can put it in the book as it adds to the story and, even at this stage, I still need all the help I can get and hopefully I think I'll make it. Having said that, let me say this, there seems to be a slight problem with the old running sheet, yes folks, it's stopped, but knowing me I ain't gonna let a little thing like that slow me down.

Chapter
27

So about now I'd been out with Marion (Marie's sister) a few times. I do remember one date we had, Brooke Bonds ran an excursion to London (I don't know why, but they did) so the six of us (Marion and myself, Bill and Marie, Terry and Beryl) decided to go and have some fun, we certainly did and it was great. There should be a photo in the book, there we were lined up with those pigeons on our paws (I know they would have been alright in a pie with some mushy peas), after they'd flown away it was hard to get the grit off your cuff, yes, I said grit. Anyway, it was an excuse to nip to the nearest Hedy Lamar (bar) for a spruce up and we'd shout back to the girls, "You can come in if you like, but trust us, you look alright."

Marion, me, Bill, Marie, Terry and Beryl

It's funny that you'd tell them they look good and they'd say, "Do we?" Then it's a wonder that no one is killed in the rush as they're off to the powder room. So while that was going on we could have a quick pint for the road, well you never know, it could be a long road and who's to know where the next watering hole is. So we wouldn't worry about it for a while, as there were sights to see and places to go, such as the (famous) Underground. By the time we'd done all that a vote was taken to grab some grub and a pub, or both. We hit the jackpot with The Thornbury Castle, which was only staggering distance to the station (see map), we might have been from up north but there were no pigeons on us (as it was later now). So we got stuck into the slops and a Mickey Mouse (grouse) time was had by all.

 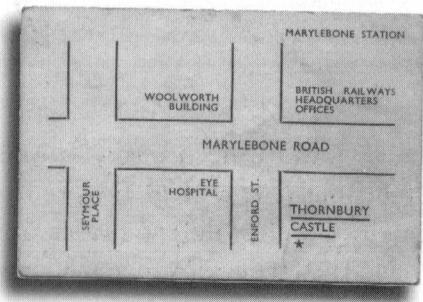

Now, we'll call it October, as that's a good name for a month. I've only got to think of another eleven and then I can go into the calendar business. Then there was a new group on the scene (you've most probably heard of them) and they were a bit of alright too, I might add. They just happened to be Lancashire lads (obviously), not only did we like them but the girls took an interest (I couldn't think why). It was then that we found out via the grapevine that they had made a record in Germany, backing Tony Sheridan on "My Bonnie" and they went under the name of The Beat Brothers, they'd gone through all sorts of names for the group and, of course, they settled on The Beatles.

Then on October 5th "Love Me Do" (on the front side) and "PS I Love You" (on the backside, you know what I mean) is released. In fact, I liked that one better than LMD and they both got plenty of air-play on Radio Luxembourg, which in those days was very unusual as you normally only heard the A side, but this was two for the price of one (what a bonus), plus they wrote their own songs. But at this stage we'd only read about them in the newspapers as they were full of them and, of course, we'd seen them on the news but hadn't seen them singing. We didn't have to wait much longer because on the 7th of November they appeared on the Granada television show, People And Places, singing "Love Me Do". About half way through the song Mum sings out, "Come and get it, your tea's ready."

And the reply from me was, "Yeah, yeah, yeah, I'll be there in a minute, The Beatles are on the telly."

She said, "There's a small brush and shovel under the kitchen sink and there should be a jam jar, sweep them into that, then on Saturday night I'll take them down to St. Marks."

I couldn't help myself, I had to ask, "Why?"

"Because they're having a Beatle Drive, and that's one to me."

Then after seeing them we just knew this group wasn't going to be a five-minute wonder, no, they would last a lot longer than that. As most folk will remember in the early sixties, America had a stranglehold on the music scene until the Mop Tops came along and their dreams were to change all that, and did they ever. And that opened the door for other groups and, I must admit, some of them weren't bad either. I read somewhere that a couple of days after they arrived in the States (The Beatles that is), they performed on TV to an audience of seventy-odd million (and goodness knows how many more watching on radio). And at press conferences they were constantly asked, "What do you think you'll be happy with when The Beatles thing is over?"

And I think it was Paul that said, "All I really wanted was a hundred quid, because with that I could buy a house and a guitar plus a car."

Well, I think he's done a little bit better than that, don't you? And he's still going strong. The reason I mention this, as I lead into that Paul and John wrote "Getting Better", and I'd read that Jimmy Nicol, who played the drums when they did the Centennial Hall (Adelaide), afterwards he was asked, "What's it like being a fill-in Beatle?"

And, of course, his reply was, "Getting better," so for the fans who didn't know it, that's where they got the title from.

Now, in the back of my mind a "Little Voice" (good film that) said, "Why don't you try and find out what became of Mr JN?" I love a challenge like that and I don't need telling twice so I put all my Beatle books into the bath and I plunged in. It didn't take long for the periscope of my "Yellow Submarine" to find the right book and it said, after his fifteen minutes of fame with The Beatles (it was a bit longer than that, actually) he then went on to form his own group, The Shubdubs (which doesn't really roll off the tongue), they didn't have any success and he just faded from the spotlight.

I read somewhere that there were over 300 groups (most of them were young hopefuls) that played in the halls and clubs around Merseyside (and for good measure I'll chuck in some of the others). A lot of them will be covered in cobwebs and there could be quite a few that have turned their winkle-pickers up. So if I can just get me mitts on the spade that I had earlier in the book, you lot moan and groan, and we'll see what I uncover, starting with…

The All Stars; The Applejacks; The Avengers; The Big Three; Billy J Kramer And The Dakotas; The Blackjacks; The Black Nights; The Brooke Brothers; The Cascades; Cass And The Casanovas; The Chants; Cliff Bennett And The Rebel Rousers; The Collegians; The Colts; The Cruisers; The Cyclones;

The Dallas Jazz Band; The Diplomats; Earl Royce And The Olympics; The Echoes; The Escourts; Faron And The Tempest Tornadoes, they appeared on the same bill with The Beatles at the Hambleton Hall, Liverpool and, to be honest with you, I don't think opportunity knocked for them, could it have been their name that held them back, they most probably had trouble fitting it on the old Ludwig (drum kit).

The Fentones; The Four Jays, changed to The Fourmost; Gerry And The Pacemakers; Group One; The Hi-Cats; The Jaywalkers; The Jets; Jim McHargs Jazzmen; The Kestrels; Kingsize Taylor And The Dominoes; The Merseybeats; Mike Cottons Jazzmen; The Overlanders; The Pathfinders; The Pontiacs; The Pressmen; The Raiders; The Red River Jazzmen; The Remo Four; Ricky Gleason And The Top Spots; The Roadrunners; Rory Storm And The Hurricanes; The Saints Jazz Band; The Sapphires; Scaffold, if you remember they had a couple of hits with "Thank U Very Much" and "Lily The Pink" and, of course, Mike McGear is Paul's brother.

Next are The Searchers; The Silhouettes; The Silkie; The Sorrals; The Spidermen (no, I didn't read about them on the website); Tony Smiths Jazzmen; The Trends; The Undertakers, I bet when a lot of groups snuffed it they did a roaring trade; The Vikings; The Wanderers; The Yorkshire Jazz Band, they played at The Cavern with The Beatles; and the last three of this lot are The Zenith Six; The Zodiacs; and The Zombies.

And while I'm here and my pen is tuned in I'll try and name as many of the others I can and hope I don't leave any out, I suppose I can always come back to them later. I'm not really a perfectionist but I do like things to be reasonably right, so if you're ready, have a listen to these…

The Alan Price Set; The Animals; The Bachelors (they'll all be married by now); The Barron Knights; Brian Poole And The Tremeloes; Dave Dee, Dozy, Beaky, Mick And Tich (what a mouthful), or to their close friends DD-D-B-M-T; Emile Ford And The Checkmates; then bouncing onto the stage it's Freddy And The Dreamers; they make way for Georgie Fame And The Blue Flames; Hermans Hermits; The Hollies, Bernie Calvert and Bobby Elliot are from Burnley, while Tony Hicks was born in Nelson.

There was The Honeycombs with the girl drummer, Ann (Honey) Lantree; up next is Joe Brown And His Bruvvers; The Kinks; Lonnie Donegan And His Skiffle Group (of course, he was a big influence on The Beatles); Manfred Mann; The Mindbenders, I think I should have shoved them in earlier, I know my secret is safe with you; The Moody Blues get there "Go Now"; Procol Harum have been waiting that long they've gone "A Whiter Shade Of Pale"; The Rolling Stones, and according to the tabloids they're still performing (then it went on to say, occasionally they sing together); The Shadows weren't a bad outfit, they had a lot of hits with (and without) Cliff; The Small Faces; there was Sounds Incorporated; The Spencer Davis Group, how unusual to have a surname for a Christian name, boy, I bet he's glad the Vicar didn't have a stutter (at the font) or he could have finished up being called Spencer Spencer; then there's The Springfields with Dusty; The Temperance Seven, I think there was about nine of 'em at the last roll-call, it's a wonder there wasn't someone killed in the rush when their royalties came in.

Here's one for you, do you remember (the singer) Paul McDowell, he was the one with the megaphone, he could've always got a job (on the boating lake) at Thompson Park, I wonder if he got that idea from Neddie Seagone (that well known tide that went out) as you know he used the old speaking trumpet and did you know when Tommy Steele started out his backing boys were The Vipers Skiffle Group. Then there was The Who (pardon), The Yardbirds and last but not least, let's have a drum roll for The Pete Best Combo, unfortunately they didn't have much luck at all, then the group changed to Pete Best Four and in July (1964) they released "I'm Gonna Knock On Your Door".

Now then viewers, if you'll excuse me I'll just turn the music down a touch and I'll tell you about December 1962, that's near enough to where we were. These next two events happened on the football scene which, I can tell you, shocked many supporters. The first one was a certain newspaper released details about three players from Sheffield Wednesday that had taken bribes in a game against Ipswich and SW had lost the match 2-0. Those players involved were Tony Kay (and the ironic thing about that was the same newspaper gave him the man of the match award), David 'Bronco' Layne and, of course, Peter Swan, the England centre-half, and they were all given prison sentences.

The second one, which took place at Turf Moor on the 29th of December, the thing about this was the visitors were Sheffield Wednesday, Burnley had no trouble beating them 4-0 in front of twenty-odd thousand, it most probably weakened their team with those three good players out as they weren't a bad side, but for those fans that saw the match they witnessed Jimmy Mac's last League game for The Clarets then, of course, he was transferred to Stoke City and, like I said in 'My Hero, My Friend', thousands vowed never to go through those turnstiles again and I was one of them.

So I was going out this one day and Pop gives it, "Where you off to then?"

I said, "Peel Park."

"What on earth is on there?"

"It's Accrington Stanley's ground," I said.

"There's no doubt about you," he replied, "you go down to London to watch Burnley and now to Accrington, you certainly get around."

I sang out, "I've Been Everywhere, Man," and I was gone.

But the funny part about this story (it's all true), I had to ask what colours Accy played in, what an embarrassment, and not only that, I think they got thumped into the bargain. I was back watching Burnley quicker than you could say supercalifragilisticexpialidocious, I bet Jack Robinson would have a fair amount of trouble with that. And just before I wrap up the bit about Accrington, I thought, I wonder how many times they played Burnley over the years and here's what I found out. They met ten times and from those meetings they both won three and the other four were drawn and they both scored seventeen goals, so you could say they were evenly matched.

This next story I'm not sure about the exact dates, but I'll take a punt and say it was early sixties that the cinemas in and around Burnley (and there were quite a few) were closing their doors. The Coli was no exception and as you will remember it later opened as the Cabaret Club, and if you made yourself a member (I did) you could also use your membership card to get into 77 Club at Brierfield (and we did that).

Looking back now I think it was closed for a while before it was reopened as the club. I remember it was strange going in for the first time, seeing it like that rather than the flicks and I'll tell you something, whoever had the contract and did the alterations, it was very well done. There was the show area, downstairs it was well set out with plenty of tables and chairs plus the great big bar, then the gaming room was upstairs, I used to like the roulette and did alright I might add. There were the one-armed bandits, now they're known as the pokies and they still rip you off. I saw many good acts (and some lousy ones) and had some great nights but the best idea was to go down midweek, it wasn't as busy but the drawback with that was you had to get up for work the next morning.

I suppose in one sense I was lucky, Pop was my alarm clock, no matter what time you wanted waking you could rest assured (so to speak) you wouldn't sleep in. Mum always said, "There's no chance with Pop, he's up that early he wakes the birds."

Sometimes I'd have a bit of fun by putting my hand behind his back and pretending to wind him up saying, "I've set the clock for 6.30."

He was always bright-eyed and bushy-tailed and I was in no mood to be leaping outta bed if I was right in the middle of a good dream, then the patter would go along these lines, "Wakey, Wa_a_a_key," and straight away I thought, what on earth is Billy Cotton doing in my bedroom.

So I said, "Yeah, I heard you," but in me mind I'm saying, please, just one more minute, that's all I wanted.

They were just about to present me with the Cup (at Wembley) after scoring a hat-trick for Burnley and I was only the goalkeeper (and I'd played a blinder) but now my fifteen minutes of fame had been spoiled, Pop stood there saying,

"Here's the cup (of tea)."

I'd mumble something like, "Thanks, Your Majesty."

Then kissing the winners medal that had been placed around my neck I was off to do a lap of honour with the lads and, of course, the fans were going berserk, chanting, "Michael, Michael."

Now at this stage, anyone having a guess (at what's coming next) I'd say you're spot on, it wasn't the crowd at all but Pop shouting, "Michael, you're going to be late."

I sang back, "But I'm drinking my tea," then it was back for a few ZZZ's.

In a minute I'd get another call and this time I'd say, "I'm up and dressed."

But unbeknown to me he was standing on the landing, anybody not familiar with that expression, it's the area at the top of the stairs, then he pushed the door open, stuck his head in the room and said, "Guess who's sleeping in your bed, and he's the spitting image of you."

Right folks, I don't think I can get any more out of that, the scary part now (with this writing caper) is if I don't write ideas down (while they are fresh) will they come flooding back when I want to use them in a story. I suppose that's a chance I'll have to take. So trying to put a year on this…

By now we would have to be
Well and truly into 1963

And I think that our courtship had come to an end, but two romances had started in the family and, of all things, Grandma had met a man, Albert, not that there's anything wrong with that. Also, Bob had met Pat and they'd started courting. Mum was so funny, telling everybody who'd listen (as if they had a choice) that Grandma had gone fishin' and had caught herself a well-to-do smartly-dressed chap and she told people that Grandma would be set for life as he had four figures in the tin tank (bank), yeah, £1 1s 1d ½ penny. I don't know if that comes across written down (I just hope it does), I don't think it was Mum's original but whoever gave birth to that saying it was a very clever one, and I dips me lid.

Now, I'll just fix me lid back in place and we'll be on the way again, which leads me to this next little story (depending on how I can drag it out). In many parts of the country you had an electric meter, which you had to feed money into whenever the house was plunged into total darkness, so this one night we were sat there in the middle of whatever when the lights went out, I don't know if you've been in the middle of whatever and your lights said, "That's it, we're going out," but if you have you'll know what I'm on about. The thing was, you only had to find a shilling but at the same time the search would be on for the candles, so whoever had a shilling or knew where one was (usually a couple would be left on the mantelpiece in case of an emergency) would tell the others and that saved everyone from bumping into each other.

So this time we'd found the candles but not the coin in question, I volunteered to go next door and try to get one, everybody cheered and off I went, but unbeknown to me, Mum or Pop had found a bob, made a cup of tea then called it a day and went to bed. There I was, in next door nattering (as you do) and after a while I said I'd better go now as Mum and Pop will be wondering where I've got to (but they weren't). Of course, I tried the front door and to my surprise it was locked, I thought, what are these two playing at, they must be thinking I'm out with me mates and I've got my key but I hadn't, that meant I had to go around the back.

When I got there that was locked too, I couldn't believe what was going on, if it's April Fools Day they're a bit late. Now, as you lot will know, most of the terraced houses had a sloping roof over the kitchen that led to the back bedroom window, which in this case was Mum and Pop's room, and seeing as they were both a bit Mutt and Jeff (deaf) it would be a complete waste of time knocking or shouting, but how do I get in, or (better still) get their attention? There's only one way to solve this, I thought, it's by climbing up the roof (that I just told you about) and knocking on their bedroom window.

As soon as I'd said that to myself I just couldn't stop laughing because I knew that once I'd tapped on the pane Pop would say, "There's someone at the window."

And knowing Mum she'd say something like, "The window cleaner must be working night shift."

So I managed to stop laughing for a couple of seconds then I tapped and heard Pop say, "Margaret, somebody's knocking on the window."

Well, as soon as he said that it started me off giggling again, Mum said, "If it's the window cleaner and he's got a chammy, ask him to do those top corners, he missed 'em last time."

Then Pop said, "Who is it?"
"It's me, Chammy Davis Jr."
He drew the curtains (and did a good job, I might add) then took one look at my face and said, "What do you want?"
I said, "Seeing as I live here I'd like to come in or should I blacken my face and go to a fancy dress as the singing coalman?" and here comes the pay-off lines, "I could give them a couple of bars of 'What Kind Of Fuel Am I' or 'Coal Me Irresponsible'."
Mum shouted, "Where's your key?"
I said to Pop, "It's on the mantel as I only went next door for a shilling, if you remember?" but they didn't.

Now folks, I can assure you that's a true story and it was very funny, it's just a pity I can't remember it word perfect but over the years we had a lot of laughs by re-telling it. Things were going along nicely at work and I'd made a lot of good friends, I mentioned earlier about the outings, the best one of all was a day at the races (not to be confused with the Marx Brothers film of the same name), which we went to annually. The only trouble was you seemed to be wishing your life away as you couldn't wait for the next trip to come around, anybody who never went on one missed a great day. The best part of it was you paid what you could afford on a weekly basis (and that was given back to you on the day of the trip). I think most of the blokes would chuck in about five bob so they would end up with about thirteen pound, which wasn't to be sneezed at. I tried to put in ten shillings or a quid and if I'd had a bit of luck on the gee-gees (along the way) I made sure I put in extra and then when the day came I'd say to myself, "This is going to be one great trip," so climb aboard readers and let's have a day out.

They usually stopped for breakfast and as someone had snuck a few bottles on, once we got to the pub it would be a mad rush for the toilets. I don't know how many the coach held but it was so funny, you've never seen anything like it in all your born naturals, three-quarters of the blokes diving for the dunny. After all that had been taken care of we'd be seated and ready for the meal, which was nearly always ham and eggs, yummy, and plenty of it. Once the grub was finished it would be time for a cigarette and then on the road again. I think we used to get dropped at the nearest pub to the track, we'd have a couple of jars then someone would shout, "Let's go and belt those bookies!"

I remember this next bit like it was yesterday, but for the life in me I couldn't tell you the horse's name, I'd checked the race book and managed to narrow it down to about three but the more I looked at them I couldn't decide which one the folding stuff would be riding on (so to speak), the bookies were shouting the odds while tic-tacking to the bloke on the food stall to send over a couple of pork pies. So with only about a minute to go I remembered Pop's words of wisdom 'when in doubt, take the top weight' and I thought, why not, as it's a bit pointless backing three in the same race. Then with a quick glance at the boards, most of them had it at 10/1, I saw this other bloke and it was 12/1 so I thought, that'll do me and if it does go down I can only lose a couple of quid.

> *Yeah, I came to have a good day*
> *So I'm gonna risk a £ each way*
> *The bookie smirked and said "Ta Shortie"*
> *I said "That's okay, I'll see you shortly"*

But little did the jockey know that I would be up there with him and I'd be riding for dear life, the only problem was, could the horse carry all that weight over the line? Once they'd got underway I kept my eyes on him, he was always nicely placed, I hadn't told too many of the others what I'd backed but now I thought, he's got a good chance to win this. He hit the front at the right moment and I was jumping up and down by now as I couldn't see too good but I let out a yell as numero uno saluted the Judge. A couple of the fellas were amazed (as they thought the favourite was good thing) and said, "Where did you pick that from?"

I told them about the 'when in doubt' trick, they said, "That's a load of cobblers."

"I couldn't care less, it worked for me and that's all that matters, now I'm playing with their money and I'm over the moon."

They said, "You'll have to come back to earth and collect as there's correct weight."

Well, you should've seen the bookies face, he wasn't smiling now, in fact, he looked like he'd been hit in the mush with a wet kipper, so with the stake back I picked up seventeen smackeroonies and quietly said, "How long's this been going on then?" Of course, it was off to the nearest bar and checking the form guide to see if I could find another good thing. It's marvellous you know, just because you've backed a winner (and had a bit of luck) some blokes think you're an expert. This is what I say, tell them nothing because if it goes down they'll blame you. I had a couple of small collects from ones that ran second or third, I didn't win a fortune but I came out well in front on the day.

Then it would be into a club for the night where there'd be a card game going (and that would do me), I didn't mind Pontoon (or Blackjack) but I love Nine-card Brag. Sometimes it didn't take long and there would be a few quid in the kitty (where's that knife) then before we knew it they were shouting last orders. After downing what we could it was onto the coach and back home and it turned out a good trip, one which we'd talk about for a long time.

When I started to tell you that last story I had this joke lined up which I thought was okay but there was no way known I could wangle it in without you lot being a bit suspicious. Now hold on to your garters as it goes something like this; there was a coach going to the races, the bloke who was running the trip and the driver were standing on the footpath having one last smoke and counting the punters as they climbed aboard. It was almost time to go but there was one missing, the bloke said to the driver, "What should we do?"

The driver said, "If I were you and wanted to make the number up I'd just grab the first person that goes past, it seems a shame to waste a seat."

So the bloke spots the chimney sweep just going to work, he sings out to him, "Cecil, do you want to go to the races for the day, all expenses paid?"

Cecil said, "It smells a bit fishy."

The bloke said, "It's nothing like that, Archie hasn't turned up, so throw your gear in the back and you can take his place."

Now that all the seats were filled they hit the road and five minutes into the journey one chap sings out, "Who's going to be first in the sweep?"

And Cecil yells, "I knew there was a bloody catch!"

Then we got some very bad news, which I think came via telegram. I mentioned earlier about Pop's brother, Kenneth, being in the Forces, he was stationed in Germany. This one night he'd gone out with his mates (and Kenneth was a bit of a speedster), I don't know if he was driving but there was an accident and sadly Kenneth was killed. There was nothing we could do being so far away, the funeral was all organised and took place over there, they buried him with full military honours. It would have to be a few weeks later that we received a letter of condolence and photos of the service and I think Kenneth had been given a gun salute (I'm not sure if it was 21 or not). It was hard to look at those photos without getting a lump in your throat, I remember seeing Pop and he unashamedly cried and this wasn't the time or the place to try and cheer him up, especially me being the emotional one (I'd cry at the drop of a hat), I had great difficulty holding back the old waterworks.

Then after a couple of weeks things were normal again and as they say, life goes on. Then something came outta the blue (which we couldn't believe at first), we were told by Grandma and Albert (who seemed to be very compatible) they had talked things over and, as the old saying goes, two can live as cheaply as one, so they'd decided to get married.

The day of the wedding came, I do remember I was without a date (but not desperate), I'd asked one girl to go with me but she reclined and, I must admit, from where I was standing she looked good in that position (isn't that what they call nine-tenths of the law, or is it possession, I always get those two mixed up). So the wedding was performed and then it was followed by the reception, which was a very enjoyable nosh-up, but unbeknown to us we were in for some more good news as Bob and Pat announced that they had become engaged, so all in all that topped off a very good day.

Grandma's wedding

Now, I'm just not sure how this next bit came about, so I'll go this way and hopefully I'll get through it. A lot of people knew Bob and Lydia Bird (I think that's how you spell her name), from the chippy, and they had a chalet at Roughlee, which they let us use. Then we found out that the one opposite was up for sale, so Mum and Pop bought it. It wasn't as nice as B & L's but still a great weekender and, of course, they were on what I call the lakeside (site). There were also some chalets and little bungalows on another site which you could get access to somewhere behind the pub, which did great meals and also pie and peas (that you could take-away). Then Grandma and Grandad (Albert) bought one on that site, a lovely little cottage, I think there was a couple of residential ones on there but if I remember right Grandma and Grandad didn't live in theirs, they only used it when they wanted to.

Now we'll move along, I know I've got my facts right with this so I hope I can explain it this way, as it didn't surface till much later but it first started in July 1963 when a young girl went missing and then, over a period of time, five children had disappeared and they'd been murdered and, of course, it became known as 'The Body On The Moors' case. Then two people were charged with their murders, they were Ian Brady and his so-called girlfriend, Myra Hindley. They were sentenced to life in May 1966 and nobody knows how those parents must have suffered, not only at the trial but the agonising years that followed. I reckon they (Brady and Hindley) should have been hung, drawn and quartered and not necessarily in that order, or better still, let the mums and dads get their hands on them.

During the early stages of the trial no photos had been in the papers but, oh boy, when we did see those mug shots, didn't they look a suitable pair. So they were locked away where they couldn't get their hands on any more kiddies and, according to the police, they were hoping to go back to the crime scene (Saddleworth Moor). Then it wasn't until 1986 that the case was re-opened and not long after that the first victims body was found, but they couldn't find the third one.

Do you know something, I never thought I'd write about it, but I did, seeing as it happened in my lifetime and subconsciously it's been there all these years. I know it wasn't a nice subject to be writing about but it's really amazing what the old mind stores (or throws away) sometimes, after saying all that, the first part of the next story is a bit vague but knowing me I'll get around it.

I think we were on a train trip to somewhere (sounds like a good title for a film) when I saw this vision of loveliness (I'd better say that or she'll belt me) and straight away I thought, cor blimey, who's dat den? I haven't seen her before and me not one for being short of a word, I went towards her to introduce myself and said, "C'est Magnifique."

She said, "Why do you speak with fork tongue?"

I replied, "It's just a little something I picked up while at Prestige."

And before I had a chance to say anything else she said, "Are you enjoying the trip, Mick?"

"Yes," but I was baffled as to how she knew my name, I said, "listen snookums, I don't know who you are but I'd crawl over broken glass to get to you."

Quick as a flash she said, "One look at your dial and I thought that's what you had done," with that she whipped an eyeliner out of her top pocket and said, "do you mind if I join the dots?"

"Be my guest, as long as you let me put that pencil thingummybob back in your pocket."

She replied, "You're so cheeky."

"Listen to the pot calling the kettle, but more to the point, where have you been all my life?"

She gave me a wink then said, "Well, for the first half I wasn't even born," I was still trying to work out who she was, then I saw the glint in her eyes, she could sense I was struggling and continued, "you don't know who I am?"

Then I realised it was Audrey and, like I said before, you were used to seeing the girls in their work gear, plus those little hats they wore and I just couldn't believe how different she looked because I didn't think I'd seen her outside of work, but if I remember right it was a while before we started going out together.

When I first put this onto paper I thought, what the heck, I'm going to have some fun and why not?

> *Here's what I love about this*
> *And that I'm able to ad-lib*
> *Can say whatever I want*
> *Then even throw in a fib*

Now I can assure you folks, these next few lines are true, we are still in July and, of course, the day finally came when I turned twenty-one (which is a bit pointless really because if you turn 21 it becomes 12, as most of you will know). I had organised to have the birthday bash at The Junction (in The Grove) which was only staggering distance (good thinking, Michael) to where we lived. I got lots of presents, there was plenty of grog at the do and a great time was had by all, among the gifts I received there was a couple of bottles of aftershave and a day or two later I was telling Mum that when you splash the stuff on it don't half sting and I'd hit the roof in record time. Mum said, "For goodness sake, don't tell Pop or he'll have you papering the ceiling while you're up there."

Now, do you know that this happened in August 1963 so I'm on the right track and, of course, I'm talking about the Great Train Robbery, which I thought was a very clever plan. I do remember having a bit of a chuckle when it came out in the papers and reading about their antics. If you, the readers, were anything like me you would have loved Monopoly (with many hours of fun), but these blokes went one better than that, they played with real money (that would have been a laugh) but I reckon they were a bit doolally, if it had been me the first thing I would've done was to go straight to the Cabaret Club, I wouldn't have worried about passing 'Go' and they could have kept their measly £200. But I suppose I'd look a bit conspicuous stood standing at the roulette table with a sack over me shoulder that has 'Royal Mail' stitched on it, while singing to the croupier, "'Life Is A Cabaret' old chum."

Right, let's get back to the courtship, we'd had a couple of dates and I started seeing a lot of Audrey (I had some powerful binoculars). I remember one night we'd been to the Odeon and afterwards we went for a Chinese meal (that's the way to impress 'em). Yes, there were restaurants in those days and not just chippys, I said to her, "Have you been out with a man before?"

Then without batting an eyelid and putting on her Mae West voice she said, "Not one so old," I had to pay that.

I think Audrey had met my folks before I met hers, we were sat there one night and Mum said to her, "Michael likes you."

Audrey sorta blushed then said, "How do you know?"

Mum replied, "Because he just loves squeezing blackheads." (That is a gem and just had to be added).

Audrey had a bigger family than ours so I'll cover this now (it's not that I don't know how to write it) and I hope I don't tread on anyone's tootsies. So for starters I'd better slip these clogs off and approach on tippy-toes, I'll put their partners names in brackets. There was Mum and Dad (Rhoda and Wilf) then came Jean (Roy), Joyce (George, who I already knew through going in the Bridge Inn), Connie (Jimmy), Maureen (Peter) and, of course, I knew Maureen as she worked at Brooke Bonds. Audrey was next, then came Billy and Ann, (I know I've spelt that one right (I checked with Audrey), then there's Arlene, Barry and Marie.

Now, I don't know how many of you noticed, but I mentioned 'clink' in one of my stories, I know that over the years I've used the word not knowing where it came from, so I thought, blow this for a game of soldiers, I'll find out by doing some reading (and in situations like this I can't get enough of it) so here's what I found out. The name comes from Clink Street Prison in Southwark, London. I don't know if it's still there (or used), I've got no intentions of going to any sort of a slammer (that's another name for it) unless, of course, I get sent there for writing something taken the wrong way within these pages (that would be my luck). So viewers, to be truthful, I don't really know how some of this reads (but it seems alright to me when it leaves the brain) so I'll just have to take your word for it, what do you mean 'lousy'? You could have picked a better one than that.

Let's move forward a couple of months and that will bring us to November of the same year. Did I hear a 'don't know' from you lot? Well in reply to that, all I can say is, it's a good job I'm driving this book or we'd be well and truly at the printers without any pages. These next stories have stayed with me (forever and a day), the first one happened on the 10th and that was James' eighth birthday. We'd asked Audrey to come down and, as it was Sunday, normally the entertainment on the telly came from the London Palladium, but this night it was the Royal Command Variety Performance, from The Prince Of Wales Theatre, which had been recorded six days earlier (weren't they sneaky?). Of course, on the bill were The Beatles and in attendance were the Queen Mum, Princess Margaret and Lord Snowdon and, if you remember, when John was introducing one song ("Twist And Shout") he came out with the classic, "Would the folks in the cheap seats clap your hands," and then with a cheeky nod towards the Royal Box, where the dignitaries just happened to be sat sitting, he added, "youse can rattle your jewellery."

I think Mum and Pop enjoyed them (well they said they did) but then Mum, not short of a line (or two), turned to Audrey and said, "Our Michael is just as funny as they are and he doesn't half 'Twist And Shout' when he's shaving."

There would have to be a million stories in me noggin, that was one of 'em, but now it brings me to the second event and one that shocked the world which happened on Friday the 22nd. I'd worked overtime (as usual) and made arrangements to go out with Bill for a few sherbets. I got home, grabbed a quick bite, then had a Dad and Dave (shave) followed by a catlick (as they called it) then I was booted and suited and ready to go. When all of a sudden they interrupted the TV programme for a newsbreak and when they did that you seemed to know something bad had happened (or is it just me?). Even to this day, when they say, "We interrupt this programme to bring you a newsflash…" straight away I fear the worst, so the statement was read saying that the President Of The United States had been shot while riding in a motorcade through Dallas and they had rushed him to hospital, there will be more details when they come to hand.

The goosebumps raced from one end to the other, we sat there in disbelief then the dreaded news came through that he'd died. When Bill came we both agreed to go and have a game of horses and carts (darts), once we got into the pub every man and his dog must have had the same idea, I think the darts went by the wayside as the talking point was JFK and most of the patrons were trying to work out why it happened, then it came through that a lone suspect had been taken into custody and he was Lee Harvey Oswald.

I think we only had a couple more pints after that then called it a night. But later there would be another shock on top of the first one and it was just like something out of a gangster film as LHO was gunned down in cold blood. So, in a sense, that put an end to the case but it came out later from some of the witnesses saying that shots had been fired from what was known as the Grassy Knoll area, which was in front of the motorcade, whereas Oswald was in the building behind the President. Then we saw the funeral, which was beamed around the world, who could forget John-John (bless his little cotton socks), playing soldiers and saluting his Daddy's coffin.

And now to bring this to an end, there were quite a few similarities between Presidents Kennedy and Lincoln; Lincoln was elected to Congress in 1846 while Kennedy was elected in 1946; Lincoln was elected President in 1860 and Kennedy in 1960; their surnames both have seven letters; Kennedy's secretary was called Lincoln and, you guessed it, Lincoln's was called Kennedy; both Presidents were killed on a Friday, being shot in the head; Lincoln was killed by John Wilkes Booth and Kennedy by Lee Harvey Oswald, both were known by their three names and both names had fifteen letters in them; both Presidents were assassinated by Southerners and were succeeded by Southerners who were both named Johnson; Andrew Johnson, who succeeded Lincoln, was born in 1808 and Lyndon Johnson, who followed Kennedy, was born in 1908; they had thirteen letters in their names, John Wilkes Booth was born in 1839 and Lee Harvey Oswald was born in 1939; Kennedy was hit while riding in a car (a Lincoln) and Lincoln was shot at the (Kennedy) Theatre; JWB escaped from the theatre but was caught in a warehouse, while LHO went from the Texas Schoolbook Depository (a warehouse) and he was nabbed in the theatre; last but not least, both of the assassins were killed before they could stand trial.

Well, that should bring us near to the end of another year, they're flying by now and I'm dinky-doo (twenty-two) next birthday.

So then Christmas came
And of course it went
All my hard earned money
Was so quickly spent

Now, a darts match was always a great night out (with plenty of gags doing the rounds) and there were a lot of good darters at Brooke Bonds and most of the works had a team. Then after the game was over the Publican used to put a supper on (and plenty of it, I might add), but the only problem was, with being mid-week, it was work the next day so on the night of the match the last thing I said while on my way out, "I might be a bit late so could you set the alarm, Pop?"

(They didn't sorta worry too much as long as I had my key), and he'd reply, "Would Prince Michael like breakfast in bed as well?"

I said, "Now that sounds good, but not if it's going to be a lot of trouble," and with that I darted out the door.

Audrey's birthday came up in January, so I'd give her a quid and say, "Go and get yourself something nice from the market," where will all this expense end, folks.

I'd read in the papers, and also seen via the box, a young up and coming boxer by the name of Cassius Marcellus Clay who said he was the greatest, and by seeing a few of his bouts he certainly had the Dave Sands (hands) to back his mouth up. He was only seventeen when he won the AAU Light Heavyweight Title, after that he went on to win the gold medal in the same division at the 1960 Olympic Games. Then in February 1964 he proved how good he was by beating Sonny Liston for the Heavyweight Championship and, for what it's worth, I thought he was great. Now here's a couple of bits (while still in February) at no extra cost, Sonny Liston and Joe Louis went to The Beatles show then on the 18th the four lads visited Clay while he was at his training camp.

Well, gee whiz, I seem to be getting plenty of mileage out of this spade and you know what? Sometimes I amaze meself with what I dig up, and while I'm in the groove I'm just going back to something I said before. Do you remember when I was telling you about those songs (somewhere between page 1 and here) that were doing the rounds? Now don't just say 'yes' for the sake of it or I'll have to strap you to the old lie detector to see if you're really telling the Sister Ruth (truth).

So one of those songs I mentioned was "Gilly Gilly Ossenfeffer Katzenellen Bogen By The Sea" which sounded to me a lot like a Welsh Railway Station, well, knowing me as I do, my curiosity got the better of me as I thought, let's take this one step further and see if I can come up with the worlds longest name for a station. Now trains haven't stopped there since the sixties but that doesn't stop people from visiting (not by train, of course), especially the village store (Pringles), which does a roaring trade by selling woollens and souvenirs. Plus you can even get a platform ticket with the name of the famous station on it.

So just stand back folks and I'll shout into my speaking-type megaphone (once used by Neddie Seaside, that well known holiday resort) then it should come out something like this:

Llanfairpwllgwyngyllgogerychwyrndrobwyll-llantisiliogogogoch

I might have missed an L or two but who the L is gonna notice, unless some of you are from Wales or a very observant postie, and seeing as you're a nice bunch I'll translate it 4 U and it means:

The Church Of Mary In A White Hollow By A Hazel Tree Near A Rapid Whirlpool By The Church Of St. Tisilio By A Red Cave

If by chance you live there you can most probably get away with the abbreviated version, Llanfairpwllgwyngyll. Could you imagine the Station Master shouting out the name then translating for the people who don't speak Welsh, the old choo choo would be well and truly on its way by the time he spit that bibful.

Now, never in my wildest dreams did I think I'd have to do so much research (not that it worried me), I've got to be honest with you it was exciting, as when I went into that story the foundation was already there, it just needed to be built into a storey (story). So I said to myself, if you think you can write it, make sure you've got your facts right and hopefully you should be able to use it. I'm normally not one to blow my own trumpet (I have been known to honk the horn on me bike before today), now is this lad good or what? But please, no applause just yet, you can save it for the end in case it's a weak finish.

Chapter
28

Now, getting back to the courtship, we used to baby-sit a couple of nights a week, as long as it wasn't too late (because I'd have to take Audrey home), and this one night Mum and Pop wanted to go to bingo and they asked us to look after Jim. So after thinking it over for a few minutes I demanded payment in advance. All I got from Pop was a raspberry and Mum chipped in with, "I'll see you right when I get me glasses on," I doffed my hat to that and off they went.

Then when they came home Pop said, in his Mr Plod voice, "Hello, hello, hello, what's going on here then?"

And Audrey said, "We're reading."

Mum said, "What, without the lights on?"

I added, "Yeah, lip reading."

Like a lot of other couples did we'd write love letters to each other, Audrey's were always good (and to the point), while mine were not only drawn out but the writing was terrible in the bargain.

Now, if you remember, on the back of the envelope you'd write something like 'postman, postman, don't be slow, be like Elvis, go man go'. Then there were a lot of abbreviated ones, Audrey used to put SWALK, which stood for 'sealed with a loving kiss'. While I always wrote on mine YTTCCH 'yours till the cows come home'. Then this day I got one from Audrey and on the back she'd written KISS, I thought that's a nice touch, I liked it but she had me bamboozled as to what on earth it meant. So the next time I saw her I said, "Thanks for the letter and how sweet of you to put KISS on the back but you've got me stumped, what does it mean?"

She said, "Keep it simple, stupid."

Now you will know how they say wine improves with age, I wonder if writing has the same effect, not that mine will be vintage but you would have noticed there's quite a bit of old stuff doing the rounds between these pages, and here's more…

This was great for us young un's as the pirate ship Radio Caroline was launched and started broadcasting in March. And then in July, just a couple of days before my birthday, that's maybe why this story has stayed with me for such a long time, it was a tragedy that shocked the football world and the player in question is John White. He left Falkirk in October 1959 and joined Tottenham Hotspur. During his career he won twenty-two full caps for Scotland and he was the inspiration of the Spurs 1961 side who, of course, did the League and Cup double. He made over two hundred appearances, he was known as The Grey Ghost but tragically he was killed (on the 21st of July) while at his peak and it happened through a freak million-to-one chance.

This day he was out playing golf (alone) near to his home when a torrential storm broke and he was struck down by this flash of lightening and it was reported later that in the fierceness of the storm the heat had melted the wedding ring on his finger. His body was found under the tree where he had sheltered till the storm blew over, he was only twenty-six and to finish on this note it proved what a valuable player he was to Spurs, they only won one of the fifteen games he missed during the time he played for them.

We'll get back to the family side of things, normally I can close my eyes and, as strange as it sounds, I see (the outline) more clearly that way, I suggest you don't do it or you could miss a line or three. But I'm just not quite sure how this story came about and I'll try by going down this path. Now I know that Grandma and Grandad had bought a lovely caravan on-site at Knots End or Poulton, I thought it was the latter, it's not really embarrassing, but more annoying as we went there one weekend (here's where that diary would have been useful) and all the family was pleased for them as they'd done very well with the deal, and I'll just go out the tradesman's entrance by saying 'wherever' it was.

Then we found out that Pats parents, Gerard and Betty, and Pat were going back to Australia as they'd been out there for a few years before and, of course, Bob was going. Drats, I had hopes of being there first but I suppose it wasn't meant to be. We'll move forward and Bob is leaving, little did we know it would snowball after that.

Bob's farewell

So I heard a muffled voice say (it was Pop's), "That bulging trunk looks heavy, and why is Michael's Claret and Blue scarf sticking out?"

Once they opened the case both questions were answered, yep, I was inside with the garment around my neck, so quick as a flash I said, "I was just checking to see you've got everything and it seems to be present and correct and it's a good job I did, fancy trying to skip the country with me scarf as a memento," I don't think they bought it, I thought it was good though.

Now, I can't remember the exact arrangements but I think it went something like this, a few days before I'd asked Mr Rush (or Milne) for a couple of hours off on that day and they said that wasn't a problem. So I'd gone to work (on my bike), then when the time came I caught the bus down to the bus station and met up with Bob and Brian, as Brian was travelling down to London with him.

Now this is where the hard part came into it, I had to decide whether to wait there till they'd gone, or say farewell and start walking, then hopefully the bus would pass me somewhere along the way, plus the walk would do me a power of good. Then I sang out, "So Long, It's Been Good To Know You," we shook hands and embraced and that was only me and Brian.

Bob said, "When you've quite finished, if you don't mind, it's me that's going." So after the tomfoolery, which eased the tension, the moment of truth was upon us and I'd been dreading it.

I can't remember what was actually said but I think there were more tears than words on my part. The old Adams apple was like a black pudding. We wished each other all the best and with that I took off. I don't think I looked back as I was scared I'd walk smack bang into a lamp-post. Once I got walking I was alright, I just had to keep looking over my shoulder to check if the bus was coming and I was hoping it would pass me before I got to the Mitre as I had to take the high road and, of course, they'd take the other. I checked my watch, I had plenty of time so if it was going to be a photo finish I could prop there for a while.

Then another sken and yes, the bus was on it's way, as it went speeding past we were all waving frantically, even the bus driver got in on the act, he gave me a wave and then they were gone and the tears flowed again, more so this time than before (as I'd forgotten to get that quid off him that he owed me). I carried on walking with all these confusing thoughts swirling around in my head. Then before I knew it Capriccio Italien was on the turntable of my mind. If I hadn't thought of that I would have been into the first pub, it was very tempting. I got back to work still a bit teary-eyed and promised to drown my sorrows at the end of a very tough day.

I raced home, grabbed some tea, then got changed. Mum said, "What's on tonight?"

I told her it was beer and lotto, she said, "That's new."

"Yeah," I said, "I'm gonna get blotto."

I'd started going in the New Inn as quite a few of the blokes from work went in there, it was a bit far from home but it was always a good night. If there weren't many in we'd go in the Tap Room and then there was a chance of playing cards, darts or dominoes. Other times we had great sessions when we gave the old jukebox a hammering. I don't know about you (musical) lot but I wish I could get my hands on the complete list of the songs on the JB at the time (I might dig into that a bit more later), there would have to be say 100 songs or more (at a rough guess). When I got the idea for this in the first place there was only a bit in the vault but by giving it a lot more thought it started to trickle back and then digging out my records and dusting them off I can tell you, I thought, oh boy I'm going to enjoy this, I don't care if it takes me all day (it could if I'm not careful).

Now, isn't it funny how I've come back to music again (well, I think so), here's some of the artists that were on at the time, I'm not going to sort them out into nationalities, I'll let you do that. If there are a few singers that you're scratching your heads about I'll put their songs in brackets then it should come back to you, there's most probably some you've forgotten (died a death, so to speak). Now, if you're sitting comfortably I'll press a couple of buttons and we'll hear from…

Little Richard as he belts out, "A Wop Bop A Loo Bop A Lop Bam Boom," followed by; Chris Andrews; Paul Anka; Frankie Avalon; John, Fred And His Playboy Band (Judy In Disguise); Teddy Bears (To Know Him Is To Love Him); Acker Bilk; Cilla Black; The Beach Boys; The Everly Brothers; The Righteous Brothers; The Walker Brothers; The Browns (The Three Bells); Chubby Checker, when at the Blackjack table sang "Lets Twist Again"; Pet Clark; The Coasters; Eddie Cochran; Sam Cooke (Cupid), he was shot dead in 1964; Bernard Cribbins (Right Said Fred); Johnny Cymbal (Mr Bass Man); Jimmy Dean (Big Bad John); James Darren (Goodbye Cruel World); Karl Denver; Dion; Charlie Drake (My Boomerang Won't Come Back); Donovan; Craig Douglas (Only Sixteen); The Drifters; Bob Dylan; Duane Eddy; Little Eva (The Locomotion); Fabian; Marianne Faithful; Toni Fisher (West Of The Wall); Connie Francis; Billy Fury; Jimmy Gilmer (Sugar Shack); Peter And Gordon; Lesley Gore (It's My Party); Rolf Harris; Clarence Frogman Henry (But I Do); Engelbert Humperdink; Frank Ifield; Kenny Ball And His Jazzmen (March Of The Siamese Children); Terry Lightfoot's New Orleans Jazzmen (King Kong); Tom Jones; Eden Kane; Jerry Keller (Here Comes Summer).

Now, if someone would get a round of drinks I'll put another nickel in, in the nickelodeon and we'll get music, music, music from; Ben E King (Spanish

Harlem); Carole King; Kathy Kirby; Brenda Lee; Peggy Lee; Lulu; Jet Harris and Tony Meehan (Diamonds), they branched out from The Shadows (wait for it, it's a good un), they went out on a limb.

Next up is Roger Miller; Ned Miller (From A Jack To A King); Guy Mitchell; Matt Monroe; Chris Montez; Ricky Nelson; The Newbeats (Bread And Butter); Anthony Newly (Pop Goes The Weasel); Roy Orbison; Crispian St. Peters (Pied Piper); Gene Pitney; Sandy Posie (Single Girl); PJ Proby; Jim Reeves, who died in a plane crash August'64; Tommy Roe; Julie Rogers (The Wedding); The Ronettes; Billy Joe Royal; Bobby Rydell; Mike Sarne (Come Outside); Frankie Vali And The Four Seasons; Del Shannon; Helen Shapiro; Sandie Shaw; Allan Sherman (Hello Muddah Hello Faddah); The Rooftop Singers, they were the group with the twelve string guitar and they sang "Walk Right In"; Percy Sledge; Cat Stevens; Nino Tempo and April Stevens (Deep Purple); Millie Small (My Boy Lollipop), I heard somewhere that Rod Stewart played the harmonica on that track.

Right folks, They've just shouted last orders so I'll get you lot one more for the frog and toad (road) then you can listen to these; The Lovin' Spoonful; Diana Ross And The Supremes; The Surfaris (Wipe Out); Johnny Tillotson (Poetry In Motion); The Tokens (The Lion Sleeps Tonight); The Tornadoes (Telstar); The Kingston Trio (Where Have All The Flowers Gone); Conway Twitty; Bobby Vee; Gene Vincent; Bobby Vinton; Mary Wells (My Guy); and Stevie Wonder. Now here's two I'm not sure about but I'll take a gamble and say Ol' Blue Eyes could have been there with "Fly Me To The Moon", which was recorded in June 1964, and Dino with his big hit "Everybody Loves Somebody", recorded in March 1964.

I bet you're thinking, he's been that busy "Jive Talkin'" he's forgotten to mention such and such, well I haven't, so here is the first which is Elvis, he would have had songs like "Devil In Disguise" and "Puppet On A String", not to be confused with the Sandie Shaw one. Then there was "Viva Las Vegas" and we'd sing 'sausage and mashed potatoes', many a true word sang in jest. The other 'such' is The Beatles, this is just my guess of their songs that were on the jukebox and, of course, we'd always give the flipside 45 revolutions per minute; "Love Me Do"; "PS I Love You", October 1962; "Please Please Me"; "Ask Me Why", January 1963; "From Me To You"; "Thank You Girl", April 1963; "She Loves You"; "I'll Get You", August 1963; "I Want To Hold Your Hand"; "This Boy", November 1963; "Can't Buy Me Love"; "You Can't Do That", March 1964; "A Hard Days Night"; "Things We Said Today", July 1964.

Now, as luck would have it, when I was going through the collection I came across a three-CD set of the sixties which was a great help, then I dug out this five-record set and it's the Greatest Hits Of Rock'n'Roll and, can you believe, 114 of 'em. I had lots of fun listening to some again (after many years). I also borrowed a rock'n'roll encyclopaedia from the library, I had it three times a day after meals, I digested as much of it as I could, some nights I'd burn the midnight oil and I thought, this is no good, I've got to get the electricity connected.

I said before I wouldn't mind a list of the songs, well I must have named all the performers (and some) which surprised "Little Ol' Wine Drinking Me". I shall bring this "Magical Mystery Tour" to a close (for now) by saying I've seen and stored lots of things over the years but one of the silliest things I've ever heard was some twit who said that The Beatles and Elvis wouldn't have made it without Brian Epstein and Andreas Cornelius Van Kuijk (Colonel Tom Parker). I thought, what a lot of rot, there's thousands of singers and groups that have hit the big time, I must've named over ninety and I wouldn't have a clue who manages them.

Now I'll throw in a 'did you know' that the King and the Fab Four (clown princes) met at his Bel Air mansion in Los Angeles. They spent a few hours together where they talked and fooled around musically, it was stated but not recorded, unfortunately.

Hands up those viewers who know what year it is. Guess what? You're right, it's this one, but not for much longer. Now, unbeknown to you I had a breakthrough, I'd been hoping to get this out of the way for a long time so I got my head into gear, and then gathered most of the notes which were on scraps of paper. It's not only me but I've heard other people do this, I think it was Mae West, one interview said she scribbled things down on tiny pieces of paper (mostly men's phone numbers, she ad-libbed) then when she thought there was enough for a story it would be time to get them all together, use what was needed, and that was how she did it. So I grabbed a folding chair and took most of the material with me and went over to the beach, just writing in a different place is like a tonic (not that I suffer much from writers block, touch-wood).

I managed to work out a few ideas that I had, but here's what I started to tell you and that is I must have got rid of at least twenty-odd bits of paper, which I'd transferred onto one big miscellaneous sheet, and that will make it a heck of a lot easier in the long run as I was getting snowed under and frightened of leaving something out.

I know I could always go back to it (return to the scene of the crime) but if it's really important I'd prefer it in the right place at the right time, comprende? I made myself laugh (as I relaxed), maybe because I'd finally done it and I felt like an enormous weight had been lifted. So I gave it this title "Mickleaneous One Man And His Ideas", that sounds like a good name for a book or a Goon Show (what, what, what, what, what), said Neddie Seabreeze, that well known wind.

Terry, me Beryl and Audrey

So with another Christmas just around the Johnnie Horner (corner) then came the works annual dinner dance and that was always a great meal and a night with plenty of laughs, plus you got to meet your friends from work and their wives and husbands and girl or boyfriends, respectively. I think it was the first dinner dance I took Audrey to, there were lots of different kinds of food, some that we weren't used to, I said, "Would you like to try some scampi?"

She said, "Yuk, no thanks!"

So I asked her, "What about the prawns then?"

"Go on," she said, "I'll have a bash at those," then licking her lips she said, "yummy, they were a bit of alright."

So I told her it was prawns done in batter, better known as scampi, she said, "You sneaky snackeler," I never did know what she meant by that but she used to use it quite often.

That just about ends another twelve months, now hang on a minute while I put a bullet in me biro and I'll finish the year off with a bang. Just getting back to Johnnie Horner (which I used a few lines ago), I always thought it was Jack, because wasn't he the one that sat in the corner? But in the book I've got (about rhyming slang) it's Johnnie, so at this stage I'm not going to lose any sleep over it and I suggest you don't.

Now, we used to go up to Roughlee, it was always a good getaway and there was the boating lake plus plenty of good walks, we'd take Jim and Audrey's cousin, Sylvia. As you know, it wasn't all that far from Burnley but you got away from the smoke, and the air up there seemed so much fresher. Other times we used to go away with Mum and Pop, which I didn't tell you about (but I will now), and mostly it would be in a caravan park somewhere as they were always cheaper than digs.

At Roughlee

There were lots of stories that came from our holiday experiences, they were the situations where you had to be there, then with barrels of laughs where we'd finish up crying, I'd give anything for a page out of a diary. I think one of the best we ever had would have to be when we went to Ocean Edge, near Morecambe. We had this van and Mum said, "It's not bad in here, as it's a bit parky outside," but she spoke too soon because out of the blue (or black) the heavens opened and the rains came and with the wind swirling around we thought the place was going to take off.

Jim was scared and tried to get under the table, I said, "Get out you coward, there isn't room for two of us."

Soon it was dripping in from everywhere, you could have a shower without going to the toilet block. We had pots, pans, buckets and all of a sudden it had gone cold so Pop said, "I've got a brainwave," after we all waved to his brain, he continued, "very funny, but if I light the oven and leave the door open it'll give out some heat."

It was one of those that took ages to light at the best of times and you could tell it was getting the better of him. Audrey said, "It's a good job you're not a Doctor, you've got no patience," (see, I'm not just writing a book, I've got to do lines for the others).

It wasn't going to beat him but I think by this time the sun had come out and it was cracking the flags (as they say up north). He took one of the shelves out, said, "Let the dog see the rabbit," stuck his head in, struck a match and then, without warning, boom!

Mum said, "It's a wonder you didn't blow us all to smithereens."

"It's most probably a lot drier there," replied Jim.

Pop said, "I can't hear anything."

We all said, "Pardon?"

Then he turned around, all his moustache was singed and he had half an eyebrow missing, after we stopped laughing, which was a while, I said, "Is you Amos or Andy? And don't you dare give me a black look."

Mum said, "You look like you've been burnt at the stake, I hope the steak's alright, I was thinking of doing it for tea, I just need a volunteer to light the oven."

I think it was Audrey who said, "Hands up all those in favour of fish and chips."

We also had some fun times playing bowls. It would be a miracle if we all managed to follow the same Jack, a lot of the other bowlers didn't seem to have our sense of humour (can you imagine another family like our clan? I shudder at the thought), but to us it was only a game and we were having a ball (bowl). It was like watching a Chaplin film, people were being skittled every which way. I think Jim was aiming for them half the time and the other half he had no trouble hitting 'em and they were hobbling around like the walking wounded and Jim thought this was hilarious. Pop said, "If we were in the wheelchair business we'd do a roaring trade."

Mum tried to be serious but the more she concentrated she just couldn't get it to go straight. Audrey said, "You wouldn't be any good at Ten Pin Bowling."

Mum said, "Ten, I have trouble with one," then she said, "that's it, I'm taking my ball and going home," so with that we called it a day (and a good one).

Then after tea we'd go over to the Club Room, they had bingo on a couple of nights a week. Now, I don't know if they had a jukebox but they did have a Joanna (piano) and we'd have a bit of a sing-a-long as Audrey had a lovely voice, yes, we had many a good night and on a few occasions they needed dynamite to get us out (or was that Pop lighting the oven).

I'm not exactly sure where this came in but we'd started playing tennis (somewhere along the line and also the double ones), which we enjoyed. There was one time, after I'd won a point, Audrey made me laugh as she stood there, hands on hips and fuming, while shouting, "You don't play fair, Mickey Plum."

I asked, "Why's that then?"

She yelled back, "Because you always hit it to where I'm not," (I thought that was the main aim of the game).

I said, "Well, if I knock it to you all the time that gives you a better chance to win the point, and," I added, "all's fair in love and war, Awdrey."

She said, "That's Audrey with a U or you will be out of love and right in the middle of a war, so don't push your luck," and with that she fired this screamer which whistled past my lugholes, then said, "game, set and match to me, so thank-you linesmen and ball-boys," and that was the end of it.

Under my breath I said, "Now I know why they name cyclones after women."

Other nights, after tea and once the table had been sided, the dishes washed up and put away, we'd get a deck of cards out and play what we called Newmarket, while some people would call it Find The Lady. As you know (those ones of you who played it), if the kitty had doubled, and the Queen as well, there would be quite a bit of money if anybody won the two pots. When Pop managed to win, Mum said, "What did you do that for, you daft ha'peth, I was just getting the hang of it."

It's funny now, just thinking back, if you did win a few games during the course of the evening you'd finish up with a pile of copper and it's been a while since I've thought about those pennies. Weren't they cumbersome things and sometimes, if you had a few of them in your sky rocket (pocket) and if you happened to run for a bus, you sounded like a Blackpool donkey trotting along.

Now, Audrey and myself had planned to get married some time in the following year, and so we got engaged, and the plan was to try and save, as a lot of our friends (who had taken the plunge) had told us that it was better to start off with some money behind you. I was paying board so I could put a couple of quid away a week and as it turned out, lady luck seemed to be on my side with the nags.

Chapter
29

Then came a chance at work, I had worked a couple of times with the Blenders but then I don't know how this came about, I was just in the right place at the right (tea) time I guess. I got asked if I'd like to work there permanently, it was a very hard job as it was piecework but the money was great...

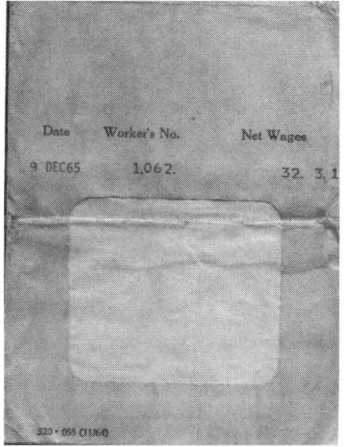

Pay packet

So let me be your artist
And paint a picture for you
Now most of this did happen
With me and the blending crew

What a bunch of characters they were and I've never come across a gang like 'em since and it was an experience, which will live with me for many years to come (I hope). So what I'm going to do now is to name most of them, some of them would come under the title of Checkers, but I'll put them all in together and go from A to Zed; Bill Allen; Albert Baker; Alex and Ronnie Bannister; Bill Barker; George Burnett and his dad, Bill, he was our Boss and had the job of trying to keep us under some sort of control, come to think of it, I suppose we did get away with quite a bit but there were times when we were caught in the act. Gus Callaghan; Alan Cook; Vinny Dolan; Jimmy Dunleavy; Terry Goad; Alan Hibbert; Brian Hoy; Harry Parkinson; Carl Pert; Ken Shepherd;

Jock Strother; Ken Taylor; and Eddie Walker.

Now most of these blokes were older than me, so they were more like father figures and they'd line up in order to wallop me (often). I'd be sat there minding my own business and twiddling the thumbs while waiting for a truck to come in, you'd hear them say, "Has Mick been belted today?"

The reply would be, "Yeah, but it wouldn't hurt to give him another, that's if you can catch him as he's a slippery little sucker and watch out, his nails are sharp."

Well, c'mon now readers, do you blame me for protecting myself, they should have picked on someone their own size. You'd hear them talking and when they mention GMT it had nothing to do with Greenwich, oh no, it was more like Get Mick Time, so I was off like a bat out of hell and I'd live to scratch another day.

There were two types of jobs with the blending crew, I'll try to explain them as best I can. The hardest part was opening the tea chests which had been laid out on the floor, the gangs had a claw-like hammer but, instead of being curved, the claw part was straight so that you could knock the metal off quite easily. There would be a sudden shout of, "Duck," when someone let go of their hammer. The chests had been lined up so that you could work with the grain, then you could get away with opening only three sides of the lid, as most of the time they were packed in together to save space.

There was a hand-trolley that you would use to wheel the boxes to where there was a platform with a cage either side, which was fitted with a small hoist, then you would put the chest on it and normally it was Ken's job (on the platform) to put the pedal to the metal (so to speak). When it got to the top he'd grab the chest and help to tip the contents into the big sieve, can you "Imagine", all that tea and dust floating about the joint, it didn't half get up your hooter. When you blew your nose it wasn't snot that came out, it was more like iced tea, that sounds disgusting doesn't it? Yeah, that's why I threw it in!

Then when the box was empty it was chucked onto some rollers, which led to the chute that went down to the Reclamation Area that I told you about earlier. Anybody coming into the gang for the first time would be told to go on the platform and give it a bash, well unbeknown to him, the lads would set him right up. So picture this if you can (as the video isn't available just yet), an empty tea chest had been fitted with a lid, which was a couple of inches from the top, then a few pounds of loose tea was poured on it (I hope you're taking all of this in, I might put you on the spot later), so that anyone on the platform looking down into the cage would see this and presume it was a full one and, of course, it didn't matter to the hoist, it still came up at the same speed, then when it got to the top the (muggins) bloke would grab hold and fling it in and it went with such a force.

By the way, if his Mum had told him to put clean undies on when he left that morning he most probably sang back, "I'm only going to work and I'll try not to get hit by a double-decker," but I reckon that little incident could have had the same effect. I had it done to me a few times, I might add, but it's nice to see someone else on the receiving end. Of course, the lads would be rolling about as if they'd never seen anything like it before and there was always quite a few watching as the word would get around that it was going to be on (it's a wonder they didn't have tickets printed). It was always interesting to watch the different reactions, some blokes took it well, then with a nod of approval said, "Good one," while others would do their blocks and sling the thing to the scheissenhausen, if you'll pardon my French, as that's in loo of.

Now, if you're anything like me and on occasions you have done your block, you'll know it can be quite painful (it could bring a tear to the eye) and it takes a heck of a long time to remove the splinters. Another part of the job with the Blenders (you'd take it in turns) was that you had to go upstairs and do what they'd call a 'mix' from there and, believe me, it was very hard work, but once you got into it with your head down and bum up you could keep in front. So after having got the tea chests out of the stacks, that's where the Checkers came into it, as they told you which one to use next, then they would tick them off on their sheet.

Then, of course, they all had to be opened, once that was done it was just a matter of getting as near to the pipeline (I'll call it that) so when you had tipped three of four down it then went at a reasonable pace and that would give you a chance to get rid of the empty TC's, which you would cob down the chute and then that joined up with the one downstairs (and when you think about it, it was a very clever idea). Sometimes, when the other lads had managed to get a few minutes up their sleeve, they'd come up and let you go for a couple of drags. Meanwhile, back downstairs, accidents happened quite a lot with the tea being spilt, so to someone new on the scene they were told to sweep it onto a lid, when he asked what should he do with it, right on cue, a couple of the lads would strum on an imaginary guitar then give it their best Elvis sneer and chorus, "You can 'Return To Blender'." There were always plenty of those flying around, mind you, most of them were as old as them thar hills but still good for a laugh.

Now here's something I've just come up with and that is, wouldn't the workhouse be a dreadful place without humour. What if Hitler was the Boss (I'm in charge), it could go something like this… you shall graft all day without so much as a titter, anybody caught sniggering shall be shot at dawn and if Dawn so much as chuckles she'll be gunned down also. While we're talking about the Fuehrer (I thought I'd spell it like that, rather than Fuhrer, just to confuse you). I love the one that Peter Sellers once told in an interview about, of all things, painters. He went on to say that Sir Winston Churchill couldn't paint to save his life but Hitler, there's a painter for you, in fact he could do an entire apartment (two coats) in one afternoon.

Here's one thing I know about Adolf and that is he was a lousy golfer, because after a couple of shots he was still in the bunker. I don't know what brought that on so I'll move right along. I do know that I told you before about the aluminium foil being used for missiles, of course it went on with the Blenders and for no reason at all you'd get belted on the bonce, it would have been no good having eyes in the back of your head as they could've had one of 'em out.

I suppose it wasn't really all that bad if they did happen to hit your body because the clothes lessened the pain and if one did manage to hit you on the bare skin (ouch!), believe me, they didn't half sting. But the funniest part of copping one of those, if you could see the funny side of it, you would look behind you and there were four blokes pointing to the others and saying, "It was him!"

Anyone who witnessed the water fights between yours truly and Jimmy, they were once seen, never to be forgotten. We were very good mates but there were times when we clashed, or more like splashed, we would stir each other just for something to do, so in the toilets there were two wash basins plus two toilets, trap 1 and trap 2, and a Hew Rinal (a Welsh chap in the corner and everybody peed on him), just my little joke. Now with trap 1 you could manage to reach over and push down the ball cock (yeah, that's what I said, cock) in the cistern and it didn't matter who went in there, as everybody was fair game and, of course, if T1 was empty you could stand on the loo then reach over and flush T2. Many a time you'd be sat sitting minding your own business (a good place for it) and studying the racing form with your overalls at half-mast, then when you were least expecting it, whoosh! The floodgates had been opened and there would be a yell of, "Godfrey Daniels!"

I suppose, in a sense, you could say that we were the first ones to have a bidet and 'too late' was the cry as the undercarriage was wringing wet and there was no way known you could let it drip-dry. So you'd pull up your trews as quick as you could, by this time you had trampled all over the racing page, then when you flung the door open five or six of them would be stood there, shrugging their shoulders, saying, "It wasn't me."

Then one of 'em piped in with, "Could you hear us in there, because we certainly heard you."

I'd take one look at Jimmy, even if it wasn't him he couldn't keep a straight face so I'd launch into my Bobby Darin impersonation and sing "Seamus"…

> *Splish splash you're heading for a bath*
> *And it's nowhere near Saturday night*
> *He sang Bobby boy I got news for you*
> *Now just trust me you'll get one too*
> *That signalled the start of the fight*

Well, you've never seen blokes scarper so quick at the sight of a bit of H_2O, we threw it about as if it grew on trees and if any of the others got in the road, so be it. Some would shout, "Don't muck around."

I yelled, "Who's muckin', I don't know about this chap but I'm deadly serious!"

We certainly got stuck in and tried to dunk each other into that basin but with slippin' and slidin', if you weren't careful you could finish up out of sync. Then when we'd both had enough, as we were like drowned rats, we would call a truce then shake hands and those little outbursts happened on the average of once a week. If there are any of the readers that used the Blenders bogs and at one time or another had been flushed out, I can't tell a lie, it was me or one of the other lads. I'm just thinking that it's a pity nobody had a video camera in those days, I'd love to see something like that again, but I suppose I should be greatly thankful that it's in my minds eye.

And while I'm on the subject of the mind, let's see how this comes out on paper. So if you weren't (in the gang) on the opening side of the job (I think you had three days each) the rest of the gang took care of the tea (chests) as it came in. But before I go any further I'll tell you this, Brooke Bonds was a strict place but the blokes could go to any area, even the girls room. Mind you, Miss Browning wasn't too keen on that idea and she would look daggers at them and if they didn't get the message that it was time to go back to their department she'd come marching over and want to know why.

But this is what I'm really getting at, and that is some of those girls could have worked there for many years and not known what some of the fellas actually did. I don't think any of the girls ventured to where the Blenders worked as it was dangerous (with missiles flying around). Of course, if I wanted to see Audrey we'd meet in the canteen at lunchtime or I'd pop down there and dodge the knives, to which Audrey would say, "What on earth are you doing here, you sneaky snackeler, you'll get me stabbed."

Back to the main story, I think I can say most of the tea came from Manchester (by truck) then when they'd taken their tarps (tarpaulins) off they would back into the loading bay and get as close as possible to the conveyor belt. Then one or two of the gang would always help the driver man-handle the boxes, which were pushed onto the belt on their sides, so when they went onto the gantry (which was christened Elmer, after the Burt Lancaster character in the 1960 film) they would be stood up and when they hit the rollers on the EG they travelled a good way. Then they got to the scales, that's why they were stood standing so you could read the name and weight, and believe me, half of them were a gobful. After you'd done your best with the name, that you had shouted to the Checker, he made sure it weighed-in alright then checked it against his sheet and yelled back a number, then with the piece of chalk that you just happened to have in your hand you wrote the number on the box and sent it on it's way into the hurdy-gurdy (I wish I had a photo), which I'll try to explain because, when you think about it, it really was a marvellous machine.

The idea being it took the chests to the floors where they were stored till needed. They came off at a steady pace, say one every couple of minutes, so that gave whoever was doing the job a bit of breathing space. Then when they did come off they ran onto rollers then you could drop them onto the deck without damaging them. If you did get into strife you could hit the 'stop' button or the lads would muck in, as they were a mucky lot at the best of times. If a box had been put on that was busted, someone down below would shout that one was on the way or there was a message written on a couple of boxes before, mind you, lots of things were written but most were unprintable and I won't even mention the guilty one's, so when the chest in question arrived you just used your noggin and a bit of TLC.

Now you would have four or five on the floor and you just waited for the right number to come off and then you'd pair them up, it was best to wear gloves (plus you could throw them now and again). So you had a few boxes there and the other lads had their hand-trolleys revved up and ready to take on "The Long And Winding Road", anybody who's never wheeled a couple of tea chests on a trolley (you don't know what you've missed). It wasn't just a case of being able to handle the weight, but there was plenty of walking involved.

The best thing about working on the same floor as the opening crew was that when the lift wasn't being used, both gates were opened and you could walk through (otherwise it was a good hike), then when you got to where the boxes had to be stacked you built the stack as you went along. Most of the time the two you had on the trolley would be run straight in but then some had to be thrown on top of these, so once you worked out with your mate what you were going to do, nine times out of ten it was plain sailing.

There were a couple of ways you could lob them up, it was either straight (meaning just that) or muscle, which was cut short to muss, and that meant both of you lifting the box up then grabbing it underneath with your other mitt and it was tipped into the spot where it had to go. Say, for instance, you had to throw about ten, it would be up to one of the crew to call the shots so if you, the viewers, will come a bit closer to the speakers, we'll make sure the big uns will be at the back and the not so tall at the front. You should hear something like this, "Sound off, straight, straight, muss, muss, muss, straight, muss, straight, straight, muss," and when you got two blokes in full flight it was good to watch them do it with ease and, I suppose, it's like everywhere hard work is involved, there's a knack. And I can tell you, at the end of some days we were well and truly knackt.

I bet this is bringing back a lot of memories for some, I know it is for me, it's been a few years since I've thought about this and I'm really enjoying it so I'll keep going and see how much more I can come up with. We had to wear safety shoes (with the built-in steel toe caps), which we always called toe-tectors and boy, they were heavy. It was funny to see the Checkers wearing them and we'd have a dig, saying, "What are you doing with TT's on?"

Quick as a flash they'd say, "Have you any idea what damage you'd do to your foot by dropping a pencil on it from a great height?" while shaking their 2HB at you.

"I get your point," I said and added, "they don't half draw your feet."

One thing you looked forward to when you were working on the hurdy-gurdy was the box with the magic word written on it, which was 'smoko', and then the tea break would either be staggered or all together. So staggered meant that the trolley gang went over and did the opening job, while they went for their break and if it was all together, we did just that.

So in the canteen there would be ten or more and a couple of tables had been pushed together and sometimes it was bedlam, most of the gang brought sandwiches or somebody would shoot across to Farrers, which was mostly muggins as I was the right calibre. And what we had back in the canteen, I don't know its proper name but I'll call it a currant bun, which was sliced open, then toasted and marge or butter was applied (with a trowel). To be honest with you it wasn't a patch on a bacon butty but a couple of those certainly hit the spot and if you did happen to be in the second gang to go for your break you had to ask one of the others to order a couple for you, otherwise they'd go like hot cakes. Then with another quick cuppa and a smoke, one last look at the nags that I'd had a glance at earlier, and then it was back to work. But it wasn't all that long and before we knew it someone was shouting, "Lunch," I thought, I'll be in that, they don't need to tell me twice.

The canteen used to put very good meals on but it wasn't my cup of tea, I was always out and about and not one for sitting in there all the time (Mum always reckoned I had St. Vitus Dance). So after I'd eaten whatever I fancied on the day, the SP bookies weren't all that far away and there was a good chance of winning some dosh, so the bets had been placed and I thought, well I've done my bit, it's up to them.

Now, back at work we were always clowning around (we got the job done though) and I'd knock out funny ones that Mum used to trot out (wouldn't have a clue where she got them from). Like this… I'm a little teapot, short and stout, here is my handle and here is my handle, curses, I'm a sugar bowl! The blokes said that I was a raving loony (a lot of you will be agreeing with 'em), I'd say, "I was born like this, what's your excuse?"

Then with a quick glance at the watch I had to find out how the horse had performed, so I'd shout down to one of the lads to try and find out what won the 2:15 at Ayr, and they would yell up, "What did you back?" And of course, like an idiot, you'd tell them. Now that's the biggest mistake you could ever make because the pranksters (for want of a better name) would tell you that one won as they had nothing to lose.

So let's just say the horse was called Lucky Mickey, which I'd shouted down, then three or four tea chests later the message would read '2:15 at Ayr, Lucky Mickey, won at 5/1'. Oh boy, was I jumping up and down, that was great news, then a short time later I'd have to get another result, you don't have to be a Rocket Scientist to work out what's coming next but I'm going to tell you. So (again) I'd tell them my horse, which was called Dusty Carpet (well, I thought it would take some beating). Then the box arrived '2:50 at Doncaster, Dusty Carpet, won at 11/4'.

A lot of the bets I had I would take what they called an accumulator, which included a round reverse, double, treble and a roll up. Now a few of the chaps could work out to a penny how much you had to collect so the word was passed around that I'd got a double in and still had a few more going for me and wouldn't that be a nice little windfall if they all came up. So there was plenty of back-slapping going on while some would sing, "For he's a jolly gorilla."

Then when knock-off time came the first stop would be the betting shop and then you would look at the board and the 2:15 at Ayr, Lucky Mickey didn't even make it into the first three. Then with a glance at Doncaster, not a mention of Dusty Carpet (I'd been taken to the cleaners with that). I checked behind the counter then knew that I'd fallen for the three-card trick, I should have held mine closer to my chest (and not told them what I'd backed). Hey, don't get me wrong, it wasn't just me that got my leg pulled, for anybody who had a bet there was a good chance they would be lead up the garden path. It would get to that stage where a conversation would go like this:

First person, "Did you have a flutter?"

Second person, "Yes."

FP, "What did you back?"

SP, "Mind your business."

I told Audrey once about some of the antics they got up to, she said, "If I were you I wouldn't trust 'em any more, as they're nothing but sneaky snackelers."

So now I was settled into The Crazy Gang, I don't know how this next bit came about but we started drinking (guzzling) in The White Bull, maybe because it was nearer the bookies (than the New Inn) and there we would have some great sessions while playing cards or dominoes. The card game we played was FK (nobody knows) or what we called Cockerwallah, I don't know if that's spelt right but it's near enough for me and the blokes will know what I mean.

The idea being you had to follow suit (when possible) or you could change it to another suit as long as you had the same number or picture card and if you just happened to have an ace in your hand you could then change it to any other suit you wanted. There were always shouts of Burtons or John Collier and, if you remember, their slogan was 'John Collier, John Collier the window to watch'. Of course the lads on The Turf changed it around and chanted 'John Connelly, John Connelly the winger to watch', quite good for its time.

Now I'll try and explain the game we played with the dominoes and it was called Honest John and the person with the highest double went down first, then you would go clockwise and all the players made their own line and they had to play on that till someone got rid of all their dominoes. If someone couldn't go you had to borrow off the next bloke, so on a good round you could dish out about three and it was better still if you gave them a double, all the time making sure you could go yourself. It did take quite a bit of working out and then the first one to chip (finish) was the winner and the rest would have to count up how many spots they had left and we'd normally play for a penny a spot, which might not have seemed much but if you were caught with a fistful it could work out a bit expensive.

Just a couple of things about work, the first one is, and we'll go back to the opening gang, with having to use the hammer so much it put a lot of strain on the wrist and the medical term was Tenosynovitis (today it's called RSI). After a while you'd have a small lump, which wasn't sore to touch, but would cause you a bit of pain. So you'd go and see the wrist specialist at Carr Road, Nelson. He was very good, you had to hand it to him (his brother had a business next door, it was a second-hand shop and, if I remember right his wife was called Rose). So we'll say it was me (why not) who had been and got a certificate for a few days off (longer if it was the drinking hand). So you'd take it into work and the lads would say, "What did the specialist say?"

And I'd tell them, "I have Tenosynovitis."

They would all chorus back, "Itsasignoflazyitis," (that's a clever one).

The other thing I want to tell you about (and most of you should remember), was when they reduced the working hours, so instead of knocking an hour off here, there and everywhere they bundled it all together and we finished at lunchtime on Friday, unless a couple of trucks rolled up late then it went into overtime.

I think it was about now that Jock and myself had formed a strong friendship, so if we had managed to have a couple of nights in the pub with the other boys during the week, when Friday rolled around, and if the weather looked anything decent, well it would seem a pity to be sat in the Tap Room, we got into B-MG-S-T-P and not necessarily in that order. I suppose I'd better do the right thing and decode that for you and it's bowls, mini-golf, snooker, tennis and pictures. With the B-MG-S-T we never really took it that seriously and we had plenty of fun.

This one day we were playing bowls and it was my turn to send the Jack on its merry way so I burst into song with "Hit The Road Jack", it looked good when it left the hand, even the follow-through was spot on but I'd given it a bit too much oomph and, of course, it trickled into the gutter, just where this little old fella was sat sitting on a bench. He most probably enjoyed watching bowls (boy, was he in for a shock), he picked the ball up and sent it back, we shouted, "Thanks."

Then I had another go and would you believe it went off the green again, this time it took him a bit longer to get up, having done that he rolled it back, "Thanks a lot," we said. Then lo and behold, kerplop, off it went again, Jock said, "Three out of three, at least you're consistent." The old chap picked it up, plonked it on the green, then walked away. And that's a true story, which is just as clear in my mind today at it was all those years ago.

Now, the mini-golf was at Towneley, it might have been called pitch and putt, if I remember right it was only 9 holes and they were par 3's (but you could still get in trouble), and I think you went around twice. I honestly don't know why we didn't play (the proper) golf, maybe because of the cost of the clubs and the membership. And that brings us to the snooker, which we used to play in the Concert Artists and it wasn't a bad pint down there and the frames were always close so it made a good day.

The tennis was alright but more energetic than the others. We'd both have to be keen before we gave it a go and, of course, at least once a month there would be a good film showing so that's where the flicks came in. When I told you about snooker, here's one for the lads (if I've got the name right), The Carlton Billiard Hall, which you got to by going down about four flights of stairs, or there could have been a lift, I haven't thought of that place in years and it could have gone out of the bacon rind (mind) if I hadn't mentioned snooker.

Now I am just thinking, what with talking about Brooke Bonds and the things we did, I reckon I've described it to a tea, I could tell you a lot more stories (believe me) but most of 'em would have trouble getting past the censors. Just think, this could encourage somebody to put pen to paper (or Shaeffer to sheet) and write their side of the story. C'mon lads, you can do it, and here's a bit of advice (for what it's worth), if you're looking for something to get you started you could take a (tea) leaf outta my book, that should do the trick and get the tea flowing through your veins. And if you're anything like me, I know those were the best years of my life, which I wouldn't have missed for all the tea in (Brooke Bonds) China.

One night, with Pauline and John, Audrey and I went to see Acker Bilk at The Cabaret Club and during the interval we managed to have a chat with AB and that was the icing on the cake, it made it a great night. Just a couple of other artists we saw were The Searchers at the 77 Club and Freddie (parrot face) Davis.

Now folks, it's time for a 'guess what' but you won't guess this in a month of Sundays. We were flitting again because Pop was working at Nelson and I think the travelling was getting a bit too much. So the brains trust had met and they were going to solve that by moving nearer to his work, and further away from mine and then, of course, Australia. It's a wonder they didn't move to John O'Groats and have done with it, then we would've been going around the world backwards.

I said to Mum, "You've had more moves than a chess champion," which I thought was clever but it didn't do a blind bit of good, the committees decision stood, they were going. So then it was up to me to find the best way to get to work, as Pop did when he was doing it from the other way. Don't get me wrong, it wasn't a million miles away, but just a little awkward, I had a few options, I tried it by push-bike a couple of times, which wasn't too bad getting there, I think my PB (personal best) was about an hour, but going home it was a hard slog, plus there was a lot more traffic which I steered clear of at all times. So if one day I did go on the bike I could get the bus home (then bike it back the next day, or after work, whenever I felt like it).

The other way I tried was the train, which was twenty minutes walk to the station, then I had to get off at the barracks and again another ten to fifteen minutes to walk to work. Or the other one was the bus, which I could get from Hilldrop and that took me right through to Gannow Top (Hilldrop, Gannow Top, I didn't mean it to rhyme like that, it just came out, as it does a lot of the time). Or I could get the bus from Walton Lane, which they called the limited stop (meaning that), so I had to get off at Burnley then get another to Gannow Top (it seems all roads lead to GT). Once I got into some sort of a routine it was easier than I first thought, plus one of the lads from work, Hughie, gave me a lift a few times and on those minus mornings we were freezing but we always managed to get to work on time, so that was the main thing.

I can't remember when this actually happened (but I do know it should go in between the next few lines) so it'll be told now, and that was I'd started knocking around with Gus. He came from Liverpool and, of course, anyone from that neck of the woods were called Scousers. He had a great sense of humour, it was almost as good as mine (ha ha), some of the things we used to come out with, I don't know about keeping a diary, a tape recorder would've been the right way to go.

I'd say to him, "Can you teach me to talk Scouse?"

He said, "Ewe gorra lern yerself, ar kid."

So from then on in I was hanging on his every werd, if we spotted someone a bit dolly dimple (simple) he would say, "That bloke would forget his bum if it wasn't riveted on," or again, if anyone was off colour or a little pale (that's not a small bucket), he'd give it, "I've seen more blood in a banana."

I said, "I like that, it has appeal," and I'd been saving that fer an occasion like this and, of course, he shrugged his shoulders and that's all he sed.

So it prompted me to have a go, in my best Pickering voice (Wilfrid Hyde-Whites character in "My Fair Lady"), "I say there old chap, that was a joke," and adding, "wersia sensa yuma?" (where is your sense of humour).

And Gus sang back as loud as he could, while doing his Professor Henry Higgins act, "By Jove, I think he's got it," and I can tell you folks, he frightened me to deaf.

By the way, MFL was taken from "Pygmalion", the music was supervised and conducted by André Previn (that well known supervisor and conductor), there were some great songs from the film, we had a bit of fun with a few of them; "On The Street Where You Live" (I have often staggered home drunk before); "The Rain In Spain" (always flows down the drain); "With A Little Bit Of Luck" (my Littlewoods might just come up); "I Could Have Danced All Night" (that's what the pregnant ballerina should have done); "Get Me To The Church On Time" (come ed, we've got to get to the pub on time); "I've Grown Accustomed To Her Face" (I've thrown a custard in her face and she's a trifle deaf); and "Wouldn't It Be Lovely" (all I want is a pint somewhere).

I heard that Gus had been in Burnley since 1962, I asked him one day what brought him here, he said, "The bus (and it worked out a lot cheaper) as I've always wanted to travel." But in all seriousness I'm glad he did, otherwise our paths may never have crossed.

This one day a young lad was putting up a sign outside Brooke Bonds when his Boss shouted, "Joe, come down, it's smoko."

"I'll be there in a tick," he said, "I just want to finish this bit."

So after he'd done that he gave it a tick of approval then realised he was stuck. Now, the only obvious way he could get out was to squeeze through one of the O's, he said, "Good thinking," and that's what he started to do.

But then, when he was half way, he lost his footing and as he'd gone past the point of no return he plummeted towards the pavement and went splat, like a big dollop of strawberry jam. One of the truck drivers from the loading bay was first on the scene, he eased him up very gently, while cradling his head and said, "What happened?"

Joe croaked, "I don't know, I just got here meself," and the next news was he'd snuffed it.

As a few of the lads knew him they went to see his Dad after work. By this time the police had been and told him what happened but his poor Dad was still in a state of shock, so the lads made a brew (as that seems to fix everything) then said, "If you buy a headstone, we will pay for the inscription and we'll come back in a couple of days time and you can tell us what you want to put on it."

After a day or two had passed they had a whip round at work, and in a couple of the pubs, then went to Joe's Dad and asked him what he wanted on the stone, this is what he said…

> *Here lies the body of our son, Joe*
> *He'd liked to have stayed but he had to go*
> *He's gone to a land far far better*
> *He went as he came, through a hole in a letter*

I don't know if you're going to believe this or not (maybe not), but I heard that joke when I first started work and that was rude, or blue (very clever though), back then. But these days I suppose it's quite tame, I've wanted to use it for the longest time and I reckon that was the best place to work it into the story.

This next little bit, I'm not sure of the dates, and that was Grandma and Grandad moved to a caravan park in Haslingden and it was a lot more central for them. Now I was just thinking, there could be all walks of life reading this, so if there's any of you lot interested in the Kings of Egypt (it's your lucky day), well this one should be right up your alley.

In this year (1965) King Farouk had gained more weight (he always had a battle with the bulge), he'd lost all interest in life and didn't want to tour any more, or anything else for that matter. His family and friends were very concerned for his health, but he wouldn't listen, he just kept making pyramidic butties that were plastered with peanut butter, of course it killed him, he was forty-five and his Mummy was devastated (if any of you smell a rat, have you got nothing better to do than go around sniffing rodents).

There were a few more that died this year; Sir Winston Churchill put his cigar in the ashtray; Nat King Cole closed the piano lid, he was forty-seven; Gracie Allen (George Burns' wife) aged fifty-nine; and Jimmy James (English comedian) aged seventy-three. If I've got all the facts they shall be passed on, otherwise it'll just be the year and their age so I'll end this one with that and hope you have a holly jolly Christmas, then we'll move into 1966.

Now, if you hold that thought (year) and remember when I told you earlier about those responses (and of course, you've already seen one) well at long long last, and it's taken me a while, I thought that deserved an extra 'long'. Yes folks, I was almost at my wits end and about to throw the towel in when I remembered those nine words of Sir Winston Churchill's 'Never give up, never give up, never give up'.

So I thought, c'mon lad, just go to the well once more and lower down that bucket of good hope and with that I got the breakthrough I'd been looking for (and finally the permission to use it) and another piece of the jigsaw was put in place. If you want to know more about how I managed this, and I'm sure there'll be quite a few of you that's scratching your heads, all questions or queries must be submitted in writing. Now it's time for a cuppa cha, so I'll leave you to read…

Thanks For The Memories

Hello Mr Spencer, what a surprise
I just read your ode bringing tears to my eyes
I have lived in London for forty-odd years
But I never forgot my happy childhood years

I too remember the shops at Rosegrove
And reading the comics while having clogs ironed
We never had shoes but they didn't slide
Nor did they spark when scraped down one side

Our toys were fun
Or so we thought
Making a tail of a rabbit disappear up your coat
Or the foot of a chicken that we could make walk

What about hopscotch with pieces of pot
Then top and whip and colour chalks too
On a cold winter's day now't tasted better
Than Mam's stew, big suet dumplings – I always had two

Back out to play
With a tin full of holes
With burning band in
Old socks on our hands not to burn on the tin

We played jumping the river and often fell in
I loved climbing trees and tore all my dresses
My knickers were navy and down to my knees
Elastic wasn't strong so a pin came in handy

I remember the "Coli"
Noisy but fun
And for money I took back milk bottles
After pleas to my Mam!

I went to St. Augustines just down the road
Played on the canal bank with boys from Rosegrove
The Ginny was fun and ran past our door
I lived on Griffin Street – never thought we were poor!

We had a tin bath and plenty to eat
And were just as well off as any on our street
At 14 years old I worked in the shed at Nuttall & Crookes
So we aren't all dead

I have been round the world
And seen rich and poor
Great joy and deep sorrow have knocked at my door
Back home now in Burnley, I'm happy to be
Alas there's no Ginny for my son to see

No trace of Little Cornwall
Where we used to live
But folks are still kind here
And help they will give

So thank-you Michael for making my day
My hair is now turning with small streaks of grey
But just for a while I ran down the street
With an old bicycle rim and clogs on my feet

And I would like to thank Catherine Frankland for that, I also love both their titles, the first one was "Treasured Memories" and that was "Thanks For The Memories". I was rapt being thanked like that, I feel I've achieved something knowing that someone has written about their past, we all have a story to tell.

If you noticed one line that Catherine used, which read 'my knickers were navy and down to my knees', I had a good old-fashioned belly laugh when I read it. Remember the girls tucked their dresses in them when they were about to topple and the boys would try to give them a hand, but got a slap across the chops, followed by, "I'm telling on you, so there." Weren't the bloomers massive, there was more material in those than the Union Jack. I don't think they got them from the Army & Navy Stores, it was more like rent-a-tent, and while I'm still within striking distance of The Grove, in "In The Grove Again" (tribute) I mentioned Little Cornwall with Griffin, Hapton and Valley Streets and I just thought it was ironic that Catherine lived on Griffin Street, May was born on Hapton Street and, of course, June used to live on Valley Street and how these three people would come into my life.

Chapter
30

When I was talking about smoko at Brooke Bonds the words 'bedlam' and 'butty' were used, Mum would say, "It's like bedlam in here," we knew what she meant but never thought any more about it, now I'm going to do some digging and see what I come up with.

So, for those of you that don't know, bedlam is an early word for Bethlehem and it relates to St. Mary's Of Bethlehem in London, founded in 1247 (that's old), which was later used as a lunatic asylum and then it was transferred from Bishopsgate to Moorfields in 1676 and since 1815 it's been St. George's Fields, Lambeth. Maybe that's where they got "Doing The Lambeth Walk" from. I honestly don't know if it's still there (what do you mean, I should be an inpatient, that's nice, you lot can't hurt my feelings, I've been insulted by experts).

Now here's what I found out regarding butty, or sandwich. It's normally two slices of bread, with butter, and any sort of fodder that you can get your grubby mitts on and it was first introduced by the Fourth Earl Of Sandwich (1718-92), who used his loaf and made a snack that he could munch on so he didn't have to leave the gaming table (I wonder (loaf) if crusts were trumps) and lose his dough. By the way, Earl Of Sandwich was not to be confused with Lord Bartholomew Butty who had the same idea (as the Earl) but he turned to cannibalism and devoured the EOS and then the butty was born, which I suppose is food for thought.

By this time we'd been saving quite well and looking for somewhere to set up home, as we were getting married and had set a date. We looked at one house in The Grove but we thought the asking prices in and around Burnley were much higher than in Nelson and by now I'd got used to travelling (which wasn't all that bad). So it was nothing against Burnley, we just liked that area of Nelson and it was near Marsden Park, which had tennis courts and lawn bowls, and I think that more or less tipped the scales.

I think we only looked at two places and we fell in love with one straight away, then we had to talk turkey (I got a drumstick) and the deal was done. We put down the deposit of £90, which was a lot of money, but we'd done well in the saving department and that was a good feeling as we were about to start on life's journey together.

Let's have a short break, I've just caught up with the running sheet and I can tell you it took some catching, but now I'm going to beg for your forgiveness (Mum would say you don't have to beg as you're old enough to steal), I should have told you this ages ago but what's a few years between (school) friends.

So come with me, we'll be there before you can say back to the past and I'll tell you about the report book and I shouldn't have any trouble with that and hopefully there should be a photograph somewhere in between these pages to back up this story. I have the item (report book) and I honestly don't think there will be too many in existence and it's a matter of whether I can get the photo to do it justice.

Report Book

It says on the cover 'Take great care of this book', it's not in the best condition so I didn't look after it all that well but I've still got it, I must have known it would come in handy one day, and (boys) if you remember, it not only had the teachers signatures but their comments as well, then you would take it home at the end of each term and it was signed by one of your parents (in my case, Mum). I was just thinking, if this was a video I'd have no trouble in showing you what I mean.

It would be about now that we meet Mick and Jenny and their son, David. Mick worked with Pop, Jenny was Mum's Avon Lady but we didn't know them that long then they went to Australia, not that there's anything wrong with that.

When I was writing before about talking Scouse I thought, where's that lemonade (spade), I need something to dig with and that's better than the biro. According to one of my dictionaries, the werd Scouse is short for lobscouse and then you've got to flick back a few pages to look that up and lobscouse is a stew or hash with veggies or biscuit, or a seafood dish also known as Lob's Course, and I'll settle for that, I don't need to go any further and I suppose in Burnley it would be called a potato pie. So who said you can't teach an old dog new tricks, just now in my life every day is a learning experience, mind you, on the other hand, at times I'm as thick as two short planks.

Here's something a little different, there was a program on TV, the Alfred Hitchcock Hour (or Theatre, you'll know the one), and Mum wouldn't stay up and watch it unless I did as it was a bit on the scary side, plus we'd try and frighten each other but most times, after "A Hard Day's Night", before long I'd be knocking the old Z's off. And this one show, I'd done just that, then the next thing I knew someone was tapping me on the shoulder, I opened my eyes expecting it to be the chap from the pools because in my short kip I was just checking the coupon but the first thing I saw was the carving knife. I almost screamed the place down while trying to scramble onto the mantelpiece, then I said, "What on earth are you doing, Mum?"

She put on her AH voice and said, "I'm putting Pop's bait up and what do you want on your butties, ham, lamb, spam or jam?" And that's a true story, as most of 'em are.

Now I'll continue about the house, all the paperwork had been done (signed, sealed and delivered, which was the normal procedure) and then the keys were handed over, there was a bit of work to do and one job was to take the fireplace out as it was a bit old, in fact it was ancient, it had a time piece but it was more like a sundial, we checked with the funds and we had some money to spare so we could afford a super dooper model. Pop knew how to put them in and he had done a few in his time. We struck a bit of trouble getting the old one out as it was quite heavy and it took a bit of muss, but once that was done the new ones were a lot lighter so it was more or less straightforward.

We'd also decided to decorate from top to bottom, I still had my portable record player and was always up to date with the latest singles so I would try to buy a couple each week (I've still got most of them) and by this time the Beatles had four LP's out which, of course, we'd bought. Then they brought out "Help" and three singles were taken of this LP and they went to number one, "Help", "Ticket To Ride" and "Yesterday". George chipped in with "I Need You" and "You Like Me Too Much" and Ringo got the spotlight shone on him with "Act Naturally", yeah, we really clogged that LP, we'd give it a bit of volume, not blaring, but loud enough and with the house being empty it didn't half echo. On odd occasions I'd been known to sing out...

> *There was a Priest the dirty beast*
> *And they called him Alexander*
> *I won't go any further with this*
> *Or Audrey'll give me a backhander*

Then this one day we were in between LP's and it was my turn to flip it over (I'll tell you this off the record), Audrey was whistling this song, I said, "What's that called?"

She said, "I don't know."

I rolled my eyes towards the heavens, then I asked her, "Who sang it?"

Of course I got, "I don't know."

"Audrey, I'm a very patient man but I think this one is going to test me," I said, "just whistle (down the wind) a few more bars."

After she'd done that she said, "Have you heard it?"

"I don't know."

She said, "Give us a minute and I'll concentrate."

So I took my watch off and handed it to her saying, "Take all the time you need," she threw the watch back, I said, "time flies when you're having fun."

I thought she was going to clock me but she ticked me off instead.

Then suddenly, in her Audrey Hepburn voice, she sang out, "By Jove, I've got it, it's called 'Kelly'."

"Right, we're half way there and from here on in it should be all downhill," I said, "is it a singer or a group?"

She said, "Don't expect miracles and you're always well up on most stuff, so have you heard it or what?"

"Or what," I said, while ducking from the flying paintbrush. I did a quick check in my noggin, trying to remember the top twenty, so I thought, this could take some time but I'm not going to let it beat me. I'd asked a few of the lads at work and they'd never heard of it, so I thought I've got to have some think time or I'm going to go round the bend.

> *I need some inspiration*
> *Then I'll work out my plan*
> *I'll play a bit of Copland*
> *"Fanfare For The Common Man"*
> *That should do the trick*
> *Yeah, good thinking Mick*

I listened to Thursday's request show on Radio Luxembourg or I tuned into Radio Caroline every chance I got. I even read the New Musical Express from front to back and did the reverse journey just to be on the safe side. Some of the TV programs at this time were "Juke Box Jury", "Big Night Out", "Top Of The Pops", "Here Comes The Pops", "Late Night Line Up" and "Thank Your Lucky Stars", these always kept you up to date in the music world and the Beeb had the "6.25 Show" while Granada called theirs "Scene At 6.30".

As you know, in those days, there were no remote controls, we had a way of getting around that by saying, "Jim, turn the TV over."

He'd say, "I'm not that strong." I thought, where on earth does he get that from?

So half the time I would be sat in front of the telly flicking back and forth, Pop would say, "What's the matter, are you having trouble finding anything that you like?"

I said, "I'm looking for Kelly."

"She was at the bingo the other day and someone spit in her eye."

Then Mum shot in with, "Which Kelly, Grace or Gene? And you'd better hurry up and find the one or you'll have those cameramen dizzy."

I'd been into the record shops, I even checked in Woolies, they had their own label (Embassy) but it would have been easier to go to NEMS (North End Music Store) and ask Brian Epstein, just like that other young lad (Raymond Jones) had when he was looking for "My Bonnie" (by The Beatles). I thought, this is going to kill me (just like I'm killing you softly with this song), if that's the case I hope Audrey finds it then she can play the flipping thing at my funeral, by the way, RJ was later an original member of The Dakotas.

So the next time I was in Pollards I had a brainwave, I'd remembered our Bob went in there once when he was after a Pat Boone EP and he said to the girl, "Can I have 'A Closer Walk With Thee'?"

She said, "I don't get off till five, then as soon as I finish I've got to dash up to the hospital, all my family's in there, Dad's got a slipped disc, Mum has a tape worm, Grandad's got an LP (large pen) and me bruvver has CD (chronic diphtheria), by the way, my name is Cassette Case, but I'll go to the flicks with you one night." He thought, she's a nut case and he was out of there in record time.

By now I was getting nearer to the counter (but not the end of the story), there was a little old lady who was next, she said, "Excuse me young man, do you have 'Jingle Bells' on a twelve inch?"

Without missing a beat he said, "No, but I've got danglers on a ten inch."

She asked him if that was a record, he replied, "I don't think so, but I reckon it's not bad for a nineteen year old."

With that she stormed out, mumbling, "Cocky blighter."

Then I enquired about "Kelly", he said no girl had been in today with that name, but he'll look out for her. I said to myself, he might be funny but he's a couple of slices short of a loaf. So I explained to him (the best I could) and was it possible to order it for me, he said that was a good idea and why didn't he think of that. I thought, of all the cheek, I'm the one writing this story and if there's any brilliant ideas floating around I'm going to make sure this little black duck takes all the credit for it. I popped back in after a few days, he said, "You're in luck, we've got the song for you," and there before my eyes was the record in question (it was on the Pye label) with "Kelly" written on it and it was by someone called Wayne Gibson With The Dynamic Sounds.

Audrey was coming up that night so I raced home, I couldn't wait to get it on the turntable then when Audrey arrived I threw the record at her, I think I invented the Frisbee. She played it none-stop, I thought I should never have got the record but it made her day and that was the main thing, but I reckon there were only two copies sold, this muggings bought one and his mother must've purchased the other. Well, I certainly milked that, now I'll have a quick drink of cow juice as I'm up to my biro with the stuff.

So after we'd finished decorating we had some paint left over, then we went out and painted the town and we did a couple of the surrounding villages for good measure, then another night we were on our way down to John and Pauline's. Now, most of you lot will remember how the bus used to turn right into Owen Street (from Liverpool Road) and you would drop off the back and run a short way, making sure you kept your footing. Well, we must have done this many times, like everybody else. Audrey said, "I'll go first," and I'm not sure if she slipped but there was a car right behind the bus, which neither of us had seen. Then I watched in horror (I'm cringing right now just thinking about it and those goosebumps have gone from top to bottom and back again), all she could do was scream as she went smack bang into it. It was one of those things you could see about to happen but could do nothing. As luck would have it no bones were broken but she was very badly shaken (not stirred) and, of course, the car had to be put down. If I'm not careful I'll get a battering but she's got to catch me first.

Now folks, this was not long before we were going to get married (as most of the plans had been made), we weren't sure if we would have to postpone at this stage or not. I think the only thing left to do was to go to the church for a rehearsal, now this is a funny bit (all true, mind you) and with Audrey still being a little sore I told her I'd go and see the Vicar. So off I toddled down to the church and I told the Vicar the story, then after all that he said, "Would you like a rehearsal while you're here, then you can explain it to Audrey and hopefully we won't have to postpone?"

So I nodded, which I tend to do at a good idea (it's just giving credit where it's due, I suppose), with that he said, "I'll get one of the women to fill in for Audrey."

I thought, if she's a bit of 'hows your Father', Audrey could get left at the altar and I nearly said, "Grab one for yourself and we'll have a party, I won't tell anyone and I'm sure you're not in the habit of confessing," so he popped out the back and came in with the cleaning lady. I thought, I've hit the jackpot this time as she had a head full of rollers under her turban and she was wearing a pinny (most probably going raving later), which she was trying to undo, I took her by the hand and whispered, "Leave it on, I'll always remember you like this." I don't think her name was "Sadie" (anyone not familiar with that record, it was a big hit for Johnny Farnham in Australia and he was English from way back).

Now, can you picture this, there I was waddling down the aisle with this woman on my arm and she was polishing a pew or two on the way through (just like a woman), she couldn't help herself, I had to tell her to stop and she could do it after we were wed, only for a few hours a week as I didn't want her working full-time.

Mind you, while we were stood at the altar I couldn't help looking over my shoulder in case her husband walked in, she could sense I was tense and asked why, so I told her I was a bit worried about her old man barging in, she said, "Nay, don't worry about 'im lad, it'll be a miracle if he does, he's on the mantelpiece in an egg-timer, I had him cremated when he died because he hadn't worked for the last twenty years so I make sure he does a little bit every day, even if it's only for three minutes and that way, when the grand kids come down they can play with him," and with that she squeezed my hand, I said to myself, this one's funny, she should be writing the book then I'd have someone to blame for all those old gags.

And then the service had been performed and I thought, for goodness sake, I hope he doesn't say you can lift the turban and kiss the bride. I said, "If that's it then, I'm off."

She said, "I wondered what the smell was," and while she was busy cleaning the collection plate with a bit of spit and polish and elbow grease, while all the time checking on her reflection, I was saying the lines over and over as there was so much to remember and I had to relay it all back to Audrey.

But I don't want to get married just yet so I'll solve that by putting it on hold…

Chapter
31

Now, can you remember when I was telling you about (my love) the films, I got stuck when trying to find out about The Three Stooges, now it's 'have bum will travel' and as I carry one with me (at all times) I'll start by putting mine to the grindstone, on second thoughts, that could be a pain in the backside and I could finish up with it in a sling.

Right, there were three brothers, Moe Howard (real name Horowitz) and Jerry (he was known as Curly) and the other one was Shemp, plus Larry Fine (real name Feinberg). Shemp had left early after starting with Ted Healy where they made 10 films from 1930 to 1934. Then Curly, Larry and Moe made 104 between 1934 and 1946, these were mostly about eighteen minutes.

Meanwhile, Ted Healy was murdered in 37 (the Police came and questioned the people in 39 but they said they'd never heard a thing). Then in 1947 Curly had a stroke and with that Shemp came back, he joined Larry and Moe, they made 78 from 1947 to 1955 (Curly had died in 1952, he was only forty-one).

Joe Besser took over from Shemp (he died in 1955, he was sixty-four) and with Larry and Moe they made 15 between 1955 and 1958. Then Larry, Moe and Curly Joe Derita did 10 from 1955 to 1965 then in 1963 they made an appearance in "It's A Mad Mad Mad Mad World", then they were in "Four For Texas" (1964), so all in all they made 40-odd films plus 200 shorts and over 160 cartoon episodes.

There were a couple of Directors who were involved with The Stooges films, now I haven't seen these names in yonks but as soon as I saw them something just clicked in the old memory bank and it all came flooding back. The two blokes were Del Lord and Jules White (I remember him more so). DL directed 38 from 1935 to 1948 and JW did over 100, they must have been gluttons for punishment. The different teams worked for 50 years, Moe and Larry both died in 1975, M was eighty and L was sixty-four. It's no wonder I used to get confused with The Stooges and if you were like me and got mixed up with Eenie, Meenie, Miney, Moe, it should all be as clear as mud.

Yes, those three were a fine pair if ever I saw one, and to sum 'em up in two words, N'yuk N'yuk. So if something gets me thinking (which it normally does) and I can't solve it, it won't be my lifes work but I guarantee I'll try to find out as much as I can (that's if it's look-upable), besides, it keeps me quiet for a couple of days, plus I can't get into trouble that way.

Right, I suppose I'd better get into tying the knot, most of me mates had done it and they said it's alright, plus it's a bonus if the ball and chain knows how to drive a can opener. I'd slept quite well knowing that when I woke up it would be the big day, but somewhere along the line I must have had a "Midsummer Nights Dream" as that music was the first thing on my mind.

The last time I saw Audrey (yesterday) she said she felt okay, and all being well she'd try to get to the church on time, I said, "If I'm not there, start without me as Burnley are at home." So the nerves had set in early, I was smoking like a trooper, I thought a bucket of brandy wouldn't go astray, then saying to myself, I'd better not or I'll be legless and I was still having trouble trying to "Relax-Ay-Voo".

The clock showed a different time whenever I looked at it (has anyone else noticed that, or is it only me?), then before I knew it I was stood standing (and doing a lot of shaking) at the altar (I bet you lot would give anything for a pen like mine and be able to zoom zoom from one place to another in seconds flat). Then the organist pulled out all those stops and started to play "The Wedding March", I laughed to myself as I had visions of Reg Dixon rising up from under the floorboards. Then someone whispered, "She's here." I thought, I hope it's not Sadie, then I sneaked a peek and there was my Audrey, not only had she made it but she looked gorgeous (in fact, we both scrubbed up well).

I took her by the hand, I was bursting with pride (I knew I'd have to get this belt fixed), then saying, "I didn't know if we would have to postpone the wedding."

She replied, "I was going to go on the market, but I suppose I could do that any Saturday!"

Now as you know, there's a lot of vows that you are supposed to abide by in a marriage (sixteen in all) and here's how I remembered mine; for better, four worse, 4 richer, and the same number poorer. So once we'd got over that hurdle the Vicar said, "Do you, Muckle, take Awdry for your bedded, er, I mean wedded wife?"

I said, "Do I, yes, I do," I knew my lines backwards.

Then he said, "Do you, Whatsit, take Oojah for your awful, sorry, lawful old man?"

She looked around and said, "No one's putting their hand up so I suppose I'll have to."

Then the Vicar said, "If there's anyone who can give reason that these two should not be lynched, hitched, speak now or forever hold your peashooters."

I half expected Sadie to pipe in with, "He's mine!" Then he continued...

Now folks let us pray
For those Clarets today
They're playing at Turf Moor
In the sweep I need four

I thought, this chap(lain) has been into the cooking sherry, then he staggered into the Christening vessel and mumbled, "I now promote you Wusband and Hife."

We both said, "He's got that back to font."

He added, "You may lift the veil and kick the bride," I thought, please don't let this be a bad dream and it's Sadie, of course it wasn't, so we both puckered then pecked as newlyweds do.

Have you ever noticed at weddings (and it happened at mine) how little old ladies would go up to some young man who was unattached (they always knew the single ones) and say, while wagging their finger at them, "You're next, Sonny."

Now I overheard this woman say it to our Jim, he gave me a quick nod saying, "I'll fix her."

"How are you going to manage that?"

"Easy," he said, "because the next time I go to a funeral I'll dig her in the ribs and say 'it's your turn next, Dearie'."

After the family, plus friends, had wished us all the best it was off to the reception, which was held at The Marsden Cross. I'd no sooner got through the door and a glass had been shoved in me mitt and, oh boy, I can tell you it never touched the sides, by gum, I needed that as I had a thirst you could photograph. I was nearly sozzled in half an hour but I soon sobered up. So after the meal and everybody had been thanked we headed for our home to get changed and leave for the honeymoon. When we got there it was time for the old heave ho over the threshold trick, so I carried her purse in first, had a quick smoke while putting the kettle on, then I went back for the missus before the rain got any heavier.

Our wedding day

We got inside, it was one small step for me and a big surprise for Audrey because, unbeknown to her, there in the corner of the lounge room was a brand spanking new television (I had to do a lot of spanking to get that), which I'd organised without her knowing. I said, "How do you like that, my little chickadee?"

I don't think she was expecting anything like that, she quickly grabbed me by the lapels and called me a sneaky snackeler, then kissed me passionately till I told her to stop as the kettle was boiling it's hat off. With that she whispered those three little words, "Make a brew."

Mind you viewers, the telly was only a black and white one, but there again, we were married in black and white, as that's how most of the photos came out way back when. So while I was making the tea (I was well trained) I shouted from the kitchen, "How do you like the television?"

She yelled back, "It's just great."

I thought, I won't tell her yet but the second payment is due at the end of the month.

We'd decided to go to marvellous Morecambe for the honeymoon, it seemed like everybody else went to Blackpool and it was always busy there, no matter what time of the year you went. So a good friend of my parents, a man named John, whose surname escapes me, said he would run us there. I said, "I'd prefer it if we go by car."

And Audrey said, "You tell him, Mickey Plum, as you've got to conserve your energy." I wondered what she meant by that, maybe there would be a lot of stairs at the digs (who knows).

Then we were in the car and after waving to everyone I said, "Morecambe, my good man, and don't spare the horses. Unless, of course, we see a betting shop," (as it was Grand National Day). It was a great feeling to be getting away after all the worry that the day was going to be alright. After a while we voted for a pit stop as a butty and a cuppa wouldn't go astray. At this stage I was jumping outta my skin, I thought, I'd better get back in as I'd forgotten to pack my pyjamas and I'd have nowhere to sleep tonight. Then I threw the wallet on the counter (frightened half of the moths to death) and said, "I'll get these." So we ordered, I handed over a fiver, didn't get much change (only a wink) but I do remember getting a Scottish pound note. I thought, you could have written your name and address on it for the next time Burnley's playing away, but there again, they don't get to this neck of the woods too often.

About the (quid) note, I've still got it, it's most probably only worth a penny these days, which reminds me about the two blokes who were fighting over a penny and that's how copper wire was invented. Then we were on our way again and it wasn't long before we got into Morecambe, we'd always liked what was known as Sandylands Promenade so that's where we headed. When I said before about it being quieter, a few of the places had the 'No Vacancies' signs but we managed to get into the Langdale Hotel.

So we said goodbye to John and Audrey said, "Cross his palm with silver."

I thought, where on earth am I going to get a gee-gee from this time of the day, surely John's not so silly as to put his hand on the floor while some stallion stamps on it. So I slipped him a ten bob note and said, "Hang onto this because one day it could be worth a lot of money if I put it into a story."

'Langdale Hotel'

73 SANDYLANDS PROMENADE
MORECAMBE, W.E
TEL. MORECAMBE 669

30   3   19·6·6

					£.	s.	d.
Name		Mick and Audrey					
Address							
Arr 26		Dep 30		Room No. 2			
2	Adults	£.1 per day			10	0	0
	Days Full Board at						
	Children at						
	Bed & Breakfast						
	Dinners		Teas				
	Extras						
			Total				
	Less £ / /		Deposit				
		Amount Due	£		10	0	0

After we settled in, the Landlady said, "Would you like some food?"

I said, "No thanks, we're going for a walk, then we'll grab something."

So off we went, I said to Audrey, "What about we go for a four-course meal?"

"Yummy!"

I said, "Yeah, and hang the expense, let's have three chips and a fish!"

After the nosh-up we went for a couple of drinks, I toddled off to the toilet and there was a Chinese bloke in there, I could tell he'd just been married (bloody idiot) as he had fried rice here there and even some in his hair (it didn't suit him at all). I wished him good luck as I was picking confetti off his shoulders, he said, "Tank U."

I said, "Yer velcome," (I bet you wish you had a pen like this that speaks any language).

When I got back Audrey was under the table, she'd lost one of her earrings, we quickly found it and then set off for a walk on the prom. I started singing (the best I could), "'I Do Love To Be Beside The Seaside', with my new bride."

When we got back to the hotel we were asked if we'd like a nightcap, I said, "I never wear them but if you've got a Claret and Blue one I will."

Audrey raised her eyes to the heavens and said, "It's been a long day."

When we got upstairs Audrey climbed into the cot and I was looking out of the window, after a couple of hours she said, "Aren't you coming to beddie-byes?"

"No, because me Mum said this was going to be the best night of my life and I don't want to miss a minute of it."

With that she threw the alarm clock at me and then she turned off the bedside light, so I said to myself, "I'd better turn in then."

I felt my way to the bed, pulled back the sheets and jumped in, but as I did I bumped Audrey with my elbow and she went, "Ooh."

I said, "What's that?"

"What's what?"

I thought, it's marvellous, remember when I was telling you about Wilf, he said once you're married you'll know what's what! How right he was, I suppose a lot of the readers will check on that to see if it's right, well it should be, unless the printer has been having fun and games.

We started kissing then she asked, "Will you love me when you get old?"

"Of course, my dear."

She said, "For goodness sake get hold then."

Her arm moved towards the lamp, she just couldn't quite reach but she fumbled around till she found the small packet that was on the bedside table. All the time she was kissing my forehead, her tongue ran along my brow, it must've been fit because it ran back again, then it tickled as it went over my eyelash and for good measure she lashed the other one. I thought, I'm going to have to draw her a map or hopefully she'll find my lips before morning. I felt her warm breath on my neck and was it the fragrance from her perfume that was lingering under my nostrils (or could I smell carbolic). Then her lips kissed my ear, her breathing was getting heavier, she nibbled on my lobe then slowly raised herself above my heaving body, I could see her silhouette as the moonlight lit up the room. It was then she said (and the words will live with me till my dying day), "You greedy pig, you've scoffed the Liquorice Allsorts."

Oh boy, was I in the doghouse, then the strangest thing happened, a terrible storm hit and, of course, she was frightened to death saying, "Mick, hold me tight."

I said, "Where is it?"

She said, "Just there."

And that lightening came at the right moment and it put me back in the good books, then before we called it a night I said to Audrey, "Rev Kev's prayers were answered, he got the sweep."

"How do you know?"

"Because I heard that Burnley had won 4-1 and Willie Irvine banged in a hat trick."

To which Audrey replied, "I don't wish to know that."

Next morning, while we were having brekkie (I'd gone down earlier to get a paper to read about Burnley's win), Audrey said she went past this room and the door was wide open and she couldn't help but notice there was a woman squatting on a po while playing the harp (if you get a mental picture of that it wouldn't be a very pretty sight). I said, "Yes, I know, I bumped into her husband at the paper shop and he was telling me she loved chamber music."

The Landlord heard this and told us about the honeymoon couple who were in last week and nobody had sighted them at meal times for a few days, so he said, I knocked on the door and enquired, "Are you two alright in there?"

And a voice said, "Yes."

Then he asked, "What are you doing for food?"

And a woman yelled, "We are living off the fruits of love."

"Well tell your husband to stop throwing the skins outta the window because they're choking next door's ducks!"

Then before we knew it the honeymoon was over, we both were a little nervous and excited at the thought of going back to our new home, and you know something folks, looking back now we didn't have a fridge, telephone or a car and like a lot of other people we just took it in our stride and managed. Nobody forced us to do without those things, that's the way it was, which is a far cry from today.

I remember this like it was yesterday, when we got home we knew there wasn't much food in, but the first thing to do was to get a fire going as the house was a bit on the cold side (being locked up for a while) and we hadn't tried the fireplace (that Pop built), so hopefully we wouldn't be smoked out or have the Fire Brigade pay us a visit.

Then it wasn't long before it was (home sweet home) nice and cosy, I snapped my fingers for the pipe and slippers while pointing at me mouth and feet. I always said Audrey had strawberry kisses but it didn't do a blind bit of good as all I got from her was a big fat raspberry (and I didn't know they were in season). Then we decided to do a quick check on the cupboards and make a list of what was needed, having done that we had a race to see who could get to the corner shop quickest. Audrey was half way through the list by the time I got to the counter as I still had me slippers on and the pipe in the gob, and everyone knows you shouldn't be running with a P in your G or you could have someone's eye out.

We somehow managed to stagger back with our arms full of goodies while tittering like a couple of school kids who'd just raided the tuck-shop. There was more food than you could throw a tin opener at as we had stocked up big time, so we were on the road to married life (it must have been about the only one that Hope and Crosby never filmed) and I can tell you, it was a nice feeling sat there in our abode, munching on Liquorice Allsorts, well one of us was, as I had to sign an affidavit because Audrey used to say, a verbal contract is not worth the paper it's written on.

Chapter
32

Right listeners, if you're ready to read some brilliant writing I suggest you pick up another book (maybe a tad late for that) as this one will just keep plodding along till it comes to a screeching halt. So I'll leave you to view this next bit and I'll try to put the remaining stories in their right order and as long as I keep a few paces (or in my case, pages) in front of you, that's all that matters.

When I did that bit on those composers it got me thinking, there are some famous people that I wanted to write about but just couldn't get enough on them (for my liking) to put it into a tribute and, as you lot should have gathered by now, I love the films and their stars. So I thought I'll combine the three and see what I can dig up, I've got nothing to lose (it should be fun) and I assure you it's not a history lesson, it's a test for me, and if just one person gets something outta this then that's my reward in itself. There will be snippets or gossip (on the stars), whichever way you look at it and, of course, it shall be done (on earth as it is in heaven) in my screwball style and if anybody does manage to get under my guard (I'll sack him for not doing his duty) I can always slot them in somewhere else, so grab yourself a drink and a couple of bickies and I'll start with the best.

And that's Alexander The Great, he was a mighty warrior and at only twenty he was the King of Macedonia. In 1956 they made a film A The G with Richard Burton, Frederick March, Stanley Baker, Clair Bloom, Peter Cushing, Michael Hordern and Harry Andrews. Alexander died young from fever (or was it the dreaded Lurgi) aged thirty-three.

Well, we're off to a flying start and now I'll keep in that vein and you can "Come Fly With Me". The next person, John William Alcock, born in Manchester, was an aviator and he teamed up with Arthur Whitten Brown, he was also a British aviator and, of course, they flew non-stop across the Atlantic. They left from Newfoundland and arrived in Ireland in just over sixteen hours. Sadly, six months later, JWA was killed when his plane crashed in France, he was twenty-eight. They made a film about him and John Holmes played the lead role in the cockpit. "Come Fly With Me" could be heard throughout the film, sang by Frank Martin or Dean Sinatra, I always get confused with Italians.

Here's one that made me sit up and take notice (as I was falling outta my rocker), it's about Countess Elizabeth Bathory 1560-1614, four films were made of her life, it's alleged she killed over 600 girls and women and used to bathe in the blood of virgins to keep her skin white (I'll disappear after this as my bath's ready), she was kept under arrest till her death. I can tell you that's true, if you don't believe me, look it up in your Funk & Wagnall, and seeing as I've had my head down and bum up in their reference books while digging some of this up (they are always at my fingertips and they come in handy for sitting my coffee mug on), I thought I'd give them a mention. In 1877 Isaac Kauffman Funk founded IK Funk & Co, he was joined by Adam Willis Wagnall in 1878, so IKF and AWW, as they were known by their friends, formed Funk & Wagnall in 1890 and the rest, as they say, is history. By the way, Mr Wagnall lived to be one hundred and one.

I should have put this one in earlier about Eddie Acuff (you might ask, who?). He was in "The Petrified Forest" but better known for his role as the Postman in the Blondie and Dagwood films, he was only forty-eight when he died and not surprisingly, I suppose, as he copped a battering every other day. His sister-in-law was Emily Stamp, the local Postmistress who was a spinster. When she went to the dead letter office (in the sky) they put on her tombstone 'returned unopened'.

Brendan Behan, 1923-64, "The Quare Fellow" was his only play to be filmed. Alexander Graham Bell, 1847-1922, invented the telephone and suffered a lot from depression because nobody ever rang him as he was the only one with the phone on. Spencer Gordon Bennett, 1893-1987, he was a stuntman and a silent actor, he made a few films then went on to direct serials and there was James Gordon Bennett, 1795-1872, a Scottish journalist, he went to the States and started the New York Herald and when he died it was the most valuable newspaper in the US. His son, James Gordon Bennett 1841-1918, inherited his dad's paper and later (after he read it) he founded the New York Evening Telegram, plus he was the one who commissioned Henry Morton Stanley to find David Livingstone, the explorer, and Stanley said, "Of all the cheek, why don't you get Alexander Graham Bell to give him a ring?" The reason I brought that up (and I feel better for it), if you remember in "Steptoe & Son" they used to say 'Gordon Bennett' and I didn't know which one they were talking about, mind you, I still don't but I've narrowed it down to three and just to bring this to a close JGB Sr. and Jr. both died aged seventy-seven.

Billy Bennett, 1887-1942, he was a Music Hall comedian and used to wear hobnail boots. Sarah Bernhardt, 1844-1923, made a few films and was played by Glenda Jackson in "The Incredible Sarah" 1976. Ward Bond, 1903-60, made lots of films but it was through TV with "Wagon Train" that he became a star, he died of a heart attack. Daniel Boone, 1734-1820, a few films were made about him and Fess Parker did the TV series. Fanny Brice, 1891-1951, she made 6 films, 4 were done of her life story and one was "Funny Girl" in 1968 by Barbra Streisand, and with a name like Fanny, I wouldn't touch that with a seven-foot pole, and my Polish mate, Mikolaj Kochanouski said he wouldn't go near it either.

Paul Carpenter, 1921-64, a Canadian who spent a lot of time in England, two of his films I liked, "Albert RN" and "The Sea Shall Not Have Them". Kit Carson, 1809-68, he became a legendary figure and a few films were made about him. Enrico Caruso, 1873-1921, he was in some silent films and he was paid $100,000 a film, that's a nice little earner and in "The Great Caruso" Mario Lanza played him. By the way, how did Caruso sing in silent films? Did they turn the subtitles up!

Giovanni Casanova, 1725-98 (I always thought that was a pizza), in "Casanova's Big Night" (a Bob Hope comedy), Vincent Price played Mr C. Catherine The Great, 1729-98, it's a pity she didn't marry Alex (The G), they would've had great kids. Here's something different and it's Champion The Wonder Horse (Gene Autry's), three horses were used in the films, the first was in the thirties, number two and three were father and son, they were in films in the forties and fifties.

There was Cleopatra, Claudette Colbert played her in "The Queen Of Egypt", Rhonda Flemming was in "Serpent Of The Nile" (I always thought Denile was a river in Egypt), Hedy Lamarr did "The Story Of Mankind", Vivian Leigh was in "Caesar and Cleopatra" and who could forget Liz Taylor's performance. Then the Carry On crew did their version, could you imagine Cleo reclining on the chaise longue with a gobful of grapes saying, "Friends, Romans and Caesar, you can all kiss my asp."

Thomas Alva Edison, 1847-1931, Mickey Rooney played "Young Tom Edison" (1939) and Spencer Tracy in "Edison The Man" (1940), where would we be without Mr Edison, most probably watching television by candlelight. Douglas Fairbanks, 1883-1939, the original swashbuckler who swashed and buckled his way through many films, by the way, his second film was made in 1916 entitled "Double Trouble", another one was called "The Mystery Of The Leaping Fish", sounds like a Goon Show title, and this one made me laugh, "Knickerbocker Buckaroo", imagine saying that when you're seven sheets to the wind.

I bet some of you lot think I'm tugging at one of your lower limbs with half of what I dig up, I can assure you I'm not. Sid Field, 1904-50, a great Music Hall comedian who finished up making a few films and he once said, "It took me thirty-odd years to become an overnight success." Barry Fitzgerald, 1888-1961, a great character actor, he made over 40 films. Ian Fleming, 1908-61, he was played in "The Secret Life Of Ian Fleming" by Jason Connery (son of Sean). George Formby, 1904-61, made over 20 films and wrote most of his songs, too many to mention. Sigmund Freud, 1856-1939, "Freud" was made in 1962 by John Huston and it starred Montgomery Clift. Will Fyffe, 1884-1947, made over 10 films, most famous for his song "I Belong To (Glesga) Glasgow".

Sid Grauman, 1879-1950, famous for his Chinese theatre, which he opened in 1927 on Hollywood Boulevard. Samuel Goldwyn, 1882-1974, a great producer who did lots of good films, he also produced SG Jr. and he followed in his dad's footsteps in the film business and then he produced Tony and, of course, he was Sam's friend in "Ghost" and he turned out to be a baddie (boo, hiss). Jean Harlow, 1911-37, made over 30 films and she was married three times, her last husband committed suicide a couple of months after they were married and, as you would have noticed by the dates, she died young. I might have to phone a friend on that one, oh curses, that's out of the question as we haven't had it connected yet.

Joan of Arc, 1412-31, there were a few women played her on screen and they all said, "Is it hot or is it me?" At her last meal they asked her, "Now, how do you have your steak and would you like fries with that?" Al Jolson, 1886-1950, he did the first talkie and made 14 films, one of which was "Rhapsody In Blue" and who could forget Larry Parks in "The Jolson Story" (1946) and "Jolson Sings Again" (1949). Buck Jones, 1889-1942, starred in Westerns, mostly in the twenties and thirties. Spike Jones, 1911-65, and "His City Slickers" among those were Mel Blanc, Doodles Weaver and Billy Barty. Could you just imagine being with that lot, it would be a riot, Spike died from emphysema.

Alan Ladd, he was only 5ft 5in, he made over 50 films, he made three good ones in 1953, "Botany Bay", "The Red Beret" and "Shane", his last film was "The Carpet Baggers" (1966), he died after taking quite a few sleeping tablets mixed with a lot of alcohol (that'll do it every time), he was fifty-one. Lillie Langtry, 1853-1929, British actress who charmed a few men in her time, a couple were Edward VII and Judge Roy Bean, in the film "The Life And Times Of JRB" Ava Gardner played LL. Mario Lanza made 8 films, he died in 1959, being the result of a weight problem, he was only thirty-eight and his wife was shattered by his death and she died six months later, she never got over the shock.

Charles Laughton, 1899-1962, he made over 50 films, I'll just pick two, "Witness For The Prosecution" and "The Hunchback Of Notre Dame". This one night Quasi came home from work and said to Mrs Modo, "Any messages?"

She said, "Alexander Graham rang, he wants you to give him a bell."

Quasi said, "I'll do that later as I want to listen to the play on the radio 'For Whom The Bell Tolls'."

She said, "You'll never hear it."

"Pardon?" And it was then he noticed the big wok on the table, he said, "Are we having Chinese for tea, my Dear?"

"Don't be such a nincompoop, I've just ironed your shirt."

Now here's another one for you, what has four wheels, five doors and it hangs around French cathedrals? The Hatchback Of Notre Dame.

Arthur Lucan, 1887-1954, original Music Hall comedian who struck fame as an Irish washerwoman "Old Mother Riley" and made 14 films with Kitty McShane who played his daughter. Bella Lugosi, 1882-1956, he made 40 or so films and of all things he was in "Mother Riley Meets The Vampire", I think every time he came on the screen he used to scare me to death and I'd disappear under the seat, when I told you earlier about wetting the bed, it's a wonder I never coloured the sheets. Douglas MacArthur, 1880-1964, the famous General who said, "I shall return," he went in 1964 and hasn't been sighted since but was played on the screen by Laurence Olivier in "Inchon" and Gregory Peck in "MacArthur". Jeanette MacDonald, 1906-65, made nearly 30 films, 8 of these with Nelson Eddy. Victor McLaglen, 1883-1959, he made a lot of silent films (here and there, mostly there) then did well in Hollywood. Kitty McShane, 1898-1964, I just mentioned her a few lines back, she played the daughter of Old Mother Riley, in fact, in real life she was the wife of Arthur Lucan, I bet not many people knew that, it came as a surprise to me. I think I'll have a break here as I'm about half way through and that will give me a chance to get the rest of the alphabet in order.

So things were going along nicely in the marriage stakes, Audrey said, "You'll hear the pitter-patter of tiny feet."

I said, "Why, have we got a mouse?"

"No silly, I'm having a baby, and with another mouth to feed we'll have to tighten our belts."

I thought, if I'm not allowed Liquorice Allsorts, neither is the new addition. My Mum was excited with the news but it's marvellous, isn't it, as soon as someone is expecting, people start frantically knitting, I was no exception and Audrey said she'd try and help me, which I thought was good of her. After that the countdown was on and, as a lot couples will remember this, that's the time when the baby kicks, I used to say I'll be able to retire when he's old enough to play for Burnley.

Seeing as I've got back to football, about this time England was the host country for the World Cup. So I'll keep it short and sweet, I think a lot of people were surprised they made it to the final but were pleased to see them win and become World Champions, mind you, they haven't done much since, so c'mon lads, it's about time you won another.

Now I'll carry on where I left off so there's Somerset Maugham, 1874-1965, most of his works have been filmed. Louis B Mayer, 1886-1957, teamed up with Sam Goldwyn and formed MGM. Max Miller, 1895-1963, (The Cheeky Chappie) made over a dozen films, I think most of his patter was censored, he always said to his audience, "There will never be another after I'm gone," well I reckon there has been quite a few and just to mention a couple of 'em, Billy Connolly and Robin Williams.

AA Milne, 1882-1956, he wrote "Winnie The Pooh" and many more. Carmen Miranda, 1913-55, famous for her fruit arrangements and most of 'em were eaten at the wake. Tom Mix, 1880-1940, supposedly a US Marshal, made 400 films, someone once said he rode like a part of the horse, of course, they didn't say which part, he was killed in a car accident and you'll see by the dates he was dead and buried a long time before we started watching him in the late forties.

Rin Tin Tin, 1916-32, supposedly he was one of five pups found in a trench by a Lieutenant in WWI, he took him to California and there RTT (as he was known to the other dogs) earned over $5 million and when on the casting couch he barked at Lassie, "How would you like a Schmacko, shweedheart?" It was reported he passed away with his head in Jean Harlows lap, what a way to go, lucky dog, he was sixteen (or one hundred and twelve). His son, R Double-T Jr. followed in his dad's paw prints and some of the films to his credit were "The Postman Always Rings Twice" (and gets bitten once), "A Tree Grows In Brooklyn", "The Last Post" and "Dog Day Afternoon", he also had a bit part in "Lassie" and they called it "Puppy Love". Yep, he was a pup off the old dog, in fact, he was so clever he used to play cards in the breaks, the only problem was when he got a good hand (or in his case, paw) he wagged his tail!

Mike Todd, 1907-58, he gave us Todd AO, was married to Liz Taylor and he died in a plane crash. Leo Tolstoy, 1828-1910, "War And Peace" and "Anna Karenina" were both filmed. Henri Toulouse-Lautrec, 1844-1901, the famous painter who loved "Little Women" and most of them would ask him to paint 'em in the nude, his reply was, "Yes, but can I leave my socks on?" or, "I'll have nowhere to stick me brushes." Ben Turpin, 1874-1940, the cross-eyed comedian who would walk into a room and most of the people would yell, "Who are you skenning at?" Mark Twain, 1835-1910, he wrote "Huckleberry Finn", "Prince And The Pauper", "Tom Sawyer" and more. Rudolph Valentino, 1895-1926, made over 30 films, several women committed suicide when he died suddenly aged thirty-one. Vincent Van Gogh, 1853-90, he was the tormented artist, he went mad and was about to shoot himself, his wife was laughing at him while dusting off the insurance policy, he screamed at her, "Go ahead and laugh, but you're next."

When I was telling you about that record (Kelly), I mentioned a Pat Boone one and, as a matter of fact, I still have it and it's an EP and the tracks are:

"A Closer Walk With Thee", "Peace In The Valley", "He'll Understand" and "Steal Away". It was on London Records. You know, I've searched high and low for a better copy (mine still plays), and if you haven't heard these for a long time try the library. By the way, there is a double CD of Elvis (his sacred performance) with over fifty tracks, he sings "Peace In The Valley" and "How Great Thou Art" and speaking of HGTA, I think George Beverly Shea was the first to do it. I have it floating around on a tape somewhere. I must try and get the Best Of GBS on CD, there should be something available by now, so just a minute folks as I make a note of that on the back of my hand as I need the writing paper to finish the story.

Chapter
33

And now I'll get back to the other one where our baby was due any tick of the clock, so most days I was dreading going to work (but we needed the money) and getting a phone call to say Audrey had gone to the hospital. It had been a lot of years since I'd lived with someone that was having a baby (meaning Mum with Jim) and I'd forgotten how big they got. So I knelt up in bed to see if it was morning, it was then that Audrey said those three little words, "Me waters broke."

I said, "Don't blame me, I didn't break it," then as quick as a flash I whipped out my hornpipe and gave her a burst of Handel's "Water Music" and that seemed to soothe the savage breast, or was it beast? I always get those mixed up. I knew the song "If I Were A Carpenter", but I thought it would be ideal if I were a plumber and I've come to fix your pipes.

Now, the suitcase had been on standby so it was just a matter of getting there, which we did, then after doing a few tests they said she wasn't ready just yet but they'll keep her in so I stayed with her till she was settled. In those days they didn't like you hanging around too long but they gave me the phone number and said, "It's alright to keep ringing." I wished Audrey all the best and left.

I didn't get much sleep but next morning I was up bright and early, I rang as soon as I could, they said she wasn't far off and they'd set the dynamite so ring back after the explosion. I rang about an hour later, the news was mother and daughter were doing well and you can come in as soon as possible. I was there before she hung up, I didn't have time to get the cigars (they'll do later) but I managed to grab some flowers, and then what a moving experience to see your baby for the first time. I knew my Mum had gone to Rosegrove to get her hair done and she'd given me the phone number so I rang to say, "Would you tell Margaret when she comes in…"

The voice interrupted, "You can speak to her yourself, she's here now."

When the phone was picked up I asked her, "Are you sitting?"

"Yes."

Then I said, "Audrey and (your granddaughter) Angela are doing well."

I think Mum was back in Nelson before I hung up. Then I carefully cuddled Angela and said, "You're beautiful and you'll look gorgeous in Claret and Blue but I don't think they'll sign you on."

With that Audrey raised her eyes to the heavens (you'd think she'd know me by now) and slung the bedpan at me. I ducked, so that was alright but the woman in the next bed wasn't too pleased, she was using it at the time. The young nurse came over to see what the commotion was and, most importantly, to see where the commode was, I nearly burst into a song with "Won't You Commode Bill Bailey" but changed my mind at the last minute because Mrs Bailey was in the bed opposite and her husband, William, was sat with her so they wouldn't have been too pleased. The nurse looked at Angela, then at me, and said, "She looks just like you."

Audrey said, "Well at least she's healthy," and with that the baby in the other bed burped, filled its nappy, yawned, then went back to sleep. Audrey said that's him to a T.

Now folks, I enjoyed that, I suppose it was leaning more towards toilet humour but it was only a bit of fun and as long as I didn't drive you around the S-bend. I managed on my own for a few days and I fixed it up at work to take time off to be there when they came home. We had a briquette heater in the front bedroom, so on the day both fires were going and the house was shipshape and Bristol (or Nelson) fashion. By the way, we lived at 62 Hendon Road and seeing as I mentioned the other addresses I should put that in, they might be famous one day (ha ha). So it was nice having a family, yeah, it was a great feeling as the weeks and months passed, the little ones are so funny, they're changing all the time.

Now if you remember when I told you about the jukebox, I've done a bit more searching as I didn't know too much so it was only a guesstimation (on my part), that's an estimation and a guess, or for those of you that like to be politically correct, a guess and an estimation. So I fed a Lady Godiva (fiver) into the machine and pressed IP (information please) and I listened to what the man said and he spoke volumes, but I'll only pass this onto you (as it was my money in the first place) and that's the JB came out in 1927, there are quite a few different models that did the rounds (I won't bore you with those details) but most of them hold between 100 and 200 singles. 'Jukebox' is taken from 'Dzugh' which is a West African word meaning wicked.

Now, seeing as I've got some money left from that five spot, I'll press CK and that should bring up Carole King, I was amazed at how many songs she had under her belt, she met up with Gerry Goffin and they later married. So here's some of them and one of her biggest, which I liked, would have to be "It Might As Well Rain Until September". Then there was; (you make me feel like) "A

Natural Woman"; "I Feel The Earth Move"; "It's Too Late"; "Pleasant Valley Sunday"; "So Far Away"; "Some Kind Of Wonderful"; "Song Of Long Ago"; "Up On The Roof" (The Drifters); "You've Got A Friend"; "Chains", sung by The Cookies (The Beatles did that on their first LP); "Don't Bring Me Down" (The Animals); "Go Away Little Girl" (Steve Laurence); "Hi-De-Ho" (Blood Sweat And Tears); "Wasn't Born To Follow" (The Byrds); "I'll Do My Crying In The Rain" (The Everly Brothers); "Take Good Care Of My Baby" (Bobby Vee); "One Fine Day" (The Chiffons); "Will You Love Me Tomorrow" (The Shirelles); "I'm Into Something Good" (Hermans Hermits); and "The Loco-Motion" (Little Eva), who, by the way, used to baby-sit for them and was always dancing "The Loco-Motion" and, of course, Neil Sedaka dedicated the song "Oh Carole" to her. Just going back to the first song, we used to sing "It Might As Well Rain Until October" (and sometimes Septober). I think Terry came up with that so we'll give him the credit for it.

When I told you about those famous people (or film stars) here's a few more that left us in 1966, so that'll bring you (and me) up to date. Buster Keaton, he did over 70 films. Sophie Tucker, she once said, "I've been poor and I've been rich but I can tell you, rich is much better." Lenny Bruce, aged forty, Dustin Hoffman played him in "Lenny" in 1974. Ronald Shiner, aged sixty-three, English comedian, he did lots of stage work. Montgomery Clift, he died young at forty-four. Linda Darnell, she died in a fire, also aged forty-four. One of my favourites was Alma Cogan (the girl with a laugh in her voice), here are some of her songs that I liked; "Bell Bottom Blues"; "Little Things Mean A Lot"; "I Can't Tell A Waltz From A Tango"; "Dreamboat"; "Twenty Tiny Fingers"; "Why Do Fools Fall In Love" (the Frankie Lymon hit); "You Me And Us"; "This Ole House"; and "Cheek To Cheek". She also did a great version of "Yesterday", if you haven't had the pleasure, try and get a copy, there are a couple of CD's available and she died young aged forty.

It would be about now we decided to go up and see my Dad, as I don't think he knew about Angela. I knew he was living up Harle Skye so I got the address off John. When we got there I think he was very surprised to see us but I could tell he was pleased that we'd called. So we had a couple of hours with him and then we had to leave but when I came away I thought, he must be a very lonely man. So, on that note, it'll just about bring another year to an end. Grandma and Grandad had been over for Christmas and it was a good time, then we were into the New Year and not knowing what it would bring us but we were about to find out.

Christmas photo

We'd been to Mum's one night for tea and they told us their news that they were on the move again (here comes the body blow) but this time their sights were set on Australia. So I said, "The three-ring circus, Barnum and Bailey and Bozo are going to pack their tent and pitch it on browner pastures."

And with that Jim belted on the pots and pans and sang, "So here we go again, ummmm, 'Catch Us If You Can', ummmm," then he said, "what's Ringo got that I haven't?"

I said, "Would it be a drum kit?"

Then Audrey said, "That's a long way to go and it's not as if you know a lot of people out there."

Mum said, "Bob and Pat are there (and they were married by this time), plus Gerard and Betty and we have friends in Wolloomooloo."

I said, "Gesundheit!"

And she added, "We know a couple in Wagga Wagga."

I said, "Well make sure you get that stammer fixed before you go, and why are you going now all of a sudden? You should have gone when I was still at home and then I could have tagged along."

"I'll tell you why," she said, "because when we were talking about going, this was brought up at one of the board meetings and we thought we'd wait till we got rid of you, er, I mean till you were married, and then once we got there we would save you a spot."

I think we were still surprised at the news as it was a big move and they were both in their fifties, not that there's anything wrong with that. I looked at Audrey and she looked at me and that's all that was said. I don't think we had any intentions of going but I suppose it was worth thinking about, I said to Jim, "You'll have to watch out for low-flying boomerangs. And what do you get when you cross a sheep with a kangaroo?"

"I don't know"

"A woolly jumper!"

Yes, they were as old as the hills (Pendle and Hameldon) but he hadn't heard them. I said to Pop, "What are you going to do for work?"

He shook his head and said, "It hurts when I do that."

Audrey said, "Well don't do it then."

"But Angela likes it and she thinks it's a rattle."

I couldn't resist this and said, "Let her play with your noggin, you don't use it, and that's one to me," then I said to them both, "you'll miss your little Granddaughter."

Pop said, "No we won't, we'll hit her before we leave, and that's one to us."

So I got back to talking about work and said, "You might get a job cleaning Ayers Rock but it'll take a couple of weeks to put the scaffold up, so if you want me to come over and give you a hand, just stand on the top and shout 'cooee', and providing you're facing the right way I should hear you, if not, yell back later."

So they were counting the days and, of course, they were zooming by and when it got down to the last month they came to stay with us and that gave Audrey and me a chance to get out a few times and catch up with the cinema. I just snuck that in because it'll be coming up again shortly, according to my notes, so I thought I'd better give you a word of warning.

So it came to the day they were leaving and it was dreadful weather, absolutely bucketing down (as they say). Now, anybody that's travelled on the assisted passage scheme would know that they gave you your rail pass. I thought of going down to London with them but it would cost me an arm and a leg (I needed them for work), so I decided not to. Then a taxi came to take them to the station, it wasn't a case of 'no time for goodbyes' (if only I had said this or that, would it have made the Bon Voyage any easier). Once the front door was closed we wondered if we'd ever see them again.

I know one thing I forgot to tell you and that was where Mum and Pop lived, there might be some folks interested, it was 4 Brentwood Road, and as long as it doesn't offend the people living there now, and the same applies to the other places I've lived at, that's my excuse and I'm sticking to it. In fact, all those houses are still stood standing, except for 76 Rosegrove Lane. I'm not normally lost for words but now I've got to make sure that all this comes together, what do they say, if you can remember the sixties, you weren't there. Well with me, a few things are a bit vague so I might have to approach with caution from here on in. Believe me, I'm not trying to pull the wool over your peepers, if that was the case I think I should take it off the needles first or I could have someone's eye out.

I don't know how these next few lines are going to read but I'll go this way, and that is if I wrote about Mum and Pop, not forgetting Jim, going 12,000 miles in a couple of lines then there's nothing to stop me going forward a month or two, and what's a month or two between friends, especially if your name is Calendar. So having said that, I'll say it was then that we got some bad news that Grandad had died, so when we got to know the details for the funeral I said to Audrey, "It's too far for you and Angela, and it'll be a race to get there on time, so I'll go."

And then the day came, and as luck would have it I made it with about twenty minutes to spare. Grandma seemed to be holding up well but it must have been hard for her to go through that again. The service was nice and then it was back to Grandma's and, as always, there was plenty of food. Then before I knew it, it was time to make tracks as it would be dark before I got home, but Grandma wouldn't let me go without giving me a bag full of goodies. The trip home wasn't bad but it had been an emotional day.

Now another football season has ended and it's been a while since I've talked about them in detail so I'll keep it short. The first year Jimmy (Mac) left they finished ninth in the League, the next season twelfth and then third, that was a good one, and finally fourteenth in this one (1967). So things weren't looking too good, plus Angus and Elder were the only two left from what I called The Great Team and I'll finish on that note.

Which brings me to this story, when I looked back on all those films I'd seen, I enjoyed it so much that now I'm gonna do it again (hooray from me and, most probably, your shouts won't be printable), if you want to tag along that's fine, they won't be in alphabetical order, you'll just have to take them as they come. I finished on 1957 so I'll go from there to 1967 and I'll start with this, as it's appropriate; "Your Past Is Showing", Dirk Bogarde did about eight Dr. ones and, in a way, I think they were the forerunner for the Carry On ones (and didn't they just). Most of the Dr. ones were directed by Ralph Thomas, while Gerald Thomas did the Carry On's but I don't know if they were related.

Here are some more; "The Wrong Man"; "Admirable Crighton"; "April Love"; "The Brothers In Law"; "Witness For The Prosecution"; "Will Success Spoil Rock Hunter"; "Campbells Kingdom"; "Tom Thumb" (really a kids film but too good for them); "Too Many Crooks"; "True As A Turtle" (was that Tommy from Lowerhouse? I always wondered where he got to); "The Colditz Story"; "Up The Creek"; "Vertigo"; "The Vikings" (great film); "Cat On A

Hot Tin Roof"; "The Defiant Ones"; "Dunkirk"; "Gigi" (with the song "Thank Heaven For Little Girls"); "Farewell To Arms"; "The Fastest Gun Alive"; "The Golden Age Of Comedy"; "Gunfight At The OK Corral"; "Island In The Sun"; "The Matchmaker", later done as the musical; "Hello Dolly"; "The James Dean Story"; "Man Of A Thousand Faces", biography on Lon Chaney, played by James Cagney; "Houseboat"; "Merry Andrew" (he wasn't like that, it was just his name, mind you, he walked with a lisp).

"Hell Drivers", great cast, Stanley Baker, Herbert Lom, Peggy Cummins, Patrick McGoohan, Jill Ireland, Gordon Jackson, David McCallum and Sean Connery; "The Horses Mouth"; "The Hunchback Of Notre Dame", with Anthony Quinn and Miss Wollabridgeider (thank heavens for Esmerelda); "The Incredible Shrinking Man"; "The Inn Of The Sixth Happiness"; "Rooney"; "Battle Hymn"; "A Night To Remember", which I thought was just as good as (Titanic) the 1953 one; "The Pyjama Game"; "The One That Got Away"; "The Old Man And The Sea", retitled "Son Of A Beach", which I just threw in; "Robbery Under Arms"; "The Pride And The Passion"; "The Prince And The Showgirl"; "Run Silent Run Deep"; "Ten Thousand Bedrooms"; "Sweet Smell Of Success".

"Teachers Pet"; "A Tale Of Two Cities"; "The Story Of Ester Costello"; "The Spirit Of St Louis"; "St Louis Blues"; "Some Came Running"; "The Smallest Show On Earth"; "Slaughter On Tenth Avenue"; "The Silent Enemy"; "South Pacific", we had to go to the Gaumont at Manchester to see this one because the cinemas in Burnley didn't have the facilities. "The Sheepman", he tried to pull the wool over their eyes, Mum warned me about blokes like that; "The Buccaneers"; "The Safecracker", that's one smart cookie, always wears a condom as he doesn't want any crumbs; "I Was Monty's Double"; "Kings Go Forth"; "Look Back In Anger"; "Bell Book And Candle", Tony Bell played for Man City and I think that's how their half-backs lined up.

That just about takes care of 1957 and 1958 so it's into 1959, The Brighton Line, but before I go on (like I tend to), here's one for you and it's testing me a bit. Cast your minds back to the early days of TV, when the Beeb Beeb Ceeb had a few minutes up their sleeve they used to show a train going from London to Brighton and it was speeded up so that it only took about four minutes to travel a couple of hundred miles. I think it was something like 'Go Slow On The Brighton Line', it seems to be flooding back (so I suppose I'll have to mop it up) about the Brighton Line 59, I'm sure they used to say that at bingo, I'll look into it, said he, whipping out his rear vision mirror which comes in handy for glancing into the past.

Here are the next ones for you, starting with; the big bossman "Al Capone"; "Room At The Top", followed by "Life At The Top" (1965) and then "Man At The Top" (1975); "The Five Pennies"; "The FBI Story"; "Follow A Star"; "Pillow Talk"; "Tiger Bay"; "The 39 Steps"; "Guys And Dolls"; "Some Like

It Hot", if that's the case pop it into the microwave; "The Gene Krupa Story"; "Sleeping Beauty"; "I'm Alright Jack"; "The Diary Of Anne Frank"; "The Sheriff Of Fractured Jaw", Kenneth More and Jayne Mansfield, who sported a great pair of 45's and KM was always ogling 'em, and the other half of the time he was just dying to gets his mitts on her Arsenal. One day on the set the pistol packing mama fell over and with being a big girl (thank heavens for big girls), she couldn't get up, the crew thought, she's going to rock herself to sleep, but then the director got four men to lift her, yeah, two abreast.

"The Mouse That Roared", followed by "The Mouse On The Moon (1963); "The Devils Disciple"; "Up Periscope"; "The Wreck Of The Mary Deare"; "The Young Philadelphians"; "Rio Bravo"; "Never So Few"; "North By Northwest"; "No Time For Sergeants"; "Operation Petticoat"; "Porgy And Bess"; "The Remarkable Mr Penny Packer"; "On The Beach", which was filmed in Melbourne and it was supposed to be where the world would end; "Shake Hands With The Devil" (not for a very long time yet, I hope); "A Summer Place"; "Ben Hur", I wasn't too keen on Benjamin but I loved Hur; "Journey To The Center Of The Earth"; "The Mating Game"; "Solomon And Sheba", Tyrone Power died during the filming and Yul Brynner took over; "The Great St Louis Bank Robbery"; "The Man Who Could Cheat Death"; "Carlton Browne Of The FO", changed to "Man In A Cocked Hat", then he was told to FO.

Now we'll travel into the sixties on; "The Time Machine"; "The Entertainer" (will be); "Spartacus", did I hear; "The Angry Silence", I was expecting that, next is; "The Adventures Of Huckleberry Finn"; "The Alamo"; "The Battle Of The Sexes"; "Two Way Stretch", both Peter Sellers; "Jack The Ripper"; "Saturday Night And Sunday Morning"; "Expresso Bongo" (Cliffs first film); "League Of Gentlemen", and playing the part of a ballet dancer is Oliver Reed; "Oscar Wilde"; "Oceans Eleven", with The Rat Pack, they went on to do "Sergeants Three" (1962), "Four For Texas" and "Robin And The Seven Hoods", some people did say that those numbers from the films 3, 4, 7 - 11 were the ones Frank used on the crap tables. If you ask me, it sounds like some sort of cologne or one of those convenience stores.

We're still in the sixties with; "Kidnapped"; "The Great Imposter"; "The Magnificent Seven"; and who could forget "Psycho", if you took a girl to see that they didn't half cuggle up; "The Rat Race"; "Tunes Of Glory"; "Elmer Gantry" and boy, didn't he have the gift of the gab, he could talk the hind leg off an elephant, mind you, when it comes to hey boys hey, I suppose I could give a nephelump a bit of an ear bashing; "The Sundowners", filmed in Australia; "Sword Of Sherwood Forest" with Richard Greene; "Sons And Lovers"; "The Day They Robbed The Bank Of England", I'll have half; "Dentist In The Chair", then they were back with "Dentist On The Job", retitled "Get On With It".

"Circus Of Horrors"; "The Concrete Jungle"; "Too Hot To Handle"; "Village Of The Damned", followed by "The Children Of The Damned" (1964); "Can Can"; "North To Alaska"; "The Rise And Fall Of Legs Diamond"; "The Story Of Ruth"; "School For Scoundrels"; "Swiss Family Robinson"; "Song Without End", the director, Charles Vidor, died during the filming, it was finished by George Cukor; "Make Mine Mink"; "Inherit The Wind", that's my complaint after beans on toast; "Ice Cold In Alex", retitled "Desert Attack"; "Portrait In Black"; "The Millionairess"; "Sink The Bismarck", one day this woman went into the scullery and there was her son soaking his shirt tail in the dolly tub and he said to his Mum, "Can you guess what film this represents?"

"I wouldn't have the foggiest."

So he says, "Sink The Bizzmark."

Folks, here's some from sixty-one
If you're ready then read on

"Come September", Rock Hudson, Gina Wollabridgeider (I love a calendar girl), Bobby Darin and Sandra Dee, young Bobby sings a couple of songs, "The Devil At 4 O'clock", "Circle Of Deception" and "Town Without Pity", the title song was a big hit for Gene Pitney; "West Side Story"; "Voyage To The Bottom Of The Sea"; "Whistle Down The Wind"; "Twist Around The Clock", which was a remake of "Rock Around The Clock", Dion sings "The Wanderer" and "Run Around Sue"; "The George Raft Story"; "Guns Of Navarone", great cast; "Breakfast At Tiffanys", I've had breakfast at Macca's; "The Absent Minded Professor"; "The Hustler"; "Mein Kampf"; "Man In The Moon"; "Bird Man Of Alcatraz"; "Billy Liar"; "One Hundred And One Dalmatians", that would be one hell of a job when it's walkies.

"Judgement At Nuremberg"; "The Misfits"; "Payroll"; "The Parent Trap"; "Pocketful Of Miracles"; "Splendour In The Grass"; "A Taste Of Honey"; "The Long And The Short And The Tall" (bless 'em all), great cast, plus John Mellion, the Aussie actor; "Lover Come Back"; "Victim"; "The Second Time Around"; "On The Double"; "The Pit And The Pendulum" and that's all on that year.

So now we can view
These from sixty-two

And we'll; "Damn The Defiant" with Alec Guinness, Dirk Bogarde, Maurice Denham, Nigel Stock, Richard Carpenter and Anthony Quayle; "Waltz Of The Toreadors"; "The Wrong Arm Of The Law", both Peter Sellers; "Gypsy"; "The Miracle Worker"; "To Kill A Mockingbird"; "The Wonderful World Of The Brothers Grimm"; "Don't Knock The Twist", with the song "Duke Of Earl"; "Dr No", the first James Bond film and I must admit, I thought Sean Connery was the best and he went on to do "From Russia With Love" (1963), "Goldfinger" (1964), "Thunderball" (1965), which was remade and renamed

315

"Never Say Never Again" (1983) and "You Only Live Twice" (1967). I'm convinced it's true, Bonds have more fun.

"Four Horsemen Of The Apocalypse"; "State Fair"; "The Scarface Mob"; "The Music Man"; "The Man Who Finally Died"; "Advise And Consent", Charles Laughton's last film, he should have been in the one before, that would have rang true; "Mutiny On The Bounty" and, of course, Charles Laughton was in the 1935 version; "Crooks Anonymous"; "The Quare Fellow" (not that there's anything wrong with that); "On The Beat"; "Requiem For A Heavyweight"; "Only Two Can Play"; "The Doc Brief", both Peter Sellers but later was changed to "Trial And Error" and "I Like Money" was directed by PS; "The Loneliness Of The Long Distance Runner"; "Geronimo"; "The Longest Day" (all star cast); "Kind Of Loving"; "Lawrence Of Arabia"; "Lolita"; "How The West Was Fun".

Now these are from 1963, starting with; "Under The Yum Yum Tree"; "This Sporting Life"; "Tom Jones"; "Toys In The Attic"; "The VIP's"; "The Birds", after seeing that I can tell you it was a while before I trusted the flipping feathered things; "The Victors"; "Come Blow Your Horn"; "Cleopatra"; "Gigot", directed by Gene Kelly, if any of you lot haven't seen this one, put the book down right now and try and get a copy, Jackie Gleason is absolutely brilliant and the scene at the fair, it's a classic, I laugh to myself just thinking about it.

"Move Over Darling" your tootsies are cold; "55 Days At Peking"; "Donovans Reef"; "Love With A Proper Stranger"; "Heavens Above"; "Diary Of A Mad Man", hey, what do you mean, that's what I should have called this book; "The Man Who Shot Liberty Valance", did the mad man do it and, if so, was it written in his diary; "Irma La Douce"; "Summer Holiday"; "Sweet Bird Of Youth"; "It's A Mad Mad Mad Mad Mad World", very funny film but, oh, how that title has so much meaning these days; "The Great Escape"; "The Running Man", maybe it was him who shot Liberty Valance; "The Nutty Professor", Stella Stevens, no wonder the professor was nutty, I don't mind telling you I was nuts about her; "Call Me Bawana" (call me bananas); "The Hook", music by Larry Adler; "Spencers Mountain", now that's a good book title; "Bye Bye Birdie", no, its not about a golfer who misses a vital putt.

These are from 1964, you can't keep her down; "The Unsinkable Molly Brown"; she was "Mans Favourite Sport"; "The Yellow Rolls Royce"; "Zulu"; "Zorba The Greek", I used to work with him; "Becket"; "Your Cheating Heart"; "Comedy Of Terrors", Vincent Price, Peter Lorre, Boris Karloff and Basil Rathbone, what a cast; then we got a different kind of a western with "A Fist Full Of Dollars", then "For A Few Dollars More" (1966) followed by "The Good The Bad And The Ugly" (1967), great music; "Father Goose"; "Sex And The Single Girl"; "My Fair Lady"; "The Pumpkin Eater"; "Send Me No Flowers".

I loved these ones; "The Pink Panther" (1964), "A Shot In The Dark" (1964), "The Return Of The Pink Panther" (1975), "The Pink Panther Strikes Again" (1976) and "Revenge Of The Pink Panther" (1978); we're still on 1964 with "Rattle Of A Simple Man"; "Nothing But The Best"; "Mary Poppins"; "The Long Ships"; "The Carpet Baggers", Alan Ladd's last film; "MGM's Big Parade Of Comedy"; "Marnie"; "A Hard Day's Night" with the all star cast of John, Paul, George and Ringo; "I'd Rather Be Rich"; "Dr Strangelove" or "How I Learned To Stop Worrying And Love The Bomb", with a title like that they'd have a bit of trouble putting it on a theatre ticket.

That's the end of another year, so let's get into 1965 with; "Those Magnificent Men In Their Flying Machines"; for any of you that has a fear of going up there you can take "The Train"; which was "Von Ryans Express"; "Dear Brigitte"; "Battle Of The Bulge", that sums up Brigitte; "The World Of Abbot And Costello", which has the 'who's on first' routine; "The Nanny"; "A Patch Of Blue"; "Return From The Ashes", no, it's not about the English cricket team and don't laugh, they'll come good one day, I just hope I live to see it; "Having A Wild Weekend" were The Dave Clark Five while singing "Catch Us If You Can"; "The Pawnbroker"; "None But The Brave".

"The Sons Of Katie Elder"; "Sound Of Music"; "What's New Pussycat"; "Major Dundee"; "In Harms Way"; "Marriage On The Rocks"; "The Hill"; "The Ipcress File"; "Cat Ballou"; "Inside Daisy Clover"; "Harlow"; "Hush... Hush Sweet Charlotte"; "Ferry Cross The Mersey" with Gerry And The Pacemakers, Cilla Black, The Fourmost and Jimmy Saville; "Ghengis Khan"; "The Amorous Adventures Of Moll Flanders"; "The Great Race"; "The Greatest Sioux Massacre"; "Doctor Zhivago", he would have been able to tend to the ones that were massacred; "Do Not Disturb"; "Shenandoah"; "Help" the Beatle boys are at it again.

Now I'll take you into 1966 so; "Walk Don't Run", Cary Grants last film; there was "Alfie" and we found out what it was all about; "The Bible" with a cast of thousands, much better than the book; "The Trap"; "Torn Curtain"; "The Wrong Box"; "The Family Way" with Hayley Mills and her dad (John) and the music was done by Paul McCartney; "Georgy Girl"; "The Ghost And Mr Chicken; "Gambit"; "The Great St Trinians Robbery"; "Hawaii"; "After The Fox"; "Madame X"; "A Man For All Seasons"; "Modesty Blaise"; "Fantastic Voyage", good for its time; "The Jokers" with Michael Crawford and Oliver Reed; "Texas Across The River", two great films that were shown on the same bill; "Rasputin The Mad Monk"; "Stop The World I Want To Get Off" remade as "Sammy Stops The World" and, of course, with the great song "What Kind Of Fool Am I"; "Skywest And Crooked", retitled "Gypsy Girl"; "The Silencers"; "Ten Little Indians"; "Stagecoach"; "One Million Years BC"; "The Oscar"; "Who's Afraid Of Virginia Wolf"; "What Did You Do In The War, Daddy"; "A Funny Thing Happened On The Way To The Forum";

"The Professionals" and that brings to an end the ones from 1966.

Now watching and talking about films
Yeah, I'm in me seventh heaven
So folks its lights camera action
And you'll see the ones from sixty-seven

That's "How To Succeed In Business Without Really Trying"; and we'll be "Far From The Madding Crowd"; with "Thoroughly Modern Millie"; "Bonnie And Clyde"; they're "Two For The Road"; and "Guess Who's Coming To Dinner", which was Spencer Tracy's last film; we'll carry on with "Ulysses"; "Fitzwilly"; here's "A Guide For The Married Man"; "Enter Laughing"; after "A Rough Night In Jericho"; "Doctor Dolittle"; "Poor Cow"; "The Reluctant Astronaut"; "St Valentines Day Massacre"; "The Taming Of The Shrew"; "In The Heat Of The Night"; "I'll Never Forget What's 'Is Name"; "How I Won The War" with Michael Crawford and John Lennon; "Cool Hand Luke"; "Half A Sixpence"; "Bedazzled"; "Barefoot In The Park"; "Camelot"; and last but not least "The Graduate", so here's to you Missus Robinson.

Chapter
34

So summer was approaching, the only thing was, we didn't know which day it would fall on this year, but hopefully we'd have some good days and, of course, Mother Nature came good, it wasn't 'cracking the flags' stuff but it was okay. We went up to Marsden Park quite a bit and had some fun playing bowls and tennis, Angela was the central umpire (propped up in her pram) but she slept through most of it, which was a shame really as there were some unbelievable shots played and I managed to get a couple in.

Mum's airmail letters (which we looked forward to), told us they were enjoying their new home but a lot of things were different to England. So Audrey and I talked it over about going Down Under, should we give it a go? We've got nothing to lose and maybe so much to gain in the lucky country. I was a gambler, so I'd take a punt and for £20 entrance fee (10 each and Angela free) it was cheap at half the price and we could always come back. But there again, if we'd gone to all that trouble in the first place why would you want to return? It was nothing against England (like we'd had enough of it), but this was to start a new life and we weren't the first and most probably wouldn't be the last.

So we sent away for the papers and in a couple of days they were filled in and returned PDQ. Then the wheels were in motion to travel across the ocean (or two), now you could either go by ship or air, we talked about flying because the sailing part would take a month plus spending money. It looked like the plane was the way to go as we would be there in just over a day and with a bit of luck maybe get some work in the first week, and I said to Audrey, "Don't worry love, we'll be alright and I'll keep me eyes open for a job," so then it was a matter of waiting.

Now, back to the music scene. By this time The Beatles had more or less taken over the world, then didn't we get a shock, Brian Epstein (their manager) was found dead, aged thirty-two. At this stage we didn't know a lot about the great man's personal life, it would all be revealed later. With him taking drugs and battling depression it was all too much, you know he had money and success but was still searching for more, it's marvellous how little things can topple a big man, and life is short, we should enjoy it while we're here, we may never pass this way again.

There were a few more that left us this year; Vivian Leigh was one, she battled with poor health, was married to Laurence Olivier, and she died aged fifty-four; Donald Wolfit, at sixty-six, English actor, made over 30 films; Nelson Eddy, sixty-six, singer who acted with Jeanette MacDonald in a few films; Jayne Mansfield, thirty-five, was killed in a car crash, she once said, "All men are creatures with two legs and eight hands," and David Niven nicknamed her Miss United Dairies; Spencer Tracy, sixty-seven, the great actor and he did over 70 films; Woody Guthrie, fifty-five, he wrote "So Long, It's Been Good To Know You", "Do-Re-Mi", "The Grand Coulee Dam" and "This Land Is Your Land"; and Otis Redding, twenty-six, was killed in a plane crash.

When I mentioned before about flying to save us some money, we'd done a quick check on the funds and there was enough in the kitty to get away for a few days, so we both said, "Why not?"

We then told Angela to pack her (Claret and Blue) bucket and spade because we were going to show her those sun-drenched beaches of Morecambe. She said, "Goo goo," we thought, that's near enough to choo choo, if that's what she said she meant. So it didn't take long to get there, in fact, we did it in record time, we travelled by gramophone (it's the only way to go, folks) and as luck would have it we got the same digs.

Then the Landlady said, early on in the piece, if we wanted to go out one night that would be alright and she would baby-sit Angela, she thought she was so cute. With that I breathed on my fingertips then rubbing 'em on my lapel, as you do when you're chuffed, I said, "She's just like me."

Now you know when two people say the same thing at the same time, well that's what Audrey and the Landlady did, and that was, "At least she's healthy!"

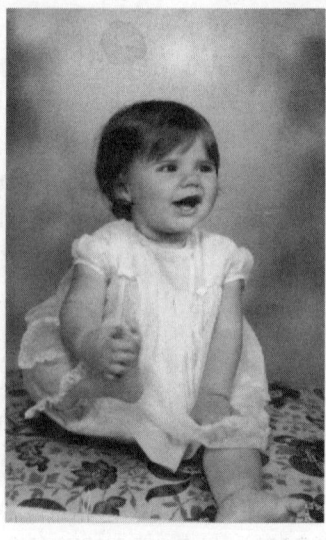

So cute

So this one day we checked the paper and "Doctor Zhivago" was showing at one of the cinemas, we asked the Landlady if it was okay to go and she said, "Yes, but leave the phone number because sometimes, once Mum and Dad leave, the little ones seem to know."

Now, if you know what's coming, don't tell the other lot as it would be a shame to wake them. So there we were in the flicks, almost half way through the film and the snogging and, I must admit, the film was running second (and not even close) as it spanned a few decades and we only had a couple of hours to snog, then all of a sudden the Usher came down the aisle (he wasn't ushing) and he was saying, in a loud voice, "Would Mr and Mrs Spencer please report to the foyer."

I couldn't really let Audrey go alone, while I saw how the film ended, so I thought I'd tag along. When we got there the Manager was waiting for us and he said the Landlady had rang asking him to pass the message on that Miss Jekyll (after her bottle), had turned into Mrs Hyde and we'd know what she meant. I thought, curses, I was hoping the call had come from Littlewoods telling me that my 'any 8 from 11 perm' was the only correct entry. We were just about to leave and he said, "Would you please accept a couple of complementary tickets and you can come back any time," we thanked him for that, then when we got outside Audrey started racing back to the digs.

I said, "Let's go on the beach."

"This is no time to be building castles in the air, we'll go down after breakfast and you can make some for Angela."

At Morecambe

We got back and there was (the culprit) Angela, she was sat on the Landlady's lap, laughing and blowing raspberries like it was all a big joke, there were a couple of noises from the other end, I didn't know if the Landlady was a ventriloquist or what was going on and I thought, I'm not game to ask. The LL said, "She's still so cute, but she can be very noisy."

Under my breath I said, "I know which side of the family that comes from," and here's a tip for the fellas, you never say things like that out loud, otherwise objects will be cobbed at you from all directions which could result in therapy, but you'll notice the purse doesn't move an inch, most probably too heavy.

Audrey didn't want to risk going back to the cinema in case the same thing happened again, she said, "You go."

I said, "There's nobody here called Hugo."

She gave me the ticket followed by a black look and said, "Disappear, Houdini."

Now I don't know if there's many of you that have been to the flicks on your Todd Slone (own), it's a bit of an embarrassment sat on the back row with all the cuggling couples, in fact, the Usher said to me, "What are you doing in between those two girls?"

I replied, "Nothing, honest Guv."

He quickly said, "Here, hold me torch."

So I showed a few people to their seats and watched the end of the film then made tracks and half way home I thought, that was a waste of time, but at least I got a torch out of it.

So we'd had a few good days there, then we had to say our goodbyes, they wished us all the best for our new life Down Under. The Landlady's daughter grabbed hold of Angela's cheek with her finger and thumb, then said, "TTFN little cheeky chops," I thought, I bet she doesn't do that to me, and she didn't, maybe just as well because Audrey was watching her like a hawk, yeah, with talons at the ready and she could have someone's eye out.

It was nice to get back home, Audrey said, "Will you check the post?" I thought, why didn't I think of that, she's right, it would look better in black and white. And now folks, it's sock it to U time so I'm going to belt you with this one and I've saved it for last as I think it's fitting, and what I like about it is it'll fit in here…

> *We've got to go for the interview*
> *And a few more things to sort out*
> *So while we're doing that*
> *You viewers can read all about…*

A Place Close To My Heart

I've written before about The Grove
As you know that's where it began
I mentioned shops and places
Which I saw when sat in me pram

That's My Rosegrove was part 1
In The Grove Again number 2
So this is the anthology
Now let me talk you through

You don't have to say grace
Or for that matter a prayer
It won't cost you a red cent
As I have the correct fare

If you're sitting comfy
I've got a story to tell
Come into my imagination
Hark, there goes the bell

At five I went to Junior School
Oh yes, this was great fun
Much better than nappies
And I had a cleaner bum

I was a little tough nut
Just as rough as the others
But then in times of twouble
I'd hide behind me bruvvers

The Grove was our playground
Yeah, we never had a care
Every day we were mucky
And did anything for a dare

Now there were a few in our gang
And in the sawdust we'd play
We jumped in stark naked
On a balmy summers day

Other times we were cowboys
Frightening dogs and cats
Shooting imaginary Injuns
Folks thought we were bats

Then when down Molly Brook
Tried to jump it for a bet
Oh look out, splash, he's in
Finished up wringing wet

We'd drink Fennings Fever Cure
And then suck on Victory Vee's
Yeah, on a cold and frosty morn
They certainly did please

Now here's some other places
The big Rosegrove Station
Foundry buses on Owen Street
Off to a different destination

There was Dorothy's and Elsie's
Heaps had a fish and chip shop
There's the Four Lane Ends
Where the coaches would stop

Thomas Edmondson Monkhouse
He named his crisps TEM's
Weren't as good as Smiths
But a lot cheaper than thems

There was Bailey's Chemist
And of course Spencer's Mill
Also The Grove character
He was called John Bill

We'd read the deaths in the Express
And some had a black border
Now why did people have to die
Especially in alphabetical order

Do you remember Comeandhavealook
Their real name was Corellars
They sold shoes, socks and jocks
For kids, women and fellas

We spent time at the flicks
Which wasn't that far away
Just a hop, skip and a jump
Where we'd go on a rainy day

Us kids loved the cinema
And we'd go to The Coliseum
All our idols are there
Let's go in and seeum

Once the doors opened
We'd scramble and rush
It was bedlam I tell you
Plus an elbow in the mush

So now we're here inside
Let's race down the aisle
Grab yourself a pew
And sit down for a while

Then once you were settled
You knew where to put your feet
Yes, you sat there last time
Your choddie was under the seat

I was as happy as a pig in muck
Sat sitting in the pictures
Coppers chased the robbers
I munched on Dolly Mixtures

There was always a kid in front
His finger up his nose and pickin'
It was every lad for himself
Once he started flickin'

Girls dragged me to the back row
You know folks it didn't seem right
They were all over me like a rash
Honestly, I was too pooped to fight

There was so much noise
Oh what a commotion
Then the curtains opened
And the film was in motion

I saw "Down Among The Z Men"
Those idiots var var vavoom
I was only a whippersnapper
But a truly converted Goon

We had Mickey & Minnie Mouse
Bugs Bunny and Donald Duck
Plus Huey, Duey and Louie
Boy didn't they run amuck

Betty Boop and Barney The Bear
Woody Woodpecker was good
Then came wabbit season
Exclaimed Elmer J Fudd

Chilly Willy The Penguin
That skunk Pepe Le Pew
Sylvester and Tweetie Pie
And the bumbling Mr Magoo

Heckle and Jeckle were funny
And Casper The Friendly Ghost
He'd already had brekkie
But you couldn't see the toast

Daffy Duck plus Foghorn Leghorn
Popeye, Olive Oil and Bluto
Spaceships outta this world
Zooming towards Pluto

Where Flash Gordon was in strife
Now what on earth would he do
Yeah, he's right up the creek
And with a barbed wire canoe

All the kids loved Flash
While Ming copped the jeers
Then when FG got free
You'd hear our cheers

There was The Three Stooges
Ma & Pa Kettle and Bowery Boys
Great belly aching laughs
More fun than playing with toys

We would emulate our heroes
"Brother Can You Spare A Dime"
Hitchcocks "Dial M For Murder"
It seemed a perfect crime

Robert Newton was Long John Silver
Remember the kid from The Fold
Always shouting "Aarrgh, Jim me lad"
Just call me Short Tom Gold

Tarzans Weissmuller and Barker
Both had a muscular chest
I wanted to take me shirt off
But I had on a dirty vest

George Burns and Gracie Allen
WC Fields, Crosby and Hope
Then the Movietone News
Always showed The Pope

Arthur Lucan was Old Mother Riley
With his daughter Kitty McShane
And little Brandon De Wilde
Through "Shane" he shot to fame

"Stalag 17" was a favourite
The way those Germans spoke
Ve hav vays and ze meanz
Of making U Eeenglisher tolk

There was Paramount and MGM
J Arthur Rank plus RKO
Martin and Lewis were "Pardners"
So were Ceesco and Pancho

Lots of actors played cowboys
Galloping around on the screen
I shot baddies with Gene Autrey
I was allowed, it was my dream

I sang along in "Calamity Jane"
With Howard Keel and Doris Day
She made a brew in "Tea For Two"
Not for me but Gordon McCrae

There was "Annie Get Your Gun"
And 'ah so' Charlie Chan
In "Casablanca" Bogie said
"Er, play it again Sam"

Peter Cushing, Vincent Price
They'd star with a vampire
We'd go to The Palace and Odeon
The Grand or The Empire

Some were called Bug & Scratch
And there you would itch
Then if you went upstairs
You were looked upon as rich

Edmund Purdom, Alec Guinness
Spencer Tracy, Kate Hepburn
Curly top Shirley Temple
Made me wittle heart yearn

Carole Lombard, Susan Hayward
Betty Grable, Betty Hutton
I couldn't get enough of their looks
Yes indeed I was a glutton

Rita Hayworth, Maureen O'Hara
Loretta Young, Audrey Hepburn
Lana Turner in that sweater
She made many a head turn

Dale Evans and Roy Rogers
I'll even throw in Trigger
There was Sophia Loren
Yabba dabba doo what a figure

Judy Garland, Ava Gardner
Grace Kelly, Barbara Stanwyck
Boy this is exhilarating
But you're doin' well Myck

Jean Simmons, June Allyson
Greta Garbo, Natalie Wood
Who could forget Mae West
When she was bad she was good

Vivian Leigh, Ginger Rogers
Janet Leigh, Jean Harlow
And what about these two (or four)
Miss Mansfield and Miss Monroe

Victor Mature, Van Johnson
Clifton Webb, Forest Tucker
Burt Lancaster, Nick Cravat
He was a funny little fella

Gilbert Roland, Randolf Scott
Cornel Wilde "The Greatest Show On Earth"
Charlton Heston "The Ten Commandments"
You certainly got your moneys worth

So the show was finished
And no it wasn't a dream
With cap in hand we'd stand
Then sing "God Save Our Queen"

The Grove was the place to live
I'm proud to come frae there
Now after the third time around
They could make me Mayor

Well folks I must close now
The dreaded night is falling
Who knows if I'll attempt another
Before the grim reaper comes calling

You've had a guided tour
But alas we've got to part
For now I'll say goodbye to
A Place Close To My Heart

That was a tribute to those stars that I used to look up to (on the screen) and "My Way" of saying "Thanks For The Memories".

Another thing that's been in the think tank for what seems like a lifetime are the names of all the cinemas in Burnley. So going from A (onwards) they are: Alambra, Coliseum, Continental, Empire, Empress, Grand, Imperial, Kings, Majestic, Odeon, Palace, Pentridge, Roxy, Savoy, Temperance and Tivoli.

Chapter
35

Let's get back to the home front (situation), while you were reading that everything has happened all at once, the interview went okay, we had the passport documents done and we'd put the house on the market (we had a helluva job to move it there, but we managed) and any day now we should get the D(eparture) date.

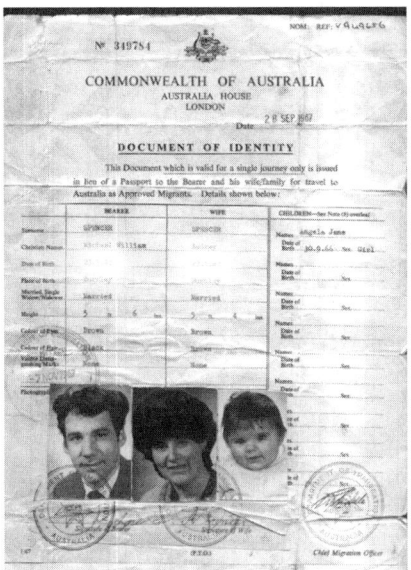

We'd had an offer on the house which we decided to take so that was a weight off our minds, then not long after that we got the date for our departure (late October). Then we moved in with Maureen and Peter till it was time for us to leave old England forever.

Now, you'll just have to bear with me half a tick as I rack the old Mark Twain (brain) to see that I haven't forgotten anything. I know there have been little bits left out, not for personal reasons, it was just that I couldn't string them together to make a story but they're still stored away somewhere in the archives of my mind, so who knows, they might surface later (have spade will travel). I know one thing and that's I've fired a few broadside but I've also put meself down plenty of times. Mind you, I have had a load of laughs at my own expense, in fact, it cost me nothing at all and it was worth every cent so you, the listeners, have been able to read throughout how I've loved comedy films and, of course, music (from a very early age). If I had my life to live over (or this book to write again) I wouldn't change a crotchet for anybody and now to get the chance to write about them, in many ways I do feel very fortunate.

In some of the stories you would have noticed how I put animals in, or talked about the ones we had, I won't name them all, I do know I told you about the geese but I hope you weren't taken on a wild goose chase. Now I must point out that none of them were harmed during the making of this, it was only the English language that got slaughtered on my journey.

I think this is a good time to go back to work as there are a few loose ends to tie up, and maybe one last water fight for old times sake. I won't be able to sling it around so freely out there as they're in the middle of a drought and it's only spring so that doesn't sound too good, but we'll worry about that when we arrive (only if we have to).

Now, most of the lads at work suggested we have a bit of a booze up, a sorta farewell drink, so they didn't have to twist my arm or ask me twice but I said, "Never mind a bit of one, lets go the whole hog."

They said, "That's typical of you, you're a real pig for punishment," I thought, the swines they're on to me, but one thing is for sure, I won't let 'em shove their trotters in me trough.

> *I think a few watering holes*
> *Had been thrown around*
> *And The Cabaret Club (good)*
> *Yeah, that won hands down*

I do remember that some of us had met in The Red House, which was only a hop(s), spit and hiccup away from the club. So once we got inside we soon caught up with the rest of the gang, I think there were about twelve or fourteen of us, we had a word with a couple of the blokes who were on the staff and they arranged to put three or four tables together so, to anyone who knew the set up of the club, they'd made a spot for us down the left-hand side, right near the stage (and not all that far from the stage door).

We knew beforehand who was on but I couldn't wait to see (him), none other than Michael Bentine. So we were having a great time and the beer was going down well, plus watching the supporting acts. Then it was time for the top of the bill and you could feel the excitement because, most probably half of them (like me) were Goon fans and to see one of them, especially in the old cinema where I'd seen him in "Down Among The Z Men", spooky. Then the Compere introduced him and the hairs stood up on the back of my neck (just like they are now as I relive it), and there he was, in living colour, I never thought I'd see one of those Goons, let alone be so near. I was still applauding after the others had stopped and he said, "Don't clap on your own, they'll think you're a seal and throw you a fish." I thought, I've got to try and meet this fella if it's the last thing I do.

Then he was into his act, he did a lot of impressions and, of course, the one with the bicycle tube, which I'd seen him do on the telly but still good. So by this time the place was in uproar and beer mats were being flung for a bit of fun, then before long they were going every which way. He finished his act, the crowd was going crazy, he came back for a couple of encores then he was gone.

In the meantime, and unbeknown to me, John (brother) had put a few feelers out to try and get Michael (what a great name) to come and say hello. So there I was, with a pint and a cigar in me gob, as I'd stopped smoking (cigarettes) but still enjoyed a cigar on special occasions, when a voice said, "G'day cobber," and there he was with his arm outstretched waiting to shake my hand.

I warmly shook his, as I still had the cigar in me hand, he said, "I've just thought of one more thing I can do with that inner tube, but not in front of a live audience."

"Very good,' I said, then I told him I enjoyed the fish gag and that I'd heard it before but I gave it the seal of approval.

He asked me where I was going to in Australia and I told him Melbourne, he said, "You'll like it Down Under and the Aussies 'They're A Weird Mob'."

I said, "That sounds like a good title for a book, and maybe I'll write one some day."

He said, "You never know, young lad, as stranger things have happened and here's one for you to tell the Aussies, what's the best way to get rid of a boomerang?"

"I'm all ears."

He said, "I've noticed, and that's one to me."

"Tell me," I said, "what is the best way to get rid of a roomerbang?" as by now the beer was starting to take effect.

"You chuck it down a one-way street," he said, and with that he shook my hand again (checking to see where the cigar was) and wished me all the best for the new adventure in the lucky country, then he was gone for good this time.

I've mentioned before about a diary, but gee, I wish somebody had a camera on that night, then I could have shown you the photo because that's a true story and I just had to have some fun with it. Now, only the jokes have been updated to protect the old ones and imagine Mickey Plum writing lines, and reasonably good uns, he said modestly. I did talk to you (lot) earlier about names and not being able to remember a few, here and there (but I don't think I've done too bad). Also, you will have noticed while you were flicking through these pages that this is not your average book (I'm not saying it's above that either).

And to anyone who thinks they've been left out I can assure you it wasn't intentional (there's still some names I'm checking on) but one way to even things up would be that you write about your life and leave me out, there, I can't be any fairer than that. I said something down the track about a pay-off, I reckon this is just the spot for a PO, so here's the thing, if anyone knows more verses to the Dead Donkey (one) or the Mickey Plum (that's me) with the gas tar bum or, don't forget lads, if you have a report book or if anyone recognises themselves in the school photo and didn't get a mention or anyone else wants to get in on the act with a poem about their childhood in Rosegrove or Burnley, this is my way of asking for material (not that I haven't got enough), and who knows, it might lead to a third book (that's a thought). I'll have the final say on what goes in, plus it'll have to get past the censor.

Now I've got you right where I want you, and that's near the end of this, and here's an afterthought, if I do give anybody a mention the cunning plan is you're going to buy the next book (and that's one to me).

So the train ticket arrived in the mail and the last few days were spent going around saying goodbye to as many people as we could, I missed seeing a lot of mates because of work commitments. We caught up with Uncle Ted and Aunty Alice, Uncle George and Aunty Mona, then John and Pauline and the lads. We'd promised Grandma we would go over and see her and, of course, when we got there she put on this spread and spoilt us as usual, we had a good few hours with her but we knew it was going to be hard to say "The Last Farewell" to dear Grandma. Then came the time and it was hugs and kisses all round and Audrey quickly said, "Not with me, you fool." Well, I thought it was worth a try, then Grandma wished us all the best and gave us a few presents and some money for Angela.

Then we were on our way and not sure what the future had in store as we had packed the crystal ball with the rest of our stuff and the boxes were already on their way. There was only a couple of things to do now, the first one was I had to go to the bank and have our money transferred to the State Bank in Melbourne, the staff were very helpful and it was done in no time. I wished we could get there as quick and the money didn't have to pay its ten quid like we did, there should be a law against that.

Now, I don't know how this is going to come out (so you'll just have to go with me) but I know it's got to be dealt with and I haven't told this story to anybody before, so it could be quite painful (but what the heck). If I can write it out it should ease that pain that has been there since day one (which I've already told you a little bit about). I had to go up and say goodbye to Dad, correction, I didn't have to, I wanted to (there's a difference). I remember it was cold and I said to Audrey, "You don't have to come with me if you don't want to," so that was alright. Then when I was on the bus I had all these questions for him (would I get the answers), there was so much pain inside it was hurting just thinking about it, like, why didn't he give me his love? I'd rather have that than a leathering, and from what John and Bob had told me (over the years), I didn't think I got belted as much as they did, but a cuff here and there so I wouldn't feel left out, I suppose he was generous (with a thump) to a fault. So when I told you in the early part of the book about the tributes, you might not be able to pick a lot of it up but little Mickey Plum is nevertheless running through most of the verses and loving it.

Now with me being the emotional type, by the time I got to the door there was a lump in my throat and I was having second thoughts (I thought I shouldn't have had that black pudding), but I knocked on the door, I heard him shout, "Who is it?"

I couldn't help myself, I shouted back, "Rent," then quickly said, "it's Michael."

He opened the door and asked me in and said, "Would you like a cuppa?"

"Yes please," I said, showing him I had the manners that one of my parents had taught me and thinking, why is this sarcasm coming out this way, maybe because it's all in the same place.

So when you bottle things up you should use different containers, otherwise it could be dangerous if it's all stored together. I do sometimes think that humour is very sarcastic and I'd rather be hurt by an ad-lib than to have no love. We both wanted to say so much (but didn't), but he was pleased for me going to Australia. I stayed about an hour then said, "Well, Dad, I must be going," but it was so hard to call him 'Dad', for the simple reason I didn't know him in that role.

When we went to the front door I didn't know what to do so I just shook his hand and said, "Goodbye," he said the same and saying good luck I noticed his eyes were a bit moist and I said to myself, "it's not the answer I was looking for but at a time like this it'll do." Phew, that was hard but I'm glad I got rid of it.

We'd had a bit of a shindig at The Junction, it was a good night with plenty of back-slapping and it was me that copped most of it. Then the day had arrived and, as we were leaving that night, family and well-wishers would meet us at the station. So we got there with time to spare and decided to have a swift one for somewhere "Over The Rainbow", which wasn't a bad toast, one with bacon on would have been better. Jock from work had turned up and (our) John was going to travel to The Grove with us, so that saved one goodbye for later. Most of Audrey's family were there and Angela thought it was great fun with plenty of coochee-coo's. Then it was time to say au revoir as the train chug-a-lugged and we were on the way. But before we knew it we got to The Grove and John had to say goodbye to me, like I did with Bob. I said, "Adios Amigo, I'll see you when Burnley get to Wembley and I'll meet you under The Culvert."

He said, "It'll be nice to get the cup off the King (good one), but I hope it's not that long."

We knew we'd only have a couple of minutes at The Grove and the ironic thing about it was that's where we first became a family and now it was my turn to leave, so it was a quick hug and a wave and now we were on the journey of a lifetime, I just sat down and I was so relieved, I said to myself…

We take the rough with the smooth
And then the good with the bad
You can take this boy out of The Grove
But not Rosegrove outta the lad

Audrey said, "Are you alright? You seem to be in deep thought."

I looked at her and said, "Elvis has vacated the building, now Mickey Plum has left The Grove."

She said, "I should have left you deep in thought, or fried."

Then it didn't seem all that long before we got to Preston where we had to change, by this time we were a bit tired, then after about fifteen minutes we were off again and the journey was long and cold and, of course, we didn't get much sleep. We got into London the next morning and saying, hopefully, we'll be able to knock off a few Z's on the plane, and it was good to stretch the legs and have a cuppa then it was off again. We got to the airport in good time but Audrey was quite concerned because Angela was sick, we made a few enquiries and they said they would get the Doctor to have a look at her. We waited around for what seemed like ages, then the Doc saw us, he advised us not to fly, just in case she got worse and they would have to bring the plane down. Straight away, I thought, I'm a gambler but I'm not all that keen on those odds. He asked us where we had to go back to and we told him Burnley, he said, "Don't worry, they'll give you some more train tickets to go up and then come back, that's as soon as Angela is better. We'll give you a phone number to ring and keep in touch, you can reverse the charges."

I said, "Can I ring me Mum?"

He asked, "Where is she?"

"Australia."

Audrey said, "Just ignore him, he should drop off soon."

The Doctor said when you get back up north go and see a Doctor and once he gives the all-clear, just ring the number and they'll get you on the first available flight. We were very disappointed but what could we do and it made it a bit easier the way they looked after us, plus there was a car to take us back to the station. Then we had to do the long trip back, and at this stage we had no idea where to go (as in, who to stay with). One good thing about the situation was we had plenty of time, but not the options, we tried to get some sleep but that was out of the question as it was peak hour and the train was packed. We felt a bit better once we got to Preston, by this stage we were over-tired, and it was then we decided to go to Grandma's as we didn't know how long we would be there.

The only problem was how to get from the station to the caravan park as it was going to be late, plus the fact that Grandma would be in bed. Then when we got off the train we were lucky enough to get a cab, we told the driver our story, he didn't seem the slightest bit interested and he showed his true colours by charging a fortune, I was furious (and it takes a bit to get me going) because it was only a few bob on the bus. Audrey said, "Bugger him, just pay it," while saying to the driver, "thanks for nothing."

The caravan park was very dark, I said to Audrey, "It's a good job we know where Grandma lives or we'd have to ask a wolf."

She said, "You and your sense of humour, but it's a good one." So then we banged on Grandma's door and knowing she was stone deaf it was no good throwing any, by this time we were thumping and shaking the van. Then, one by one, the lights of the other vans were switched on to see what all the commotion was about, one bloke shouted, "Hoy, whatcha doing?"

I said, in my Al Jolson voice, "You aint heard nuttin yet, we've got to get Grandma to hear us."

He said, "With a racket like that you'll wake the dead."

After a few more minutes Grandma's light came on, she opened the door and couldn't believe it was us and, of course, she didn't have her hearing aid in. So once that was taken care of and the kettle was put on and a quick sandwich made she wanted to know what had happened. We told her the story and, of course, she said we could stay there till we got another flight. At this stage we were having second thoughts, like it wasn't meant to be, but what could we do? So then it was time for bed, we were drained as it was nearly midnight. Grandma put some whisky in Angela's bottle, I said, "I'll have one of those."

Audrey said, "No you won't, now get to bed and warm my side, there's a good lad."

With that I toddled off and next morning we had to go out and send a telegram to Mum so they wouldn't show up at the airport, we left Angela with Grandma. So after we'd been there a couple of days, Grandma got a letter from Mum, which was posted before we were supposed to arrive and telling Grandma that everybody was excited and they'd organised all this food, then Grandma made us laugh by saying, "What about all that food being wasted?"

I said, "It wasn't our fault," pointing at Angela.

Audrey said, "They're having a drought, not a famine."

Oh that was a good one folks, I should have said that myself but I'll make sure I get the next one.

We went to the Doctor and he said Angela should be okay to travel so we rang London (Temple Bar, I think), they said the rail tickets will be sent then once you get everything in order let us know and we'll get you on the first flight. The tickets came the next day and I rang them straight away, they said ring back tomorrow and we'll have a date, I said, "That's very good of you but I'll have to say no because Audrey will kill me," (that was alright, so I'll keep that for myself). So the next time I rang they said, tomorrow, the 5th of November, so now it was all systems go and hopefully second time lucky, or something like that.

When the morning came we were up early and now we had to say goodbye to Grandma (again), which was just as hard as the first time, but we got over that hurdle then we were off again. One good thing about the trip this time, it was an evening flight, so that meant we could travel down during the day, we were happy with that and this time everything was running smoothly. Then it was time to climb aboard and once we got on the plane we couldn't believe the size of the thing, we'd never seen a plane so close before, let alone been inside one. It didn't take long to get settled and then the engines were roaring and the 'no smoking' signs were flashing, I would have given anything for a smoke. Then Audrey said, "I'm a bit scared."

I said, "Don't be silly, get under the seat with me, I'll look after you."

And then we had lift-off and once we'd levelled out it was plain sailing, or flying. Then the Pilot told us to look out of the window and we would see the lights of Paris, Angela had her fingerprints all over the window and didn't know what all the fuss was about but the look on her face was enough to say, are we there yet?

Before we knew it we were landing in Rome, I said to Audrey, "I could kill for a bacon butty and a pot of tea."

"Don't be silly," she said, "you'll never get that at this time of the night," but you could get a bacon butty, and that's one to me.

It was good to have a walk, I strolled across the lawn area singing, "It's good to touch the green, green grass of Rome."

We couldn't believe how hot it was and then we were told to go back to the plane, we were in our seats and just about to take off and Audrey sang out, "Arrivederci Roma."

We didn't seem to be on the plane all that long and we were going to have another stop, this time it was bread and butter (Calcutta), well, we thought Rome was hot, but this place was stifling and the toilets weren't the best. It was good to get back on board and by this time I'd been chatting to a couple of Aussies that were sitting behind us. One of them passed over a can of Fosters, which I quickly handed to Audrey saying, "Here's a lager for you," because a lot of women used to drink lager and lime.

I said to the blokes, "What's the beer like that you drink Down Under?"

They replied, "That's it, Fosters."

"But isn't that a lager?"

They said, "It might be called that but it's still pretty powerful stuff and if you had about sixteen schooners under your belt you'd be legless."

I thought to myself, lagers and schooners, I'm not game to ask what the pubs are like, whether there's a Tap Room or could you get a pie and mushy peas. I know Slim Dusty sang "A Pub With No Beer" and I thought, blimey Charlie, that'll never do. But for now let's deal with this...

Rhymes have been a theme throughout
And now I'll throw these ones about
As I'm nearly outta paper
And writing against time
To my Shaeffer I dips me lid
For being a pardner in rhyme
Who knows where this is going
Ecky Thump, it could be a success
I'd be rapt if it's reviewed
In the Burnley Express

We're on the yellow brick road
Coming in on a wing and a prayer
To that great big land of Oz
We'll "Advance Australia Fair"

So now the hoity-toity types
Oh yeah, they can kiss me bum
I've really enjoyed penning
The Life And Rhymes Of Mickey Plum

As you know, when we started I stuck something on the back of the stove, well it's nearly boiling, so "With A Little Help From My Friends", "Sergeant Peppers Lonely Hearts Club Band", "All Together Now"…

Should old acquaintance be forgot

And never ever brought to mind

Down Under we'll meet and guess what

You can read what I have rhymed

And remember in life, you should think much, speak little, and write less, so I'll leave you with…

The End

Epilogue

Now we're well into the home stretch and I'd better start cracking the whip as I've got to get to the post before you lot and I could be on a winner with this. Now, you don't have to be a Rocket Scientist to fathom this out but there will be another (work of art) book, not too far behind and the good news is it should be a lot cheaper unless, of course, this doesn't sell and then you'll have to pay through the nose.

I said earlier on in the piece that you were an intelligent lot, well please don't fail me, if you're going to tell your friends about this book, for goodness sake don't lend 'em your copy, let them buy their own and that way the second one will be a reasonable price. Yep, no doubt about it Mickle, your blood's worth bottling (but I don't think there'll be a market for it).

I know I mentioned on the first page about going down the old (memory) lane, I think you'll have to agree it's been more like "The Long And Winding Road" (or in some cases the path of insanity), but I reckon on most of these pages I was up front and personal (very much so). I think there's been something for everyone, if there's anybody out there who didn't like it, yer very hard to please, but to the rest of you I sincerely hope you enjoyed the rhymes and reason for putting it all together in a book format. Over the years I've read plenty of terrific books and, on the other hand, some were rubbish, so I suppose this could be classed as reasonable garbage.

Well, I've done the hard yards to put my (life) story (or part of it) in print. It was a slice of life but really a piece of cake and I can assure you I have no intentions of being rich and famous (as a lot of people seem to strive for that, these days) so at this stage of life I'll just settle for wealthy and well known, yeah, that'll do it.

References

Beatlemaniac (page 36)

DB	Dave Brubeck
E	Elvis
EK	Earl Klugh
FS	Frank Sinatra
G	George
J	John
MH	Mary Hopkins
P	Paul

The September Of My Years (page 208)

B	Beatles
BC:GK	Bing Crosby:Grace Kelly
CL	Cindy Lauper
DM	Dean Martin
E	Elvis
NKC	Nat King Cole
NS	Nancy Sinatra
RCG's	Rose Coloured Glasses
SB	Shirley Bassey
WN	Willie Nelson

Acknowledgements

Bookmark, Burnley, England

Burnley Express, Burnley, England, review by *Andrew Greaves*

Burnley Library, Burnley, England

Catherine Frankland *Thanks For The Memories*

Centreforce Digital Design & Printing, Mornington VIC Australia

International Express (Express Newspapers), London, England, review by *Graham Ball*

Joel Rothman, two limericks taken from *1000 Limericks* © Joel Rothman 1985, reproduced by kind permission of Joel Rothman

Keith Fort, for his permission to use the photograph of *The Engine Shed*

May (Hoyle) Feathers *Treasured Memories*

Morningside Printers, Mornington VIC Australia

Record City Collectables, Frankston VIC Australia

Rosebud Library, Rosebud VIC Australia

Text Management, Mornington VIC Australia

This England, Cheltenham, England, review by *Edmund Whitehouse*

My best efforts have been made to include all appropriate thanks and acknowledgements but should anyone be omitted or mis-credited I offer sincere apologies and undertake to amend any further editions.